The Collected Poetry of Malcolm Lowry

ALTHOUGH HIS LITERARY REPUTATION rests primarily on his novels, Malcolm Lowry considered himself to be a poet, and he composed an extensive poetic canon. Yet, until now, unless one had access to the special collections of libraries, reliable texts for Lowry's poems were unavailable. It was this problem, and increasing critical interest in all aspects of Lowry's life and work, that prompted Kathleen Scherf to prepare this complete edition of his poetry, which includes the texts for 481 poems – most of them hitherto unknown – written by Lowry between 1925 and his death in 1957.

The sections of Lowry's text are chronologically arranged to reflect his artistic development, and are preceded by short essays describing the specific issues raised by his poems. Each poem is located, identified, dated, arranged, collated, annotated, and explicated by biographical, critical, and textual introductions. Chris Ackerley's explanatory annotation, which follows the main text, provides a rich and comprehensive guide to the poems. Appendices contain sections of song lyrics and undated fragments, as well as a remarkably coherent group of love poems written between 1949 and 1957.

This meticulously edited work makes accessible the latest determinable authorial versions of, as well as the textual histories for, Lowry's poems. Scherf's intelligent treatment of the material, combined with her full scholarly apparatus, offers the reader a unique perspective on Malcolm Lowry's literary sensibility.

KATHLEEN SCHERF is an assistant professor in the Department of English at the University of New Brunswick.

The Collected Poetry of Malcolm Lowry

Edited and introduced by Kathleen Scherf

WITH EXPLANATORY ANNOTATION BY CHRIS ACKERLEY

UBCPress

VANCOUVER

Introduction, notes, and editorial apparatus © UBC Press 1992
Poetry © The Estate of Malcolm Lowry
Printed in Canada on acid-free paper ∞
ISBN 0-7748-0362-2

Canadian Cataloguing in Publication Data

Lowry, Malcolm, 1909--1957.
  The collected poetry of Malcolm Lowry

  Includes bibliographical references and index.
  ISBN 0-7748-0362-2

  I. Scherf, Kathleen Dorothy, 1960-
II. Ackerley, Christopher John, 1947-
III. Title.
PS8523.096A17 1991   821'.912   C91-091251-3
PR9199.3.L69A17 1991

This book has been published with the help of a grant from the Canadian
Federation for the Humanities, using funds provided by the Social
Sciences and Humanities Research Council of Canada.

Design by Arifin Graham, Alaris Design

UBC Press
University of British Columbia
6344 Memorial Rd
Vancouver, BC V6T 1Z2
(604) 822-3259
FAX (604) 822-6083

With admiration, for
William E. Fredeman

Contents

EXPLANATORY ANNOTATION

APPENDICES

Appendix A: LOVE POEMS, 1949–57   319

Acknowledgments

ANY LARGE EDITING project requires the contributions of various experts. I thank the following people for their generous help with the preparation of this edition: Frederick Asals, Earle Birney, Susanna Blackburn, Kathleen Bourne, Peter Bourne, Gordon Bowker, George Brandak, Sally Brown, Adrienne Case, Ralph Case, David Deaton, Victor Doyen, Elizabeth Emond, Ian Fairclough, Jane C. Fredeman, William E. Fredeman, Peter Friesen, Charles F. Forbes, Joselyn Foster, G.C. Houghton, Sidney Huttner, Joseph Jones, Holly Keller-Brohman, Greg Laikin, Diane Loik, J.B. Lyons, William McConnell, D. Lorne Macdonald, Peter Matson, William H. New, Harry Porter, Robin Ramsey, David Ray, Laurie Ricou, Herbert Rosengarten, George Scherf, Helga Scherf, Nick Scherf, Cynthia Sugars, Hilda Thomas, Mark Thomas, Philip Thomas, Paul Tiessen, Ian Willison, Jean Wilson, Priscilla Woolfan, and Anne Yandle. I am particularly grateful to Sherrill Grace for her warmth and support, and, especially, to Chris Ackerley for sharing his humour and for contributing his extensive knowledge of Lowry's imaginative universe.

To Dan Silk and Robbie Scherf, I owe a debt beyond words. I also wish to acknowledge – with deep appreciation – the encouragement provided by my colleagues in the Department of English at the University of New Brunswick. I am grateful to the Estate of Malcolm Lowry for its permission to edit and publish this edition. I thank the following institutions for their kind permission to reprint items from their collections: the Special Collections Division of the University of British Columbia Library, Vancouver; the Houghton Library, Harvard University; the Huntington Library, San Marino; the Harry Ransom Humanities Research Center, University of Texas at Austin; and the Department of Special Collections, McFarlin Library, University of Tulsa. The lyrics for 'I've Said Goodbye to Shanghai,' copyright 1927, B. Feldman & Co., are used by permission. Parts of the introductory essays to this edition have appeared in *Canadian Literature, The Malcolm Lowry Review,* and *Papers of the Bibliographical Society of Canada.* Full citations appear under my name in the bibliography. Every attempt has been made to secure and acknowledge individual and institutional permissions; any errors or omissions are, of course, my responsibility.

Abbreviations

Introduction

Malcolm Lowry and His Poetry

ALTHOUGH MALCOLM LOWRY'S literary fame and reputation rest exclusively on his fiction – particularly his 1947 novel *Under the Volcano* – he considered himself to be primarily a poet. He composed poetry during most of his adult life, and his correspondence reveals a consistent concern with his poetry. In 1937, a depressed and paranoid Lowry wrote his Mexican friend Juan Fernando Márquez:

> The English are sufficiently stupid but the stupidity and hypocrisy of your detectives and the motives which are behind their little eternal spying – their activities – completely transcend any criminality and stupidity I have ever encountered anywhere in the world. Have these guys nothing better to do than to watch a man who merely wants to write poetry? (SL 13–14)

Almost a decade later, in January 1946, when Lowry posted to Jonathan Cape his well-known and widely quoted defence of the structure and style of *Under the Volcano,* he again highlighted the importance of poetry in his creative imagination. With reference to the problems the publisher's reader found in the novel, Lowry suggested that the situation was 'irremediable': 'It is that the author's equipment, such as it is, is subjective rather than objective, a better equipment, in short, for a certain kind of poet than a novelist' (SL 59). His essential interest in poetic composition continued until the last year of his life, when Lowry wrote from England to Ralph Gustafson, who included two of his poems in the 1958 *Penguin Book of Canadian Verse:*

> Sometimes I think I've never been able fully to understand the most elementary principles of scansion, stress, interior rhyme and the like with the result, by overcompensation, that my poems such as they are *look* as though they had a kind of wooden monotonous classical frame...All this is very sad and complicated to me because I think of practically nothing else but poetry. (SL 408)

The number of poems he composed and the significant position poetry held in his consciousness argue strongly for more critical and scholarly attention to Lowry's poetry. This edition seeks to make such scrutiny possible by providing, for the first time, accurate texts and textual histories for Lowry's complete poetic canon.

Unless they have access to the manuscripts in the UBC Library, critics interested in Lowry's poetry must rely on Earle Birney's *Selected Poems of Malcolm Lowry* (1962), published in San Francisco by City Lights Books. That any of the poetic texts has been available is owing to the efforts of Dr. Birney during the early 1960s. Singlehandedly, he placed over one hundred of the poems in journals and little magazines. In those years, too, he prepared an edition of Lowry's collected poems, which, as a result of his textual disagreements with Margerie Lowry, has remained unpublished. Birney's intentions were laudable; however, there are serious problems with *Selected Poems*. Beyond its incompleteness – the volume contains only 71 poems – the structure of the collection reflects Birney's *not Lowry's*, vision of Lowry's *The Lighthouse Invites the Storm*. Birney's selection encompasses poems that date from every compositional period, yet he insists on forcing them all into the *Lighthouse* structure in the belief that Lowry intended to revise the volume to include all his poems. No bibliographical or contextual evidence for Birney' hypothesis exists; on the contrary, it is clear that Lowry thought of and treated *The Lighthouse* as a discrete volume. Furthermore, Birney expands the original *Lighthouse* structure to include four new section headings and omits two authorial headings.[1] Far more serious is Birney's editorial policy of silently emending so many of the poems. While it is true that Birney's revisions often improve the poems, they also create serious critical problems for readers who do not have access to the originals.

Malcolm Lowry's first recorded poem appeared under the pseudonym 'Camel' in a 1925 issue of his school newspaper, the *Leys Fortnightly*. During his literary apprenticeship, which spans the eight years prior to the publication of his first novel *Ultramarine* in 1933, he published thirteen further poems in the *Leys Fortnightly*, in the programme for the Cambridge Festival Theatre, and in *Cambridge Poetry 1930*, issued by Leonard and Virginia Woolf at the Hogarth Press. His poems were among the first literary efforts Lowry showed his mentor, American poet and novelist Conrad Aiken (1889–1973), and in the summer of 1929, Lowry travelled to Cambridge, Massachusetts, to study with Aiken.

In addition to poems, during his apprenticeship years Lowry produced a number of lyrics for songs, two of which, 'Three Little Dog-gone Mice' and 'I've Said Goodbye to Shanghai,' he and his Cambridge musical partner Ronald Hill had printed by a London vanity sheet-music publisher in 1927. Five years later, he wrote the lyrics for two songs for the Cambridge Footlights Dramatic Society's 1932 production of *Laughing at Love*, in which he appeared. He also experimented with jazz lyrics, several of which are included in Charlotte Haldane's 1932 novel *I Bring Not Peace*, and he is the putative author of a number of bawdy variants of traditional sailors' songs.

Lowry's attention was not focused only on poems and songs during this period. He also contributed short stories to the *Leys Fortnightly*, and from 1927 to 1933 he worked on his novel *Ultramarine*, which is modelled closely on Conrad Aiken's *Blue Voyage* (1927) and Nordahl Grieg's

The Ship Sails On (1924; trans. 1927). From 1929 to 1932, Lowry studied at Cambridge with varying degrees of diligence. He managed to convince his examiners to consider *Ultramarine* in addition to his English tripos requirements, and his graduation in 1932 marked the commencement of a two-year Bohemian period he spent in England, France, and Spain. His next period – perhaps more accurately, his first period – of serious writing took place in New York between 1934 and 1936, where he started to compose *In Ballast to the White Sea*, later lost in a fire (1944), and the novella now known as *Lunar Caustic*.

Lowry's taste for popular music, evident in his juvenilia, remained with him all his life. His battered ukulele and his fascination for American jazz were, together with his seafaring persona and his devotion to alcohol, the characteristic features of his youth; it is not at all surprising that Lowry turned his hand to the composition of jazz tunes 'with ukulele accompaniment.' The wooden and somewhat superficial tone of his juvenilia is probably equally the result of his inexperience and of the undisciplined and undirected literary enthusiasms of his youth. The fourteen items of juvenilia included in this edition must represent only a fraction of the poems he composed between 1925 and 1933. Lowry almost certainly wrote more than the single 1933 poem this edition preserves, and additional juvenilia will undoubtedly surface as more primary material becomes available.

After leaving Europe in 1934, Lowry and his first wife, Jan Gabrial, lived unhappily, and more apart than together, in New York City. In 1936 they decided to maintain separate residences, and Lowry, desperately depressed, set up housekeeping in a run-down basement room. Alcohol was the chief cause of both his desperation and his depression. In May of 1936,'incoherent, shaking, and hallucinating,'[2] Lowry was admitted to the psychiatric wing of Bellevue Hospital, where he gathered the material for *Lunar Caustic*. Like most of Lowry's literary work, the novella is strongly autobiographical and reflects the atmosphere of his New York experience.

At some point during this New York period, Lowry conceived his first poetic project *The Lighthouse Invites the Storm*. Some poems from this collection appear on the same kind of paper as the first typed draft of *Lunar Caustic* (15-1, 2; WTP 1-25). He included all of the extant poems composed on this paper in the *Lighthouse* collection. Several of the most prevalent unifying motifs of *Lighthouse,* including imagery of seafaring and jazz, the sonnet form, and the recurring characters Vigil Forget and Peter Gaunt, make their first appearances at this time. Relatively few New York poems survive; Lowry's unsettled life made the preservation of papers difficult, but it is also significant that in New York, Lowry was – as far as writing is concerned – first preoccupied with *In Ballast to the White Sea* and then with *Lunar Caustic* (and perhaps some stories), so he had relatively little time for poetry.

In the fall of 1936, Lowry and his wife left New York for Los Angeles, and by December they had settled in Cuernavaca, Mexico. After a dismal year, Jan left Lowry for the last time in December 1937; he remained in Mexico until the summer of 1938. His nineteen-month Mexican sojourn, although by all accounts a wretched emotional experience, led to a blossoming of Lowry's poetic work.

In Mexico, Lowry wrote the missing first draft of his great novel *Under the Volcano*, for which all known manuscripts date from the Dollarton period. However, he also substantially completed *The Lighthouse Invites the Storm*, for which many manuscripts, in various states, exist. It was finished by 1939, when he probably had a triplicate fair copy typed in Los Angeles. That the *Lighthouse* was sent to at least one publishing house is evident from his correspondence; in late 1939 or early 1940, he informed Conrad Aiken that Whit Burnett, who had recently become an editor at Lippincott's, was holding the *Lighthouse* typescript (SL 24). A year later, in the spring of 1941, Lowry, unsure of the location of the 'hapless and ambulatory' typescript, wrote his agent, Harold Matson, for information on its whereabouts (SL 40). Matson had no success in selling *The Lighthouse*, and, to make matters worse, Lowry's friend, Irish writer and translator James Stern, reported a similar failure with 'Eight Poems from *The Lighthouse Invites the Storm*,' which Lowry had sent him in May 1940 in the hope that Stern would be able to sell them to *Esquire* (1-64). His contact with Stern appears to have been Lowry's final attempt to promote the collection, and after 1940 he paid little attention to it. Only three of the eighty-three *Lighthouse* poems were included in Lowry's second unpublished volume of poetry, which he assembled in 1947, and only eleven of the *Lighthouse* poems were revised at all after 1940.

The Lighthouse Invites the Storm is textually, biographically, and critically representative of the New York and Mexican periods, and therefore it can be most profitably studied in conjunction with the New York version of *Lunar Caustic* (more properly for the period 1934-6 titled *The Last Address*) and certain aspects of *Under the Volcano*, on which Lowry laboured between 1940 and 1944, but which he conceived during the *Lighthouse* period. The only extant literary manuscripts that are reliably representative of Lowry's time in Mexico are those for *The Lighthouse Invites the Storm*.

In 1940, Lowry and his second wife, Margerie Bonner, moved to a shack on the beach at Dollarton, and except for their 1944-5 visit to Ontario, their extensive American and European travels from 1945 to 1949, and a few winters spent in rented apartments in Vancouver, they remained there until their final departure in 1954. During the first part of his Dollarton tenure, Lowry rewrote and finished *Under the Volcano;* between 1949 and 1954 he wrote most of his volume of short stories *Hear Us O Lord from Heaven Thy Dwelling Place* and wrestled with the unwieldy *October Ferry to Gabriola*. In addition, Lowry wrote half of his poetic canon during the 1940-54 period. Of the 479 poems collected in this edition, 232 can be assigned by paper analysis to Dollarton. However, his Dollarton output was actually much greater: from 1949 until his death in 1957, Lowry composed many love poems for Margerie. These poems, collected in Appendix A, overlap Lowry's second Dollarton and last English periods and appear on the same types of paper, so it is difficult to determine precisely how many of the 98 were composed in Dollarton and how many in England. An analysis of the contents of the notes related to them indicates that approximately one-third can be safely assigned to Dollarton, bringing his total output there to some 264 poems; clearly, it was Lowry's most prolific poetic period.

In the middle of their extensive travels, the Lowrys made a brief eight-month return to Dollarton in 1947. While they were there, Lowry had Margerie type out approximately sixty poems; he then selected fifty-four and ordered them into a second volume of poetry. Unlike the *Lighthouse,* which is an integrated and highly structured work, Lowry's 1947 volume represents what he regarded as the most promising poems from the first Dollarton period. The selection is typically Lowryan in that it is autobiographically organized. The typescript is divided into three titled sections: 'Poems of the Sea,' 'Poems from Mexico,' and 'Poems from Vancouver.' Lowry sent the typescript to Albert Erskine, his American editor, on 7 November 1947, the day the Lowrys left Vancouver by ship bound for Europe via the Panama Canal. Although he was self-deprecating in his covering note, this typescript bears a closer resemblance to a polished collection than anything else in Lowry's poetic papers. Erskine later returned the typescript with his comments pencilled on the sheets. In light of Erskine's editorial suggestions, between 1951 and 1954 Lowry further revised forty-six of the poems, but nothing ever came of the revised selection. That he continued with his revisions suggests that he may have had plans for submitting the selection to a publisher, but there is no evidence that he ever did so.

On 11 August 1954, on a final sojourn that would take him first to New York, then to Italy, and, finally, to England, Lowry left his beloved Dollarton beach for the last time. He was in a terrible condition; the ravages of his extreme alcoholism were evident in his appearance and conduct. In his widely published 'Malcolm Lowry: A Reminiscence'[3] David Markson, who had written a Columbia University Masters' thesis on *Under the Volcano,* paints a vivid portrait of Lowry's two-week stay in New York:

> The man could not shave himself...Mornings, he needed two or three ounces of gin in his orange juice if he was to steady his hand to eat the breakfast that would very likely prove his only meal of the day. Thereafter a diminishing yellow tint in the glass might belie...the fact that now he was drinking the gin neat, which he did for as many hours as it took him to collapse – sometimes sensible enough of his condition to lurch toward a bed, though more often he would crash down into a chair, and once it was

across my phonograph. Then he would hack and sputter through the night
like some great defective machine breaking apart. (164)

It was in this condition – perhaps even worse – that Lowry was admitted
to London's Brook General Hospital in September 1955 after having
spent a year in Italy and England. He continued to drink, and in November 1955 he entered the Atkinson Morley Hospital in London for psychiatric treatment. After his release in February 1956, the Lowrys settled
into their last home, the White Cottage, in Ripe, Sussex. In June, July,
and August of that year, Lowry was again at the Atkinson Morley, and in
the fall Margerie was hospitalized for exhaustion. From the time of
Lowry's final discharge in August 1956 until his death on 27 June 1957,
the Lowrys lived quietly in Ripe, leaving it briefly only for a tour of the
Lake District just before Malcolm died.

Despite his illness, Lowry engaged in some literary work at the White
Cottage. Although he was revising the stories and composing a philosophical/political essay entitled 'Halt! I Protest,' he devoted most of his
writing time to correspondence and *October Ferry to Gabriola*. The
poems written during 1956 and 1957 were almost all a continuation of
the type of love poem that he had started leaving around the shack for
Margerie during the second Dollarton period. He sent a great many of
these little 'ditties' to his wife during her hospitalization in London.

When he died, Lowry left on both sides of the Atlantic a copious number of manuscripts in various states of disarray. He never had the opportunity to complete the grand plan he conceived for his literary canon –
'The Voyage That Never Ends' – because his own voyage ended much
too soon. Since 1960, when Earle Birney and Margerie Lowry began collecting Lowry's papers and publishing, with Douglas Day and Harvey
Breit, posthumous editions, the Lowry canon has been extended to include the revised *Ultramarine* (1962), the stories in *Hear Us O Lord from
Heaven Thy Dwelling Place* (1961), *Selected Poems* (1962), *Lunar
Caustic* (1963), *Selected Letters* (1965), *Dark as the Grave Wherein My
Friend Is Laid* (1968), *October Ferry to Gabriola* (1970), and other miscellaneous works. With the exceptions of *Selected Letters* and the unreliable *Selected Poems*, all these posthumous editions have been of prose
works – a misleading editorial and critical emphasis.

In this edition, Lowry's poetic material is organized chronologically to
reflect Lowry's artistic development accurately. His poetry falls into the
following major periods of composition: apprenticeship, 1925–33; New
York, 1934–6 *(Lighthouse)*; Mexico, Los Angeles, and Vancouver,
1936–9 *(Lighthouse)*; Dollarton, 1940–54. The poetic texts belonging
to each period are presented in separate sections, and each section is preceded by a short essay discussing the relevant issues concerning biography, context, manuscript material and history, dating, arrangement, and
emendations. The integrity of the two collections Lowry made in his lifetime – *The Lighthouse Invites the Storm* and the 1947 selection – are

preserved, and these collections appear in their proper chronological sequence. Such an arrangement of the poems is designed to be as editorially unobtrusive as possible and to facilitate critical discussion either in a biographical continuum or in relation to the prose texts on which Lowry was simultaneously working.

NOTES

1 Birney adds 'Thunder beyond Popocatepetl,' 'Venus,' 'Songs from the Beach: Eridanus,' and 'The Language of Man's Woe'; he omits 'Songs for Second Childhood' and 'The Moon in Scandinavia.'
2 Day 196.
3 *Nation* 202, 16 (7 February 1966):164–7.

Texts and Contexts: A Critical Overview

> The simple Wordsworth...
> Who, both by precept and example, shows
> That prose is verse, and verse is merely prose.
>
> (Byron, *English Bards and Scotch Reviewers*)

APPLIED TO MALCOLM Lowry, Byron's wicked, satirical stricture would be hyperbolic; but the formulation nevertheless underscores a central dilemma Lowry specialists face in attempting to evaluate his sizeable poetic corpus critically. A novelist who regarded his essential creative 'equipment' as poetic rather than fictional, Lowry left behind an enormous amount of poetry, most of it in manuscript form, but twice he prepared typescript drafts for completed volumes that he was unable to place for publication. As this edition testifies, in terms of its size alone, Lowry's poetic canon is too extensive to be ignored. More importantly, the poetry complements the fiction in so many ways – thematically, topically, and, especially, biographically – that it often serves as a commentary on the prose, illuminating the mental and emotional processes that Lowry employed in adapting, translating, and transfiguring his poetic impulses into language and strategies suitable for fiction.

With typical self-perception, Lowry's 1957 epistolary complaint to Ralph Gustafson, quoted on p. 3, strikes at the heart of his poetic problem. His comments reflect a discomfort with the *forms* of poetry, not with the type of vision it requires. It was Lowry's difficulty with 'scansion, stress, interior rhyme and the like,' not problems with poetic conception, that resulted in his poetry's 'wooden frame.' Norman Newton, a Vancouver writer, was a visitor at the Lowry shack during the second Dollarton period (1949–54). In a 1986 letter, he remembered:

> Malcolm had an intensely musical mind – his writing uses rhetorical devices in the style of an accomplished composer – but he had none of the physical endowments of the musician... All of this, of course, went to feed his hatred of his body. It simply did not respond finely enough. I feel that his lack of physical finesse had something to do with his failure to master the craft of verse. The images are marvellous, but the ear is coarse so far as rhythmic detail is concerned. He needed the larger and looser swing of prose. (Salloum 88)

Lowry's discomfort with regulated form is marked; in 1940, a year after he had completed his first volume of poetry, *The Lighthouse Invites the Storm*, Conrad Aiken advised him: 'I think it's good that you're writing poetry – but do try to keep your numbers and quantities straight – ! Freedom comes *after* mastery not before – the sonnet consists of 14 lines of five-beat iambics, rhymed ababcdcdefefgg or abbaabbacdecde: it can't just be *anything*' (1–2).

As his correspondence with Gustafson indicates, Lowry was frustrated by his lack of success in achieving poetic discipline. It is a traditional view among Lowryans that because he never considered any piece of work complete, he had to be coaxed to send a 'final' version to his publisher. This is true of the prose, but the number of first draft poems to which Lowry never returned is high. In countless cases, abandoned drafts have jotted beside them sonnet rhyme schemes with missing or half lines where Lowry could not force his poetical conception into an appropriate form.

Lowry felt, paradoxically, that writing in prose allowed him to be more poetic, that a multi-layered and encyclopaedic, rather than a formalist, approach could better couch his poetic conception. According to Lowry, *Under the Volcano* displays just such a form. In his 1946 letter to publisher Jonathan Cape, he argued vehemently, *contra* vettor, for its carefully planned 'churrigueresque structure' (*sl* 61) – a structure which is essentially poetical:

> I claim that just as a tailor will try to conceal the deformities of his client so I have tried, aware of this defect [his poetic mentality], to conceal in the *Volcano* as well as possible the deformities of my own mind, taking heart from the fact that since the conception of the whole thing was essentially poetical, perhaps these deformities don't matter so very much after all, even when they show! But poems often have to be read several times before their full meaning will reveal itself, explode in the mind, and it is precisely this poetical conception of the *whole* that I suggest has been, if understandably, missed. (*sl* 59)

Lowry clearly viewed his approach to writing as poetical, regardless of generic conventions, and he shared this view with his mentors. In a lengthy 1951 letter to David Markson, Lowry described both Conrad Aiken's *Blue Voyage* and Nordahl Grieg's *The Ship Sails On* as works of poets (*sl* 265), an indication that his sense of poetics was not limited to verse. A study of his poems and their interrelationship with his prose is invaluable because of what it reveals about Lowry's conception and use of language. In his best writing – poetry and prose – Lowry strove to weave a net of language in which associations, ideas, images, and reverberations were densely meshed and where the full meaning only gradually 'explodes' in the reader's mind. For example, to Cape's reader William Plomer's objection about the vagueness of the *Volcano*'s characters, Lowry responded:

> This is a valid criticism. But I have not exactly attempted to draw charac-
> ters in the normal sense – though s'welp me bob it's only Aristotle who
> thought character counted least...The truth is that the character drawing
> is not only weak but virtually nonexistent, save with certain minor charac-
> ters, the four main characters being intended, in one of the book's mean-
> ings, to be aspects of the same man, or of the human spirit, and two of
> them, Hugh and the Consul, more obviously are. I suggest that here and
> there what may look like unsuccesful attempts at character drawing may
> only be the concrete bases to the creature's lives without which again the
> book could not be read at all. (*SL* 60)

Lowry hoped to evoke a vision of the 'human spirit' through an amal-
gamation of all four main characters. His comments on characterization
prefigure Tzvetan Todorov's statement in the 1966 essay 'Poetics and
Criticism': 'The literary work does not have a form and a content but a
structure of significations whose relations must be apprehended' (*The
Poetics of Prose* 41). Lowry's literary language operates on the principles
of embedding, amplification, and resonance; the reader's conception of
the novel or poem depends upon the sum total of its effects, and the suc-
cess of any of his works must be evaluated on the basis of its evocative
impact upon the reader, not, as Cape's reader assumes, on the merits of
its plot, characters, and themes. Accordingly, in the 1946 letter Lowry
suggested that the vettor's appreciation of the resonant, organic nature of
the book would depend upon second and third readings. To Lowry, such
a literary work was 'essentially poetical.'

Lowry's compositional method combined his verse and prose. In the
collection of short stories *Hear Us O Lord from Heaven Thy Dwelling
Place,* for example, uncollected Dollarton poem 'Pines write a Chinese
poem upon the white-gold sun' [271] is written on the holograph manu-
script of the story 'The Present Estate of Pompeii.' Preceding the poem, at
the top of the sheet, Lowry wrote: 'Also, in II, when Downey reflects at
the top of the Wilderness steps, while they are swimming, I write this in
poetry, which it is...but I think, if a long story, its substance should be
here' (22–3). Then follows the two-page poem, after which the prose
continues.

Though the poem does not survive in the published story, it was an in-
tegral part of the story's composition and development. Thirteen of the
Dollarton uncollected poems, and many of the fragments, are parts of
prose manuscripts. Also rich in poetic fragments are the manuscripts for
Dark as the Grave and 'Through the Panama.' Though they are not pol-
ished examples of verse, these poems are nonetheless significant as evi-
dence of how frequently for Lowry the conceptual process for his prose
began in what he considered to be a poetic vision. This relationship also
exists between the poetry volume *The Lighthouse Invites the Storm* and
the novel *Under the Volcano.* According to Earle Birney:

[Lowry] was too self-centered, too inexperienced about others, to be contented with prose fiction alone; when he felt most deeply he turned to verse, especially after he came under the influence of Conrad Aiken. Indeed some of the most powerful passages in *Under the Volcano* were first written as verse. By the time he came to Dollarton he had the habit of recording whatever day-to-day experiences most moved him in poetic form, seeing an eagle, finding a strange flower. And later he would re-work some of these poems into the prose of his *Volcano* and his later novels. (Salloum 69)

Some of these initial *Volcano* versions are preserved as parts of poems in *The Lighthouse Invites the Storm*. For example, in the seventh chapter of the *Volcano,* the Consul stands musing in Jacques Laruelle's house in Quauhnahuac:

Suddenly he felt something never felt before with such shocking certainty. It was that he was in hell himself. At the same time he became possessed of a curious calm. The inner ferment within him, the squalls and eddies of nervousness, were held again in check. He could hear Jacques moving downstairs and soon he would have another drink. That would help, but it was not the thought which calmed him. Parián – the Farolito! he said to himself. The Lighthouse, the lighthouse that invites the storm, and lights it! (UV 203)

In this case the opening line of a poem and the title of the poetry volume itself have moved from the poetry into the prose. The Farolito cantina beckons the Consul throughout the Day of the Dead, and at the end of that day, he is murdered there. As Ackerley and Clipper point out (278), a lighthouse that *invites* the storm is a striking image of the Consul's self-destructiveness. The image first appears in the poem 'The lighthouse invites the storm' [87], composed in New York between 1934 and 1936, but there its purpose and effect are markedly different from the way Lowry uses it in the *Volcano*. In the poem, the lighthouse appears only in the first line 'The lighthouse invites the storm and lights it.' The rest of the piece describes a storm at sea, and the final lines offer a sonnet-like philosophical observation:

And what shall we, what shall we not, tolerate
Today from chaos, what? – by the unshot albatross and
Icarus' circus plunge?
(13–15)

The effect of the lighthouse image is weakened by its single appearance; after introducing the storm and sparking it, the lighthouse disappears. The image of the lighthouse is more resonant in the *Volcano*; it is a perfect objective correlative for the Consul, whereas in the poem, the image, though striking, is diminished by Lowry's failure to weave it into the fabric of the text. The Farolito – the lighthouse – is mentioned frequently throughout the *Volcano,* and its associations with alcohol, death, and hell reverberate and effectively remind the reader that the Consul is lighting and inviting his own storm. The collected poems and their links to the prose offer innumerable examples of Lowry's literary imagination at work.

The image of the lighthouse in these two pieces, however, signals the diminishing importance of Lowry's sea experience in his work. He never abandoned the sea motif, but as he aged, Lowry was less insistent that all his male protagonists share his seafaring past. His placement and the revised tonal shading of a favourite good line such as 'The lighthouse invites the storm' reveal something about his conception of the new work's emphasis. The sea, and all its Lowryan connotations, is certainly less vital to the *Volcano* than to the *Lighthouse.* Although both Hugh and the Consul have had nautical experiences, Hugh is the character who shares the sailing experience of *Ultramarine's* Dana Hilliot, and Lowry does not give his good line to Hugh, to be used in literal relation to the sea, as he does in the poem; rather, he gives it to the Consul, the novel's dominant, unforgettable figure, to express the Consul's essential characteristic – his alcoholic self-destruction – and all that Lowry believes it signifies about the human condition.

Motifs, such as alcoholism, that appear in embryonic form in the *Lighthouse* often come to fruition in the *Volcano.* For example, in 'Another than Wordsworth dropped his live work' [45], Lowry mentions the *Ohio,* a ship that sits 'smoking' off San Francisco. In the margin of the sheet, beside this line, the words 'Dark as' appear in the poet's hand. In *Dark as the Grave* (6–7), the ship reappears as the *Pennsylvania,* the same ship that brought Lowry and Jan Gabrial to Acapulco in September 1936. In Chapter Two of the *Volcano,* the Consul's estranged wife Yvonne arrives at Acapulco on the *Pennsylvania.* Throughout that chapter, repeated references to the ship occur. Although Yvonne remembers sailing into a harbour alive with swarms of beautiful butterflies, the undertone of the *Pennsylvania* references is very dark, like the hopeless love Yvonne and the Consul share; through Yvonne, Lowry represents the Consul's dire self-destructiveness in terms of the ship. A few moments after Yvonne has discovered the Consul in the bar, he informs her that

> 'It's really the shakes that make this kind of life insupportable. But they will stop: I was only drinking enough so they would. Just the necessary, the therapeutic drink.' Yvonne looked back at him. ' – but the shakes are the worst of course,' he was going on. 'You get to like the other after a while, and I'm really doing very well, I'm much better than I was six months ago, very much better than I was, say, in Oaxaca' – noticing a curious familiar glare in his eyes that always frightened her, a glare turned inward now like one of those sombrely brilliant cluster-lamps down the hatches of the *Pennsylvania* on the work of unloading, only this was a work of spoliation: and she felt a sudden dread lest this glare, as of old, should swing outward, turn upon her. (UV 48–9)

The tone of this passage is heavily reminiscent of 'Another than Words-worth dropped his live work,' the last three lines of which provide an accurate depiction of the Consul's morning:

> Such is the nature of his doom
> That like some infant Aeolus Dowson in Tempest's tavern,
> He claps for better thunder, wilder typhoon.

The theme of taverns and alcohol, essential in the *Volcano,* also informs much of the *Lighthouse,* particularly the third section, 'The Cantinas.' In Chapter Three of the *Volcano,* during his unsuccessful attempt to make love to his wife, the Consul asks himself essentially the same question posed at the end of the poem 'Doctor Usquebaugh' [28]:

> So well might we inquire, content to rot,
> What do you offer, love, which drink does not?
>
> (17–18)

In fact, when he realizes he is impotent, the Consul visualizes a bottle of alcohol; he cannot tell Yvonne that he loves her, but he can recite the slogan on the labels of Johnnie Walker whisky bottles (UV 95). Jan Gabrial's biographical short story 'Not with a Bang' (*Story* 29 [1946] 121:55–61), a depiction of the impossible situation she shared with Lowry in Mexico, echoes and corroborates the mood and tone of the final couplet in 'Doctor Usquebaugh.' In the *Lighthouse,* in the *Volcano,* and in Lowry's Mexican experience, drink trumps sex.

The expression of Lowry's personal conception of the essence of Mexico is an important component of the *Volcano,* as he made clear to Jonathan Cape in 1946: 'I feel the first chapter for example, such as it stands, is necessary since it sets, even without the reader's knowledge, the mood and tone of the book as well as the slow melancholy tragic rhythm of Mexico itself – its sadness – and above all establishes the *terrain*' (SL 58).

A similar concern for the land exists in Lowry's Dollarton poetry and the posthumous novel *October Ferry to Gabriola.* Lowry's ability to find the appropriate language to articulate an explicit sense of Canadian location links the Dollarton poems and *October Ferry.* It is worth nothing that the sections of the 1947 selection are geographically grouped and that roughly two-thirds of poems are contained in the 'Poems from Vancouver' section. The Dollarton prose and poetry manuscripts share the linked pattern manifest in the Mexican papers. For example, Lowry composed the uncollected poem 'Lament in the Pacific Northwest' [241], which mourns the 'progressive' changes in the Vancouver neighbourhood around Denman and Davie Streets, on the manuscripts for *October Ferry,* and a version of the poem closes Chapter 25. Certain descriptive passages in *October Ferry* are reminiscent of the Dollarton poems:

> For one fine morning near high tide they would rise to see a great wheel of carved curling turquoise with flashing sleeked spokes sharp as a fin three miles long sweeping around the bay: crash, boom: the wash of a steamer

coming in under the mist – paradisal result and displacement of that far distant and most malodorous cause, a dirty oil tanker which, with all its flags strung diagonally aloft above its bridges and catwalks, looked like a huge floating promenade. (OF 80–1)

Again, Lowry's descriptive method in this passage is poetical or 'churrigueresque': its effect depends upon the reader's 'poetical conception of the whole.' His characteristic technique of providing strings of multiple modifiers ('great wheel of carved curling turquoise') evokes the description's sense of place through imagery, so that readers are forced to interact subjectively rather than objectively with Lowry's landscape, as they must also do in the poem 'Happiness' [148]:

> Blue mountains with snow and blue cold rough water –
> A wild sky full of stars at rising
> And Venus and the gibbous moon at sunrise.
> Gulls following a motor boat against the wind,
> Trees with branches rooted in air;
> Sitting in the sun at noon
> With the furiously smoking shadow of the shack chimney,
> Eagles drive downwind in one,
> Terns blow backward

Ben Maartman, a fellow shack-dweller during the 1950s, remembers Lowry's characteristic poetic method of speech:

> When he'd get drunk Malcolm would speak with a flow of thoughts and imagery. He would look at something like the local gravel pit and tell you all the shades of history, and classics down through the times, and out of it would come a kernel of why we were all in this moment in time. His knowledge, associations, and descriptions were phenomenal. He was a poet: we could all have the same experience, but he was the only one who could capture it. (Salloum 96)

Lowry's most recent biographer, Gordon Bowker, comments 'that Lowry was actually a better poet than *Selected Poems* suggests he was. There were some very good ones in the selection, but there are many more just as good in "the whole bolus" ... I am coming to the conclusion that the poetry is of greater biographical value than I had previously thought' (letter to K.S., 25 April 1988). Most Lowryans agree that Lowry's works manifest a strong autobiographical component. The lyrical nature of the poems allows critics to gain more direct access to Lowry's mind – both his immediate thoughts and his more intimate concerns. Because a large proportion of Lowry criticism is biographical, the poetry is an invaluable and essentially unworked mine of information.

In the *Lighthouse* Lowry's devotion to various authors, including Conrad Aiken, Nordahl Grieg, and Herman Melville, is marked. Other biographical motifs include references to Jan Gabrial's desertion and

Lowry's ensuing desolation, expressed in his poem 'Delirium in Vera Cruz' [27] and described by Aiken in *Ushant*. Drinking, alcoholism, and guilt also play large roles in the collection, particularly in 'The Cantinas.' While it is true that *Ultramarine*'s Dana Hilliot feels some guilt among the rough sailors about his comfortable, middle-class background, as Lowry did on his own 1927 voyage, it is not until the Mexican period that he begins to vent his guilt about his alcoholism. Although the Consul provides a vivid portrait of this guilt, Lowry's poem 'Most nauseous of all drinks, what is your spell?' [23] is perhaps its clearest lyrical statement:

> Most nauseous of all drinks, what is your spell?
> You are cheap, you are the whore of potions;
> You are impalatable, you are the way to hell;
> You are insatiable of ravagement, you
> Are the worst of libations!
> ...
> Under your acid spell, quite wanting only you,
> Loving only you, we wait only our balm
> For the heart's next recession to its false calm.
> – But would you were only friend, not mistress too!
>
> (1–5, 16–19)

Specific allusions to other biographical events continue into poetry of the Dollarton period. In 'Xocxitepec' [129], for example, Lowry mentions the same two shrieking fawns that appear in the *Volcano*'s Hotel Canada (92). This hotel, which becomes the Cornada in *Dark as the Grave*, was the scene of Lowry's final break with Gabrial in December 1937.

In Dollarton, Lowry reached a literary maturity he did not possess in 1937; more and more of his autobiographical poems address the problems of being a writer. In 'Joseph Conrad' [118], Lowry expresses his frustration with the rigours of poetic form:

> This wrestling, as of seamen with a storm
> Which flies to leeward – while they, united
> In that chaos, turn, each on his nighted
> Bunk to dream of chaos again, or home –
> The poet himself, struggling with the form
> Of his coiled work, knows.
>
> (1–6)

In another Dollarton poem, 'Bright as the Pleiades Upon the Soul' [181], the storm motif again depicts his difficulty:

> Wrestling with iambics in the stormy wood
> I lost the joy that wind itself may bring:
> And yet the wood must struggle with the form of the gale
> As poets should with words from that quarter

> Of the plains of sense
> Bent by its fury
> The gale is
> The wood composed in peace once more the poem.

The frequency of poems about writing and writers increases in the third section of the 1947 selection. In 'Foul, Or Twenty-Five' [144], Lowry employs a rugby conceit to express the writer's struggle:

> Gloomy is this weary scrimmage
> Of my thoughts to heel some image
> Out to where the scrum half-dancing
> Of my will to write entrancing
> Poems waits to fling the fated
> Thing, that will arrive deflated
> On the tryline of abortion.
>
> (1–7)

Lowry regarded almost any idea or event as poetical fodder: while he and Margerie awaited mail from Scribner's regarding Margerie's novel *The Last Twist of the Knife,* which was eventually published by that firm in 1946, albeit without its final chapter, Lowry composed 'Scribner's Sons' [147], which records his reaction to this lack of mail. The poems are revealing autobiographical portraits because Lowry used them almost as an undated diary, recording and commenting on numerous and varied events. In an interview published in the *Paris Review Interviews* (New York: Viking 1976), Conrad Aiken, responding to the interviewer's statement '[Lowry] lived through a lot that he was able to use very effectively,' commented, 'oh, he didn't miss a trick. He was a born observer.' Lowry loved to collect and note bits of eclectic information, and he then incorporated them into one or more of his literary efforts. This methodology in part accounts for the encyclopaedic nature of his prose works and for the wide range of his poetic topics.

Related to biographical criticism, and extending beyond it, is the documentation of Lowry's imaginative universe: his reading, beliefs, fears, theories, and internal voices (or 'familiars') all inform his writing. The more critics understand about Lowry's imaginative universe, the more they will be able to trace and explain the multi-layered complexities of his work. And a study of the encyclopaedic nature of the poems and the eclectic array of information and references they contain will help to illuminate the discursive, 'churrigueresque' features of the prose.

In the 1946 letter to Jonathan Cape, Lowry dates the *Volcano*'s conception to his 1937 residence in Cuernavaca (*SL* 63). If this date is accurate, Lowry must have composed parts of the lost Mexican manuscript of *Under the Volcano* while he was writing *The Lighthouse Invites the Storm,* which accounts for the similarity of information and allusion in the two works. Direct and indirect references to the works of Melville,

Shakespeare, Shelley, Aiken, Grieg, Poe, Brooke, Bunyan, Chekhov, Dostoevsky, Donne, Ibsen, Rimbaud, and Yeats abound in both texts, as do biblical and classical allusions and references to jazz and to geography. Both texts refer to some of the same historical and political events, such as the Spanish Civil War. Lowry's emphasis on this event provides a critical context in which to study Lowry in relation to other writers of his era, such as Ernest Hemingway and George Orwell, for whom the war was an ideological and moral issue, as it was for Lowry in a poem like 'For Christ's sake and for mine' [73]. A reference book such as Ackerley and Clipper's *A Companion to 'Under the Volcano'* (UBC Press 1984), which documents Lowry's multitudinous allusions in that novel, can also be used to illuminate the encyclopaedic nature of the poetry, which stems from the same imaginative universe.

In this edition, Chris Ackerley's explanatory annotations and their prefacing essay provide a detailed analysis of Lowry's poetic encyclopaedism. These annotations are also useful for documenting aspects of his imaginative universe that are not as clearly revealed in his better-known prose and correspondence. For example, the marginal text in Lowry's story 'Through the Panama' acquires a deeper resonance when it is viewed in the light of Lowry's interest in the technological and symbolic accomplishment of the Panama Canal:

> All in all though, gentlemen, what I
> would like to say about the Panama
> Canal is that finally it is a work
> of genius – I would say, like a
> work of child's genius – something
> like a novel – in fact just such a
> novel as I, Sigbjørn Wilderness,
> if I may say so, might have written
> myself –. (*Hear Us O Lord* 62)

Lowryans unfamiliar with *The Lighthouse Invites the Storm* may not realize that its first poem, 'Peter Gaunt and the Canals' [15], which commences with the name of the canal's builder, De Lesseps, introduces the theme of the canal to Lowry's work through the volume's recurring character Peter Gaunt, an adventurer and builder of canals, the character whose mythologized biography and romantic journey the *Lighthouse* represents. Once again, the poetry illuminates aspects of the prose.

Aside from those poems important because of contexts they share with the prose works or because of their biographical relevance, there is in the canon a core of highly successful poems – works one might wish to anthologize as the best or most representative of Lowry as poet. The Dollarton group, and especially the 'Poems from Vancouver' section of the 1947 selection, are particularly good examples of Lowry's ability to capture the land and seascapes and to depict with poignant accuracy the squatter life on the beach. The best poems in this group place Lowry firmly in the tradition of Canadian nature poetry. 'Indian Arm' [164], for example, presents a vivid, natural picture of the beach on a late November afternoon:

> Mill-wheel reflections of sun on water
> And the spokes of light wheeling on the shacks,
> Such freshness of wind in a spring quarter
>
> Such radiance for November! While oil tracks
> Make agate patterns, a tanker passes
> – sudden sleeked lead boils on the beach, attacks
>
> Boats under houses, the bowed band grasses,
> Reflections are shivered, wild spokes unreel
> The day booms a song of foaming basses
>
> . . . Softly renews the round of the mill-wheel
> Sun reflections winding longer shadows
> Turn pine bough into green chenille.
>
> After the moonlight walks over windrows
> Mill-wheel reflections of moonlight later
> On water embroider waving windows.

What distinguishes 'Indian Arm' and other collected and uncollected Dollarton poems, such as 'The Wild Cherry' [152], 'Port Moody' [165], 'A Picture' [269], and 'Pines write a Chinese poem upon the white-gold sun' [271], is the poetic vision that infuses the land-sea descriptions, capturing in the process that sense of the wildness of the landscape that inspires the best Canadian nature poetry. In 'Pines write,' for instance, Lowry describes the hardness and sharpness of the land:

> Gigantic, the pines against the Chinese sun
> Illumined and embodied by light, the pines are real
> That were broken bottles guarding the hill.
>
> (3–5)

The lines echo similar sentiments in A.J.M. Smith's 'The Lonely Land' (1936), in which 'Cedar and jagged fir / uplift sharp barbs / against the gray / and cloud-piled sky' (1–4); but whereas Smith seems to be striving, in both his descriptive sparseness and the brevity of his lines, for a kind of imagist effect, Lowry's perspective, with its longer line length, is softened and more expansive, and as a result more lyrical, more personal and subjective, in a word, more romantic – a quality, finally, that characterizes much of Lowry's poetry, accounting, paradoxically, for both its successes and its failures and, also, for its fascination.

Note on the Text

MOST OF MALCOLM Lowry's poetic manuscripts are preserved in the Malcolm Lowry Papers in the Special Collections Division of the University of British Columbia Library.[1] The Lowry collection is extensive, containing sixty boxes of correspondence, manuscripts, typescripts, published works, photos, and memorabilia, as well as a full complement of critical works on Lowry. The manuscripts and typescripts for the 296 poems on the inventory are, with a few exceptions, located in boxes four through seven, which contain individual files, alphabetically arranged, for each poem. Any given file contains all the UBC manuscripts or typed drafts of a particular poem, except for the two unpublished authorial collections, which are filed separately – *The Lighthouse Invites the Storm* in box six (6–51), the 1947 collection in box seven (7–2).

The inventory arrangement of the poetic papers is logical for locating a particular poem; from a bibliographical point of view, however, the arrangement is chaotic. The most serious problem is that the integrity of the poetic archive has been violated. While collecting and arranging Lowry's poetic manuscripts and typescripts, Earle Birney and Margerie Lowry separated sheets in which Lowry had composed more than one poem, thereby destroying invaluable evidence for the cluster-dating of related poems. By disbinding four of Lowry's manuscript notebooks, Birney made it virtually impossible to restore Lowry's compositional sequence, a loss that affects not only dating, but also critical analysis. In addition, Birney scribbled – often, inexplicably, in ink – on many of Lowry's manuscripts and typescripts. Fortunately, Birney's hand is markedly different from Lowry's, so that his substantive emendations are easily distinguishable. However, it is very difficult to determine whether handwritten marks of punctuation are authorial. Editorially, this problem is especially irritating with regard to cuts indicated through lines or slashes. Equally irksome is Birney's inclusion of his own unmarked typescript versions of the poems in many individual poem files. Their presence made it necessary to examine papers in Birney's correspondence in order to generate a chart to identify the papers he typically used, to distinguish them from Lowry's, and to preclude, or lessen, the risk of bestowing textual authority, or perhaps even copy-text status, on Birney's revisions.

Lowry's own method of composition and the state of his poetic papers complicates further the chaotic nature of the collection. The fact that he tended to compose on any paper at hand, whether a restaurant menu or the back of a sheet from a discarded draft of prose, compounds the difficulties in compiling a chronological master-list of Lowry's poems. That these manuscripts can appear anywhere in the collection vitiates the value of the poetic inventory. Because Lowry also composed poems in the margins of his prose manuscripts, it was necessary to consult them to compile a complete listing of his poems. For example, the three poems included in 'Through the Panama,' published in *Hear Us O Lord from Heaven Thy Dwelling Place*, must be traced back through the multiple drafts of that story. The poems in 'Through the Panama,' as published texts, pose no editorial problem; less easy to discover, however, are unpublished poems jotted in the margins of draft versions of published prose works. Many of these 'poems' are really fragments, and as such they are questionable candidates for inclusion in this edition. A representative selection, mostly from the manuscripts of *Dark as the Grave*, is included in Appendix C.

Lowry's eclectic methods of composing and revising his poetry create a bibliographically bewildering array of manuscripts and typescripts in which little apparent pattern of consistent compositional practice is evident. Some poems exist in ten to fifteen drafts, some in only one. Some poems are incomplete – the sonnet rhyme scheme, for example, may be jotted beside a poem in which designated lines are missing – and yet still exist in multiple drafts. The chronological line of development for certain poems can be deceptively simple if the editor naively assumes that a Lowry manuscript always precedes a typescript. There is also the delicate question of Margerie Lowry's role in the composition process. Mrs. Lowry was responsible for transcribing Lowry's holograph drafts on the typewriter. A close collation reveals occasional substantive variants between a holograph draft and a typed version. In these instances, the question of textual priority must be resolved. Should the editor assume that the Lowrys discussed these variants, thereby conferring authorial status on them? Or, following Fredson Bowers' treatment of Hawthorne's text, simply view the wifely variants as non-authorial and disregard their textual relevance?[2] Or should the editor acknowledge that the variants *are* likely non-authorial, but still grant their authority on the assumption that Lowry himself welcomed, perhaps even needed, Margerie's literary input? Despite the possibility of Mrs. Lowry's editing, the final typescripts have been assigned authority on the grounds that Lowry saw them. According to both Lowrys, Malcolm composed during the night; in the morning, Margerie typed from his holograph sheets; later in the day, Malcolm would enter holograph revisions on the typescripts. Unless such revisions appear on the typescripts, I assume that Lowry tacitly approved any of his wife's changes. The hypothesis that Mrs. Lowry silently emended the poems during their retyping is difficult to prove without more evidence than survives. In any case, the number of poems that do not change from the final holograph draft to the typescript version is greater than those that do, so that the issue of Mrs. Lowry's possible emendations is not vital to the integrity of the text.

These are just a few of the problems and questions raised by Lowry's poetic manuscripts for which no simple, global solutions are possible. Accordingly, each poem is treated individually within guidelines based on a consistent overall editorial policy, combining methodological principles derived from both the humanist and the scientific schools of bibliography. This edition aims to present a reliable text of Lowry's entire poetic corpus, with copy-texts based on the latest determinable authorial versions of the poems, providing for each poem a complete record of the authorial substantive variants in every version preceding the final copy-text.

The preparation of the text for this edition has proved more onerous than originally envisioned, and it has involved five major editorial stages: location, transcription, dating, arrangement, and collation. The main contribution of the edition in the first category is the addition of some poems to Lowry's known poetic canon: the UBC inventory includes only 296 titles against 479 in the complete edition. Following the identification, verification, and transcription of each poem, the next step was to make a thorough paper analysis to determine a terminus a quo and ad quem for all manuscript and typescript variants of each title. Once the dates of each poem had been definitely, or at least satisfactorily, established, the poems were grouped according to their compositional periods to convey some idea of Lowry's artistic development. Arrangement within the chronological sections depends on the nature of that particular group of poems. For example, the integrity of the authorial volumes has been preserved, while sections of uncollected poems have been arranged alphabetically except where dating is precise enough to justify a chronological arrangement. Once the order of the edition had been determined, the task of close collation of the multiple versions for each poem in order to supply a detailed history of the poem's text began.

In the interest of providing what Lowry actually wrote, instead of conjecturing about his final intentions, which are now unascertainable, or trying to finish his poems, which is not the job of a textual editor, this edition contains few substantive editorial emendations. Silent emendation of accidentals is restricted to initial line capitalization, which Lowry sometimes ignored in drafts but generally used in his final typescript versions, expansion of abbreviations, including ampersands, correction of spelling errors, and restoration of lineation where paper width forced Lowry or a publisher to break lines in the poems 'For Nordahl Grieg Ship's Fireman' [12], 'Fyrbøterer' [94], and 'Where Did That One Go To, 'Erbert?' [317].

The specific bibliographical and textual details of each group of poems are discussed in the section headnotes; Appendix D contains a chart of the papers used by Lowry in his outgoing correspondence preserved at UBC, which has been invaluable in dating Lowry's poetry. The following survey, which supplements the general introductions to each section, provides textual details on the groupings of Lowry's poems in this edition.

Apprenticeship: Poetic Juvenilia, 1925–33

No manuscripts have surfaced. Copy-texts for ten of the fourteen items in this section are from published sources and may contain non-authorial compositional variants. The four poems from the Conrad Aiken Papers in the Huntington Library are, for lack of other evidence, dated 1929, the date ascribed to them either by Aiken or by the Huntington librarians.

The Lighthouse Invites the Storm

New York / Mexico / Los Angeles / Vancouver, 1934–9

The textual history of Lowry's first volume of poems, *The Lighthouse Invites the Storm,* is extremely complicated. The UBC inventory terms its manuscript 'Lowry's draft copy.' Whether this group of typescripts accurately reflects Lowry's final arrangement is uncertain given the editorial modifications made in the poetic papers. Fortunately, Lowry numbered the *Lighthouse* poems, so it is possible to reconstruct the volume's intended order. The draft copy contains seven kinds of paper; earlier and later versions – both typescript and manuscript – of the poems in this draft are contained in the individual poetry files. Also preserved in the individual files are poems that are not included in the draft but that appear with numbers on one or more of the *Lighthouse* papers. It is now difficult to determine whether the omissions are authorial or editorial and, since the numbering recommences in each of the seven sections, in which sections the omitted poems belong. A combination of paper-dating from correspondence and the New York *Lunar Caustic* typescripts and determining version priority through the tracing of authorial variants eventually resulted in a clear stemmatic lines for most of the poems. The earliest *Lighthouse* papers date from the 1934–6 New York period; the latest retyping of the entire volume occurred in Los Angeles in 1938–9.

The Dollarton Years, 1940–54

Lowry composed over half of his poetry during his residence at Dollarton, and there is a correspondingly large number of manuscripts and typescripts for this period. Lowry's lengthy and prolific sojourn in the Lower Mainland and his wide literary network in the Vancouver area are largely responsible for the extent of UBC's holdings of manuscripts for this period, because, when the Lowrys left Dollarton in 1954, they entrusted to some Dollarton and Vancouver friends, notably Harvey Burt and Earle Birney, most of Lowry's papers, a decision that, considering Lowry's unsettled life, has proved most beneficial to scholars and to the

UBC Library, into which Lowry's Vancouver friends deposited his manuscripts.

The extent of the Dollarton manuscripts and the amount of documentation available on the typescripts makes it easier to be more precise about Lowry's compositional practices during this period than about any other time of his life. At Dollarton, Lowry generally composed in pencil on cheap 8½ × 11″ newsprint sheets, which are now faded and difficult to read. During his first year there, he also used various types of 7 × 9¼″ notebooks, and although they appear infrequently throughout the rest of the period, in 1941 the frequency of notebook papers drops sharply in favour of the letter-size newsprint sheets. After one or more holograph drafts of a poem were complete, Lowry would give Margerie the draft of his choice, and she would type it out, again on newsprint sheets. Very often three to five of these intermediate drafts appear on the same sheet – or they would have, had the sheets not been severed. The poems would then undergo another round of holograph revision, after which they were typed individually on newsprint sheets or the bond papers listed in Appendix D. A frequently used bond paper not present in the correspondence is cream-coloured 8 × 10″ Voucher Bond. The fact that this paper is absent from the correspondence makes it difficult to date poems that appear on it. The variants in the Voucher poems suggest that Lowry used this paper late in the Dollarton period, as does the fact that they are typed in the elite type characteristic of the second (1949–54) Dollarton period. Because the versions are late, their significance as copy-texts is obvious. There are photocopied 8 × 10″ elite-type letters in Lowry's outgoing correspondence, but the watermark of the original is not visible and Lowry also used 8 × 10″ paper typed in elite type in England. Because of the voucher sheets' significant position as possible copy-texts, it was necessary to further research their dates.

Paper manufacturers' catalogues reveal that Voucher Bond paper was manufactured in North America during the 1950s. However, Lowry could have taken a store of this paper to England in 1954, so that an English period date for these versions is not impossible even though Voucher Bond paper does not appear in his outgoing correspondence for 1954–7. This paper certainly post-dates 1947, when Lowry selected and had retyped the fifty-four poems that comprise his second volume of poetry, because forty-six of the fifty-four poems, plus nineteen additional Dollarton poems, were further revised and retyped on Voucher Bond. However, since the Lowrys travelled from 1945 to 1949 and since there is no evidence to suggest that Lowry worked seriously on any poetry in England, the Voucher Bond poems almost certainly fall between 1949 and 1954. In 1951 Lowry revised thirteen of the fifty-four selected poems on Victory Bond paper; ten of these thirteen were further revised on sheets of Voucher Bond, so the Voucher date can probably be narrowed to 1952–4.[3]

Love Poems, 1949–57 [APPENDIX A]

In December 1987 the UBC Library acquired from Margerie Lowry and her sister, the conservator of the Lowry estate, Priscilla Woolfan, and their friend Dr. Elizabeth Moss, a new lot of Lowry papers that they date from the England period. A content analysis of these papers reveals that approximately one-third date from Dollarton. For the most part, this lot comprises 3¼ × 4¾″ coloured newsprint sheets inscribed in pencil and blue ink. Lowry filled approximately two hundred sheets with handwritten personal messages, poems, and song lyrics for Margerie, 'ditties' that he almost certainly did not expect to publish. An explanation for their inclusion in this edition is provided in the introductory essay to that section.

Only four of the poems in this section come from sources other than UBC's most recent acquisition. The most interesting of them is 'Lusty Advice of a Fortune Teller' [354], the only single draft poem that appears on Plantagenet Bond paper, one of the last papers Lowry used, datable to 1957. It is probably the last formal poem Lowry wrote.

Song Lyrics, 1927–57 [APPENDIX B]

The fifteen items in this section come from various sources. Just under half of the lyrics date from Lowry's apprenticeship period. The copy-texts for all but one have been taken from published sources: 'Ballad' [422], for which no manuscript exists in Lowry's hand, is a transcription of a re-creation by Margerie of Lowry's verbal recitation of the poem – a kind of textual paraphrase, like an Elizabethan prompt book, it has great interest but no absolute authority. Two of the three song lyrics written at Dollarton appear in Lowry's outgoing correspondence; the third appears in the manuscripts and published version of 'Through the Panama.' The remaining lyrics are from UBC's most recently acquired manuscripts.

KEY TO THE EDITORIAL APPARATUS

The clearest way to explain the editorial apparatus is to provide a specific example:

1937   III   [19.2]

MEMORY OF THE HOSPITALITY OF AMERICAN BARMEN

We reserve the right to refuse to anyone, pal.
Yeah, and that means you, four eyes, with the wheels,
[and hell!

Don't tell me you're a diamond and put
It on the slate, or that your heart is fat,
5   Or that your landlord can't wait to break it.
What's that? It's broken already? Well, that's that.
A spade'll pick your grave if grave you merit;
A spade's a spade, that's what they call it here.
We teach 'em bully the cabbage, never you fear;
10   In God we trust – but only on the nickel.
Well, if you had a buck too bad you spent her,
– But all who ask for trust distrust inherit,
And even God is fickle.

T   19.1: [missing]
1   19.1: (– we reserve the rot to refuse to anyone, pal.
6   <u>It's]</u> its {19.1}
13 19.1: and even god is fickle. –)

In the sample, which appears in the third section of the *Lighthouse*, the
date of the poem is recorded on the left of the head line. If the date has
been determined through non-bibliographical means or if it is for any
reason tentative, it is placed in square brackets. If paper-dating indicates
one date, and content analysis another, both dates are given, with the
content date place in square brackets, as it is for 'I don't want to criticize
war' [450]. Many poems in the edition are dated only within a range of
years. The centre of the head line records the authorial title or number of
each poem. If the poem has both a number and title, the title appears on
the next line of text, and if it lacks both, the head lines remains blank.

The edition number of the poem, by which it is cross-referenced, is
placed in square brackets on the right side of the head line. The figure fol-
lowing the decimal point indicates the number of extant versions for that
poem. Unless otherwise noted by a figure in round brackets following the
number of versions, the copy-text is always the latest authorial version.

The lines of the text are numbered by fives down the left side of the
page. Any word in the poetic text of which the editor is unsure is square-
bracketed with a question mark preceding the first letter of the suggested
word. Unauthorized line breaks are marked by a single square bracket
and are not counted as separate lines.

The sigla (or record of substantive authorial variants in versions pre-
ceding the copy-text) and record of editorial emendations for each poem
are combined and immediately follow the text of the poem; they are
keyed by line number on the left. In the case of sigla, as distinct from
emendations, the next figure represents the version number of the poem
in which the variant occurs, and the variant line follows the colon.

Any words that are not Lowry's – for example, 'missing' – are placed
in square brackets throughout the edition. In the case of editorial
changes, such as line six in the sample, the emended word follows the line
number and is underlined. The copy-text reading follows the single

square bracket. If there is a justifying reference for the editorial change, for example, an authorial appearance in an earlier version of the poem, its location is recorded and appears in pointed brackets following the copy-test reading.

Any intended authorial changes indicated on the manuscripts, such as deleted or added lines, interlineations, and crossings-out, are followed and properly recorded in the sigla, as are title changes. If the copy-text lacks a title that appears in earlier drafts, it is restored from the latest titled authorial version, duly noted in the sigla. Occasionally variant versions of a poem are so different that they are impossible to collate, as occurs in 'A child may find no words for its sorrow' [185]; in such cases the parallel version is reproduced separately and follows the sigla notation. Sometimes a block of variant lines does not match the number of lines in the poem. For example, in 'A Passing Impatience with a Noble Country' [268], six lines in the text (9–14) replace a previous reading comprising the five lines noted in the sigla. To reconstruct the earlier version, the reader should simply replace the six-line block with the five-line block. Poems published during Lowry's lifetime are included in the stemmatic line; posthumous – and therefore heavily edited by Birney – publications are not.

A list of the abbreviations used in this edition is provided in the preliminaries.

NOTES

1 For a list of other libraries with significant Lowry manuscript collections, see the bibliography. For Lowry's poetry, the most interesting accession outside UBC is in the McFarlin Library at the University of Tulsa. For a further explanation, see note 3.

2 In his introduction to the Center for the Editing of American Authors' Centenary Edition of *The Marble Faun* (Ohio State University Press 1968), Fredson Bowers provides a textual history of Sophia Hawthorne's manuscript emendations, as well as his rationale for excising all traces of her work from her husband's text. This introduction sparked a controversy in the American scholarly community, including Edmund Wilson's famous 1968 attack on the Center, *The Fruits of the MLA*, originally published in the *New York Review of Books* (26 September and 10 October 1968).

3 The McFarlin Library at the University of Tulsa possesses a collection of sixty-five typescript poems by Lowry, typewritten in black elite type on the 8 × 10″ cream-coloured Voucher Bond paper. In response to a letter requesting information regarding the provenance of these typescripts, Sidney F. Huttner, curator of Special Collections at the McFarlin Library, replied: 'our provenance records are not always as complete as one desires, but reviewing them I am now reasonably convinced this group of poems was acquired in early December 1976 at a Sotheby's (London) auction with J. Howard Woolmer acting as our agent' (6 October 1987).

   That sale, located with the assistance of C.F. Forbes, the Colbeck librarian in the Special Collections Division of the UBC Library, was held at Sotheby's Chancery Lane, on Friday, 17 December 1976, and appeared as Lot 612, the literary estate of Lowry's friend, English writer and critic John Davenport

(1908–66), in Sotheby's *Catalogue* 7 (1976–7). Included in this lot was a typescript of sixty-eight poems divided by separate title pages into 'Sea Poems,' 'Mexican Poems,' 'Canadian Poems,' and 'Miscellaneous.' The lot also contained some other items of Lowryana, including letters from Margerie Lowry to John Davenport dated between 1961 and 1963. The price list indicates that the entire lot was purchased by 'Stanton' for £1,100. 'Stanton' may have subdivided and sold his lot, because the McFarlin has only the sixty-five typescript poems, without their title pages, and no letters.

Exactly how John Davenport came into possession of the typescript selection is probably revealed in Margerie Lowry's letters to him in the sale, but these have not been located. However, on 15 August 1960, Margerie, who was heavily engaged with Earle Birney in arranging and organizing Lowry's poems, wrote to Birney that Davenport would go through the poems (Birney Papers, box 64, Fisher Library, Toronto), which explains Davenport's possession of the typescript. Although Margerie and Birney retyped Lowry's poems in the early 1960s, the Voucher Bond paper certainly has a rightful place in the authorial stemma, since Lowry's hand appears on several of the Voucher sheets. The fact that these poems appear on one brand of paper, with only one typeface, probably from the same typewriter, and that they are divided by title pages that bear a striking similarity to those in Lowry's 1947 selection strongly suggests that the Voucher Bond sheets represent a third authorial collection, one which is a later and revised version of the 1947 selection – a theory further supported by the fact that forty-six of the fifty-four poems included in the 1947 selection were revised on Voucher Bond sheets. However, until more definitive evidence, such as the Margerie Lowry/John Davenport letters, comes to light, this theory is only conjectural, and although the Voucher sheets are used as copy-texts because of their late date, the order of the poems in this edition follows that in the 1947 selection preserved at UBC.

The Text

But I think I most really want to be squelched,
to be a posthumous rather than a living poet.

MALCOLM LOWRY, 1940

Apprenticeship: Poetic Juvenilia, 1925–33

LOWRY'S FIRST MAJOR literary success was the 1933 publication by Jonathan Cape of his novel *Ultramarine*. The fourteen poems here classified as juvenilia represent Lowry's known pre-1933 poetic efforts. From 1923 to 1927 Lowry attended the Leys School in Cambridge, where, in 1925, under the pseudonym 'Camel' (based on his initials 'C.M.L.'), he began contributing stories, hockey reviews, and occasional poems to the school newspaper, the *Leys Fortnightly*. In 1927, Lowry left the Leys School to spend the summer and fall sailing to the Far East aboard the SS *Pyrrhus*. After spending the winter of 1927–8 in Bonn at Weber's School of Modern German, Lowry departed for the East Coast of the United States in order to study with Conrad Aiken. He remained with Aiken from April to September 1929, and in October of that year he entered St. Catharine's College, Cambridge, where, except for a summer trip to Norway to meet Nordahl Grieg, he remained until his graduation in May 1932. *Ultramarine* was published in November 1933, eighteen months later.

The first seven poems in this section appeared in seven issues of the *Leys Fortnightly* between 1925 and 1928, three of them [5–7] after he left the Leys School: 'The Glory of the Sea' [5] is dated 'Yellow Sea, August 1927'; the two others are undated, but, like 'The Glory of the Sea,' they reflect Lowry's new-found interest in the sea and foreshadow its thematic importance in his later literary works. The four 1929 poems [8–11] – dated by Aiken or by Huntington librarians – are included in the Lowry/Aiken correspondence in the Huntington Library. Lowry sent Aiken these typescript poems before the two men met in the spring of 1929. The last three poems in this section express Lowry's infatuation with Aiken and another Lowryan muse: Norwegian writer Nordahl Grieg. 'For Nordahl Grieg Ship's Fireman' [12] was included by Lowry's Cambridge friend John Davenport in his Hogarth Press anthology *Cambridge Poetry 1930*. 'In Cape Cod with Conrad Aiken' [13] and 'Those Coke to Newcastle Blues' [14] both appeared in the programme for the Cambridge Festival Theatre in 1930 and 1931 respectively. The latter is signed as a joint effort by Aiken and Lowry.

Since all the poems in this section survive only in printed texts, the problem of copy-text does not arise, though the authority of the accidentals in the printed text is, of course, uncertain. The paucity of poems dating from this period of Lowry's career makes it possible that additions to the juvenilia may surface in the future, but there is no basis at present for projecting any substantial extension of his early canon. The fourteen poems, all datable, are arranged chronologically.

1925   DER TAG   [1.1]

(IN WHICH THE AUTHOR, HAVING, AS HE ENDEAVOURS TO SHOW,
BATS IN THE BELFRY, DISREGARDS ANY ATTEMPT TO WRITE
CORRECT POETRY.)

On every Friday afternoon,
Before the sky is tinged with moon
And stars whizz round the hor-iz-oon,
One writes from Postgate this and that
5   Of *sibi,* and of *capiat*
And all the other verbs in *at;*
Of *alvus,* and of *carbasus*
And all the other nouns in-*us;*
In Rutherford, of dear old Zeus
10   (I often wonder what's the use) –
My kingdom for a San-excuse!
Then might I willingly refuse
To state my views upon the Muse,
Sadly to wait my graphic fate,
15   Receive my weekly evening hate,
Give in my imposition late,
Obtain three raps upon the pate,
Rewrite again on paper green:
(Next afternoon may I be seen
20   Partaking not of Pork and Bean
But writing Postgate – by the ream!)
With twitching face and doddering limb
I tentatively hand it in:
'Won't do!' says He – 'Omissions... sin!'
25   Then like some Bagdadanian djinn
He wafts my efforts towards the bin:
Again I try, again I fail –
Again at all the words I quail....
Until at last with mouth afoam
30   I go, quite dippy in the dome,
Into my narrow padded room,
Where Colney warders glibly boom
At little me.... *Ah! me putes
Amentem,* quite! ('Tis cruel, very,
35   Thus to abuse a dromedary).

1926   HOMOEOPATHIC BLUES IN J.   [2.1]

Jones took the little daily dose
Of Kruschen in his tea,
And cleaned his teeth with Pepsodent,
That filmless they might be.

5 And when J. went to bed at night
   He left his windows wide,
  And slept not on his back, for J.
   Preferred to on his side.

  Again, J.'d take a dose of salts
10   On rising from his bed,
  And if he'd not a sixpenny bit
   Six pennies served instead.

  J. had a little bread-and-milk,
   Some Liver Oil and malt,
15 And finished off his breakfast with
   An 'Andrews' Liver Salt.'

  Concerning J. had I the art,
   I might for ever sing,
  If only J.'d not just succumbed
20   To septic poisoning.

1926   THE OLD WOMAN WHO BURIED CATS   [3.1]

  There was an old woman who lived in a nice
  Little house that was badly infested with mice:
  'Ah, ha!' said the woman, 'I'll have to stop that;'
  So she squandered some money in buying a cat.

5 From that cat not a mouse, nor a sparrow could hide,
  Until at long last the poor cat itself died.
  The woman donned black, as was proper and fitting,
  And wearily, drearily, wept in her knitting.

  As that cat had behaved as a cat should behave,
10 It behoved her to find it an honourable grave.
  ''Tis a difficult job, for alas!' so thought she,
  'There's nothing near here like a cats' cemetree.'

  'I can't drop, I won't drop, *my* cat down a well...'
  In the meantime the cat was beginning to shrink
15 'Aw! wheel it away,' said the cook, 'in a barrer.'
  'What'll I do?' wailed the woman, just like MISS GWEN
                [FARRAR.

  She attempted to bury the corpse in the Park,
  Quite late on a night which was reasonably dark;
  But was scared by a Robert, who, noting the time,
20 Had (naturally rather) suspected a crime.

At last in a frenzy she rang up a friend,
And asked her politely if oh! could she send
Her a dead pussy-cat; and the friend replied, 'Right,
But you must come yourself, dear; in fact, come to-night.'

25   The train it was crowded; indeed 'twas a feat
For our heroine e'en to get hold of a seat.
She had packed the poor cat in her dead husband's case,
And mem'ry brought tears with the sweat down her face.

Her friend at the station asked, 'Is this the bag?
30   My dear, you look tired, for these trains *are* a fag.
We'll just have some tea and be happy and merry:
the Cat – (oh, don't worry) – the gard'ner will bury.

The gardener opened the suitcase and said. . .
'I'm dashed!' and the mystified man scratched his head;
35   For lying inside, stark, immaculate, mute,
Was – – a perfectly pressed Pope and Bradley dress-suit.

1926   THE RAIN FELL HEAVILY   [4.1]

Among the wet and sodden grass
      A lonely little graveyard stood
      Within the precincts of a wood
Where men are seldom known to pass.

5   The wood was gaunt. I saw the wreath –
      The mourners murmuring silence kept:
      Forlorn the naked willows wept;
A toad sat corpulent beneath.

The mourners slowly crept away
10   And left me to my solitude.
      I read the legend on the nude
Small gravestone in the blackened hay.

      When I am dead
      Bring me not roses white,
15   *Nor austere lilies grimly bright;*
      But bring me from the garden roses red,
      Roses red, wind-blown, sun-kissed;
      The roses that my life hath missed –
      When I am dead.

20   *Bring roses red!* There was no sun
      To shine. The grey and yellow sky
      Wept in the month of February;
Each pine – a dripping skeleton.

1927 THE GLORY OF THE SEA [5.1]

The tramp sailed grimly on her track;
A sickly haze shut out the sky;
The air was green, the sun was black;
The sea was calm like molten lead.
5 An engineer came staggering by:
'Another Chink gone west!' he said.

'Another Chink!' The purser's tastes
Were delicate. He loathed the sight
Of bare-backed stokers, sweaty waists.
10 'By crimes, sir, don't it make you think,
That death should touch an Annamite?
That God should stoop to kill a Chink?'

'You pen-push clerk! you pursing thing!'
The chief spat out: 'you dog-eared clump!
15 You goat-skin rotten in Tin-Sing!
I'd like to throw you down the hole;
I'd see them firemen made you jump,
To sweat your lifeblood in the coal.

'I'd like to see you doss on straw,
20 And live on samshaw, fleas and rice,
Or suck the ling fish from the floor,
Or drink the fly-bejostled muck
They get for tea with foc'sle lice. . . .
Perhaps *your* soul would come unstuck.'

25 The cook stood at the galley door
To sup the calmness of the night:
His lips were parched, his back was sore
With bending o'er the galley stove.
He looked for Chang the Annamite,
30 A lad whom he had learned to love.

'Where's Chang to-night?' he asked the Third;
'It's past the time he came off watch:
Half-hour ago eight bells I heard;
I've got a cake of Kobe trout,
35 Tinned, by crimes! I bed you'd scotch –'
'Chang? Chang's dead: his heart came out.'

The panting sun dropped in the sea;
All hands but five stood on the poop:
The cook sank quietly on his knee,
40 His shadow cast upon a winch.

It was a melancholy group;
And no man breathed or moved an inch.

   * * * *

The owners lolled in office state;
The typist took her files away.
45   'Good business, Ephraim! How I hate
These rainy summers here, I guess!'
'My wife and I at Biarritz stay. . . .
A coffee? Thanks, you've said it. Yes.'

1928   THE COOK IN THE GALLEY   [6.1]

He knows the ship, its dizzy flight,
The upward thrust, the sinking plunge
Into the infinite;

When pans and dishes crash and slide,
5   When green seas crash through milk-white doors,
And stewards saloonwards staggering wide,
Knee-deep in water, splash like cows;
When wind reverberating roars
And whips his dishcloth overside
10   He knows, and, reeling, turns the chops;
The cook has served ten thousand chows;
The mad ship trembles, falters, drops . . .

He comes outside when weather's fine
To hang his singlets on the line,
15   And then returns – he needs no bell –
The scouse, or Sunday's duff to share;
The stoker's tabnabs need his care;
The sea sounds far away in there,
Sssssssh, like the hush in a conch-shell.

1928   NUMBER 8 FIREMAN   [7.1]

Blackened and firescarred,
Up from the stokehole,
Supping the wind –
Cold clean scourge of the ocean –
5   Stood No. 8. Fireman.

'Jesus in heaven
Counts sands on the seashore;
The gulls that wheel, *Klio,*

And mew round the funnel;
10   The sharks and the dolphins;
        Red sponges, fiddler crabs,
        Snouted squids umbrella-winged
        Squeezing and buzzing,
        Coiling and heaving;
15   Stars that are reeling;
        And all of his children
        He counts for His Father.

        But I have no father;
        The fire is my mother,
20   And roaring she bore me;
        She washed me in coal dust,
        And fed me on cinders;
        She parched me, then maimed me;
        And I am her stoker.

25   'As God cannot count me,
        The Board of Trade count me,
        Like winches and derricks
        Or boilers; like pistons
        Revolving and gleaming;
30   Like brass-silled white cabin-doors
        Windily creaking'.

[1929]   ALCOHOLIC   [8.1]

        I died so many times when drunk
        That sober I became
        Like water where a ship was sunk
        That never knew its name.

5   Old barnacles upon my sides
        Ringed round with pitch and toss
        Were given me by mermaid brides,
        Immaculate as moss.

        Here now, with neither kin nor quest,
10   I am so full of sea
        That whales may make of me a nest
        And go to sleep in me.

        (Those angels of the upper air
        Who sip of the divine
15   May find a haven holier
        But less goodbye than mine.)

[1929] DARK PATH [9.1]

By no specific dart of gold,
No single singing have I found
This path. It travels, dark and cold,
Through dead volcanoes underground.

5 Here flicker yet the sulphurous
Charred ends of fires long since I knew.
Long since, I think, and thinking thus,
Ignite, daemonically; anew.

Yet, burning, burning, burning Lord,
10 Know how this path must likewise come
Through multitudinous discord
The awful and the long way home.

[1929] SONNET [10.1]

This ruin now, where moonlight walks alone
Uncovering the cobweb and the rose,
I have been here before; loved each dim stone;
If there were shadows I was one of those.
5 There listening, as in a shell, I heard
Through some invisible, unlettered whole
One true, if not at all eternal, word
Wrung from the weird mutations of the soul;
Palace or hovel, ruin will at last
10 Make peace of what is waste; take for a time
The hungry future and the bloody past
Into her night. Only the moon will climb
Up broken stairs to towerd [*sic*] might have been
And rest a little, like some poor, blind queen.

[1929] SPIDERWEB [11.1]

The moment hangs from Heaven like a webbed
Bridge to that invisible wherein
Necessity's dimensions sometimes win
Harbors of air, from which the storm has ebbed.

5 But we are spiders. And with waiting eyes
We see sail by, beyond old reach and hope,
Doomed wings of distance, small as periscope,
While dining on a diet of dead flies;

The black and gold, the gross and gullible,

10   We are those spiders who of themselves have spun
Nets of sad time to sway against the sun –
Broken by secrets time can never tell.

1930   FOR NORDAHL GRIEG SHIP'S FIREMAN   [12.1]

Two Norwegian firemen, friends in the same watch,
[stand looking up at the ship,
And what do they see? They see an iron moloch
Securely waiting to swallow the lives of men. . . .
But this ship also visits lands of strange beauty
5   Where broad leaves struggle against the sun.

The hawsers drop and groan,
While the ship backs out of harbour.
She swings round and steams for the open sea.
What are these lands of strange beauty?
10   They are there surely, they are seen, but are not part of the two
[firemen,
Only the port with its cranes is part of them,
Beckoning with their bronze arms at night;
The girls laughing in linked quintets in the lamplight;
A swarm of spirochaetes,
15   Maggots hatching in the very pulse of love.

Often these two firemen remember Norway
As they gaze from the poop at the galloping clouds above;
They think of the soundless black depths of fjords;
Spring plants staring at the sun in Trondhjem;
20   Bare arms among the storm-tossed washing in Tvedestrand
As Iphigenia remembered Hellas, so do they remember Norway.

When they remember this the ship is a moloch
An iron monster that crushes seamen and firemen
In its jaws; something obscenely neuter
25   With its sides fouled with filth, that swallows their lives
Or maims them. There is no beauty about the ship.

Then one night the two firemen blackened with coal
And firescarred, up from the stokehole,
Pausing amidships in their shuddering flimsies to sup the wind,
30   Happen to be standing by the ship's hen-coop
As the cold clean scourge of wind whips them.
'Look,' one says, 'why one of the hens has got chickens!'
As they stand and watch the tiny yellow balls
Tumbling in the moonlight, so soft and pathetic
35   With their little cries, they wonder
How it is possible for them to be so alive
So tender and helpless,

How *these* could emerge from the cruel naked iron and thrive,

And they forget the murdering strength of the ship,
40   How it slays like a lion.

Nor do they think of the life of the chicken,
How shortly the warm fluffy ball becomes hideously naked
and perhaps dies,
Or is ugly, a continual harlot, a scraggy concubine;
45   They do not think of eggs beaten in Norwegian egg cups.

Lo. All is innocence.
For the moment the ship is no longer a moloch
No longer neuter: the helpless warm chickens
Bring back to the firemen a white dream of a girl's face:
50   One remembers walking through grey fields,
That time they watched the steam rising at night
From the dark Norwegian earth;
And a certain street built on an incline,
Orange squares that were windows in the evening. . . .
55   The ship staggers and wallows in the sea.

One thinks that the poor lonely ship is still in its birth-agony,
It is as though the very ship itself has given birth.

1930   IN CAPE CODE WITH CONRAD AIKEN   [13.1]

Two philosophers a thousand years from now met in a grotto
[secretly
Where bayonets of ice dripped about them and the one star shone
in a fountain. . . .
And the first said, 'Friend I have discovered a language, but so
5   complex and difficult
That it would take a thousand years to synthesise a single word.'
The other smiled in reply. 'I also have discovered a language,'
he said,
'But in *my* language one word is the equivalent of sixteen thousand
10   years.'
They sat long thus in conversation, their hands palm-downward
on their knees,
While ice melted loudly about them;
And the hours folded their wings beneath the sky.

15   I tell you this young man
So that your outlook may perhaps be broadened.
I who have seen snoring volcanoes
And dismal islands shawled in snow. . . .

T   Aiken] Aitken
7   . . . a language,'] [omits end quotation mark]

Professor J.L. Morison, Professor of Modern History at Armstrong Col-lege, Newcastle, has resigned his membership of the Newcastle Literary and Philosophical Society because the society has arranged lectures deal-ing with certain modern authors whose works he says may not un-justifiably be called 'indecent.' In an interview the Professor said: 'I ob-ject to the first three names in the list of lectures. They are D.H. Law-rence, Aldous Huxley, and James Joyce. Those three are, to my mind, responsible for some of the most indecent writing of the present day. James Joyce's book 'Ulysses' has been banned in Great Britain, where it cannot be sold; Lawrence was a man whose works were hopelessly over-sexed. Aldous Huxley is what I call a writer of dirty-minded matter. I cannot imagine a young man or woman reading Aldous Huxley's books without being the worse for reading them. . . . As an ordinary Christian man, I will fight against indecency in every form. I have appealed to the Bishop. This is not a storm in a teacup, but the beginning of a fight for decency and purity, and I shall fight to the last ditch. I appeal to the Press, to the people of Newcastle, to see that the minds of these young people are not polluted by these authors.' – from a recent *Sunday Times.*

      Let Paris read Joyce!
      Let Florence read Lawrence!
      As for me I regard them with proper abhorrence –
      Let Frankfort read Flaherty!
5   Munich read Mann!
      But Newcastle's always the nice gentleman.
      On the banks of the Tyne,
      On the banks of the Tyne,
      To the good is no evil
10   And no Gertrude Stein;
      To the pure are no sexes,
      Nor naughty complexes
      Bewilder the minds
      Of the people of Tyne,
15   Of the people of Tyne. . . .

      I appeal to the Bishop,
      The Navy, the Press,
      To help me; Lord help me to clean up the mess,
      For no matter how clever
20   *Crome Yellow* may be,
      Crome Yellow, I point out
      Means saffron to me.
      On the banks of the Tyne,
      On the banks of the Tyne,
25   To the good is no evil
      And no Gertrude Stein;
      To the pure are no sexes

No naughty complexes;
The puritan finds
30 No sub-consciousness vexes
The grey-faced boll-weevil
That lives by the Tyne,
The whey-faced boll-weevil
That lives in the minds
35 Of the people of Tyne,
Of the people of Tyne!

An appeal to the clergy would certainly fish up
Some filth from the lecherous mind of a bishop;
And one to the Press, say the *Daily Express,*
40 Might result in a campaign to clean up the mess;
And a long peroration might follow to try us
From Douglas the dimpled, the pimpled, the pryous,
That tinfoil best tinseller, pride of the pious,
And pride of the nation, sir, pride of the nation... !
45 For whatever endeavour this Lawrence has made
To rip out the grey things the grey ones have said,
Whatever the courage or price he has paid,
Shall not sever the strings of the stays of the staid,
The Northumberland strings of the stays of the staid,
50 Nor can hardly be other than vicious, I'm sure,
To hearts that are upright and minds that are pure.

[with Conrad Aiken]

The *Lighthouse Invites the Storm*, 1934–9

THE *LIGHTHOUSE INVITES THE STORM* is Lowry's first unpublished collection of poems. It is not clear when Lowry conceived a group of linked poems or a possible sonnet sequence, but he first mentioned the volume in a 1938 letter to Nordahl Grieg (*SL* 15–16). However, the recurring characters on whom the unified structure of the collection rests – Peter Gaunt and Vigil Forget – are first introduced on draft leaves datable between 1934 and 1936. Most of the poems were substantially complete by 1938–9, when Lowry appears to have had a professional typist in Los Angeles prepare a triplicate fair copy of the *Lighthouse* manuscript.[1] In 1939, some of the poems underwent a further round of revisions and were retyped at Carey's house in Vancouver on paper that Lowry also used for outgoing correspondence in that year.[2]

That some version of the *Lighthouse* text – perhaps the originals of the 1938–9 fair copy triplicate – was circulating through New York publishing houses in 1940–1 is clear from Lowry's correspondence: in 1941 he writes his agent Harold Matson to ask whether Matson is still holding 'the hapless and ambulatory' *Lighthouse*.[3] Although he toyed with it periodically during the last fifteen years of his life, Lowry appears to have left the *Lighthouse* largely intact after 1940, with the exception of those poems that he included in *Dark as the Grave* (see Appendix F). It seems clear that he intended this volume to be a discrete collection: after 1940, only eleven of the eighty-three *Lighthouse* poems at UBC bear traces of further revisions; of these eleven, only three were included with Lowry's second poetry collection in 1947. These two facts undermine the widely held view that all his life Lowry intended to work all his poetry into the *Lighthouse* structure.[4]

No finally revised copy of the *Lighthouse* exists. Lowry's draft copy of the volume, which includes some duplicate poems, some heavy authorial revisions and comments, and indications of in-process editing and reordering, is preserved at UBC (6–51). Unfortunately, this draft copy is reliable only for establishing copy-texts of individual poems because its authorial structure has been reorganized and heavily annotated by previous editors. The draft copy of the volume contains seven types of paper ranging in dates from 1934 to 1940; the individual draft files for eleven poems contain later papers that can be dated through their appearance in the correspondence.[5] The latest traceable work Lowry did on *Lighthouse* is the final version of 'Letter from Oaxaca to North Africa 1936,' which appears on paper that dates from 1957, the year of Lowry's death. Most of the *Lighthouse* papers are typescripts; manuscripts survive at UBC for only fourteen of the eighty-three poems.[6]

Given the tempestuous and unsettled nature of the two years of Lowry's life between his flight from Mexico and the beginning of the relatively calm Dollarton period, it seems likely that the missing poetic manuscripts were included with, and suffered the same fate as, the missing Mexican first draft of the *Volcano*. That the sigla drop sharply between states after 1938 suggests that the draft of the *Lighthouse* is one in which the texts were established to Lowry's satisfaction, but in which the order had not been finally determined. For example, several of the poems have Lowry's 'out' scrawled across the heads of the typescripts. This fact could indicate that a fair copy would have included fewer than the eighty-three poems originally designated for the *Lighthouse*. However, tracing Lowry's revisions reveals that he did not always revise or title the latest state of any given poem, using instead whichever state was handy to him at the time. He could easily have changed his mind about the 'out' poems, thus explaining their inclusion in the draft copy. Alternatively, the 'out' poems may have been replaced in the draft by other editors. Since it is impossible to determine whether these poems were authorially or editorially reintroduced into the draft copy, it seems prudent to include all the poems – and the titles – in the current edition.

Because some poems in Lowry's draft exist in only one state – others in as many as nine – the problem of copy-text is unusually complicated. The states for each poem were dated by their appearances on papers that also appear in Lowry's datable outgoing letters, and they were then arranged chronologically. In this edition the latest authorial state serves as copy-text except in three cases where earlier states are used. For these poems, in which a post-1940 version is included with Lowry's 1947 collection, the final states of the versions he had approved by 1940 were used as copy-texts for the *Lighthouse* and the post-1940 states were used as copy-texts for the 1947 collection.[7]

Some poems, particularly in 'The Comedian,' exist only in the Grimes triplicate fair copy state (see note 1). The dates of these poems have been bracketed in this edition because it is fairly certain that this state does not represent the first version of any *Lighthouse* poem. In a few cases the paper on which a poem appears does not match the geographical or biographical content of the poem. For example, 'Delirium in Los Angeles' [46] first appears on Champion Bond paper, which dates from New York 1934–6. Lowry had not been to Los Angeles before 1936, so the poem was probably not written earlier than that year. The same New York paper makes another appearance in the Mexican poem 'Most nauseous of all drinks, what is your spell?' [23] – a poem about tequila, a drink Lowry did not begin to consume until 1936. It seems reasonable to assume that Lowry took a stock of paper with him when he and Jan

Gabrial left New York for Mexico via Los Angeles in 1936; in this section, any West Coast or Mexican poem that appears on New York paper is dated according to geographical content.

It is not clear whether the disorder in the *Lighthouse* draft is authorial or a result of the 1960–1 collaborative work of Margerie Lowry and Earle Birney. Lowry revised the order of the *Lighthouse* poems at least three times: three separate numbering systems appear on most of the typescripts. These roman numerals, which comprise separate series for each of the seven authorial sections, are for the most part handwritten at the top of the sheets, including the Grimes fair copies; the numerals are inscribed in pencil and/or black ink, Lowry's characteristic method of making revisions to typescripts. The 1939 paper, however, has typed numerals, which, along with certain revisions, indicates that the states that appear on this paper post-date the Grimes states. There is, however, a list in Margerie's hand of one version of the *Lighthouse* order that, though nearly consistent with the foliation, does not always agree with any one set of holograph numeration (6-52). Alterations in foliation do not, however, seriously affect the order of the collection, for the inconsistencies produce gaps that serve only to collapse the order rather than change it. These gaps do raise the interesting question of the missing (or perhaps unwritten) poems, especially since no other poems in the UBC collection are numbered in a similar fashion.

For this edition, the order has been determined by the foliation; but the existence of three sets of numbers generates some unresolvable problems. Wherever there is a single numeral, it serves as order-determinant. In the case of multiple numerals, the order established by the single numeral pages provides a guide to selecting an appropriate choice of position from among the multiple numerals. The resulting order was then checked against Margerie's list. Although it is obviously not definitive, this list likely represents the order in which Margerie found the draft copy of *Lighthouse*, since it is certainly not a list of the expanded *Lighthouse* format created by her and her coeditor, nor does it match the current disordered state of the draft copy. All unsolvable ordering problems were dealt with by reference to Margerie's list, as its authorial proximity is at least reasonably reliable. Because Lowry himself had not determined a final order for the *Lighthouse* before his death and because it is impossible to know how he would have wanted the work completed, this edition aims to re-establish the latest order Lowry *had* established by the time of his death.

A version of *The Lighthouse Invites the Storm* makes one other interesting appearance in Lowry's manuscripts. A short selection of *Lighthouse* poems closes the typescript for *Dark as the Grave*, but the poems do not appear in the published edition. The works are attributed to Sigbjørn Wilderness, the novel's protagonist and Lowry's *alter ego*, and are reproduced here in Appendix F as 'Sigbjørn's *Lighthouse*.' Because the selection is a discrete segment of another test, it is given no textual authority in this section.

NOTES

1   Lowry arrived in Los Angeles from Mexico in the summer of 1938. After he met Margerie Bonner in June 1939, only she typed his manuscripts. During the month they were apart, before Margerie arrived in Vancouver, Lowry handwrote his passionate letters to Los Angeles. Lowry's own Mexican typescripts are instantly recognizable by the errors, clumsy corrections, cigarette burns, and alcohol stains. The triplicates are typed on 'Grimes Business Bond' erasable paper, which is of a much higher quality and durability than any papers that date from Mexico. Typographical errors are extremely rare on these sheets; it is therefore unlikely that they are from Mexico or that Lowry typed them. Unless Margerie typed the poems during the month they shared in Los Angeles, the *Lighthouse* had to be typed there by someone else – from their high quality, probably a professional typist – because its next round of revisions can be traced to Vancouver in late 1939.

2   A second paper, which contains 'Eight Poems from *The Lighthouse Invites the Storm*' (6–55) also dates from Carey's house. This selection accompanied a May 1940 letter to James Stern asking him to place the poems. Stern was unsuccessful in this endeavour. The eight poems are: 'In the Oaxaca Train' [101], 'Delirium in Vera Cruz' [27], 'Quartermaster at the Wheel' [79], 'The Devil Was a Gentleman' [40], 'Doctor Usquebaugh' [28], 'There Is a Metallurgy' [80], 'The Roar of the Sea and the Darkness' [97], 'Lull' [72].

3   Malcolm Lowry, letter to Harold Matson, 4 March 1941 (1–80).

4   As expressed, for instance, in Earle Birney, 'The Unknown Poetry of Malcolm Lowry,' *British Columbia Library Quarterly* 24, 4 (1961):33–40.

5   These poems are: 'Letter from Oaxaca to North Africa 1936' [16], 'At the Bar' [26], 'Delirium in Vera Cruz' [27], 'The Last Man in the Dôme' [29], 'Lull' [72], 'We likened one man to a ship adrift' [85], 'Song about Madrid, Useful Anytime' [91], 'A Poem of God's Mercy' [93], 'On Reading R.L.S.' [95], 'The Roar of the Sea and the Darkness' [97].

6   These poems are: 'I have known a city of dreadful night' [24], 'Thirty Five Mescals in Cuautla' [25], 'Delirium in Vera Cruz' [27], 'The Last Man in the Dôme' [29], 'Curse' [33], 'As the poor end of each dead day drew near' [35], 'The sun shines: where is the lyric?' [36], 'The gentleness of rain is in the wind' [37], 'He wrote for the dead, but the ubiquitous dead' [41], 'Pigling, pigling, burning bland' [48], '– – For Christ's sake and for mine and last for a child's god gone' [73], 'We likened one man to a ship adrift' [85], 'The ship of war sails in the grey morning' [88], 'Song about Madrid, Useful Anytime' [91].

7   The three poems are: 'Delirium in Vera Cruz' [27], which appears, under the same title, as [131] in the 1947 selection, 'On Reading R.L.S.' [95], which becomes 'Old Freighter in an Old Port' [114], and 'The Roar of the Sea and the Darkness' [97], which becomes 'The Western Ocean' [117].

The Lighthouse Invites the Storm

– June, too soon: July, stand by: August, you must:
September, remember: October, all over.
MARINER'S PROVERB

I. Peter Gaunt and the Canals

1936–7   PETER GAUNT AND THE CANALS   [15.3]

I

De Lesseps, he said, was not the only one,
Peer Gynt, too, climbed a world of money-bags
– they happened to be dunes in the desert –
Wearing rings and a watch or two and so forth,
5   And said it was hard, indeed it was certainly
Hard indeed, in this peculiar place,
Hard to see the Almighty's purpose
Where there was nothing life-giving, nothing
But a burnt-up waste profiting no growth,
10   An old corpse which never once said thank you
Since it was shaped. Why was it made at all?

II

The extravagance of nature took his mind;
Was that the sea, or mirage, in the east?
Whatever it was glittered like diamonds.
15   No. Sea was to the west where like a dam
Sandhills protected desert from its life.
A dam, thought Gynt, from Norway, hills are small;
A dam; why not a cutting, a canal
Through which the wise ocean, warping slowly
20   At first, would fill the plain itself with flood?
And all that desolate grave become a lake.

III

A lake, a sea itself, whose gentle crash
Of waves would show crystal against islands;
To the north, forever a new landfall;
25   To the south, snowy plumage of frigates;
While above, below, around, white harbingers,
– Since gulls are incident in salty projects –
And this is first the dream of a canal
Whose green banks roar with towns as busy trade
30   Steams from the land of Habes to the Nile,
Where, piled against a Cape, Peeropolis
Staggers, the capital city of self.

IV

Peeropolis; another Petersburg!
But peopled with Norsemen, for nothing else
35 Than Norsemen satisfy Peer Gynt; Nordic
Men for the new born land whose founder signs
And doubtless sings into some khedive's ear:
All we need is capital! Capital!
Capital! All we need is capital!
40 Ab esse ad possess! Capital
Is all we need! Nordic men! Capital!
All we need's some capital, some capital,
Indeed . . . And so on, to the 'Hall of the Mountain King.'

V

The jig, like Noah's donkey in the Ark
45 – What was that Ark if not a dream like Peer's,
Its voyage back in heart from water to sand? –
Noah's donkey in the Ark, in the Ark,
In the Ark, brays its message – asinine! –
To east, west, north, and south. Thus good Ibsen,
50 And later Grieg, and later still the six
Brown brothers, hot forerunners of the riffs.
Let this pun pass, remembering Peter Gink;
And so make way for Mr. Peter Gaunt.

VI

(What was that story of an older dream
55 But some vision of wilderness of water
And a settling of loud rodents in a dry world
Washed white? No doubt it was a Nordic world.)
But there goes Mr. Peter Gaunt, M.A.,
P.H.D., and so on – not P.H.D.? –
60 Or better still, plain Peter; or better still,
Plain Pete. Hell, are you Mr. Gaunt at all?
Whether or not you like it, whether or not
You think my reason for it is valid,
Your name is Peter Gaunt. It is solid.

VII

65 Peter Gaunt, as Gynt then, climbs a dune,
Looks on a dead world that seems to him bad,
– Though dune's but a stool in the 'Automat,'
Spelling this backwards makes Tamotua,
Pacific island in titanic surf,
70 Glutting ten thousand taverns in the town;
It was the surf of traffic round his feet
Washed him to this escape, his oasis

In the desert of Chicago, London,
Rheims, and a blest island for lovers, too –

VIII

75   And lights a cigarette, noting, far off,
The ostrich; the cigarette's a camel,
And ostrich but a reflection of himself
Wondering at the Almighty's purpose;
Gaunt, because he starves; Peter, because hard.
80   Peter is a starved rock that thinks and smokes,
Though both are discouraged here, wondering
How man should be both stone and bird at once:
And when he eats, should eat with sandfilled eyes;
How pauper lips may strangely cram with dessert
85   And paper cups brim over with sweet wine.

IX

Sees he the new city, the really better land,
Or wills he the flood on all of us
But to destroy, not slake, not fructify,
Under the bleak north star of his self-mistrust
90   He has read or not read about in Myers?
Under the maniacal lamp of the cafeteria
Lurks there the strange, the bird-haunted vision
Of the canal that lives in mankind's dream,
Ploughed through past's sand, no bitter lakes beyond
95   From Casino-Palace to Bab-el-Mandeb,
Or Caribbees to Tehuantepec,
Liverpool to Canaan via Manchester?

X

Liverpool to Manchester via Runcorn
Archangel to Kattegat and Sound!
100   A dream still living in the mind of man
Has many coloured meanings: if Gaunt sees
Sandhills obstructing desert from new life,
Thinks of dams, why now the hills are low,
Feels the wise ocean warping slowly
105   To fill the plain itself with salt sweet flow;
If, remembering Panama, he says Mersey,
Gynt, Gaunt, are they the same? If the White Sea
Was nearer Gaunt's dream in both beautifully,
I think there is no predominance of white.

XI

110   After all, the vision was like but subtly sea-changed,
Whether grave became a lake sweet or sour
The canal changed direction every hour;

Whatever Gaunt saw, whatever sloping city
Was built by free men for the free to live in,
115   Created through men for mankind by mankind;
Say at very least Gaunt thought less of self
Than thought Gynt? But is it strictly true? Truth
Lies between old facts as swamps between seas,
Or if not facts they're rationalizations.
120   The silted truth is also dredgeable,
It is this man's empowered to reclaim
For man. It is a canal in mind. And it is for himself.

XII

Let us give him the benefit of some doubts;
That Gaunt was kinder to his Solveig and Aase;
125   Must have known the difference between the two,
Scarcely would have set his mother on roof;
Hoped, at least, love without love of mankind
Was its own sepulchre. Perhaps Peter Gaunt
Died for Madrid under machine-gun fire.
130   Perhaps not. But no matter where he died,
Or even where he lived, he was Peter Gaunt,
And he was you, who may have needed capital
To the same tune and Solveig thrice a night,
But at least did not fill his star with Norsemen,
135   And, if with abstractions, not with the four horsemen.

XIII

So when flesh feels slighted by the present,
And spirit by the future, think of Gaunt
Who loves his wife and has no heart to die,
Yet masked as Jones may run Bilbao's gauntlet,
140   Cutting his own canal through brackish death
And bringing life to life, too weak to stand;
When deathward the mind makes supercession,
Consider Gaunt, who built a loyalist column
That Gaunt, ourself, might live on sea and land,
145   Free to feel slighted, free for joy or peace;
Free to laugh, love, run, walk, see, or be blind,
From Lorbrulgrud to Leningrad via Nice;
From Ithaca, New York, to Ithaca, Greece;
In Georgia, in the deep south, and in the far east,
150   And in that deeper south below Cape Horn,
From Aldeberan to Aberdeen.

36   15.1, 2: men for the new born land whose founder sings
40   15.1, 2: Ab esse ad posses. Capital
64   15.2: your name is Peter Gaunt, sir, it is solid.
65   15.1: . . . Peter Gaunt likewise climbs on a dune,
        15.2: Peter Gaunt, then, also climbs on a dune,

        15.3: Peter Gaunt, as the others, climbs on a dune,
 66   15.2: looks on a dead world which seems to him bad,
 74   15.1: [adds next line:] ah, rats live on no evil evil star –
 76   15.2: the ostrich. The cigarette's a Camel,
 78   15.1: wondering at the almighty's purpose. [line repeats once]
 79   15.1: Gaunt because he starves Peter because hard.
 81   15.2: – though both are discouraged here, – wondering too
123   15.1: Let us give him the benefit of the doubt;
124   15.1: Say Gaunt was kinder to his Solveig and Aase;
149   15.2: in Georgia in the deep South if not the far East, –

II. Letter from Oaxaca to North Africa

1936–7 LETTER FROM OAXACA TO NORTH AFRICA 1936   [16.3]

    – Martin I cannot say to you, old friend,
    Dearest of all my friends, that I can see
    You softly borne over a wayward sea
    To this alcoholic or sardonic end,
5   Or that colic shore . . . I wish I could find
    Your image studded somewhere in the void,
    Or under some shining, ocean-stormed waterproof
    Or shooting the greater horned whiffenpoof . . .
    Selah. Is no 'gnus good gnus?' Not at all!
10 (– All this I find upon an obscene wall,
    Written by one, a spy, Vigil Forget,
    And scrawled in blood and urine and his own sweat –
    Some say his name was Peter Gynt or Gaunt,
    He wrote these lines and then was promptly shot.)
15 Nyasaland with delirium tremens and stamp album giraffes?
    Spain! But here I hold my obverse laughs,
    Remembering other friends and sons of fiends,
    And how much else which dark and goodness holds,
    And hope which dies and yields, but never ends,
20 Or, when it does, its bleeding past defends . . .
    – Well – what the hell – yes, what! the giraffe has a long neck,
    And too much longitude, by all Tehuantepec,
    And infinite therapeutic and a technique,
    Demanding reciprocal exactitude in love's arithmetic.
25 Ah, *you* must be the Nubian three-horned
    To deal with one so forearmed. Be forwarned . . .
    Sincerely, I suggest she is not toothsome,
    Too much being asked to satiate her loathsome,
    Her thoughts jump like beans when you say Timbuctoo,
30 Her body's striped like boys at bleak Harrow,
    Or visions of the Aldershot tatoo.
    Or, simply like another giraffe, in another zoo . . .
    – Oaxaca? Si, Oaxaca, Oax., Mex!
    Where is Oaxaca, Vigil, you ask, what annex,
35 Niche, pitch, is this? What age is it? What sex?
    Mexico? Is it not the place of the lost?
    Goal of all Americans who want to be divorced:
    Of all Norsemen who want to be unnorsed:
    Of all horsemen, already unhorsed:
40 Licences by Lawrence, by pouncing serpents endorsed.
    – Chingarn chingarn chingarn chingarn chingarn,
    In Oaxaca I strum my bawdy tune,
    Which says, let there be happiness for you,
    But delivery, my friend, from ancient heaven,

45   For God must know it is too badgery,
      And retrospect with harps and harpies too,
      All botched and bungled with celestial grind...
      Hush hush I hear the sound of last no-trumps –
      (That strumpets bid before they go to bawd
50   Warmed by the bloodstream of Wasserman turnips?...)
      Which are the military police.
      – How long since I was last in hell, oh Lord?
      Since the last heartbreak of a broken record?
      The last memory of a lovely laughing face?
55   All lost in mistress time and virgin space.
      Ah, ghouls are nursling to this bosom,
      My heart a widowed spider trapping grief,
      Its strings are wrung with agony of Ed Lang,
      From floribundia to rose of gall and lung,
60   It knows the dungeon and must know the gun.
      Ah, Martin, would I were in Birmingham,
      With old complaints and duns upon my pen!
      I love the sun yet I would trade the sun
      For 'In a Mist' by Beiderbecke's ghost,
65   A break from 'Singing the Blues', a phrase from Bach,
      'Walking the Dog' in 1929; Liverpool;
      Frankie Trumbauer's 'Imagination', and good Gogol;
      For Birmingham-erratum-edgbaston...
      Inverted we have been from Grantchester!
70   ...Strange, I shall know death tomorrow, which siesta,
      May turn out simply just one more fiesta...)
      And the nighted storm glistening on the wet fruit,
      And Ralph and Bob and Margaret to greet,
      Quietly again, in rainy Gillot Street...

  T   from] to {16.2}

  T   16.2: [In Lowry's hand at top of sheet: 'Dedication to Martin & Ralph' – two
        of the Case brothers.]
 14   16.2: [adds next line:] – Are you in Spain, hell fire, Liberia gruesome?
 70   16.1: ... Strange, I shall greet death to-morrow, which siesta

III. The Cantinas

1936–7   I   [17.2]

How did all this begin, and why am I here
At this arc of Bar with its cracked brown paint?
Papegaai, Mezcal, Hennessey, Cerveza,
Two slimed spittoons, no company but fear:
5   Fear of light, of the Spring, of the complaint
Of birds, and buses flying to far places,
And the students going to the races,
Of girls skipping with the wind in their faces;
But no company, no company but fear:
10   Fear of the blowing fountain, and all flowers
That know the sun are my enemies,
These, dead, hours?

2   17.1: at this arc of bar with its cracked brown paint,
3   17.1: papegaai, mezcal, hennessey, cerveza,
5   17.1: fear of light, of the spring, of the complaint

1937   II   [18.2]

Above all, absent yourself from that affair.
Swedenborg had such half wisdom; thought ahead.
But Lawrence thought backward; while even Shakespeare
Shook in the dark abysm past time's maidenhead.
5   Did you know Maidenhead? The Richmond
Girls fare better in Maida Vale; in Baker Street
Take Sherlock home, visit Madame Twosores, the wax dead.
From these I expect little, least of all, pleasure;
Three beers in Charlotte Street, a Star at six o'clock,
10   And sixpences two, one bright brown shoe, and doom;
And four bad books and the thought of Vermont,
The sea would be good to have, too, but a shock
To receive. Thank you; and simply to count
No money, inspect no hotel room.

7   18.1: take Sherlock home, visit Madame Twosores; & the wax dead.

1937   III   [19.2]

MEMORY OF THE HOSPITALITY OF AMERICAN BARMEN

We reserve the right to refuse to anyone, pal.
Yeah, and that means you, four eyes, with the wheels, and hell!
Don't tell me you're a diamond and put
It on the slate, or that your heart is fat,
5   Or that your landlord can't wait to break it.

What's that? It's broken already? Well, that's that.
A spade'll pick your grave if grave you merit;
A spade's a spade, that's what they call it here.
We teach 'em bully the cabbage, never you fear;
10   In God we trust – but only on the nickel.
Well, if you had a buck too bad you spent her,
  – But all who ask for trust distrust inherit,
And even God is fickle.

T 19.1: [missing]
1 19.1: (– we reserve the rot to refuse to anyone, pal.
6 <u>It's</u>] its {19.1}
13 19.1: and even god is fickle. –)

1937   IV   [20.2]

When you were starving, you waited – how long?
Two hours? But Fernandez Passalique,
At the corner of Main, waited two years for a break.
Perhaps this is not a subject for a song,
5   But now he is starving again. It is a trick
To pass inhibitory time away? Well, the rack
Is still used in Trujillo. So be it. Ring
Out, you bleeding bells, over our time's demise;
Ring in this bad Kentucky straight Bourbon.
10 Mint Springs one pint and ninety proof of what!
Ring in, too, my corn king assassin, you distilleries,
And churches, and by Torture, Tortu, the Sorbonne,
And San Domingo, let us brew one alcoholic thought!

13 20.1, 2: and San Domingo, let us brew an alcoholic thought!

1937   V   [21.2]

Shakespeare should have come to Acapulco;
Here he would have found a timeless hell,
He who leaves all, Dean Donne said, doth as well –
(There is no rhyme for foul Acapulco,
5   Nor reason, expletive, save – Acapulco!)
  – As he who eats, devours. He would scarcely have left all
Fruits here in this 'seascape in a bottle!'
  – (Or escape into a million!) – quotes: Wells Fargo.
Paraiso de Caleta, seduce him to your bed!
10 Suppose it. He would have held no horses,
Written no plays. What creditor wants verses?
  – Globe? No Globe here, not a scenical sound.
All that could have been said is what Marston said:
Rich happiness that such a son is crowned.

1934–6   VI   [22.2]

But never fall from fealty to light,
You said, Melville? Now, by God, sir, why not?
The pall is comfortable enough; as soon rot
There as another place; once being well met
5   The beauty of the dark is there's no sight
Of that light you speak of! What lamps are lit
Save no falling from fealty to it
When once accepted wholly by the night.
It is a treachery to the powers of hell
10   To refrain as you suggest, is a treason
Against the inferno whose judgements well
Fit the crime; whose mercy is tempered
With fire – light enough for those unhampered
By day. And true to unreason.

1936–8   VII   [23.2]

Most nauseous of all drinks, what is your spell?
You are cheap, you are the whore of potions;
You are impalatable, you are the way to hell;
You are insatiable of ravagement, you
5   Are the worst of libations!

Tequila of Jalisco, of maguey, – (image of man
Tortured, and tossing gangrened hands in the sun,
Half-buried in the crepitant desert sand!); –
How is it, precisely, we call you our friend,
10   When your salty jest is to calm our nerves
And then to storm what passes for our homes?
Chingarn! As jests go perhaps this is a good jest –
To make a God of man first, then a fiend,
So that he forgets even those he loves,
15   And whither he comes.

Under your acid spell, quite wanting only you,
Loving only you, we wait only our balm
For the heart's next recession to its false calm.
– But would you were only friend, not mistress too!

1937–8   VIII   [24.2]

I have known a city of dreadful night,
Dreadfuller far than Kipling knew, or Thomson...
This is the night when hope's last seed is flown
From the evanescent mind of winter's grandson.
5   In the dungeon shivers the alcoholic child,

Comforted by the murderer, since compassion is here too;
The noises of the night are cries for help
From the town and from the garden which evicts those who
               [destroy.

The policeman's shadow swings against the wall,
10 The lantern's shadow is darkness against the wall;
And on the cathedral's coast slowly sways the cross
Which are wires and the tall pole moving in the wind –

And I crucified between two continents.

But no message whines through for me here, oh multitudinous,
15 To me here, – (where they cure syphilis with sloans liniment,
And clap, with another dose.)

2 24.2: More dreadful far than Kipling knew, or Thomson . . .

1937   IX   [25.4]

THIRTY FIVE MESCALS IN CUAUTLA

This ticking is most terrible of all,
You hear the sound I mean on ships and trains,
You hear it everywhere for it is doom;
The tick of real death, not the tick of time,
5 The termite at the rotten wainscot timber of the world,
And it is death to you though well you know
The heart's silent tick failing against the clock,
Its beat ubiquitous and still more slow,
But still not the tick, the tick of real death,
10 Only the tick of time – still only the heart's chime
When body's alarm wakes whirring to terror.
– In the cantina throbs the refrigerator,
While against the street the gaunt station hums.
What can you say fairly of a broad lieutenant,
15 With bloody hand behind him, a cigarro in it,
But that he blocks a square of broken sunlight
Where scraps of freedom stream against the gale
And lightning scrapes blue shovels against coal?
The thunder batters the Gothic mountains;
20 But why must you hear, hear and not know this storm,
Seeing it only under the door,
Visible in synecdoches of wheels
And khaki water sousing down the gutter?
In ripples like claws tearing the water back?
25 The wheels smash a wake under the jalousie.
The lieutenant moves, but the door swings to . . .
– What of all this life outside, unseen by you,
Passed by, escaped from, or excluded

By a posture in a desolate bar? . . .
30   No need to speak, conserve a last mistake;
Perhaps real death's inside, don't let it loose.
The lieutenant carried it into the back room?
The upturned spittoons may mean it, so may the glass.
The girl refills it, pours a glass of real death,
35   And if there's death in her there is in me.
On the pictured calendar, set to the future,
The two reindeer battle to death, while man,
The tick of real death, not the tick of time,
Hearing, thrusts his canoe into a moon,
40   Risen to bring us madness none too soon.

Note: Soma was mystically identified with the moon, who controls veg-
etation and whose cup is ever filling and emptying, as he waxes and
wanes.

T	25.1:	Prelude to another drink
	25.2:	Mescal
		Mescal: in an empty bar in Cuautla
		In an empty barroom
		The end
		The Calendar
	25.3:	Twenty nine Tequilas
1	25.1:	This ticking is the most terrible of all
2	25.1:	You hear this sound on ships, you hear it on trains
3–4	25.1:	[missing]
5	25.1:	It is the death-watch beetle at the rotten timber of the world
	25.2:	the death watch beetle at the timber of the world;
	25.3:	the death watch beetle at the world's timber,
	25.4:	the death watch beetle at the rotten timber of the world,
6	25.1:	And it is death to you too: for well you know
	25.2:	and it is death to you for well you know
7	25.1:	That the heart's tick is failing all the while
	25.2:	the hearts silent tick is failing against the clock
8	25.1:	Always ubiquitous & still more slow.
	25.2:	always ubiquitous and still more slow
9–10	25.1:	[missing]
10	25.2:	not tick of time.
11	25.1, 2:	[missing]
13	25.1:	And against the street the gaunt station hums.
14	25.1:	What can you say fairly of a fat man
15	25.1:	With a bent hand behind him & a cigarette in it?
	25.2:	with a broken hand behind him and a cigarro in it?
		with a cruel hand behind him and a cigarro in it?
		with a mechanic hand behind him and a cigarro in it?
16–18	25.1, 2:	[missing]
19–30	25.1:	[missing]
19	25.2:	or of the thunder in the Gothic mountains
		[adds next line:] the Cuautla towers crashing against thunder
		the Cuautla towers plunging against thunder
20–2	25.2:	[missing]

23   25.2: of khaki water sousing down the gutter
24   25.2: ripples like claws tearing the water back,
25   25.2: cats smashing wake under the jalousie,
        25.3: The wheels smash wake under the jalousie.
26   25.2: [missing]
31   25.1: Yet death is in the room, there is death everywhere:
        25.2: real death's inside no need to let it loose
32   25.1: That man carries it though I cannot see his face:
        25.2: the lieutenant carries it though I can't see his face
33   25.1: The upturned spittoons mean it, it is in the glass,
        25.2: the upturned spittoons mean it so does the glass
34 25.1, 2: the girl who refills it pours a glass of death
36–40   25.1: [contains only:]
        On the calendar, set to the future, the two stags battle
        To death: man paddles his coracle to the moon
        Which, seen also in the light, is as divisible as death.
36   25.2: On the calendar, set to the future,
39   25.2: hearing, thrusts his canoe into the moon,
        Note] [missing] {25.3}

1936   X   [26.4]

AT THE BAR

— Drunkards of salt water, thirsty for disaster,
Derelicts do not dream of being ships:
Never does calamity forsake them
For the hush of the swift and the look-out's all's well:
5   Neurotic in Atlantic of a death,
Bereaved but avid of another's breath,
Swimming with black genius under black waters,
And buried standing up like Ben Jonson,
Though eighteenpence is here a total loss;
10   And Tarquin certain of a ravishable prey;
While others grope the rails, rigid with gazing down.

T   26.1: Only god knows how

1937   XI   [27.7(5)] [131]

DELIRIUM IN VERA CRUZ

Where has tenderness gone, he asked the mirror
Of the Biltmore Hotel, cuarto 216. Alas,
Can its reflection lean against the glass
Too, wondering where I have gone, into what horror?
5   Is that it staring at me now with terror
Behind your frail tilted barrier? Tenderness
Was here, in this very retreat, in this
Place, its form seen, cries heard, by you. What error
Is here? Am I that forked rashed image?

10   Is this the ghost of love which you reflected?
    Now with a background of tequila, stubs, dirty collars,
    Sodium perborate, and a scrawled page
    To the dead, telephone disconnected?
    ... He smashed all the glass in the room. (Bill: $50.)

  7 27.1, 2, 3: Was here, in this very bedroom, in this
  9 27.1, 2, 3: Is here? Am I that rashed image?
10 27.1, 2, 3: Is this the ghost of the love you reflected?
13 27.1, 2, 3: To the dead, telephone off the hook? In rage
14 27.1, 2, 3: He smashed all the glass in the room. (Bill: $50.)

1936   XII   [28.3]

DOCTOR USQUEBAUGH

    The doom of each, said Doctor Usquebaugh,
    Quite clearly bids out loutish bones to stare.
    True, drink's unfruitful on a larger scale;
    Its music is an equinoctial gale:
5   Still, unembarrassing: and, profounder,
    Outwinds the range of Cupid's organ grinder.
    If worms are sabbatical in a drunkard's dream
    No fouler's this than love's nocturnal game,
    Since dream of love it is, love of the pit
10   For its own sake, the virginity of the present,
    Whose abyss is a womb shall not deny
    A wintry plunge to nescient ecstasy,
    Unsheathed entrance to the spirit's Tarquin,
    But featherless and free from overt din,
15   Extending a plattered Lucrece with ferment,
    Yet deeper than she, and rich with moist consent.
    ... So well might we inquire, content to rot,
    What do you offer, love, which drink does not?

1937   XIII   [29.7]

THE LAST MAN IN THE DÔME

    Where is the finely drunk? Is the great drunkard?
    This imponderable small mystery
    Perplexes me at midnight constantly:
    – Where is he gone and taking whence his tankard?
5   Where are they all gone, my friends, the great unanchored?
    They moan no more at bars, none put to sea;
    A shake of the will and they dream most easily,
    Livers at last of lives for which they hankered –
    Endless corridors of boots to lick,
10   Or at the end of them all the Pope's toe.
    Where are your friends, you fool? you have but one,

And that a friend who also makes you sick –
If much less sick than they; and this I know,
Since I am the last drunkard: I drink alone.

T]   [missing] {25.4: in Lowry's hand 'The last drunkard should I
             last man in the Dôme.'}
T   29.1: Prelude to another drink
                     29.2: The man who had not heard of the war
                           The last man at the Dôme
             29.5, 6: The Last Drunkard
I   29.1, 2, 3, 5, 6: Where is the finely drunk? Where is the great drunkard?
3   29.5, 6: confounds an ex-gob worse than history.
5   29.5, 6: Where are all gone, my friends, the great unanchored?
             29.5, 6: Where are all my friends, the great unanchored?
6   29.1: They drink no more: they go to bed at three
             29.5, 6: They moan no more at bars: though this story
7   29.1: In the afternoon yet dream more easily –
             29.5, 6: Fails to tell if they quit the Battery
8   29.5, 6: To live that dream for which their souls hankered
9   29.1, 2, 3, 4, 5, 6: Of endless corridors of boots to lick,
10   29.5, 6: Or at the end of them all the Mate's toe.
13   29.5, 6: If much less sick than they. I raise my glass –
14   29.1: Since I am the last drunkard. And I drink alone.
             29.5, 6: I am the last drunkard. I drink alone.

IV. Songs for Second Childhood

1934–6   I   [30.3]

Lead were their feet, and lead their heart and bone,
Their dreamed-of port was lead but their ships were stone;
Their houses all with leaden shapes of doom,
Were haunted in the leaden Wesleyan gloom.

5   Their childhood's scribble pencilled out their pain,
But served not obsolescence time nor gain;
Their ships were stone because their Church was rock.
Let Greek meet Greek, rock rock, now find the wreck!

Their lips were cracked and moulded half to pray
10   To genius foundered on the idiot way;
Were they lost too? None claimed them, were they drowned;
They were not lost, but neither were they found.

They were not found! No trace of them betrays
That through a sleeked and molten sea of lies
15   They sank, uncared prodigies of the dead,
Weighed down by an eternity of lead.

4 30.1, 2, 3: were haunted in the precise Weslyan gloom.

1937   II   [31.2]

The tortures of hell are stern, their fires burn fiercely,
Yet vultures turn against the air more beautifully
Than seagulls float downwind in cool sunlight,
Or fans in asylums spin a loom of fate
5   For hope which never ventured up so high
As life's deception, astride the vulture's flight.

1937   III   [32.2]

The dead man sat in the sun
And mourned what he had done;
The live man sat on the grave,
And thanked God he had been brave.

5   Live and dead men both
Exchange impartial dooms
In the dance of sunlight on earth,
In the dance of sunlight on tombs.

4 32.1: and thanked god he had been brave.

1938   IV   [33.5]

CURSE

Tender meat were you to snouted boys
– Oh little Wesleyan paying the savage piper –
Gasping in the dark by the tennis court
Jeered at for your frailty or your sex,
5   By badged boy scouts with notched totems for sadism:
Idiot be prepared but not for this
Ambush of anguish revealed by the patrol sneer
Of tiger, wolf, lion, stoat, and the dove
Quite lost whether of peace or war.
10 The whirring of the chapel bell's amaze,
Stopped the heart as never mouth stopped with kiss.
Lifting your uncracked voice in broken praise,
Your self struggling in the frozen heart's fissure –
– The ladders runged against it were woman's hands
15 That numbed in curious rings before they touched –
Or praying in icy silence for compassion,
Through burst blained fingers squinting in icy silence
At something half a face and half a bum,
You remembered the oath: against yours my worst
20 Pathfinder of moons in chapel or asylum! –
And snarled like Adams to no human beast.

T]   [missing] {33.4}
T 33.2, 3, 5: [missing]
I   33.4, 5: Tender meat you were to snouted boys
5   33.2: by badged boy scouts with totems for sadism
7   33.2: ambush of anguish advancing with foul cries
8   33.2: of tiger stoat lion wolf & purring dove
11   33.2: stopped heart as never your mouth was stopped with kiss
15–21   33.2: [missing]
20   33.4: Pathfinder
21   33.4: [missing]

1937   V   [34.3]

The stone must be rolled away from self's pain,
Or you, my dear Jones, well though you have sung,
Will become, as it were, a sort of pelican,
Who, plunging her beak in her breast, yet feeds no young
5   And all this on some sea-margin she knows barren
Of food, though dives and wheels and wheels and dives again.

1937–8   VI   [35.2]

As the poor end of each dead day drew near,
He tried to count the things which he held dear;

No Rupert Brooke, and no great lover, he
Remembered little of simplicity.
5   His soul had never been empty of fear,
And he would sell it thrice now for a tankard of beer
He seemed to have known no love, to have valued dread
Above all human feelings. He liked the dead;
The grass was not green, not even grass to him;
10   Nor was sun, sun; rose, rose; smoke, smoke; limb, limb.

6   35.1: and he would sell it thrice now for a tarot of beer

1937–8   VII   [36.2]

The sun shines; where is the lyric?
Moon, stars, etc. produce no panegyric.
Now we have the sun it's the last thing we want;
If Oswald, ('Ghosts'), had it, he would resent
5   It; would give it away to another ghost.
Somewhere, people marching . . . The world will content
Itself with itself again, thinking itself excellent.

4   36.1: if Oswald (Ghosts), had it, he would resent
     36.2: If Oswald (in Ghosts), had it, he would resent

1936–8   VIII   [37.2]

The gentleness of rain is in the wind,
Shelley's elided fragment stars the mind;
Together with Kafka's by any other route,
He would have reached the Castle. As well as
5   Some disputed smithereens by Shakespeare
Ambiguous souvenirs of James or Jones,
Cast up by a bounded ocean of thought
On blank shores where the soul seems boundless,
Like man, the extravagance of creation.
10   Phrases rejected for a trochee's sake
Bobbing like corks on margins of volumes,
May mark depths where the caught iambic glitters;
Or one flying line among such fragments
Soars on forever like the Bird of Paradise.
15   It is my joy to core the world as such
A rounded phrase in God's black manuscript
Remembered, but abandoned for a fairer,
As such, mankind's alternative of God,
Yet claimed by us, and thoughtfully conserved.

12   37.2: May mark depths where the iambic glitters;
14   Soars] Soar
18   37.1: as such mankind's alternative of god,

1937   IX   [38.2]

THE SAILORS

    – Thou promontory dreadfuller than Hatteras,
    Show us the track;
    Tell us, the sea-doomed to a stuffed mattress,
    Tell us the trick.
5   Tierra del Fuego.
    – Here is the curve when young,
    Beautiful and clear;
    This is too often sung.
          The sailors.
10   – This rather we would know before we're gone;
    Which is the cape and which the horn?
            Tierra del Fuego.
    – The trick when life is done?
    Then cape and horn are one;
15   Is that what you mean?
          The sailors.
    – No!
            Tierra del Fuego.
    – No time! There is your cape full-bellied;
20   Stride thou now for New York;
    The watches are rallied,
    And the crowd at work.
          The sailors.
    – Tell us, before –
25   The bosun.
    – Eight bells, where are we, men?
            Tierra del Fuego.
    – Your ship makes her veronica and goes,
    In Fuego this chilly bull bows.
30   Farewell till the next time!
          The sailors.
    – But –
            Tierra del Fuego.
    – Wait for no plaudits ringing!
35   Stride on, though far be the landing
    For you, and the bunting waving
    Where at the bending of the bay
    Your love is standing;
    Where ends the curve,
40   Begins the new ship's wave.
          The bosun.
    – Yes, and when the curve's squeezed out of shape,
    Where then's your horn, and which the cape?

23   <u>sailors.</u>] sailors

1934–6   X   [39.2]

He plays the piano with a razor,
The concertina with a pair of scissors;
A rigadoon for all his customers,
He is the Sweeney Todd of improvisers!
5   Though all men fear this poor relation,
His keener music gives a strange sensation;
Defying all anatomization,
Beckoning like ambiguous sounds,
Heard by those who dwelt with Cyclops and fiends,
10   And died on perfumed seas with stinking wounds...
Under the razor, under the broken light
Of this gibbering world we shall fall
Thus enticed, into the swinging chair to wait;
Read madness; watch self; accept nothing; accept all.

1937   XI   [40.3]

THE DEVIL WAS A GENTLEMAN

The devil was a gentleman,
He tried to raise his hat,
But it got caught upon one horn,
He hadn't thought of that.

5   The devil was a gentleman,
Though most anonymous,
Dantesquely loved a woman,
She proved as cold as ice.

Still, the devil was a gentleman,
10   So could not keep it on;
Grotesquely tugging, broke the crown –
And the lady had gone.
And now he was a devil
To make the whole world smile;
15   No more stalked subtle evil,
Under the infernal tile.

Bowing before a mirror,
To observe his gehennaed beard;
He started back with terror,
20   This was worse than the old fiend feared.

He knew that he had ruined
His hat, so bruised and torn,
But Oh my God, to have profaned
Not only hat, but horn!

25   So a hatless, one-horned demon

Limped sourly among men;
While the rumor slowly died quite down,
He had been a gentleman.

T   40.1: [missing]
21   40.1, 2: He knew well he had ruined
22   40.1, 2: the poor hat he had worn
23   40.1, 2: but not that he had so profaned

1937–8   XII   [41.3]

He wrote for the dead, but the ubiquitous dead
Liked their own wisdom, and preferred their bed;

He wrote for the blind, yet the polygonous blind
Had richer, thicker things just then in mind;

5   He wrote for the dumb, but the golden-voiced dumb
Were singing their own songs and could not come;

So he wrote for the unborn, since surely, it is said,
At least they're neither dumb, nor blind, nor dead.

1937   XIII   [42.2]

Oh, pyre of Bierce and springboard of Hart Crane!
I will not die here! He prayed for his ill life.
This is far from home, by Christ! to die so,
Too far from love, lane, sanity, wife.
5   He trembled. But his hurdling Olympic brain
Raced with the imponderable athlete doom,
To be of life once more the bridegroom,
And ran death down and ran him to defeat . . .
'But not defeat of such doleful wreathing,'
10   Grinned death, (a sardonic loser), 'Of faces
And English stones, with smiles and flowers, as graces
My slow prize day at home for stopping breathing,
Such as all who have been buried under the forget-me-not,
Will tell you of jovially; and well they should know.'

1934–6   XIV   [43.3]

Time entered the stuffed court, slowly swearing:
– – I have, he added, dripped my soft snow
Too long for those who find our life past bearing,
Treading down in the year's drifts their black woe;
5   And long enough have turned the day to dollar
For soldier spendthrift rogue and battered scholar,
Been spelled, by the echoing bell, in the ship's pitch,
Tolled agony to far schoolmates in green vetch,
For all that I am a fake healer of cracked hearts,

10   Vampired and counterwhored by a false name
    Most merdurinous; and so the fates
    Contrived, for a poor dream, a famous crime;
    Though love's wrenched houghs my cataplasms have known,
    Now that I love, my Lord, I must be slain.

1934-6   XV   [44.2]
    Loathing is as beautiful as the scourge
    Of wind on freighters at dawn, but more strange.
    Decency's landlord inveighs against force,
    While we detest most what we would embrace;
5   Seek, though eschewing in advance, advice . . .
    Yet now pentametre shall scan our hate
    For those whose sober and platonic lips,
    Dryer than broken trumpets in pawnshops,
    Confirm our ease among the strident worst;
10   Such lips were never made for love to bite
    That offer ashes to immedicable thirst,
    Uncalled for service both to life and death;
    Better to be salvaged by the accursed
    And succoured by the foulness of their breath.

11   44.1: [adds next line:] unwelcome service this to life and death,

1936   XVI   [45.2]
    Another than Wordsworth dropped his live work
    To listen to the wind's shriek of uprooted trees,
    And vessels' smashed backs under portentous seas
    Scrabbling with sharks as Rydal hives with bees,
5   The *Ohio* smoking in Frisco on a sharp pen
    Of rock, lightning a leash snarled by force
    At the bounding neck of God's mad dog, the dark;
    The universe snapping like hounds at some dread groom.
    I believe that Wordsworth thought of the calm . . .
10   But to another blessing chaos, since it must horridly drown
    In hurled gules of conflict's flesh, his own strike
    Of the hour, his own grief, no peaceful lake
    Lights by storm's flash. Such is the nature of his doom
    That like some infant Aeolus Dowson in tempest's tavern,
15   He claps for better thunder, wilder typhoon.

9   45.1: I think that Wordsworth thought of the calm . . .

1936   XVII   [46.2]

DELIRIUM IN LOS ANGELES

    'Informal' (dancing on the zebra floor)
    Seemed first, – it was an electric sign – 'infernal':

Then, the next street to the bar, came 'Vigil',
Which really was 'Virgil' by Vermont.
5   St. Vitus of the City of Angels!...
Wurlitzer turned 'howitzer', from its bung,
Blasted a boisterous bomb at the bar.
At the blue clock with vermilion pendule
Hangs man's 'public inquiry of the hour.'
10   The goose blue cloak swings high against the door...
In the travel agent's window, 'quest for beauty' –
Indistinct, one thinks how two sable steeds
Were lost in a circle unknown to Dante;
But delirium's on the march, we are wrong
15   Nevertheless these three dark words proved right.

T   46.1: [missing]
9–10   46.2: Hung man's 'public inquiry of the hour.'
              The goose blue coat swung high against the door...
11   agent's] agents
11–13   46.2: On that travel agents window, indistinct, 'Quest for beauty'?
              And one thinks how two sable steeds were lost
              through gaps in broken hearts unvoyaged through by Dante.

1934–6   XVIII   [47.3]

– – Where do you come from? The land of Epigram,
Or Connecticut? I am from Hinnom;
Educated, Nantucket and Bellevue;
At Cape Cod committed my first murder,
5   In a windmill. Of course, I murdered you!
What is it like to be dead? Have you a planchette?
A raspail in heaven or a bal musette?

– – If I am dead, young Judas, I've been deader
10   In your bedraggled, insectuous, country...
Further, I dwell on that declivity of life
Where weeping (Herford's) willows rock and laugh,
And lazarene hyenas softly weep
Under them, even as you, on Hebephrene's steep.

10   47.1: in your bed-wraggled insectuous country...

1937   XIX   [48.2]

Pigling, pigling, burning bland,
On Arabia's coral strand;
What immortal station pie,
Dare frame thy frightul piggery?

V. The Comedian

1937   I   [49.2]

You were in hell fire? had been all your life?
And thought that nothing had been forged there?
I see a weapon moulded from the fire
Stronger than any sword: that deadlier knife
5   Of keen wisdom which flayed your soul strife
With flame in the pit could not wholly tire.
Take that soul and strip it down to the core
With new steel as others who burnt before
For their knowledge or ours, our gain, or loss . . .
10   There is a fellowship some pilgrims think
Between all in disastrous fight, yet few
Know their truest guardians in darkness.
Get out to your tavern, drink your nauseous drink,
And read these lines, then pray to those like you.

12   49.1: know their real guardians from darkness.

1936–8   II   [50.1]

DELIRIUM IN URUAPAN

– I met a man who suffered more than I
At a street corner. Then another. Yet one more.
After, I found a blackened street of poor
Fiends who had suffered an eternity.
5   I asked the first man for his company
But he refused; so wondering why
I thought to ask the second man, whose stare
Of perfect contempt held such frigidity
I climbed the blackened street in haste to tell
10   Those who suffered most, to ask what had been done
To deserve this. But there was a curse in their laugh.
Then I remembered that I was in hell.
Yes – what had I done to earn even the damned's scorn?
. . . And turned back down the blacker street of self,
                                        knowing well enough.

[1938–9]   III   [51.1]

Love which comes too late is like that black storm
That breaks out of its season, when you stand
Huddled yet with upturned tentative hand
To the strange rain. Yet sadly no sane calm
5   Succeeds it as when all the surprised form
Of nature is restored to a surprised land,

Or the poor flowers thirst again and the sand
Sifts drily once more; and the abnormal norm
Of a parched world wholly returns. But say
10   It is like anything else: for let this love strike
You blind, dumb, mad, dead, your grotesque fate
Will not be altered by your simile.
It slakes no thirst to say what love is like
Which comes too late, my God, alas, too late.

11 51.1: You blind, dumb, mad, dead, your untimely fate
14 51.1: Which comes too late, my God, too late.

[1938–9]   IV   [52.2]

But I shall live when you are dead and damned – –
Did you say Chatterton to Chesterfield? – –
Oh, Chatterton, Chatterton, wield
In your inferno or evening land
5   Some sword for me, steal something to defend
My poor spirit: and if no sword, a shield
Does as well. I wish that spirit healed
Which is yours, though mutilated, and
My love is dead too, gone to her death bed
10   All under the willow tree: Oh, Chatterton, I cry out
That you have pity on my self pity,
My lack of genius and what I write in doubt:
Let us meet in your dark metric city,
Before I am dumb; and damned; and dead.

[1938–9]   V   [53.2]

A DRIED UP RIVER IS LIKE THE SOUL

A dried up river is like the soul
Of a poet who can't write, yet perceives
With imperfect clarity his theme and grieves
To parched death over the drought. But his goal
5   Once a wholesome sea of clearest crystal
Recedes, grows grey in hartseye, like old love leaves,
Leaves the mind altogether. He conceives
Nothing to replace it: only at the pole
Of memory flickers some senseless compass.
10   So the river, by her grey pitying trees,
Is an agony of stones, horrors which sank
But are now declared, bleached. For it is these,
These stones and nothingnesses which possess
When river is a road and mind a blank.

T]   [missing] {53.1}

[1938–9]   VI   [54.2]

There is a tide in the affairs of men
Which taken at the flood leads on to fortune.
So his brother loved to quote and importune
A crapulous sad dish whose ten
5   Feet or not by fourteen of unsold line
Was not quite even considered out of tune
With his time, and whose drunkard's rigadoon
Disgraced father, mother, sister, and then
Wife, child, home, country; and yet, and yet,
10   Costly though he proved, I have met worse men
Who took no tide, if any, at the flood. . . .
There is a story of a great poet
Who told a bishop his line was blank verse.
They laughed; the poet laughs still, in tears of blood.

6 54.1, 2: Was disastrously considered out of tune
7 whose] who's
10 54.1: Costly though he proved, I have met far worse men
     54.2: Costly though he proved, I have met duller men

[1938–9]   VII   [55.1]

A poem about a poem that can't be written
Is like true love the heart has foregone
But not lost: say both are smitten,
The real poem, and the right love, frozen.
5   Both must wander never quite forgotten
By their ghost over the iron, woebegone
Waste, grave of consciousness and heart where stone
Is foliage and builds no cross or shrine,
Where no groan's heard from dream, love, or nightmare,
10   Where death's a gift at Christmas or at Easter,
And birth a jest of vascular endeavor,
And moon and sun a maniacal glare.
Such ravagement have we known;
Such expedition, and such despair; –
15   Yet this is not us here,
Never could this be us, say it is not, say that this
                     is not us here.

[1938–9]   VIII   [56.1]

Darkness has its compensations, both
Supersensual and extramundane:
But of these not to be counted is the pain
Forget felt then in the shadow of death.
5   Life was not dear to him, yet his last

Breath he feared, and his tumultuous brain
Fought with good light against the thought of doom
And conquered it, thus avoiding the wreath
Four relatives might have given, and the burial
10   In the town on the hill where all he loved
Was the rain, one tree, and a girl
Whose loss he had long since mourned
And shall mourn till he dies, knowing too well
He lives again but lives in darkness still.

[1938–9]   IX   [57.1]

Resurgent sorrow is a sea in the cave
Of the mind – just as in the poem
It gluts it – though no nymphs will quire a hymn;
Abandon it! . . . Take a trip to the upper shore. Lave
5   Yourself in sand; gather poppies; brave
The fringe of things, denying that inner chasm.
Why, the hush of the sea's in the seashell; in the limb
Of the smashed ship, its tempest; and your grave
The sand itself if you'd have it so. Yet glare
10   Through a sky of love all day still must you receive
In the cave the special anguish of your life;
With the skull of the seagull and the wreck you may fare
Well enough but will not escape the other surf
Remorse, your host, who haunts that whirlpool where
15   The past's not washed up dead and black and dry
But whirls in its gulf forever, to no relief.

[1938–9]   X   [58.1]

You gave yourself to death but never to me.
Marvell might have laughed. I cannot weep.
Shakespeare might have quite calmly urged: Keep
All metaphysics from those who are mortally
5   Wounded. But envy the dead. A fig for that virgin Dante.
My third best bed was in the cemetery.

So you are dead who insulted my soul.
Being buried, who were not even my friend,
Buried without heather or wild rose
10   In the bleak weather as the great wind blows
Over the shining pavements, the wet magazines,
The fur scented girls, and the grass green with the new rains,
And left a tragedy here, if you can call
What hurries beyond tragedy, a tragedy,
15   For these should have a beginning and an end.

10   58.1: In the wild wild weather as the east wind blows
        In the bleak dark weather as the east wind blows

[1938–9]   XI   [59.1]

This is the end but since it is the end,
You are happy at least in this one certainty,

As you were in the eternity
Of childhood's blue summer with seagull and yacht for friend;

5   When God was good; love, true; sea, sea; land, land.
Yet dare not to base immunity

From baseness on this triviality!
The murderer once gathered sea poppies with a hand

To be scarleter, to be pressed to the blacker
10   And less amorous heart of death . . . Oh, Christ,

Wash up some bone clear memory on this bitterest coast
Where is no wreck dead beak nor feather

Though none venture here without disaster. Give at the last
One half passionate tryst with the past;

15   Some sweet joy to gather there to my salt grey breast
Though children were betrayed, and money was kissed first.

15   59.1: Some sweet joy to gather to my salt grey breast

1936   XII   [60.1]

A wounded voice over the telephone:
'Call me later. I am just tired.'
– Then, the bell shrieking in the unseen room
Filling it with the ferocity of doom.
5   'But what shall I do, my own, my lost one,
Latched back into deeper night from the dark's drone
They have called back the last, the slowest of all
                              to the asylum
Whose only thought is time, now there is none,
Now all is gone, all, all, save compassion,
10   And all is doubly gone with you gone, dear.'
– The bell still beats about that tragic room
Like a trapped bird, precursor of greater fear,
Where I imagine every book we shared,
Touched, yes, touched, smell, out of the pages of a book,
15   Out of Gogol; or your heart fluttering in my hand
But never held your heart back from denial,
Nor teeth, from my own heartsneck . . .

– The stars like silver rifles in the void
Look down their sights to their special aim.
20 They do not range the categories of our pain.
No world will plunge for tears we never saw fall,
For sorrow that was never shared at all,
That I might comfort the dead, clasp stones in the stream.

12 precursor] precurser

1936   XIII   [61.2]

Searching in a ravaged heart for anguish
You found only a dead grief? No sorrow
Could be as bad as that which quite goes by,
Ah, no, no sorrow . . . Still, to distinguish
5   It from other sorrows, extinguish
The heart first. Then call to-morrow,
Today: today, to-morrow; right, wrong: then languish
With these incorporate errors – and the live dead
Is the omission here, ominously –
10 Until you live again what dies unread:
Then remember what the Strauss song said:
Just once a year the dead live for one day . . .
– Oh, come to me again as once in May.

61.2 [Lowry's typist mistakenly appends the last two lines of 60 to the
beginning of this poem. They have been omitted here. {61.1}]

VI. The Moon in Scandinavia

1936   I   [62.2]

UKE IN PAWNSHOP

A ukelele once in pawn I saw:
Hikopale, hikopale, hilowai, oh:
Oolaki, walawalaki, waikapona.
Oh, mokuaweoweo!
5   Hikapale, hikapale, hilowai, ah.

T]   [missing]{62.1}

1937   II   [63.2]

God help those and others who
Have only thought of self,
To whom no simple truth was true,
No swift clear life was life:
5   And God help those who feel no pain
Yet live by it no less,
Since they invest it soundly in
Our stock of happiness.

8   63.1: our share of happiness.

1936   III   [64.2]

PRAYER

Give way, you fiends, and give that man some happiness
Who knelt in Wesleyan prayer to beget a fiend;
Builder of a gabled house with daffodils
Flattened by the webbed foot of false April
5   Father of four gaunt sons minus one,
Who, hearing the great guns, faltered not at all,
In church his rock, in home his Morro Castle,
In golf his chess, in poetry capital,
(And in the gulf his youngest abortive beauty,)
10   For him and for the woman of his choice
Replace the love which these most displaced bore me:
And from the wild choir over the freezing estuary
Bear him one humble phrase of love at last,
Some childhood supplication never to be lost
15   As I am lost whose lips had formed its shape . . .

5   64.2: Father of five steel gaunt sons minus one,
13   64.1: bear him again one humble phrase of love at long last
16–18   64.1: lest his fierce soul be abandoned to the gale
          and quick as the snake, the clock, [?] as death strikes,
          out of the nameless trees the nameless speak.

[1938–9]   IV   [65.2]

ON READING REDBURN

Children brave by day have strange fears at night
But when they wake in the morning light,
Their fears dissolve in sun between warm sheets,
Or, freezing in winter, become icy thoughts, –
5   The compulsory game in frost, – the impossible boast,
The Geometry lesson, the primer stolen or lost...
– Ah how often, Redburn, must lovers wake in nightmare
Bedded with what seems hatred and despair,
Only to turn to ecstasy like de Maupassant,
10   To find yet one more morning is triumphant!
– There is no constant here, such is our condition,
In dark to know conquest too, and in light no hope,
At dawn the girl, at midnight the horned owl.
– But what of the waking of the brave race of man
15   After the unvintageable terrors of its sleep,
To find the mildew still upon its soul?

T   65.1: On reading Melville's Redburn
7 65.1, 2: – How often, Redburn, lovers wake in nightmare
14 65.1, 2: – But what of a waking of the brave race of man

1936–8   V   [66.2]

A fig for 6-par-T-pak ginger ale!...
For contest winners every Friday night
And N.B.C. network, too, coast to coast contest!...
Tipi-tipi-tin out of a dead coin and hell
5   Is yours even if in God you do trust
Or piddledee or life's rot from cost to cost...
Wrecker of gardens, no nickel or Yale yell
Will ring victory now, nor speech with Everest,
Ixtaccihuatl, Popocatapetl,
10   Quetzalcoatl, jail, Xicotancatl,
Nor whaleship's blubbery education,
Soothe your rashed breast. See, they have all gone,
The names too: Oaxaca; Xanadu; Belawan;
Saigon. And the sun. You would have liked Saigon.

[1934–6]   VI   [67.2]

BLEPHARIPAPPUS GLANDULOSUS OR WHITE TIDY-TIPS

I prayed to say a word as simple
As the daisy. I have sought so long
To speak this flower goodness created,
Or recreate the daisy in song...

5   Alas, my song's again too ample,
        So, again, I am defeated.

T]   [missing]{67.1}

1936   VII   [68.3]

ON READING EDMUND WILSON'S REMARKS ABOUT RIMBAUD

        – Foreman of quarries in Cyprus,
        The granaries of genius rolled down the river,
        Stevedore of Marseilles, friend
        To soap manufacturers in the whuling Cyclades,
5   No son to engineer a dreamed-of bridge,
        Carlist, communist, dutch soldier, and
        David to no Goliath in black forest,
        Livid sleeper across real tracks at noonday,
        Absinthe manque at the Yorkshire Grey
10   Seller of key-rings, shoe-laces, self, trunks,
        Traveller with 'Springboart & Tumplingakt',
        Dreamer of railways to Addis Ababa,
        Ahab of the Abyssinian rain,
        No Onan spilling false substance of the sun,
15   But false enough to betray the moonlight,
        And fiend of the family of Verlaine,
        With balls between your shoulders and elsewhere,
        Cover up the leprosies of old walls,
        Of the soul's climb with Harrar's later wisdom,
20   Of doleful trafficking with preposterous chiefs
        And monstrous wives from Obangui-Tchari-Tchad,
        Sailed by camels who could climb St. Paul's,
        From Sokotra or the islands of the damned,
        As you may; or build, not sense, canals,
25   Poetry snapped to the waist with a snake belt
        Studded with polite lies precious as stones,
        Still will life close with Isabelle in a dream,
        Dying far from home at harvest time.

T]   [missing] {68.1}

4 68.1, 2: to soap manufacturers in whuling Cyclades,
14   68.1: not spilling false substance of the sun,
           not Onan spilling false substance of sun,
24   68.1: as you may; and build, not sensing canals
25   68.1: poetry snapped to the waist with a snake skin
27   68.1: still may life close with Isabelle in a dream,

[1938–9]   VIII   [69.2]

        The exile is the luckiest of men,
        Let million flint stones incommode his feet,

Be unstrung harps in his ears, it is sweet
To dwell in Hinnom and stride Hell again:
5   Or let it be Upper Slaughter, Aberdeen,
Xochimilco, Bodo, Chester-le-Street,
Worms, New Brighton, or Morocco,
You greet your spirit each tempestuous night to frighten
Remembered love into your loved one's tears,
10   Where drowning's incident now, you pewter Timon!
Ah, Leander, breath of winter, thronged arms of nightmares!
Lustre of sea the gleaming Arctic wears!
Better be hugged there, where grave Polar bears
Invite the soul with Borealian airs.

9   69.1: An imaged Love into your loved one's tears
12   69.1: Lustre of the sea the gleaming arch wears!

1937   IX   [70.2]

Wolf, wolf, cried the boy in the fable,
Who plagued the shepherds and the sheep alike,
To return, laughing softly, to the stable,
And fold away the hours with reed or fiddle,
5   Bleating in music for deceived shepherd's sake.
There was no wolf then. But at night one struck,
Long famished in iron hills she saw her table
Spread whitely on the green plains of Tortu.
Wolf, cried the boy. But now no herdsmen came.
10   Wolf, wolf, returned the wolf, her icy heart aflame . . .
So wolf and child were well met. But I say to you
That slept they once on never so proud an Alp, –
It is the poor wolf now who cries for help.

11   70.1: So wolf and child were well met. But some still say

1936   X   [71.3]

ONLY GOD KNOWS HOW

King Lear blinded Oedipus in a dream
And gave him Sophocles in braille to read
While robins and Cordelia drank his blood.
The fated monarch like a bird picked through
5   His scarlet story, crouching where feverfew
And agatha in an asylum garden grew.
Here no pale shepherds found him for a Priam
Eating furred peaches, counting every stone,
Each hour a tinker with the royal bone,
10   Stroking the careless waves to kingdom come
When sailor stood. Jocasta came to him
His pulped heart strewn on the rashed, embossed, scheme;

Four thousand yards of incandescent pain.
The gates grinned wide. Now smell your way to Dover!
15   Fly, fly there straight as any bobelin,
No more sing never, never never,
But slap spang as from the great bison's bung the bomb!
Cannot you hear the beach, snuff the sea-salt?
Your great blindness engulfs its own cobalt.
20   My awful son, imponderable with fate,
Who only scent the crest, shall see the womb.

T]   [missing] {71.1}
4   71.1: The fated monarch like a bird pricked through
13   71.1: [missing on ts; added in L's hand]
17   71.3: But slap spang as from the great bison's bung this bomb!
20 71.1, 2, 3: My fated son, imponderable with fate

1936   XI   [72.8]

LULL

Now we have considered these things, each to each,
The white house in the marsh, like home, the factories
With torn smoke evanescent as farewell,
The bright ship and solitary landward gull,
5   And with its special currents the bright river
(Which throws a sudden wash upon the beach)
Negotiable as a simple poem, the trees
Nameless, but friends, sentinels, and nowhere
Pandemonium of our enemies, the news
10   Of how this brother fought and that one fell
To conjure up such beauty with his blood
Shakes us with an appalling human (being theirs) laughter
Since all we know is that the wind is good
And at the end the sun is what it was.

T   72.1: Letter from Europe
              The ship sails on: for Nordahl Grieg
              Persistence of Life
          72.3: Persistence of Life
I   72.1: Now that we have considered these things with visible
                                                              [touch
          72.2: Now that we have considered these things, each to each, –
          72.3: Now we have considered these things, with visible touch
          72.6: Now we have considered these smashed chimneys
2 72.1, 2, 3, 5: The house in the marsh like home; the factories
          72.4: The white house in the marsh, the factories
          72.6: And the strewn river, (that most subtle breach)
3   72.6: That throws a sudden wash upon the beach
       72.6, 7: Which adds a sudden wash upon the beach,
4 72.1, 2, 3, 5: The swift ship, and solitary landward gull:
          72.4: The bright ship, and solitary landward gull

```
        72.6, 7: With all its currents and complexities,
  5  72.1, 2, 3, 5: And with its special currents, the river,
        72.4: And with its special currents the clear river,
        72.6, 7: Negotiable as a simple poem; trees
  6     72.6, 7: Nameless, but freezing sentinels, and each
  7     72.6, 7: A friend, and nowhere, within the heart's reach,
  8   72.1, 2, 5: Nameless, but friendly sentinels; and nowhere
        72.6, 7: Pandemonium of our enemies.
  9  72.1, 2, 3, 5: Pandemonium of our enemies.
        72.4: of how this brother fought, or that one fell,
        72.6, 7: News of that immedicable slaughter
 10  72.1, 2, 3, 5: The news of how one fought, another fell,
        72.4: to expiate such beauty with his blood
        72.6, 7: Which conjured up such landscape with the blood
 11  72.1, 2, 3, 5: To conjure up such landscape with his blood
        72.4: shakes us with a sudden, gigantic laughter
        72.6, 7: Of those who shelved the smeared Book of Because,
 12   72.1, 2, 5: Shakes us with an inward, fluctuant, laughter,
        72.3: Shakes us with a secret, gigantic laughter,
        72.4: since all we know is, that the wind is good
        72.6, 7: Shakes us with anguished, secret laughter,
 13     72.4: And at the end the sun is what it was.
```

1938   XII   [73.3]

– – For Christ's sake and for mine and last for a child's god
                                                              [gone
Stand on that declivity by University City,
Which is forever abandoned,
Stand there laughing down with
  5 Sommerfield, John Cornford, Julian Bell.
Hashish in the library behind
But rifles and tobacco well in hand.
No Grecian urn will smother your bodies' leaves
Nor twelfth street hash your lives to rags of self pity:
 10 Nor is there anguish importunes my lease
As this real death without its gilded hearse
Nodding down some dull plumed serpent of a street
That turns out at the last to be the sea.
Let I who take my sanest leave of you
 15 Phone Michigan 1951 for help.

```
  4   73.2: stand poised there laughing down with
  8   your] you {73.2}
73.1           – – for christ's sake & mine & last for a
                                 child's god gone
               stand on that declivity for ever by University City
               for ever posed there unabandoned,
               is a fixture that no Greek urn knew.
               nor shall she smother your gallant bodies' leaves
               For skulls in Spanish wars laugh long with long teeth
```

ground by tumult of bombs dropping over Madrid.
With hashish in the library behind
and John Sommerfield & John Cornford
tobacco & cracked rifles well in hand

1936   XIII   [74.3]

ONLY GOD KNOWS HOW III

Oilers for rivers: cargo ships for stars
Neoshe, Wabash: Wormwood, Arcturus;
And ocean-going tugs for Indian tribes
Narkeeta, Barnegat and Massasoit.
5   Mine layers for words of menace, Terror.
Repair ships are mythological characters
Reappearing as Zeus etcetera . . .
– Reinaugural nomenclature
Reclaims dividendless Homeric errors:
10   A rusted Helen rotting in Kow-Loon:
Menelaus riding at anchor: Agamemnon
Awash with stiff dismantled shrouds, Paris
Striding the Red Seas as stinking pilgrim
A miserable ship as ever sank Lord Jim
15   In port: And, terrible at night of Perim
Troilus and Cressida reeling, the iron
Pandarus: Vast, silent, malodorous.
– Loutish we scrubbed in chalk the dark's bulkhead;
Renamed a stone fleet for God's bereaved lap;
20   For animals, impalpables of the mind;
For children, categories of the blind;
Currencies and scavengers for women;
For man, new names for sleep.

T]   [missing] {74.1}
5   74.1: [adds next line:] Or combined with flowers, as lobelia syphilitica.
7   74.1: who reappears as Zeus etcetera . . .

[1938–9]   XIV   [75.1]

The walls of remorse are steep, there is no belay
Safe in her conquest, and one remembers
Behind a gin-fog of lost Novembers
Climbing the Devil's Kitchen, or better say
5   Not climbing it; No matter; betray
The vexed memory! Burn in some hotter embers,
Hotter than ever devil set for climbers –
That ravage the heart – and poor child, once stay
Warmest handholds here you can only freeze. Said
10   My friend in Wales when drunk with port and hope –

– I'd climb that rock again in sandshoes for sport,
And then in spikes for the glory of God!
But life gave me one chance whatever it set
You. And as well end that fall too at the end of a rope.

VII. The Roar of the Sea and the Darkness

[1938–9]   I   [76.1]

IRON THOUGHTS SAIL OUT AT EVENING

Iron thoughts sail out at evening on iron ships;
They move hushed as far lights while twelve footers
Dive at anchor as the ferry sputters
And spins like a round top, in the tide rips,
5   Its rooster voice half muted by choked pipes
Plumed with steam. The ship passes. The cutters
Fall away. Bells strike. The ferry utters
A last white phrase; and human lips,
A last black one, heavy with welcome
10   To loss. Thoughts leave the pitiless city,
Yet ships themselves are iron and have no pity;
While men have hearts and sides that strain and rust.
Iron thoughts sail from the iron cities in the dust,
Yet soft as doves the thoughts that fly back home.

[1938–9]   II   [77.1]

FROM HELSINKI TO LIVERPOOL WITH LUMBER

The old timber ship steams down the Mersey
– *Dimitrios N. Bogliazides* –
Though Lloyds refuse, a vast load of trees
From anguished lands of frozen destinies,
5   High piled on deck, 'insure' her own demise.
Can a ship turn over and yet not capsize?
If so, she'll do it, but if not, she tries.
A ship capsize yet not sink? It may be.
She hurts the heart's eye, by beauty wounding all,
10   This fabulous, overloaded, Greek ship,
Starting thoughts for leaks in the world's old plates . . .
No sweet wood there! Yet what dread load lies steep
On her ancient sides as she overweights
The estuary, lies broken against the last dock wall?

4   77.1: From lands of hope or frozen destinies,

[1938–9]   III   [78.1]

VIGIL FORGET

Vigil Forget went ten miles on a camion,
Then a thousand or more on a freighter
Trembling in every mast; no chameleon
Changed color faster than Forget from apprehension

5   Of himself. His cargo of disaster grew lighter and lighter;
     Once in a rickshaw he felt real condescension
     Towards the present, loving it, and feeling greater
     Than the ancient torturer, himself . . . Ah, new selves!
     Vigil Forget took a sampan to a far shore,
10   And an angry camel to Stalin's Samarkand,
     And then a bleak freighter home with his poor lives
     Grown self again, to board the ferry to his whore . . .
     – Columbus too thought Cuba on the mainland.

[1938–9]   IV   [79.3]

QUARTERMASTER AT THE WHEEL

     The Harkness light! Another hour spelled out,
     Struck by myself with unction but with doubt.
     A man is killed but does not hear the shot
     Which kills him; four bells kills me.
5   Lucky to hear it if I killed myself,
     Whose age haunts calendars upon the screen;
     The heroine born in nineteen eighteen,
     Who yesterday was born in nineteen eight.
     A pile of magazines assess dead love
10   On shore where one light burns no love will wait.
     Tomorrow is the sea and then the sea,
     To both least faithless when we most forsake,
     The one unscaled, the other vomitless
15   Of Jonah to his gourd or Nineveh . . .
     It is a straw to tickle blood shot eyes
     Of quartermasters soldered to darkness
     The stiff wheel and the remembrance of the crowned,
     For sinking men to suck at or to claw
20   The thought that what we saw we often hear
     Too late or not at all, or cannot bear
     To know resounding eardrums register.
     Our siren now! What ugliest ship has not
     Borne heart from heart with that deep plangency,
25   Sadder than masthead's light, a soul
     In mourning whose voice is grief gone by.
     Roll on, you witless, dark brown ocean roll,
     And light light years and grey ones let us live
     Within that gracious nexus of reprieve,
30   Between the fated sight and fatal sound . . .
     – Now leave the world to Harkness and to me.

T   79.1: Quartermaster at the Wheel
           Quartermaster
     79.2: Quartermaster: For John Sommerfield
29 79.1, 2: Within that gracious minus of reprieve

[1938–9]   V   [80.3]

THERE IS A METALLURGY

There is a metallurgy of the mind
Draws out the real of young love as fine wire
Is drawn from white-hot steel in the tall fire.
Life has no time to waste; but in the blind
5 Fastness of first love's presence, constrained
Permanence in parting, immediacy of desire,
What hint or shadow of a hint is there
Attesting to this doom so close behind,
For it is like a doom to feel love shrink,
10 Its metal cooled by friendship's failing breath?
Yet they are fools who say that true love dies,
Nor would it die as poets have us think.
Gazing at peonies is not to see death;
Nor is it death to drown in hazel eyes.

T]   [missing] {80.1, 2}
7 80.1: What hint or shadow of a hint conspire

[1938–9]   VI   [81.1]

Christ, slashed with an axe, in the humped church –
How shall we pray to you all pied with blood,
Yet deader by far than the hacked wood?
But pray we must since prayer is all our search
5 Who come in anger only to beseech.
Here kneel two creatures who believe in good,
Here stood two lovers, they believed in God,
And in thee, too, though maimed at life's touch
As by the doleful art of these dull men.
10 – Oh, ravaged by man but murdered in mankind,
Of peace a prater, yet of fire and shot
Vicarious exculpator to seventy times seven;
Image, we wish thee ill; yet alive in mind
That mind itself may live, and compassion forsake us not.

[1938–9]   VII   [82.1]

Black thunderclouds mass up against the wind,
High-piled beyond Popocatepetl;
So with force, against whose swollen metal
The wind of reason has the heart pinned
5 Till overbulged by madness, splitting mind...
Or, drifting without reason, see mind's petal
Torn from a good tree, but where shall it settle
But in the last darkness and at the end?

Who take no arms as the good wind's defender
10   You psalmists of despair, of man's approved lease,
Reason remains although your mind forsakes
It; and white birds higher fly against the thunder
Than ever flew yours, where Tchechov said was peace,
When the heart changes and the thunder breaks.

[1938–9]   VIII   [83.1]

No road in existence strikes such terror
From its blind length, from eternity to eternity
To the soul, as the deadly quality
Of the coiled heart frozen in its error.
5   The road may lead to Archangel or Gomorrah,
Its tossing stones not less moved to pity
Than this stone encompassing no city.
And if our soul's Australia knew its Canberra,
Some fixed capital to its masked archipelago,
10   Light in our darkness, in our lightness dark,
To which the only road was the sea or through the earth,
Or through this heart or through the body's woe –,
That heart would deny no passage, leaving us the black
Ocean for comfort: and fire: and death.

7   83.1: Than this stone which encompasses no city.

[1938–9]   IX   [84.1]

So he would rather have written those lines,
Those Trumpington Street lines, than take the town –
Would he, the liar? So write his name down
'Wolfe'. And the town too: Quebec. His name shines
5   In our history. Cortes' shone in Spain's.
Shines more or less for all I know or have known.
Somewhere there is some knowledge; under the stone
A message perhaps; or hidden by strange signs
In places only the stupid visit.
10   The path led to the grave? The elegiac way
Scaled Abram heights for our lupine avenger?
A worn path also for the wolf, – or is it?
– Keep wolves from country churchyards, reading Gray,
Too good a name is wolf for scavenger.

1937–8   X   [85.4]

We likened one man to a ship adrift
Broken from anchorage with skeleton crew
Of false precepts; or listing with iceberg's impact;
It was melancholy to hear him try to shift

5   The blame on us for his sure guilt: but gift
      Of clarity he lacked and in fact
      No tactile appeal for help was made anew:
      It was long before he was silent. I tried to sift
      Later the mystery of man's dissembling
10   When most he needs aid. He would have
      Given him that. I have considered it since.
      When the doomed are most eloquent in their sinking,
      It seems that then we are least strong to save,
      And pray that his proved no titanic case.

14 case.] case {85.3}

[1938–9]   XI   [86.2]

      – You cannot, must not, Orpheus, look back, my soul;
      What guards you summon yet be afraid of.
      The dead stagnate at corners from unbelief,
      Waiting for the deed that seems almost will.
5   Consider sanely our wish to be whole,
      For life must be in death as life in all.
      A sense of finitude transcends the real of grief,
      When lungs of darkness gasp in life's used oil.
      Life! Our longing for you was more than dreams
10   Of home on earth, though we traced the moors,
      The clock on the grey sand, and the path of the sea,
      Whose salt death never finally inters
      Hatreds, oppressions, phantasms, crimes,
      – With our breath, with our fate, we will help you,
15   Eurydice.

9 86.1, 2: Oh life! Our longing for you was more than dreams

1934–6   XII   [87.3]

      The lighthouse invites the storm and lights it.
      Driven by tempest the tall freighter heels
      Under the crag where the fiery seabird wheels,
      And lightning of spume over rocks ignites it.
5   Oh, birds of the darkness of winter whose flights it
      Importunes with frost, when ice congeals
      On wings bonded for flight by zero's seals
      What good spirit undulates you still like kites that
      Children are guardians of in cold blue? –
10   And what indeed ourselves, Chang, in these pursuit
      Planes, strung to a nucleus within range
      Of our polygonous enemy,
      And what shall we, what shall we not, tolerate
      Today from chaos, what? – by the unshot albatross and
15   Icarus' circus plunge?

10   87.1: and what indeed ourselves in this pursuit
11   87.1: plane, strung to a nucleus within range
12   87.1: of our enemy of the anti-aircraft crew?
            of our enemy the epicene Whangpoo
      87.2: of our enemy, the epicene Whangpoo
14   87.1: from chaos, what – by the unshot albatross and Icarus'

1936   XIII   [88.2]

      The ship of war sails in the grey morning,
      Or Vigil says so, who followed the sea.
      – The shape of this war is like that spared tree
      Over there. See how it is an awning
  5   Now, that was quite bare; a profound warning
      Of a spreading wisdom mere force can't see –
      But to go back to the ship: Vigil tells me
      The ship and war hold much the same meaning
      For him; same loyalty to fire and knife
 10   In both; anguish for home; comrades you love
      Borne to a common goal by an iron jade.
      – Well, if the end is death the field is life
      Which we shall gain, shipmate . . . Time now to move
      Toward the one good port war ever made.

1934–6   XIV   [89.2]

                    TASHTEGO BELIEVED RED

      A hand comforts held out to one who's sinking;
      And what founders deeper than a world which sinks?
      Like a lost ship it never once says thanks,
      Since no single hand shall save its timber drinking
  5   The poisoned salt its sides awash are flanking,
      Thirsty for web of weeds or sift of sandbanks,
      Its last music gunshot, its gesture pose of tanks
      Over the wood where swathes of death are ranking . . .
      But witness, the hand is no hand but an arm
 10   Curving itself with the strong swimmer's flex
      – A thousand arms which thresh against the blast
      Of a regressive ocean even whose calm
      Is derelict with that impartiality which wrecks.
      – Yet regard, regard, the red banner nailed to the mast!

  T]   [missing] {89.1}
  7   89.1: its music gunshot, its gesture poise of tanks

1937   XV   [90.2]

      Lying awake beside a sleeping girl,
        Thunder and gunfire plunging about the house,
        Lightning like an inch worm going down the sky,

The sound of the storm seems a forlorn boast,
5 And sirens muted along the iron coast
Forlorn's a word to toll us back to self?
Rather it warns us forward to the sad world,
Or to those sadder worlds beneath the sea
10 Of sense, divorced by self. Uncared by it,
It by them. Forgetting the boast of gods
That they are gods, the thunderous boast
Of an enemy gun that thinks itself a god;
Consider the ship instead who needs a light for succour,
15 – The *'Seven Seas' spray'*, (Captain 'Potato', Jones).
With eyes like gimlets her lookouts probe the night:
The cliffs, where are the cliffs, where are the cliffs?
The course to Bilbao! The gauntlet must be run
Toward the smaller sound of the braver gun.
20 – Or, considering the agony of the treacherous rocks themselves –
Which, once wrecked upon them, who would indeed consider?
And let this lead us to all stupidity and error,
The mariner's mistake, the wreck metaphysical,
The order to starboard taken as port,
25 Inconsistency of divine and human law, Kafka
In the allied blockade, (truth still asleep beside us),
And so be guided to the foul berth,
To the pretended vision, the great lie,
Told for the millionth time it became true,
30 A truth only when it was too late,
Or when one no longer believed it himself,
And new falsehood was needful as new chaos
To Saturn; though less difficult to find,
Since here it was, a denial of the false
35 Which was now true, a rationalization
Projected with such vaporous force
As launches planets, blesses battleships;
Most natural and fated birth of all,
Our world eased doubtless from such sophistry,
40 And all lying worlds that wait sunk in darkness.

17 90.1: the cliffs, where are the cliffs, where the beacon?
34 90.1: Since here it was, a denial of what had been false
35 90.1: and now was true, a rationalization
39 90.1: our world eased doubtless from this sophistry

1938   XVI   [91.9]

SONG ABOUT MADRID, USEFUL ANY TIME

Shall life be the victor,
Where we go to die;
Or has death the malefactor,
The future in his eyes?

5   Life knowing such obstruction,
       Death hopes to defy us?
       Destruction's seed is barren,
       Though it is more copious.

       Nor shall death pass to that town,
10   Where life finally stands guard;
       Though swollen death with death be grown,
       And the dead ride hard.

       Since life must be the winner,
       Though even a recruit,
15   Though but a rank beginner,
       In the musketry of thought.

T   91.1: [missing]
       91.2, 4: Life, the recruit!
           91.6: Madrid
                 Persistence of the memory of Madrid: To John
                     [Sommerfield and Julian Bell
           91.7: The Live phantoms of University City
                 The dead ride hard
           91.8: Slogan for Everyone
                 Not to be used by both sides
2   91.1: where I go to die?
   91.2, 3, 4, 5, 6: Where they go to die?
           92.3: Where my comrades go to die?
5   91.1, 3: Destruction's seed is barren,
        91.4, 5: Barren is destruction's seed
           91.8: Life, cooled in such obstruction
6   91.1, 4: Yet her fruits are overgrown
           91.2: No cornucopias
           91.3: Where her barren seed is strewn
        91.4, 5: Though his fruits are overgrown
7   91.1: See the madness of the harvest.
           91.3: But what sad harvest may this yield
           91.4: Yet his harvest may not yield
           91.5: What harvest can destruction yield
8   91.1: Where the teeth of death are sown.
     91.3, 4, 5: Where the teeth of death were sown.
9–12   91.1: [missing]
9   91.2: But death shall not pass to the town
                 But death cannot pass to the town
           91.3: But death shall not pass to that town
           91.4: But the dead shall not pass to the final town
           91.5: But the dead shall not pass to the town
11   91.4, 5: Though swollen death with death be blown
12   91.4: When the dead ride hard.
13   91.1: shall life then be the winner?
           91.2: life knows it is the winner;
           91.3: Life shall be the victor!
           91.4: Life then shall be the winner

91.5: Life shall be the winner
91.8: Sin, life shall be the winner
14   91.1: Though a recruit.
91.3: Yes, even though a recruit
91.4: It must: though a recruit
91.5: Fist clenched: though even a recruit

1937   XVII   [92.2]

THE SHIP IS TURNING HOMEWARD

The ship is turning homeward now at last.
The bosun tries to read but dreams of home.
The old lamptrimmer sleeps, the engine thrums:
Home. Lamps are set to light us from the past
5   To a near future unmysterious as this mast,
Whose bulk we recognize and finite aim.
Patient iron! But, beyond the maintruck, dumb
Blankness, or the twitch of reeling stars cast
Adrift in a white ocean of doubt.
10   Perhaps this tramp rolls towards a futurity
That broods on ocean less than on the gall
In seamen's minds. Is that star wormwood out
Among love's stars? This freighter eternity?
Where are we going? Life save us all.

3–6 92.1: The old lamptrimmer hears the engine thrum
His lamps are set to light us from the past
Into a future cold as this mast
With iron and what iron loves of kingdom come.
5 92.1: to a future unmysterious as this mast,
14 92.1: How is the compass set? Life save us all.

1938   XVIII   [93.4]

A POEM OF GOD'S MERCY

Cain shall not slay Abel today on our good ground,
Nor Adam stagger on our shrouded moon,
Nor Ishmael lie stiff in 28th Street,
With a New Bedford harpoon in his brain,
5   His right lung in a Hoboken garboon.
For this is the long day when the lost are found,
And those, parted by tragedy, meet
With spring-sweet joy. And those who longest should have met
Are safe in each other's arms not too late.
10   Today the forsaken one of the fold is brought home,
And the great cold, in the street of the vulture, are warm,
The numbed albatross is sheltered from the storm,
The tortured shall no longer know alarm

For all in wilderness are free from harm:
15   Age dreaming on youth, youth dreaming on age shall not be
                                                                [found,
        While good Loki chases dragons underground.
        Life hears our prayer for the lonely trimmer on watch,
        Or shuddering, at one bell, on the wet hatch,
        At evening, for the floating sailor by the far coast,
20   The impaled soldier in the shell hole or the hail,
        The crew of the doomed barque sweeping into the sunset
        With black sails; for mothers in anguish and unrest,
        And each of all the oppressed, a compassionate ghost
        Will recommemorate the Pentecost
25   Ah, poets of God's mercy, harbingers of the gale,
        Now I say the lamb is brought home, and Gogol
        Wraps a warm overcoat about him . . .
        Our city of dreadful night will blossom into a sea-morning!
        Only bear with us, bear with my song,
30   For at dawn is the reckoning and the last night is long.

T]   [missing] {93.2}
  2   93.2: Nor Adam reel under our shrouded moon,
  6   93.1: For this is the day when the lost are found,
  8   93.1: with spring-sweet joy. And those who should have met
  9   93.1: are safe in each other's strange arms not too late.
 10   93.1: The one of the ninety nine in the fold is brought home,
 12   93.1: [missing on ts; added in L's hand]
 15   93.1: Age pleading youth, youth dreaming on age, shall not be found,
 18   93.1: or shuddering, at one bell, on the cold hatch,
 23   93.2: And for each of all the damned & the oppressed
                And for each of all the betrayed, & the oppressed
          93.3: And for each of all the damned and the oppressed.
 24   93.2: Will draw to his salt-grey breast.
          93.3: [missing on ts, added in Margerie's hand]
 25   93.2: Ah, poets of God's mercy and the gale,
                Ah, poets of God's mercy, poets of the storm & the gale,
          93.3: Ah, poets of God's mercy and the gale,
 29   93.1: so bear with our song, for at dawn is the reckoning
 30   93.1: and all last nights are long.
          93.2: For at dawn is the reckoning. And the last night is long.

1930–1   XIX   [94.4]

                            FYRBØTERER

And on the bridge the wheel turns silently,
We follow a coast of heather, how small she is says the
                                                        [wandering lover,
I wonder how we have loved too as the ridge is lost completely:
The tall fire was beating us but now the watch is over.

5 For other watches taking the twelve to four.
The reaper sadly harvests what the wet March spent.
Sleep shadows those left. Footsteps knock against it. They are
                              [awake to dreariness once more!
But us, sea-weary, sleep overwent.

So in our lives how powerfully we move
10 Like this iron black ship back towards the Magellan of our birth,
All suns unsighted on this earth save love's or not
    – 'I have worn my jacknife in my cap to catch the lightning at
                                    [Cape Horn.'

    . . . The merchantmen hull-down creep near the shoal –
Danger they seek not though their range be dark –
15 Ah, fraught with sad freightage towards some sullen goal!
At Hatteras the wreckage drifts; and to Mount Ararat the ark.

3   94.1: the ship is a sleepwalker the ship is a silent ghost she is
                                    [eternity
4   94.1: and other watches take the 12 to 4
8   94.2: While some, sea-weary, sleep overwent.
9   94.1: so in our lives with what dark certainty we move
10   94.1: swiftly towards the magellan of our birth
11   94.1: the bourne is dangerous the noon unsighted we have
                                    [known on this earth
         94.2: All noons unsighted on this earth save love's or not
12 94.1, 2, 3, 4: [quotation marks missing; added in L's hand on 94.4]
         94.2: I have worn the jacknife in my cap to catch the
16   94.2: At Hatteras the wreckage drifts: and on Mount Ararat the
                                    [ark.
13–16   94.1: the moon hurls blindly through the storm like a silver
                                    [discus
         Saint Pierre we shall know when Montserrat seems darkest
         dark with a flood of oleander and hibiscus
         the Cedric lies at Cobh she is at rest and on mount ararat
                                    [the ark

1936   XX   [95.8(3)] [114]

ON READING R.L.S.

It had no name and we docked at midnight.
Its darkness spoke indecision and menace:
Nor could girls, laughing in linked quintets in the lamplight,
Leaven our hearts, embittered with sea salt.
5 There was no beauty about this port.
But, waking early, seeing near at hand
The very lineaments of a new land
With wharf, clock, market, road and post office,
Whose every stone seemed to conceal a secret,
10 With our own flag flying and its promise

Of news from the only one in the world –
Emergence was of Christian from Despond
And Friday's print for Crusoe in the sand.

T   95.1, 2: [missing]
6   95.1: But, waking early, to see near at hand
8–9   95.1: A city with towers clear, and the day bright
              As the first day when God saw it was good,
              The white road to the market, the post office
11 95.1, 2, 3: Of letters from the only one in the world, –

1934–6   XXI   [96.3]

LINES WRITTEN ON READING DOSTOIEVSKI

The world of ghosts moves closer every hour,
Knowing we belong to no life's order;
To those who see no ghosts no spectres are,
Yet these preserve an appetite for murder,
5   For life on the short wave, aching for Caesar.
Men leaving Tokio return as trundled cedar,
Or for 'sex fiend's tots feed alligator;'
Child bride flew through a forest to no castle,
The forest was the post, (she travelled in a parcel) . . .
10   The world of ghosts moves closer and closer,
Knowing we belong to no life's order . . .
Contemptuous of signs, sounds, furies,
Of those interwishing categories
Significant to us, (to be impartial),
15   But to the lilac sea who knows our purpose,
By carribean geometry of porpoise,
Coring to time the whirling arc's compass,
Knowing our cosmography not planetary,
Our sanctuary not sanctuary,
20   As with full swell to our ambiguous coasts
She bears to us the more ambiguous ghosts.

T]   [missing] {96.1}
12   96.1: to order contemptuous of signs, sounds, furies,
              no order contemptuous of signs, sounds, furies,
       96.2: No order contemptuous of signs, sounds, furies,
15   95.1: and to the lilac sea who knows our purpose,
       95.2: And to the lilac sea who knows our purpose,
19   95.1: [adds next line:] our misery not momentary
       95.2: [ts includes additional line, then cuts it]
21 95.1, 2: she bears to us the weary ghosts.

1936   XXII   [97.7(3)][117]

THE ROAR OF THE SEA AND THE DARKNESS

He prayed to his ghost for a vision of the sea,
Which would harbour it strictly in the mind
For all time, that he might be resigned
To it and not haunted eternally;
5   The ghost nodded his head, and said gravely:
Gaunt Forget, thus you would lose your only grief and find
You had composed your tears, landlocked your heart;
You would pray for the roar of the sea wind
And darkness, then, call us wrong or right,
10   You must always claim its unrest and its monotony;
Its mist on your breast – – His ship in harbour
Loaded sweet timber from the high-piled wharf.
He looked at her long, and then with a laugh,
Climbed on board and was seen no more.

The End.

T]   [missing] {97.2}
 6   97.1: – Friend, thus you would lose your only grief and find
     97.2: – Friend, thus you would lose your only grief and find
           But then you would lose your only grief and find
 9   97.2: And darkness, then, call me wrong or right,

Uncollected Poems, 1933–9

THE SIXTEEN POEMS in this section date from the *Lighthouse* period, but they were not included in that text, although 'In the Oaxaca Train' [101] appears in the 1940 'Eight Poems from *The Lighthouse Invites the Storm*.' Lowry probably considered the poems in this section the cull of his Mexican poetic material: fourteen of the sixteen never reached typescript form.

The first states for eight of the poems appear in the 'Pegaso' Mexican notebook, which also includes fragments from the lost novel *In Ballast to the White Sea* as well as *Under the Volcano* (12–14).[1] The 'Pegaso' paper – 8 × 10″ white, wide blue-lined and unmargined – can be assigned to 1937–8 through its appearance to Lowry's outgoing correspondence for those years (1–76). It is clear that the work in this notebook is immediate and rough; five of the eight 'Pegaso' poems exist only in one holograph draft.[2] Of the three multiple draft poems, only 'In the Oaxaca Train' ever appears anywhere other than the 'Pegaso' notebook.

The eight remaining poems appear on different kinds of paper, which further contributes to the fragmentary nature of this section. 'For *Under the Volcano*' [100] first appears as a holograph draft on 8½ × 11″ white, narrow blue-lined, three-ringed paper also used for some *Lighthouse* poems, and it later surfaces in the typescript for *Dark as the Grave* (9–1); I have used the manuscript as copy-text, as I have for 'Outside was the roar of the sea and the darkness.' 'Outside was the roar of the sea and the darkness' [105] also appears in the *Dark as the Grave* typescript; the holograph draft is scrawled on 'Argonaut' letterhead, which is probably a hotel stationery. This manuscript contains a fragment from 'Memory of the Hospitality of American Barmen' [19], of which the first typed state appears on 1937 paper; therefore, the 'Argonaut' manuscript is likely pre-1937. Although the sigla for these two poems reflect the variants in the *Dark as the Grave* typescript, the copy-texts are taken from the poetry manuscripts before they were reworked into the structure of *Dark as the Grave*. Two of the poems in this section come from a 1937 letter from Lowry to Aiken: 'Prelude to another drink' [106] and 'Prelude to Mammon' [107] are two of four poetry exercises that appeared in the letter.[3] Another poem, 'S.O.S. Sinking fast by both bow and stern' [109] comes from a 1937 letter to John Davenport in which Lowry agonizes over his treatment by, and his loss of, Jan Gabrial. The Mexican menu poem [108] mentioned in both *Under the Volcano* and *Dark as the Grave* is scrawled in two states on the 1938 menu for the El Petate restaurant (WTP 1–24). The earliest poem in this section actually appears on the newsprint paper characteristic of the Dollarton period, but on the manuscript Lowry dates the poem 1933. Given this date, the poem 'Who made this suicide pact of love?' [113] probably refers to his relationship with Jan Gabrial.

The poems in this section are arranged alphabetically because it is impossible to determine their exact chronology; approximately half of the poems appear on the same type of paper, while the papers of the other half are so widely disparate that no clear dating pattern emerges. No authorial order is apparent – for the poems are mostly untitled and always unnumbered. Because the manuscripts in this section appear to be mostly aborted drafts, the sigla are selectively recorded to show only significant line variants. Line initials are not emended.

NOTES

1   The eight poems are: 'The boatmen swing their lanterns on the Caribbean' [99], 'In the Oaxaca Train' [101], 'Midnight denies poursuivant of the dawn' [102], 'A morning coat is walking' [103], 'To Herr Toller, Who Hanged Himself' [104], 'Thoughts While Drowning' [110], 'What the Irish soldier said' [111], 'When I am in the purgatory of the unread' [112].

2   The five single-holograph poems are: 'The boatmen swing their lanterns on the Caribbean' [99], 'A morning coat is walking' [103], 'To Herr Toller, Who Hanged Himself' [104], 'Thoughts While Drowning' [110], 'What the Irish soldier said' [111].

3   The two others were further reworked and eventually were included in the *Lighthouse* as 'Thirty Five Mescals in Cuautla' [25] and 'The Last Man in the Dôme' [29].

1939   [98.3]

       And, when you go – much as a meteor,
       Or as this swaying, incandescent car
       which, like lost love, leaves lightnings in its wake,
       (And me, an aspen with its Christ in mind
5   Whose wood remembers once it made a cross
       So trembles ever since in wind, or no wind,)
       But most like Venus, with our black desire
       Which blinds me now, your light a horned curve
       First; then, circling, a whitely flaming disk,
10   Not distance, but your phase, removes the mask,
       Until you are the brightest of all stars –
       Pray then, in this most brilliant, lonely hour
       That, reunited, we may learn, forever
       To keep the sun between ourselves and love.

1   98.1: And, when you have gone – much as a meteor,
7   98.1: But more like Venus, with your dear desire
    98.2, 3: But most like Venus, with our black desire
8   98.1: Which blinds me now, your light a curved streak
11   98.1: Yet, at your farthest, you are of all stars the brightest star,
             Until you burn brightest of all stars –
12   98.1: Pray then, in your most brilliant polar hour
             And in this brilliant and forsaken hour
14   98.1: To keep the sun so, between ourselves, and love.

1937–8   [99.1]

       the boatmen swing their lanterns on the Caribbean;
       the great circle of the nameless window stares
       (the reeling circle of the unacknowledged stars)
       lovely as widows in Nantucket waiting for Ahab;
5   the sharks crawl and dance into the darkness:
       the evening darkens on the noble bottles
       where others drink their suns down under the bars
       crawling sharks swarming over the heavy-lidded porthole:
       these fears belong to well-deck of our childhood;
10   the foredeck churning with furies of water, the disjointed
                   [derrick is to be dealt with . . .
       jammed against the crosstrees like beauty in a cartoon
       a giant at sea a fool against the first mate in port
       crossed, against the tree like myth in a storm
       Judas, swinging in masthead in mid-ocean in the typhoon . . .
15   ashore the pearl fishers circle the square
       the alchemist's drogher's in reverse the philosopher's stone
       the rock which penetrates our focsle

7   99.1: where cramped elders drink their suns down under the bars
11   99.1: jammed against the crosstrees like simplicity in a cartoon
14   <u>in masthead</u>] ['in' immediately repeated]

1937–8   FOR *UNDER THE VOLCANO*   [100.2]

A dead lemon like a cowled old woman crouching in the cold.
A white pylon of salt and the flies
taxying on the orange table, rain, rain, a scraping peon.
And a scraping pen writing bowed beggarly words.
5   War. And the broken necked street-cars outside
And a sudden broken thought of a girl's face in Hoboken
A tilted turtle dying slowly on the stoop,

of the sea-food restaurant, blood
lacing its mouth, and the white floor –
10   ready for teredos to-morrow.
There will be no to-morrow. To-morrow is over.
clover and the smell of fircones, fricases and the deep grass,
and turkey mole sauce and England
suddenly, a thought of home, but then

15   the mariachis, discordant, for the beaked bird

of maguey is on the wing, the waiter bears

a flowing black dish of emotion,
the peon's face is a mass of corruption
we discard the horripilation of the weather

20   in this ghastly land of the half-buried man

where we live with Canute the sundial and the red snapper
the leper the creeper together in the green tower
And play at sunset on the mundial flute and guitar
the song, the song of the eternal waiting of Canute
25   the wrong of my waiting, the song of my weeping
betrothed to the puling vacuum and the unfleshible root
and the sound of the train and the rain on the brain outside
                            [creeping, creeping
only emptiness now in my soul sleeping
where once strutted tigers lemonade scruffy green lepers
30   liquors pears scrubbed peppers and stuffed Leopardis,
– Thus delirium. This pyre of Bierce and springboard of Hart
                                    [Crane!

Death so far away from home and wife
He feared and prayed for his sick life –
So far from home and lane
35   He feared while his standing by
'A corpse should be transported by express,' said the Consul
                    [mysteriously waking up suddenly.

T]   100.2: [missing] {100.1}
6   100.2: [breaks line into two after 'broken']
7   100.2: A tilted turtle dying on the stoop
9   100.2: Lacing its mouth on the white floor
10   100.2: Ready for terenedos tomorrow.

12	100.2:	Clover and the smell of fircones and the deep grass
18	100.2:	(The peons face is a mass of corruption)
21	100.1, 2:	Where we live with Canute the sundial and the police savant
25	100.1:	the song of my waiting, the song of my waiting
	100.2:	The song of my writing, the song of my weeping
27	100.2:	And the rain on the hair outside creeping, creeping…
28	100.1:	only emptiness now in my soul which is sleeping
	100.2:	Only emptiness now in my soul, sleeping…
28–36	100.2:	[missing]
36	100.1:	[added later]

[100.2 has no blank spaces and all lines start with capitals]

1937   IN THE OAXACA TRAIN   [101.5]

When maguey gives way to pine
What we see from the train is kinder:
'This' is England: or, of the Rhine,
'That' is reminder.

5   But when pine gives way to cactus
What we see, someone says, is 'brutal.'
To smashed maguey's patterns react us
From wooled thoughts of Bonn or of Bootle.

Then when it is dark, from the train
10   Nor forest nor field may we see,
So within from the dark flies the pain
Of the maguey, the strength of the fir tree,

To settle in toiler's faces,
In the faces of those who recline,
15   In the faces of those who have laboured
In maguey, or up in the pine.

Yet what hope in this plunging compartment!
As they sleep it is set like a sign.
A hope that still flickers in England,
20   But vanished along the Rhine.

3	101.1, 2:	'That' is England: or of the Rhine
4	101.1, 2:	We say, this is reminder
	101.2:	We say, such is reminder
	101.3:	'That,' we say, serves as reminder
		'That,' we say, is as reminder.
6	101.1:	what we see from the train may be
	101.2:	what we see from the train is brutal
	101.3:	what was 'kinder' is bettered by 'brutal'.
7	101.1:	the maguey brutal lines react us
	101.2:	To the smashed maguey's lines react us
8	101.1:	From thoughts of Bonn or of Bootle.
	101.2:	From swell thoughts of Bonn or of Bootle.
		From old thoughts of Bonn or of Bootle.

101.3: From meshed thoughts of Bonn or of Bootle.
       From gay thoughts of Bonn or of Bootle
       From wooled memories of Bonn or of Bootle.
       From meshed memories of Bonn or of Bootle.
       From gay memories of Bonn or of Bootle.

9   101.2: And when it is dark, from the train

10   101.1: Neither forest nor fields may you see
      101.2: and nor forest nor field can we see:

11   101.1: only faces reflect the pain
      101.2: within from the dark flies the pain
      101.3: So within from that dark flies the pain.
      101.4: And within from the dark flies the pain.

12   101.1: of the maguey and the pine tree

13–20 101.1: [missing]

13   101.2: Reflected in toiler's faces

14–15 101.3: In the bark of those who recline:
      In the timber of those who have lingered

16   101.3: In maguey or away in the pine.

17   101.2: While at length a hope grows
      But there is hope in this plunging compartment!
      101.3: Yet what hope for this plunging compartment!

18   101.3: As they sleep Life is set like a sign

19   101.2: A hope that rarely harboured in England
      101.3: A hope much less harboured in England

20   101.2: And never along the Rhine,
      And never one side of the Rhine,
      [ms. adds next line:] But only beneath the Rhine.
      101.3: And never along the Rhine.
      And unseen on one side of the Rhine.

1937–8   [102.2]

Midnight denies poursuivant of the dawn.
And dawn denies finality of twelve
What shall we regenerate for time
to shake our fool equation alive?

5   how shall we balance unbalanced childhood
with some fixed decency with an even tune,
to some certainty, to its holiest decembers?
when days that seem now full, upright as tulips
raged in horrible circles like cyclones:

10 the hyacinths flattened in the wood
then we forgot that tempestuous spring
which sinks the lost ship now in cold calm of order:
forget too we had seen the white whale
which now appears scarred at the other pole

15 its passage under ice our adolescence,
that engineering taught us at first hand
trigonometry failed to teach us
the magnets of the rich were clogged with sand

that machinery of Zenith's obsolescence
20   questioned clear loyalty to the cotton cities
eased on heart's trial hill the slipping gear
for those who dived for moons into the river.

3   102.1: what force shall we regenerate for numbers
7   102.1: to its certainty and its loved Decembers:
            to its certainty and its holiest Decembers
8–16 102.1: Sand clogs the magnets of the great:
            eights [?breaking] up potholes with an obsolete beat
            and laminated spring forks [?] pulley,
            Chaos was fixed then without a gear:
            that meccano and [?longer] towers strange signatures
            questioned clear loyalty to the cotton cities
            gradually eased on heart's trial hill the gear safe
            for those who dived for moons into the river.
17–22 102.1: [missing]

1937–8   [103.1]

A morning coat is walking
Along Broadway
But bright at Wall Street gleams the spat
Of affluent yesterday.

5   Ah, let the past, forsaking,
Drown in its special vat:
Richer are you in wisdom and heartbreaking
Sans coat, stick, stock, – yes, – sans hat!

And so, our friend, forbear, forbear
10   The past's felicity,
Lest we, through customs, have to wear
Our coats of mourning too.

3   103.1: And bright at Wall Street gleams the spat
5   103.1: But let the past, forsaking,

1939   TO HERR TOLLER, WHO HANGED HIMSELF   [104.1]

No swallows build their nests here my dear Toller.
Only the aspen has its Christ in mind
remembering its wood which made a cross before
trembled ever since in quest or in wind
5 I know what you loved, and know that your collar
It was a dressing gown cord
The hanged man was only hanged once and the last mile
is the last mile. And this week is beginning well
said the man going to be hung on Monday. Hell!
10 Terror smiled twice but thrice it could not smile
Horror smiled too: it will never smile again

As once it grinned upon your pen in prison
But though we are such a case too, in bad style
I see your death as no party treason
15   Your doom out of time, as good reason.
Hoppla, wir leben!

1936–7   [105.2]

Outside was the roar of the sea and the darkness
Was it? Greatest of all poets of the storm, –
outside, outside, – are you sure her form,
her shape implied there your special wilderness?
5   Your clanging Inchcape rock and your Harkness?
Your doom? what Start Point started you to your multiform
knowing of the unconsciousness's typhoon,
to the tenderness of cyclones to Atlantic's meekness
and death's leaping tarpon landscape, oh poet of god's mercy,
[poet of storm
10   of the bloody harpoon and the sperm whale at bay
Each life has for a while its Good Hope and Cape Horn.
Yet when I think of you I see the freighter
sinking for Mazatlan: and the heeling shadow of albatross
seeking forever the ancienter mariner
15   In Formosa and the islands of the damned:
and those shawled islets dying of age and snow
as I too die of the headache of my sorrow:
(lost as the huarache in the dust in Tehuantepec)
the dhow which sank, the drunk with the broken neck:
20   I think of the plunging derrick on the foredeck;
the violet of the Indian Ocean yet with no sight of land:
nor wind, asphodel; violet; gentian; sand,
and in half-memory only the tenderness of a hand:
and guardians in moonlight could not understand
25   derelicts at midnight, and hail in Samarkand:
the hangover: the dead stevedore on a blazing lighter:
– Ah dead of dereliction, snow, fire, and age
myself, my haunter of myself, I ponder your page,
(which is great –), letting me know
30   all but why the bearded ocean is outside.
For this secret you have canvassed with your pride,
or to some rare but loutish phantasy; –
why forked-radish Neptune should be admired
by you, with consciousness; and the ox-eye daisy
35   to glow through me, – dead, feverish, and tired.

4   105.2: Her shape implied there your special wilderness
5   105.2: Your clanging Inchcape Rock and your Harkness
7   105.2: Knowing of the unconscious typhoon
8   105.1, 2: To the tenderness of cyclones and Atlantic's meekness

11   105.2: (Each life has for a while its Good Hope and Cape Horn)
13   105.2: Sinking off Mazatlan: and the heeling shadow of the albatross
14   105.2: Seeking forever an ancient mariner
16   105.2: And other islands dying of age and snow
17   105.2: As I of the burden of my sorrow
18   105.2: [missing]
20 105.1, 2: The plunging derrick on the foredeck
21   105.2: Violet of the Indian ocean with no sight of land
22   105.2: Nor asphodel, violet, gentian, sand
24   105.2: [missing]
26   105.2: The dead stevedore on the blazing lighter –
29   105.2: Letting me know
31 105.1, 2: For this secret you have conserved to your pride
35   105.2: Glow through me, dead, feverish and tired.
        [105.2 capitalizes the beginning of lines]

1937   PRELUDE TO ANOTHER DRINK   [106.1]

Is this an airplane roaring in my room?
What is it then, an insect, god knows what:
God probably does know which is the point;
Or did know – leave it at that – some sort of hornet.
5   Airplane or aeroplane or just plain plane, –
Some hint of something more than this is here.
Insect, vision, or terrestrial visitor, –
Some hint of something more than this is here.
Some hint is here and what should it be but this?
10   To watch this guest, to see what it does.
It taxies like an Avro skidding through the flying field
Rises like a Sopwith, flits into a rage
Bangs against the light, settles on the printed page
Soars: then falls: then can't get up
15   When I try to help him his hands evade my help –
I myself seeing the only possible exit.
So God watches us with lids which move not.
But this is a repetition of an 'idea'
Before the terrible delirium of God.

1937   PRELUDE TO MAMMON   [107.1]

Sir: drinking is a problem without doubt:
Whether or not we like it, whether or not
The goddamn thing will put you on the spot
With heebiejeebies hebephrene or gout:
5   Or lumbago will set you tapping out
On brass ferrule to stool, to rest, to rot.
Though rotting's a fine pastime for a sot
It seems when we excrete we should not shout;
While even when we rest it's more discreet

10   That we should unambiguously rest.
      What others think is one torment of drink
      But these have dung not dew upon their feet
      Whose dry concern for us is manifest
      In the ubiquity of the parched soul's stink.

1938   [108.2]

      – Some years ago he started to escape; –
      and has been escaping ever since –
      Not knowing his pursuers gave up hope
      Of seeing him dance at the end of a rope
5   Hounded by eyes and thronged terrors now the lens
      of a glaring world shunned his defense
      and attack, reading him in the preterite tense
      spending no money thinking him not worth
      the price a government pays for a cell.
10   There would have been a scandal at his death
      Perhaps. But imagine it as soon over. Some tell
      hellish tales of this poor foundered soul
      Who once fled north.

    1   108.1: A year ago today he started to escape
    3   108.1: But long ago in distant light years pursuers gave up hope
    5   108.1: Now pursued by his fears now the lens
    6   108.1: of the glaring world shunned even his defense
    7   108.1: She read him strictly in the preterite tense
 8–10   108.1: made no further effort, took no chance,
              spent no money, to secure him, thought him not worth
              even the price the government pays for a cell
   13   108.1: who suffered the agony of his own birth.

1937   [109.1]

      S.O.S. Sinking fast by both bow and stern.
      S.O.S. Worse than both the Morro Castle
      S.O.S. and the Titanic –
      S.O.S. No ship can think of anything else to do when it is in
                                                [danger
5   S.O.S. But to ask its closest friend for help.
      CQD. Even if he cannot come

1937–8   THOUGHTS WHILE DROWNING: [110.1]
         BUT TRY TO ELIMINATE THE ARGUMENT

         let others quarrel alone about my grief
         raven like wolves over a cache of meat
         my grief is now the property of the state
         long self-starved, it is on relief;

5   many of these with surfeit of happiness need it

the evening darkens with a sense of guilt
like a thunderstorm blackening the promontory
smearing remembered headland of a life
with a child's scowl of chaos against the night
10   the tourists wait with fatuous smiles of triumph
with bereaved arms upon the gossiping shore
having known the corpse they are for a moment great.

1937–8   WHAT THE IRISH SOLDIER SAID   [111.1]

Jesus here has got something to answer for
Tear him down from that cross
stand him over there boys by the barrier
Franco won't notice the loss.

5   Nine hundred and thirty years
you've given the world the run around:
Time we gouged out in blood and tears
And Plato in bleeding ground.

Haven't you got something to answer for
10   Aren't you our myth ancestral land?
Jesus aren't you hunted and tortured?
Where will you ever find a friend?

'I did not come on earth
With such a ministry as I have been given.
15   What I have been credited with here,
Is debated in heaven.'

For Christ's sake give us the strength then
To fight against yourself.

1937–8   [112.2]

When I am in the purgatory of the unread
of the backward, of the wandering attention
What will survive must go back to Pier Head.
It will not be a spirit worthy of mention:
5   Not one to recommend or help the out-of-work sailor.
Nor will it be a ghost to help my gallant father
flying behind his bowler hat to work
As he chased his new school cap.
I shall not be looking for those I can help
10   For the salt gray prop looks after itself.
Even ghosts help with metaphors. I am in no poet's hand.
Nor is my work upon the remotest shelf.
I have thought too much of wounds which never mend

of ships which sail in rain and never come back
15   I lived with sadness: then I shall be stern.
Such sadness I lived with.
I shall watch them sail;
to Saigon the Equator or Port Said

3   112.1: What will survive will go back to Pier Head with the tide
5   112.1: Not one to recommend the down-and-out sailor:
[adds next line:] Struggling in the gale with this poor new news-
paper
8–9   112.1: As once before to race his new school cap.
I shall not be looking for anyone to help,
11   112.1: Nor shall I be a metaphor in a poet's hand
I shall not stir a metaphor in a poet's head
12   112.1: My work shall not be upon the dustiest shelf
grown greyer than the dust on his bookshelf
13   112.1: I thought too much of wounds which never mend
I spoke too much of wounds which never mend
I remember too much of wounds which never mend
I spoke too much of the dead for their good.
15   112.1: But I shall watch them sail still: But without heartbreak:
16   112.1: For I shall be lost before they are gone.
For I shall know, before they are gone.
17   112.1: I lived with sadness: then I shall be stern
with anguish once my joy: I must be stern
18   112.1: This is a letter I shall never send.
As this dead letter I shall never send.

1933   [113.1]

Who made this suicide pact of love?
Nor you nor I, we were not moved to the act.
The Lord made it, and he is invisible.
The devil signed it, and he is incredible.

Dollarton, 1940–54: Selected Poems, 1947

FROM 1940 TO 1947 THE LOWRYS lived in a shack on the beach at Dollarton. They visited Gerald Noxon in Ontario during 1944–5, and afterwards travelled for two years, arriving back at Dollarton in March 1947. In November 1947 they embarked on a European journey from which they did not return until 1949. The Lowrys continued to live in Dollarton until 1954, when they again left for Europe, this time not to return. During the two Dollarton periods Lowry composed over half of his extant poetry, approximately 264 of 479 poems. Sometime in 1946 Lowry decided to assemble from his Dollarton poems a second volume of poetry. On 22 June 1946 he wrote Albert Erskine: 'I've got masses of poems left... enough to make two volumes I'd thought of calling *The Lighthouse Invites the Storm* and *Wild Bleeding Hearts*' (SL 114).

One year later, on 24 June 1947, Lowry again mentioned the poems to Erskine; by this point Margerie had 'some fifty' typed out, but they required 'more weeding' before Lowry could send him the poems. *Wild Bleeding Hearts* is probably the 1947 typescript preserved at UBC; Lowry possessed the paper used for the poetry typescript by the time of his June 1947 comment to Erskine; it appears in correspondence from Dollarton through April and May of 1947. Lowry sent the fifty-four poems, less than one-quarter of his Dollarton output, accompanied by a covering note, to Erskine on 7 November 1947; therefore the tentatively titled *Wild Bleeding Hearts* must have been assembled sometime between July 1946 and November 1947.

Although Lowry included only three of the poems from *The Lighthouse*,[1] he arranged the 1947 selection to reflect his major stages of literary composition up to that point, as the section headings indicate: 'Poems of the Sea,' 'Poems from Mexico,' and 'Poems from Vancouver,' the latter of which comprises the bulk of the volume. Except for the three revised *Lighthouse* poems, none of the material in this volume was written before 1939–40, and most of it was composed after 1940. The selection was never published.

There are manuscripts and multiple drafts for poems in the 1947 selection. The earliest manuscript states appear on $7 \times 9\frac{1}{4}''$ notebook paper. During the initial organization of the UBC collection, Earle Birney disbound the notebooks in order to create individual files for the poems, but it is nonetheless evident that Lowry used at least four, possibly more, distinct notebooks during 1940: blank newsprint; blue-lined pink-margined newsprint; blue-lined unmargined newsprint; blue-lined pink-margined white paper. At least two of the notebook papers are datable to 1940,[2] and close holograph drafts for some individual poems, including 'Stoker Tom's Ukulele' [115] and 'Joseph Conrad' [118], appear on several of the papers, which indicates the close dating proximity of the notebooks. Lowry probably wrote the notebook poems during a very concentrated period of time: a tight network of drafts criss-crosses the notebook sheets. For example, the six holograph drafts of 'Freighter 1940' [162] include drafts for 'A Quarrel' [135], 'I met a man who had got drunk with Christ' [226], and 'My hate is as a wind that buffets me' [252]. Although this evidence strongly suggests that Lowry used the notebooks simultaneously, infrequent examples of notebook paper occur in the 1945–6 correspondence. Therefore, to address all possibilities, the notebook paper poems are dated '1939–40; 1945–6.'

In 1941 the occurrence of the notebook paper drops sharply in favour of the cheap 8½ × 11″ newsprint paper most characteristic of the first (1940–7) Dollarton period.[3] Intermediate states for many poems are datable from their appearance on clearly watermarked white bond papers that also appears in Lowry's outgoing letters between 1942 and 1946. The 1947 hand-annotated original copy of the 1947 selection, which Lowry sent to Albert Erskine in November 1947, is preserved at UBC (7–2).[4] Erskine returned the typescript with his comments pencilled on the sheets.

Most of the poems in this selection were further revised into the 1950s. Retypings for thirteen poems appear on 'Victory bond' 8½ × 11″ paper, datable to 1951.[5] Between 1952 and 1954 Lowry revised forty-six of the fifty-four poems in this selection, as well as nineteen additional Dollarton poems. This retyping appears on 8 × 10″ cream-coloured 'Voucher Bond' paper inscribed with elite type. This set of sheets is particularly interesting because Lowry evaluated with a letter grade most of the poems included. It is quite likely, perhaps even probable, that Lowry intended this final major retyping of his poems to be a revised edition of the 1947 selection. However, since further evidence of this hypothesis has not yet come to light, this edition is based on the discrete 1947 format. For individual copy-texts the latest-determinable authorial text of a poem is used.[6]

Problems of copy-text are rare in this selection: paper dating is well documented in the correspondence of this period, and the later typescripts are readily identifiable through revisions as well as paper-dating. There is no numeration in the selection; it lacks a table of contents, and the poems are unnumbered and the pages unfoliated, so no grid exists for determining the authorial order of the selection. However, the original typescript at UBC appears pristine enough to provide the only justifiable basis for ordering the poems.

The poems are dated according to their first extant drafts. Poems which first appear on 1947 paper are dated 1947, but the dates are square-bracketed since it is unlikely that the 1947 state is their first. Many poems in this selection are dated simply 1940–7. Without external or contextual evidence, it is impossible to be more precise because the first drafts appear on the newsprint paper that Lowry used throughout the 1940–7 period. Some of the poems whose multiple holograph drafts appear solely in the notebooks possess a stemma which is indeterminable through paper-dating or revisions; many of these drafts, such as 'The Canadian Turned Back at the Border' [167], which has several variants for almost every one of its eighty lines, are incomplete or fragmentary. For those notebook poems whose early states manifest an indeterminable order, line variants have been provided under a generalized sigla notation. For example, the notation '1 167.1-5:' indicates that the variants listed for line one of poem 167 all occur in the first five drafts, but that it is impossible to determine the order of composition for the first-line variants in those drafts.[7]

NOTES

1 See note 7 for '*The Lighthouse Invites the Storm, 1934–9.*'
2 The white blue-lined pink-margined paper appears in outgoing correspondence for 1940 (1–79); in a handwritten note Margerie dates the newsprint blank paper 1940 (21–8). One type of notebook paper also appears in correspondence for 1945 (2–2).
3 This paper also appears, for example, in the 1941 typescripts for *Under the Volcano* (boxes 28 through 31).
4 There must have been a duplicate typescript because carbons of the 1947 retyping, on identical paper, exist for five of the fifty-four poems. These poems are: 'Jokes in the Galley' [125], 'Outward Bound' [126], 'Mr. Lowry's Good Friday under a Real Cactus' [130], 'Death of an Oaxaquenian' [132], 'Nocturne' [134].
5 The thirteen poems are: 'Old Freighter in an Old Port' [114], 'Stoker Tom's Ukulele' [115], 'Bosun's Song' [116], 'The Western Ocean' [117], 'Xocxitepec' [129], 'Kraken, Eagles in British Columbia' [140], 'About Ice' [141], 'Deserter' [155], 'The Dodder' [157], 'Freighter 1940' [162], 'Warning from False Cape Horn' [163], 'Salmon Drowns Eagle' [166], 'The Canadian Turned Back at the Border' [167].
6 For example, the copy-texts for two poems are included in two of Lowry's 1957 handwritten letters: 'Sestina in a Cantina' [127], to David Markson (DM 1–9), and 'Happiness' [148], to Ralph Gustafson (3–13).
7 The six poems thus affected are: 'Stoker Tom's Ukulele' [115.1–7], 'Joseph Conrad' [118.1–5], 'Deserter' [155.1–9], 'The Dodder' [157.1-10], 'Freighter 1940' [162.1–9], 'The Canadian Turned Back at the Border' [167.1–5].

Poems of the Sea

1940   OLD FREIGHTER IN AN OLD PORT   [114.8][95]

It had no name and we docked at midnight.
Nor could girls, shadowed at the dead car halt,
Laughing in linked quintets in the lamplight,
Leaven our hearts embittered with sea salt.
5   There was no beauty then about that place.
But waking early, to see near at hand
The wharf, road, and market, friendly clock face,
– The very lineaments of a new land –
Our flag run up the post office in spring,
10   Whose each stone seemed to promise news from one
Loved, and from our rusted bow the soaring
Car lines burning straight-ruled into the sun –
Emergence was of Christian from Despond
And Friday's print for Crusoe in the sand.

T   114.4: [missing]
2   114.4: Nor could girls, shadowed in that vault,
            Nor could girls, circling a vault,
3   114.4: Laugh in linked quintets in the lamplight.
6   114.4: But waiting early, seeing near at hand
            But waiting early, to see near at hand
7   114.4: The wharf, clock, market road, and post office,
            The wharf, clock, market road – ah –
9   114.4: Whose every stone seemed to conceal a postcard
10 114.4: With our own flag flying, and its promise
11 114.4: Of news from the only one in the world
12 114.4: [missing]

1939–40   STOKER TOM'S UKULELE   [115.11]

Tom left his seabag behind and this uke,
Beautiful as all I don't know about art.
Rosewood parable of the unsubtle heart!
From it he struck the fondest harmonic.
5   Many who claimed this was dingy music,
Who never saw beyond the second fret,
Said disowned chords spoke now at night, apart,
Which argued the nature of heartbreak.
Each snapping string a hawser to Tom's soul:
10   First the taut B broke, strangely held F sharp,
And last the frayed D twanged off like a gun . . .
I used to feel it waited then with all
Its sounds and echoes for his heavy step.
But now I think it waits for me to learn.

T   115.1–7: [missing]
                 Tom's Ukelele
       115.8: Hawser Tom's Ukulele
3   115.1–7: This rosewood parable of the heart
                 It said much more than some might orchestrate
                 Sanguine pouring of the unsubtle heart
       115.8–10: Sanguine pouring of the unsubtle heart
4   115.1–7: It reached something of the nature of heartbreak
                 For all that they accounted it a freak.
                 Yet he would strike the fondest harmonic
                 From it was once struck the fondest harmonic
                 From which he struck the fondest harmonic
5   115.1–7: There are those who say it was dingy music
                 But those who claimed it made dingy music
                 Many who claimed here was dingy music
                 But some who claimed this was dingy music,
                 But some who claimed here was dingy music,
6   115.1–7: To those who get beyond the second fret
7   115.1–7: [missing]
                 Admitted it spoke chords, now none played it
                 Said later there spoke chords, now none played it
                 Said ownerless chords spoke at night, apart
8   115.1–7: [missing]
                 That argued of the nature of heartbreak.
                 Which argued the nature of heartbreak
       115.8–10: Which argued the nature of heartbreak
9   115.1–7: First the B string went/snapped, one night in Darien
                 First the B string went/snapped, one night in Berne
                 First the B string went/snapped, one night in Lucerne
                 First the B string went/snapped, one night in Rouen
                 First the frayed B string went off like a gun:
10   115.1–7: [missing]
                 After, the A broke, strangely held F sharp:
                 First the taut B broke, strangely held F sharp,
11   115.1–7: Each breaking string a passage of his soul
                 Each breaking string a chapter of his soul
                 Each snapping string a chapter of Tom's soul
                 Each snapping string a hawser to Tom's soul.
                 For next the frayed D twanged off like a gun . . .

[1947]   BOSUN'S SONG   [116.3]

        Here on the poop each lousy night I stand
        And watch the twirling log, the foam, the moon,

        And what would I not give for a hand
        In mine? Even a dog's! But they'd as soon

5   All of them, see dead, old Mr. Facing
        Bloody Both Ways! Just hear that engine cry,
        Hating me too: why not? Hear her racing?

        Lonely: lonely: lonely: lonely: lonely:

Bloody thing. And through the fireman's skylight
10   – Queer thoughts men have with power over others –

A blackened Chink stands naked as daylight –

Sometimes I think all men could be brothers

Hating me, whose only friend is the foam
Here, and atop a tankard way back home.

1940   THE WESTERN OCEAN   [117.7] [97]

He begged his ghost a vision of the sea
That would compose it stilled within the mind
Forever, so that he might be resigned
To it and not haunted eternally.
5   The ghost shook his head and said gravely,
'You would have lost your only grief, to find
You prayed then for the roar of the sea wind
And the darkness,' they turned toward the quay,
'That you had landlocked your heart to compose your tears.
10   Its unrest will claim you as on this wharf
Its mist on your breast.' His ship in harbor
Loaded sweet timber from the high-piled piers.
He looked at her long and then with a laugh
Climbed on board and was seen no more.

T   117.4: The Roar of the Sea and the Darkness
1   117.4: He prayed to his ghost for a vision of the sea,
2   117.4: Which would harbour it strictly in the mind
3   117.4: For all time, that he might be resigned
5   117.4: The ghost nodded his head, and said gravely:
     117.5, 6: The ghost shook his head and said, quietly,
6   117.4: 'But then you would lose your only grief, and find
7   117.4: You had composed your tears, landlocked your heart;
8   117.4: You would pray for the roar of the sea wind
9   117.4: And darkness, then, and call me wrong or right,
     117.5, 6: ' – Had landlocked your heart to compose your tears.
10   117.4: You must always claim its unrest and monotony;
12   117.4: Loaded sweet timber from the high-piled wharf
14   117.5, 6: Climbed on board swiftly and was seen no more.

1940   JOSEPH CONRAD   [118.9]

This wrestling, as of seamen with a storm
Which flies to leeward – while they, united
In that chaos, turn, each on his nighted
Bunk to dream of chaos again, or home –
5   The poet himself, struggling with the form
Of his coiled work, knows, having requited
Sea-weariness with purpose, invited

What derricks of the soul plunge in his room.
Yet some mariner's ferment in his blood
10   – Though truant heart will hear the iron travail
And song of ships that ride their easting down –
Sustains him to subdue or be subdued.
In sleep all night he grapples with a sail!
Yet words beyond the life of ships dream on.

T   118.1–5, 7: [missing]
2   118.1–5: Which flies to leeward, while they
3   118.1–5: United in that chaos, turn, sea-weary
4   118.1–5: Each on his bunk, to dream of fields at home
5   118.1–5: Or shake with visions Dante never knew,
          The poet knows struggling with the form
6   118.1–5: of his quiet work knows too, having requited
          of his labour. He too has requited
          The poet himself knows, struggling with the form
          The poet himself wills, struggling with the form
          The poet himself feels, struggling with the form
7   118.1–5: Sea-weariness with purpose, indited
          of his quiet work. What derricks of the soul
8   118.1–5: To himself, by strife, some reward. Not calm!
          Plunge in that muted room, adrift, menacing?
9   118.1–5: For now that awful derricks of the soul
          When truant heart can hear the sailors sing
10   118.1–5: Plunge in that dark room, adrift, menacing?
          He'd break his pen to sail an easting down.
11   118.1–5: What fireman in the blood crams all steam on?
          And yet some mariner's ferment in his blood
12   118.1–5: Or then all night grapples with a sail,
13   118.1–5: Or then all night hears some sailor sing
14   118.1–5: But words beyond the life of ships dream on.
          That words beyond the life of ships dream on.
        118.6–8: But words beyond the life of ships dream on.

1940–7   JOKES ALOFT   [119.5]

I never picture an immedicable grief
Without some fifty bottles for relief,
And five and fifty taverns in my path
Of sorrow, on that day of wrath.
5   From which it seems I fear such grief per se
Less than that lack of means might make it grey.

T   119.1–3: Consolation

1940–7   DANISH SAILOR'S SONG   [120.8]

It was blowing a storm in the red light district.
It was blowing so hard that not a sailor
Was blown off the sea but a pimp was blown

Off the street. It blew right through the windows.
5   And it rained through the roof.
But the gang chipped in and bought a pint.
And what is better,
When a bunch of soaks are together,
Even when the roof is leaking?

T   120.1–3: From an old Danish song
1   120.1–3: It blew a storm in the red light district
4   120.1–3: Off the street. It blew through the windows –
5   120.1: And it rained through the roof but the gang chipped
6   120.1: In and bought a pint and what is better
     120.2: But the gang chipped in
7   120.1: [missing]
     120.2: And bought a pint – [adds next line:] And what is better,

1940–7   JOKES AMIDSHIPS   [121.3]

There is no pity at sea
And isn't that a pity
The bosun's mate said to me

I said yes I sure agree
5   (We lay at Jersey City)
There is no pity at sea.

Yet I think that that must be
Else we'd need a committee
The bosun's mate said to me

10   To say who needs it, we
Don't with this in the kitty
There is not pity at sea

Though. Eight bells there, time for tea
But you go find a titty.
15   There is no pity at sea
The bosun's mate said to me.

1940–7   JOKES ON THE POOP   [122.5]

No one waits for me
Beyond the white wake
Aft, beyond the sea.

I want no pity
5   But make no mistake
No one waits for me.

Is it that you flee
The past, as dawns break
Aft, beyond the sea?

10   No, myself lonely,
        It is for my sake
        No one waits for me.

        Till my doom shall be
        Like a lost snowflake
15   Aft, beyond the sea.

        I think of one tree –
        But no one, nobody,
        No one, waits for me
        Aft, beyond the sea.

10–12 122.1: No, eternity;
       It is for its sake
       No one waits for me
  17 122.1: The thought is a fake.

1940–7   INJURED CHORIANT OR PAEONIC   [123.4]

        The sea
        Pouring
        Harmlessly
        Past the port
5   Is yet the
        Menacing
        Tyrant of old
        That the
        Drowned
10   Know.

1940–7   REFLECTION TO WINDWARD   [124.5]

      A grey day of high tempestuous seas
      As seaward rolls the Dimitrios N. Bogliazides
      Each weary hand a sweat-ragged Ulysses.
      This ocean out of wedlock was begot.
5   The fireman's fo'c'sle ships the bastard lot.
      Small wonder that the ancients, I confess,
      Made Venus rise from such a bloody mess.

 2 124.1, 3, 4: As northward rolls the Dimitrios N. Bogliazides
    124.1, 2: As homeward rolls the Dimitrios N. Bogliazides
     124.3: As starward rolls the Dimitrios N. Bogliazides
 6 124.1–4: No wonder the ancients, I confess
     124.2: No marvel if the ancients, I confess

1940–7   JOKES IN THE GALLEY   [125.5]

      There is no pity at sea
      Unless you should die like me

Then they'll wash your clothes
With fearful oaths
5   With terrible oaths
They'll wash your clothes
But there is no pity at sea.

T 125.1, 3: Rondelet
    125.2: The Sea
    125.4: Jaunty Song
3–6 125.1: There is no pity at sea
        But over the hard faced men
        Comes a supple sympathy
        Of some kind it may be.
5–6 125.2 Oh they wash your clothes
        With terrible oaths

1940–7   OUTWARD BOUND   [126.6]

On the poop of a ship
I watched each night
The fluctuant hope
Of the moment before.
5   The wood drifting,
The torn smoke,
All the beauty,
The sadness of the sea.
These words are stronger
10   Than images:
The simple fact
Of bewilderment
Than what it meant to another.
The twilight cold
15   The sail gone
And home far
And abaft the beam
The Pillars of Hercules.

T 126.1–4: [missing]
2   126.2: I watched recede
4   126.1: of the moment.
        [adds then deletes next line:] I prayed for words
    126.3: [adds then deletes next 2 lines:] Vanish from sight
                        And be born once more
5   126.1: [missing]
   126.2, 3: The weed drifting
6–13 126.2: When bells strike
        You grind duty.
        My life was waste
        And the rape of the world
        Swept it away with blood.
7–18 126.1: The trimmer was lonely

As the watch ends
Bucket on arm
Bells struck.
I prayed for the words
As clean as death
White as bone
To say all this

Poems from Mexico

1943   SESTINA IN A CANTINA   [127.5]

Scene: A waterfront tavern in Vera Cruz at daybreak.

LEGION

Watching this dawn's mnemonic of old dawning:
Jonquil-colored, delicate, some in prison,
Green dawns of drinking tenderer than sunset,
But clean and delicate like dawns of ocean
5   Flooding the heart with pale light in which horrors
Stampede like plump wolves in distorting mirrors.

Oh, we have seen ourselves in many mirrors;
Confusing all our sunsets with the dawning,
Investing every tongue and leaf with horrors,
10   And every stranger overtones for prison,
And seeing mainly in the nauseous ocean
The last shot of our life before sunset.

ST. LUKE (A SHIP'S DOCTOR)

How long since you have really seen a sunset?
The mind has many slanting lying mirrors,
15   The mind is like that sparkling greenhouse ocean
Glass-deceptive in the Bengal dawning;
The mind has ways of keeping us in prison,
The better there to supervise its horrors.

SIR PHILIP SIDNEY

Why do you not, sir, organize your horrors
20   And shoot them one day, preferably at sunset,
That we may wake up next day not in prison,
No more deceived by lies or many mirrors,
And go down to the cold beach at dawning
To lave away the past in colder ocean?

ST. LUKE

25   No longer is there freedom on the ocean.
And even if there were, he likes his horrors,
And if he shot them would do so at dawning
That he might have acquired some more by sunset,
Breaking them in by that time before mirrors
30   To thoughts of spending many nights in prison.

LEGION

The fungus-colored sky of dawns in prison,
The fate that broods on every pictured ocean,

The fatal conversations before mirrors,
The fiends and all the spindly breeds of horrors,
35   Have shattered by their beauty every sunset
And rendered quite intolerable old dawning.

The oxen standing by this door at dawning –
Outside our tavern now, outside our prison –
Read through the wagon-wheels, jalousies like sunset
40   Swinging now in a sky as calm as ocean
Where Venus hangs her obscene horn of horrors
For us now swaying in a hall of mirrors –

Such horrid beauty maddened all my mirrors,
Has burst in heart's eye sanity of dawning,
45   No chamber in my house brimful of horrors
But does not whisper of some dreadful prison,
Worse than all ships dithering through the ocean
Tottering like drunkards, arms upraised at sunset.

RICHARD III (A BARMAN)

Vain derelict all avid for the sunset!
50   Shine out fair sun till you have bought new mirrors
That you may see your shadow pass the ocean,
And sunken no more pass our way at dawning,
But like on the cold stone sea floor of some prison
A chunk of sodden driftwood gnawed by horrors.

LEGION

55   At first I never looked on them as horrors;
But one day I was drinking hard near sunset,
And suddenly saw the world as a giant prison,
Ruled by tossing moose-heads, with hand mirrors,
And heard the voice of the idiot speak at dawning,
60   And since that time have dwelt beside the ocean.

EL UNIVERSAL (EARLY EDITION)

Did no one speak of love beside the ocean,
Have you not felt, even among your horrors,
Granting them, there was such a thing as dawning,
A dawning for man whose star seems now at sunset,
65   Like million-sheeted scarlet dusty mirrors,
But one day must be led out of his prison?

LEGION

I see myself as all mankind in prison,
With hands outstretched to lanterns by the ocean;
I see myself as all mankind in mirrors,
70   Babbling of love while at his back rise horrors
Ready to suck the blood out of the sunset
And amputate the godhead of the dawning.

THE SWINE

And now the dawning drives us from our prison
Into the dawn like sunset, into the ocean,
75   Bereaving him of horrors, but leaving him his mirrors.

ST   127.1: veterio vestigia flammare
          127.2: Scene: a waterfront cantina in Vera Cruz.
        127.4, 5: [missing]
4   127.1: But clear and pure and delicate like dawns of ocean
12   127.1–4: The last shot of our life before the sunset.
14   127.1, 4: the mind has many slanting staggering mirrors
16   127.1: Cool, prepared, in the Bengal dawning
21   127.1: As we may wake up next day not in prison
22   127.1, 2, 4: No more deceived by lies nor many mirrors,
23   127.1–4: and go down to the cold beach at dawning
35   127.1, 4: Have ruined by their beauty every sunset
37   127.1, 2: The oxen standing at this door at dawning
38   127.2, 4: Outside our tavern, our insatiate prison,
40   127.1: Swinging in a sky as calm as ocean
52   127.1, 2, 4: Which sunken shall not pass our way at dawning
57   127.1: And suddenly saw the world as a great prison
65   127.1–4: Like a million-sheeted scarlet dusty mirrors,
66   127.2, 4: No. I see myself as all mankind in prison,

1940–7   *SUNRISE*   [128.6]

Sober I rode into the brand new dawn
With steady hand grasping the single rein
New shod new shrived and all but newly born
Over the smiling illogical plain.

5   Surcingleless as heaven ran my steed
And true to heaven rose my simple song
Ah, the years behind seemed lost and lost the deed,
As pommel and stirrups unheeded I cantered along.

– But what cactuses are these on every hand
10   Wild dogs and spectres, all enveloping?
And came again into that evening land
– Galloping, galloping –

Bound to that unrelenting fatuous horse
Whose eyes are lidless and whose name, remorse.

T   128.1: [missing]
4   128.1–5: Over the smiling grandiloquent plain.
12   128.1, 3–5: Galloping, galloping, galloping

1940   XOCHITEPEC   [129.5]

Those animals that follow us in dream
Are swallowed by the dawn, but what of those
Which hunt us, snuff, stalk us out in life, close

In upon it, belly-down, haunt our schemes
5   Of building, with shapes of delirium,
Symbols of death, heraldic, and shadows,
Glowering. . . Just before we left Tlampam
Our cats lay quivering under the maguey;
A meaning had slunk, and now died, with them.
10   The boy slung them half stiff down the ravine,
Which now we entered, and whose name is hell.
But still our last night had its animal:
The puppy, in the cabaret, obscene,
Looping-the-loop and soiling the floor,
15   And fastening itself to that horror
Of our last night; while the very last day
As I sat bowed, frozen over mescal,
They dragged two shrieking fawns through the hotel
And slit their throats, behind the barroom door. . .

T   129.1: [missing]
       129.2: The animal kingdom
              Lupus in Fabula
              Mescalitos
       129.3: Lupus in Fabula
       129.4: Patience of Beasts
              Lupus in Fabula
1   129.4: Strange animals which follow us in dream
2   129.2–4: And mean I know not what! But what of those
       129.4: Are, – (one might say) preferable to those
3   129.2, 3: That hunt us, snuff, stalk us out in life, close
4   129.2: In upon us, belly-down, haunt our scheme
14   129.2, 3: Looping-the-loop, and dirtying the floor
       129.4: Looping-the-loop, and soiling all the floor
17   129.2–4: While I saw bowed, frozen over mescal

       129.1: Animals that follow us in dream
              And they mean I know not what.
              The cat lay quivering under cruel trees
              And then was thrown down the ravine.
              The chihuahua puppy, in the cabaret,
              Looping the loop, and dirtying the floor:
              The goat that glowered with savage
              With hatred eyes then charged
              Me, who would have petted it
              This was a warning: avoid tragically
              Worthless history: and the day you went,
              Horror beyond horror beyond horror
              They dragged two shrieking fawns through the hotel
              And slit their throats behind the barroom door.

1940–7   MR. LOWRY'S GOOD FRIDAY   [130.4]
              UNDER A REAL CACTUS

              Because I am a fraud
              Because I am afraid

                Because I must evade
                The dictum of the Lord,
5   And then, again, deride Him,
                Yet be crucified beside Him
                And then, once more, evade . . .
                Because I must decide,
                Because I should not do so,
10   Because I am like Crusoe
                But shipwrecked on a grief
                That passes all belief.
                I am dead, I am bored,
                Because I am a fraud,
15   Because I am afraid . . .

T   130.1: Genet
            The Cashier
            Poem
            The Thief at Sunset
    130.2: Guilt
5–6 130.1: And yet, again, deride him.
            Yet be crucified beside him.

1947   DELIRIUM IN VERA CRUZ   [131.7] [27]

        Where has tenderness gone, he asked the mirror
        Of the Biltmore Hotel, cuarto 216. Alas,
        Can its reflection lean against the glass
        Too, wondering where I have gone, into what horror?
5   Is that it staring at me now with terror
        Behind your frail, tilted barrier? Tenderness
        Was here, in this very retreat, in this
        Place, its form seen, cries heard by you. What error
        Is here? Am I that forked rashed image?
10   Is this the ghost of love which you reflected?
        Now with a background of tequila, stubs, dirty collars,
        Sodium perborate, and a scrawled page
        To the dead, telephone disconnected?
        . . . He smashed all the glass in the room. (Bill $50)

1947   DEATH OF AN OAXAQUEÑIAN   [132.4]

            So huge is God's despair
            In the wild cactus plain
            I heard him weeping there

            That I might venture where
5   The peon had been slain
            So huge is God's despair

            On the polluted air
            Twixt noonday and the rain

I heard Him weeping there

10   And felt His anguish tear
For refuge in my brain
So huge is God's despair

That it could find a lair
In one so small and vain
15   I heard him weeping there.

Oh vaster than our share
Than deserts of New Spain
So huge is God's despair
I heard Him weeping there.

11   132.2: My heart with useless pain
13   132.2: Yet how may I now dare
14   132.2: To say I heard, again
18–19   132.2: I heard him weeping there –
So huge is God's despair.

1946   SONG   [133.4]

Pity the blind and the halt but yet pity
The man at the bank in the pitiless city
The man at the bank who can't sign his name –
Though he call on his courage and posthumous fame –
5   This man with the terrible shakes far from home.
Ah, pity this man with his pitiful income
Arrived now from far, from far sources of shame,
For a man at the bank who can't sign his own name,
Though he sweat till the ultimate Manager came,
10   – Pity the blind and pity the lame
But pity the man who can't sign his own name.

T   133.1: Self pity
Prayer for humanity, me.
133.3: [missing]

Poems from Vancouver

1940–7   NOCTURNE   [134.4]

    This evening Venus signs alone
    And homeward feathers stir like silk
    Like the dress of a multitudinous ghost
    The pinions tear through a sky like milk.
5   Seagulls all soon to be turned to stone
    That seeking I lose beyond the trail
    In the woods that I and my ignorance own
    Where together we walk on our hands and knees
    Together go walking beneath the pale
10 Of a beautiful evening loved the most,
    And yet this evening is my jail
    And policemen glisten in the trees.

T 134.1: [missing]

1939–40; 1945–6   A QUARREL   [135.7]

    The poignance of a quarrel in the post!
    That threat, flung at myself into a pillar
    Which could have been as a white bird loosed
    Homing, with news of reprieve, to your heart –
5   Would that the tyrannous thing might be lost,
    Or sorted into the dark, by some eerie scrivener. . .
    The wind is high tonight in Canada,
    A viaduct is drifting out to sea,
    Ground lightning felled a tree across the street
10 And direst portent's here for all save me.
    For still the wheels cry out against the iron
    And frozen platforms race back into day.
    Ah, that I could believe, when wires are down,
    That venom such as mine could lose its way.

T 135.1–3, 6: [missing]
2   135.1: This threat, thrown at myself into a pillar
3   135.1: that should have been as a white bird loosed
        135.6: Which could have been a white bird loosed
6   135.1: To be sorted into the dark by eerie scrivener
      135.2–4: Sorted into the dark, by eerie scrivener. . .
9   135.1: A tree crashed on a man and broke his head
10   135.1: For all save only I, is hideous portent!
            For all save only I, is direst portent!
14   135.1: That venom such as mine might lose its way
      135.2–6: That venom such as mine would lose its way.

1940–7   THE GLAUCOUS WINGED GULL   [136.4]

The hook nosed angel with spring plumage
Hunter of edible stars, and sage
Catsbane and defiler of the porch,
Dead sailor, finial, and image
5   Of freedom in morning blue, and strange torch
At twilight, stranger world of love,
Old haunter of the Mauretania,
Snowblinded once, I saved. And hove
Out of the rainbarrel, back at heaven
10   A memory stronger than childhood even
Or freighters rolling to Roumania.

T   136.1, 2: The Herring Gull
1   136.1: The angel that walks like a sailor
           [adds next line:] Pure scavenger of the empyrean

1941–6   NO TIME TO STOP AND THINK   [137.6]

The only hope is the next drink.
If you like, you take a walk.
No time to stop and think,
The only hope is the next drink.
5   Useless trembling on the brink,
Worse than useless all this talk.
The only hope is the next drink.
If you like, you take a walk.

T   137.1: [missing]
       137.2, 3: Triolet
5   137.2, 3: Hopeless trembling on the brink
8   137.4, 5: If you like, *you* take a walk.

       137.1: No time to stop and think
               What I stopped at or was taught
               The only hope is the next drink

               No time to say I cannot sink
               Lower, – this is the drink I've bought
               No time, no time to stop and think

               What hopes stand trembling on the brink
               Might launch way without a wreath
               The only hope is the next drink

               And then the next, another link
               In the debased impersonal myth
               No time to stop and think

               No time to expand nor to shrink
               Oh lonely man of Nazareth
               The only hope is the next drink

1940–7   VILLAKNELL   [138.5]

But now I see myself a fool
I used to say with real dismay
For I was born in Liverpool

I used to mourn fat boy at school
5   That Mersey wasn't Tiger Bay
But now I see myself a fool

Or on Pier Head my heels I'd cool
Gazing at freighters far away
For I was born in Liverpool

10   Dreaming of Constantinople
Beyond the seas beyond Cathay
But now I see myself a fool

Which was not at that time Stamboul
In this our life which we call grey
15   For I was born in Liverpool

I always knew I was a ghoul
My friends were satisfied to stay
But now I see myself a fool
For I was born in Liverpool.

T   138.2: [missing]
4   138.1–3: I used to mourn dull head at school
7   138.1–3: Or on Pier Head my heels to cool
8   138.1–3: Would gaze on freighters far away

1940–7   WHAT SIGBJØRN SAID   [139.4]

My only triumph is the challenge cup
My mother wears upon the mantelpiece,
My soul perhaps roves back to Skjellerup –
My mother's mother was a Viking's niece.
5   But though all this must make a doleful hymn
No Viking's heart have I, beneath the fat
That cushions every slight and palsied limb,
Remote from the maelstrom as the Kattegat.

It is not true, I hear some Sigbjørn say,
10   Ridiculous and squalid though you are,
You yet are you! If nothing you can own,
You yet have strength to drink your strength away –
To stand up in a corner of some bar
And grapple with your bourgeois hell alone.

8   139.1–3: [missing]

The heagles how they fly in great circles!
Nature is one of the most beautiful
Things I ever saw in my life. Why, the
Heagle went around to get his bearings
5   To look over the country. Two mile wide
Hin great circles. Pretty soon you'll see crabs
Under these stones and then it will be spring,
Some crabs in spring no bigger than a fly.
Have you ever seen how an elephant
10   Was constructed? Where did the old Romans
Get them shields but from the rooster's wings?

II

Take in the desert now – the Sahara –
Where camels stamp with hooves like great spitoons
Upside down. One day they built a railroad.
15   But hinsects heat up all the wooden ties.
So now they make the ties out of metal
Shaped like camel's hooves. And soon the birds,
And pretty soon the crabs will bring the spring;
And the deer swimming right across the bay
20   With their hantlers beautiful sticking up
Like branches on a floating tree, swimming,
Swimming across to the lighthouse in spring.

III

Then see dragon flies like flying machines
Back-pedalling! But crabs. I had a friend,
25   A diver – thief he was in private life,
Never come home without somethink even
If it was only a nail, ay, basement
Like a junkyard! – well, this time he goes down,
Down, down, down, you know, deep! Then gets scairt: why?
30   – Migrations of billions of crabs –
Climbing all around him, sir, migrating
In the spring, aclambering around Sam
Aswallering and stretching their muscles!

IV

And you might say the diver's mate's like God
35   Who pulls him up, if you see what I mean,
And like as not pulls up a pouncing fiend.
Praps they see somethink *else* down there – who knows?
You know. Because Sam was so crazy scairt
He wouldn't speak to no one for two weeks.
40   But after that he sings like nightingales

And talks the head off any wooden duck!
... In great circles how they fly the heagles,
One of the most beautiful things ever
I saw in my life is nature. That's true.

1940–7   ABOUT ICE   [141.3]

(A STORY TOLD BY A CANADIAN FISHERMAN.)

When you speak about ice, do you mean live ice
Which is blue, or dead ice, white as chalk?
The blue will hold the mountain in its vice,
Crawl up it, swelling, sing down at a walk.
5   But white is dead so cannot climb at all
And lies in valleys where it sings no more.
One island held that not unusual,
Familiar with white along her shore,
Thinking all ice lay thus, motionless, dead,
10   The blue ice came and calmly ravished her
Of all her beauty of trees and moss, bled
Her lichen to the rock, leaving her bare
As that door. Stone was that island's surplice,
Who thought ice meant merely her kind of ice.

T   141.1, 2: To You, Declaiming Generalities
2   141.1, 2: Which is blue or dead ice, sir, white as chalk?

1940–7   THE MAGIC WORLD   [142.6]

The magic factory chimneys stand in rows.
Bored Prosperos decree a magic war.
And every club contains a magic bore.
The magic peasants delve with magic hoes,
5   The magic factory chimneys stand in rows,
The magic peasants delve in magic tilth,
At night lie down to sleep in magic filth.

T   142.1: Dream
    142.2: A Magic World
4–7   142.2: The magic peasants dig in magic tilth
       The magic paupers walk the magic streets
       At night they sleep in magic filth

1940–7   KINGFISHERS IN BRITISH COLUMBIA   [143.7]

A mad kingfisher
Rocketing about in the
Red fog at sunrise

Now sits

5   On the alder
Post that tethers the floats
Angrily awaiting his mate.
Here she

    Comes, like a left wing
10   Threequarter cutting through toward
The goal in sun-lamped
Fog at Rosslyn Park at half
Past three in halcyon days.

T 143.1: Kingfishers in Columbia
10 143.1: Threequarter cutting dawnmists
11–12 143.1: [missing]

1946   FOUL, OR TWENTY-FIVE   [144.6]

Gloomy is this weary scrimmage
Of my thoughts to heel some image
Out to where the scrum-half dancing
Of my will to write entrancing
5   Poems waits to fling the fated
Thing, that will arrive deflated
On the tryline of abortion.
Poet, gloomy is thy portion.
Poet, cease to be a poet.
10 Poet, cease. Should I shout go it
After everything that's happened
To this bird so sadly wappened?

Gloomy is this world and tawdry
(But shot through with shafts of bawdry).

T 144.2: Incomprehensible Statement
144.3: Twenty-five!
Foul!
144.5: [missing]

1940–7   FISHERMAN'S RETURN   [145.5]

– In the city got a little exercise.
Been sitting humped up in the old boat.
I never saw a street flusher.
They just letting the old grime go.
5   The street cars are getting
So humpy and dumpy.
I ran into a couple of bottles of rye.
I thought a little walking would speed
The old ticker...

1–6 145.1: Middle of July I had two light Union suits
Never used no belt. In the city

Got a little exercise, been sitting humped up
In the old boat. I never saw
A street flusher. They just letting
The old grime go. The street cars
Are getting so humpy and dumpy.

1940–7   GHOSTS IN NEW HOUSES   [146.4]

There's something dreadful about ghosts in new houses:
Ghosts in old houses are bad enough:
But ghosts in new houses are terrible.
The very newness of these new desolate houses
5   Would be terrible enough without the ghosts.
But the ghosts are new too.
Blue girls in blue blouses
And people at their Sunday roasts
In broad daylight, within these new houses
10   On streets where men are sweeping broken glass.

1946   SCRIBNER'S SONS   [147.6]

There is no mail
There is no hope
There is no sail

Beyond the veil
5   Our senses grope
There is no mail

Stupid to rail
Senseless to mope
There is no sail

10   Futile to wail
Stupid the rope
There is no mail

Yet I might fail
Once more and tope
15   There is no sail

A feeble tale:
There is no soap
There is no mail
There is no sail.

T]   [missing] {147.5: Scriveners and Sons}
T   147.1: Scribners
                Publishers
                Poem for the eternal writer waiting for the eternal rejection
                                                                        [slip
        147.2: Scribners

The eternal writer waiting for the eternal rejection slip
147.3: Poem for the eternal writer waiting for the eternal rejection
[slip
    Publishers!
147.4: Publishers!
147.5: Scriveners and Sons
7   147.1–5: Useless to rail
8   147.1, 2: Fruitless to mope
11   147.1: Senseless the rope
    147.2: Futile the rope

1940–7   HAPPINESS   [148.6]

Blue mountains with snow and blue cold rough water –
A wild sky full of stars at rising
And Venus and the gibbous moon at sunrise.
Gulls following a motor boat against the wind,
5   Trees with branches rooted in air;
Sitting in the sun at noon
With the furiously smoking shadow of the shack chimney,
Eagles drive downwind in one,
Terns blow backward
10   A new kind of tobacco at eleven,
And my love returning on the four o'clock bus –
My God, why have you given this to us?

T   148.1: Ecstacy
1   148.1: [missing]
3   148.1: And Venus and the golden moon at sunrise
4   148.1: Forty slow gulls following a motorboat against the wind
6–7   148.1: Sitting in the sun at noon with the furiously
                  Smoking shadow of the shack chimney
6–7 148.2, 3: [both on one line]
8–10   148.1: Eagles drive downwind in one, terns blow
                  Backward; a new kind of tobacco at eleven
                  Blue mountains with snow and blue cold rough water

1940–7   [149.5]

Alas, there is no still path in my soul,
I being evil, none of memory;
No path, untenanted by fiend or ghoul,
Where those I have loved best touch wings and sigh,
5   And passing enter silently the place
Of dream, illumined by bright fruit, and light,
That circles from the always brightest face
Of love itself and dissipates the night.

There is no path, there is no path at all,
10   Unless perhaps where abstract things have gone
And precepts rise and metaphysics fall,

And principles abandoned stumble on.
No path, but as it were a river in spate
Where drowning forms, downswept, gesticulate.

1940–7   POEM TO BE PLACED AT THE CONCLUSION   [150.3]
            OF A LONG OBSCURE PASSIONATE
            AND ELOQUENT BOOK OF POEMS

          I know no poet's use of words
          My sufferings are unique
          I see the emblematic birds
          But have no wit to speak.

5   Yet that I see them thus at all
          Sustains the gloomy hope
          Which I peer at, beyond the pall,
          As through a telescope,

          That someday, somehow, something there
10   Will kindly not confuse
          My delegation of despair
          To the bedraggled muse.

T]   [missing] {150.1}

1940–7   [151.3]
          There is no poetry when you live there.
          Those stones are yours, those noises are your mind,
          The forging thunderous trams and streets that bind
          You to the dreamed-of bar where sits despair
5   Are trams and streets: poetry is otherwhere.
          The cinema fronts and shops once left behind
          And mourned, are mourned no more. Strangely unkind
          Seem all new landmarks of the now and here.

          But move you toward New Zealand or the Pole,
10   Those stones will blossom and the noises sing,
          And trams will wheedle to the sleeping child
          That never rests, whose ship will always roll,
          That never can come home, but yet must bring
          Strange trophies back to Ilium, and wild!

1940–7   THE WILD CHERRY   [152.4]

          We put a prop beneath the sagging bough
          That yearned over the beach, setting four stones
          Cairn-like against it, but we thought our groans
          Were the wild cherry's for it was as though
5   Utterly set with broken seams on doom

It listed wilfully down like a mast,
Stubborn as some smashed recalcitrant boom
That will neither be cut loose nor made fast.
Going – Going – it was yet no bidder
10   For life, whether for such sober healing
We left its dead branches to consider
Until its sunward pulse renewed, feeling
The passionate hatred of that tree
Whose longing was to wash away to sea.

8   152.1: That can neither be cut loose nor made fast,
13   152.1: the wooden passionate hatred of that tree
14   152.1: Whose longing was to be washed away to sea.

1940–7   HARPIES   [153.4]

Harpies pied with virgin faces
Squatting on the window sill
Harpies going through their paces
Harpies healthy, harpies ill.

5   Harpies, angry, on the ceiling,
Harpies, savage, late at night,
Harpies reading, harpies squealing,
Harpies sober, harpies tight.

Harpies gnashing on the table
10   Harpies who can hardly speak
But yet maintain a muted babel,
Harpies sending their last cable,
Harpies, who've been dead a week...

1939–40   HUNGER   [154.3]

The spirit blows from the home cliff with gulls
Questioning the old shore and the steep face,
And now the horizon with its lone trace
Of bronze smoke, and wheels over sunken hulls
5   With them, or seems to, as they reel back – pulls
Off once more, to eat, perhaps, Lycidas;
They set a far too mouth-watering pace
Though for no better reason my soul mulls,
That all this time thinks past red pub curtains
10   To mountains of gravied beef, portentous,
Rare, blooming with sprouts, of making merry
With an endless procession of Burtons,
A slab of cheese like the side of a house,
All of which is quite imaginary.

T   154.1: [missing]

154.1: The heart blows from the cliff with gulls
Questioning the shore, and the steep face
And now the horizon, with its fine trace
Of smoke, and the one ship, wheels
And returns, like a child's kite, sails
Hunger for the sea, for the unknown white
Calm of death, maybe.
And for no better reason my soul proves
That death is nothing less than beef
Had this not given me an appetite
Meantime the body will be fed on steak
And Yorkshire pudding, and potatoes with gravy –
And beer
Hypocrites, that would feed the soul on air
A plague upon such as they
The way to god is through the sunday joint.

1939–40   DESERTER   [155.13]

In a refrigerator car at Empress,
Then, lying on bare boards in a small room,
Dead... 'Should be in England?' 'Home for Christmas?'
'There wasn't even a sheet over him.'
5   Guilty papers in his army greatcoat –
His father came from Coquitlam to see –
Brought his body down from Medicine Hat
That had been placed in Category B.
'Surely he didn't have to bum his way – '
10   Thus pass from old to New Westminster!
He wrote he would be back for Christmas day.
... This is a tale that clangs an iron door
Shut on the heart, freezing sense, and pity,
For a tragedy, beyond tragedy.

T   155.1–5, 10: [missing]
        155.8: Hero
1   155.1–9: Dead in a refrigerator car at Empress, –
                Dead in a refrigerator van at Empress,
                Dead in a refrigerator at Empress
3   155.1–9: His father came from Coquitlam to see –
                'There wasn't even a sheet over him.'
5   155.1–9: Brought his body down from Medicine Hat
                Brought his lovely body down from Medicine Hat
                Red tape in his army greatcoat
                Military papers in his army greatcoat
6   155.1–9: That had been placed in category C.
7   155.1–9: Military papers in his army greatcoat
                Frozen to death in the refrigerator
8   155.1–9: – 'Should have been in England?' 'Came home for
                                            [Christmas?'
                He wore his greatcoat, carried military papers

9   155.1–9: – And did he have to bum his way back home? –
               Who could have thought he'd bum or work his way
               But did he have to work his way back home?
               He wrote he would be back for Christmas day, –
               He wrote his mother that he would be back

10   155.1–9: Pass somehow, from old to New Westminster.
               Thus pass, from old Westminster to New!
               Thus passed a soldier from old Westminster to New.

11   155.1–9: How worry now he meant to bum his way?
               Here is a tale that clangs an iron door shut

12   155.1–9: Against the heart, freezing sense: for pity
               Shut on the heart, freezing sense, and pity

13   155.1–9: Cannot follow to the accusing root
               May not follow to the accusing root
               On pity, which may not pass to the root of the tree

14   155.1–9: Of this tragedy, beyond tragedy.

1940   WHAT THE GARDENER SAID TO MRS. TRAILL   [156.4]

       – And now they turn poor poetry outdoors.
       But in the olden time it was not so,
       For it was once the language of man's woe,
       And, through the tongues of prophets, of God's laws,
5   And, through the tongues of angels, of that cause
       For which great souls have burned, and dwarf oaks grow.
       I, who am friend to love-lies-bleeding, know
       A healing in that name, and for these shores.
       But now they use hard words for simple things,
10   For the wild flowers, and the flowers of the lake.
       Gayfeather, blazing star, are words that move
       Few today, yet have more than a seed's wings,
       If ever sinful man like me can speak
       With God who humbly calls such names with love.

11   156.1: Gayfeather, tansy, blazing star – they move
12   156.1: Men no more, yet these words have a seed's wings,

1939–40; 1945–6   THE DODDER   [157.14]

       The early flowered everlasting,
       The hooded violet, the branching white
       Wood-violet, that, brooding in May night
       Sends petals forth even in Spring's wasting,
5   – Sped by the monkish cellarage-tasting
       Of cowled cuckoo-pint, jack in the pulpit! –
       All of these, where there was but one poet,
       In Katchewanook, lacked no contrasting.
       If I seek that which, poor, leafless, rootless,
10   Twined with goldenrod in ill-repute lives,
       It is, for exiled passion's sake, comfort
       Here, on Stony Lake: nor is it fruitless

What faithful coils are goldener than leaves
To share, what blossoms parasites support.

3 157.1–10: Wood violet, that broods all summer night,
Wood-violet, the jack-in-the-pulpit,
Wood-violet, that brooding in summer night,
Wood-violet, that, brooding all May night,

4 157.1–10: Sends blossoms forth even in spring's wasting,
Or cuckoo-pint, that clocks and drinks the Spring,
Sends blossoms out even in spring's wasting

5 157.1–10: Sped by the cowled monkish cellar tasting
The sooner for jack-in-the-pulpit tasting,
Hastened by the monkish cowled cellar tasting
– Is it the other's hooded spathe shrouding
The sooner for the arum's drunken tasting

6 157.1–10: Monkish, of March's cellarage. But yet
The spadix, like a monkish cowl, twinkles bright
The spadix, like a monk's cowl, winks bright
The spadix, like a monkish cowl, wears bright
Of cuckoo pint, jack in the pulpit. – yet

7 157.1–10: On March soil, names it? – these, were one poet
These when there was but one poet
On March soil? these, when there was but one poet
In March soil, would, were there but one poet
And all these when there was but one poet
All of these where there was but one poet,
Would never like poets, were there but one poet

8 157.1–10: In Katchewanook, never lack praising
In Katchewanook. But if I go seeking
In Katchewanook, would not lack praising
In Katchewanook, would not lack singing

9 157.1–10: If I seek now what leafless, rootless
If I seek the dodder, who, leafless, rootless
If I go seeking the leafless, rootless
For the lonely, the leafless and the rootless
If I go seeking rather the leafless, rootless

10 157.1–10: The poor Dodder, twining round narrow leaved
The poor Dodder
Who twined with goldenrod like goldthread lives

11 157.1–10: Twining the narrow leaved solidago on Stony Lake
Solidago, that lives on rocky shores
Solidago, that lives on molten shores
Entwined with solidago, it is not for comfort

12 157.1–10: There, on Stony Lake: nor is it fruitless
Of Stony Lake, it is not to comfort his fruitless

13 157.1–10: And golden coils, fidelity, and aversion to death

14 157.1–10: Given meaning to a poet in like case . . . a rootless life.
To note what blossoms parasites support.

1940–7   MEN WITH COATS THRASHING   [158.4]

Our lives we do not weep
Are like wild cigarettes

That on a stormy day
Men light against the wind
5   With cupped and practised hand
Then burn themselves as deep
As debts we cannot pay
And smoke themselves so fast
Once scarce gives time to light
10   A second life that might
Flake smoother than the first
And have no taste at last
And most are thrown away.

T   158.3: [missing]
7   158.1, 3: [adds next line:] Nor, reckoned, are our debts

1940–7   POEM INFLUENCED BY JOHN DAVENPORT   [159.3]
AND CERVANTES

A child, I thought summer would solve all things,
But this illusion passed with unseen springs.
The flowers that bloomed at home were dead at school,
And youth was born to die in Liverpool,
5   Or in Sierra Leone, with the shakes.
The yearning reappeared as spring in books,
The poem read in drugstore magazines,
Half understood – the glass holds what it means –
Then vanished with girls who never turned round,
10   Fled palette faces sucked into the ground.
The sea came then, cobalt or whiskey brown,
The disused longing settled on a town
Always far, and by a different name,
Archangel, Surabaya, or Tlampam,
15   Or merged in emblems of freedom never
Redeemed by the will, nor have they ever,
And then I saw that death was all my search,
But reigned up on the threshold of the church,
Angry with hope that one secular dawn
20   Might bring with it at last enlightened scorn.
Yet for all this I am still at suckle:
The tavern is the centre of my circle.

T   159.2: Reading Don Quixote
20   159.1–3: Would bring with it at least enlightened scorn.

1940–7   [160.4]

– You think you are a man shaking the hands of that dog
Like that, but I hate you.
Nor do I like the manly way in which you poke that log.
Nor will I imitate you.

5   The truth is you wouldn't have shaken that dog's paws like that
If you hadn't seen Bruce do it.
Nor would you dress as you do or bang doors like that
– Well, a truce to it.

Nevertheless I shall go on – because Bruce wouldn't do things
[like he does either
10   If it hadn't been for that O.C. of his during the war.
Neither would that O.C. of his have behaved as he did, neither
Would whoever it was *he* saw

Do something in a way that impressed him when he was young.
It seems to me no one behaves quite as he might
15   If he had sprung up naked in this world alone among
Stones, with no fool in sight.

T 160.1, 2: Or pool in sight
15   160.3: If he had sprung up naked in this world among
15   alone] along {160.1}
16   160.1: Stones, with no pool in sight

1940–7   [161.4]

A pilgrim passes through the town by night
An ignorant, an insignificant man.
He was a pilgrim when the world began
To read strange huntsmen in the infinite.
5   The cliffs are on the left, while to the right
The sea is like the sea whose rumour ran
Once in his childhood through the thundery plain.
The sea was hope then, and the rumour bright.
The cliffs are high, the sea is far too deep,
10   The town is just a lie, twitching with lies,
– Would that I had the courage not to sleep,
I may not follow, when may I arise?
Teach me to navigate the fjords of chance
Winding through my abyssal ignorance.

1940   FREIGHTER 1940   [162.9]

A freighter builds in Birkenhead where rain
Falls in labourers' eyes at sunset. Then
She's launched! Her iron sides strain as merchants gaze;
A cheer swoops down into titanic ways.
5   A hope of something odd is in each throat.
The ferry, quite as Charon's boat, knows death.
A gangway, medieval, spans the moat.
Pier Head, and the bells prance out. We are careful

Looking up. Gulls, bombs, manna, all may fall.
10   Below the sea, in the tunnel, men breathe.
The ship sails on a biting Saturday;
Grey ship, grey day, but the heart is not grey.
God may not bless thee dear, but may sustain;
Farewell! . . . Now she is a long way away.

T   162.1: Birkenhead
     162.8: In Birkenhead
3 162.1–9: She's launched! As merchants gaze her iron sides strain:
            The she is launched. Her iron sides strain
4 162.1–9: As merchants gaze. A cheer swoops down
            A cheer swoons down into the Mersey ways
            A cheer looses down into titanic ways
5 162.1–9: A hope of something strange is in each throat
6 162.1–9: Two stand on the ferry, silent as death.
7 162.1–9: Pier Head, and the bells pounce out: a gangway
            Ghosts in the fog. Bells jangle. A gangway
            Pier Head, and the bells prance out. A drawbridge
8 162.1–9: Below the sea, in the turmoil, men breathe
            Mediaevel, spans the moat. We are careful
            Mediaeval, spans the moat.
9 162.1–9: Between ship and wharf. This is the abyss.
10 162.1–9: But that there may be devileries about
11 162.1–9: On a biting Saturday the ship sails
12 162.1–9: Grey ship, grey wharf, grey day – yet all is not grey!
13 162.1–9: God may not sustain her, but can bless
            God may not sustain her, might not bless

1939–40; 1945–6   WARNING FROM   [163.7]
                         FALSE CAPE HORN

I turned my eyes from the drifting body,
The cross that floats downstream in stinging dawns,
The deer embrangled in one another's horns,
Lest these impose an attitude on me.
5   A writhing fixed, appallingly, bloody,
By these dread postures upon the will, spawns:
Some infernal portent of such actions
There as might beget unique tragedy.
Yet, friends in publike places, if you would
10   Hackle the blatant beast and call him tame,
Sound Melville deep to grapple your white whale,
First you must live with corpses three months old.
No Kraken shall depart till bade by name.
No peace but that must pay full toll to hell.

T 163.1–3: [missing]
     163.4: To Three in London
            To a Friend in London
            To the ghost of William Blake somewhere in London

To a friend in London beyond pity
163.5: To Three in London
        Advice from the Delirious
        The voice in Maximilian's palace

1	163.1:	I have turned my eyes from the drifting corpse
2	163.1:	The cross that floats downstream from the sawmill
		The cross that floats downstream in dreadful dawns
	163.2:	The cross that floats downstream in awful dawns
		The cross that floats downstream in jaundiced dawns
	163.3:	The cross that floats downstream in frightful dawns,
3	163.1–7:	The deer embrangled in another's horns
5	163.1:	Yet well I know that hell's the only way
6–9	163.1:	[missing]
6	163.2:	By these postures, upon the will, spawns
7	163.2:	In the heart some portent of such actions
	163.3:	Some infernal portent of those actions
8	163.2:	Which like a curse begets such tragedy
9	163.2:	Yet do I know what rank hell is – if you would
10–12	163.1:	If you would hackle the blatant beast and call him tame
		Sound Melville deep to tackle the white whale of Kraken
		Pardon if I think your beast is no more real
13	163.1:	Than you endure and violate
14	163.1:	Nor will Kraken go lest called by name
	163.2:	Nor live in peace till rent's been paid to hell.

1940–7   INDIAN ARM   [164.5]

Mill-wheel reflections of sun on water
And the spokes of light wheeling on the shacks,
Such freshness of wind in a spring quarter

Such radiance for November! While oil tracks
5   Make agate patterns, a tanker passes
– sudden sleeked lead boils on the beach, attacks

Boats under houses, the bowed band grasses,
Reflections are shivered, wild spokes unreel
The day booms a song of foaming basses.

10   . . . Softly renews the round of the mill-wheel
Sun reflections winding longer shadows
Turn the pine bough into green chenille.

After the moonlight walks over windrows
Mill-wheel reflections of moonlight later
15   On water embroider waving windows . . .

T]		[missing] {164.4}
T	164.1:	[missing]
	164.2, 3:	The Lake Dwellers
4	164.2, 3:	Such radiance for November! While oil tracks
8	164.2–4:	Reflections are shivered, will spokes uncreel,
9	164.2, 4:	The day booms a song for foaming basses.

12   164.2–4: And turn the pine bough into green chenille.

164.1: Mill wheel reflections of sun on water
The spokes of light wheeling on the shacks
The oil with dust and sawdust an agate pattern in the fjord
pansies and timber and bottle, a drowning leaf,
– an oil tanker passes, trumpeting
like a Leviathan
turn the pine tree to green chenille
soft cords of green strike down to the water
from the boat moored under the shack
make the day and the freshness moving
with the motion of the millwheel
with the motion of moonlight
with the motion of eternity.
The dogwood in autumn is hung with copper pennies
with chrome and scarlet coins, with beauty and radiance
A gull soars upside down in a brown toned pigment
A broken cup is stuck in the sand where a huge crab crawls
Another crab is drowning on the opaque surface
Sunlight sunlight.

1940–2   PORT MOODY   [165.3]

Over the mauve there is smoke like a swan
Pouring from the chimney of the sawmill.
In our yellow and red boat we drift on
While broken bottles of pine guard the hill,
5   Sitting still as two round unspeaking forts.
Red hammers beat on xylophone keys,
Under the sunset, of the tiered retorts –
The loveliest of oil refineries.
Power lines rule the west; three kinds of smoke:
10   Brown smudge, pure white from buildings, gentian
From the stiff incinerator, evoke
The music of our inattention.
Oil preens the water with peacock feathers.
So we have sat drifting in all weathers.

6   165.1, 2: Red hammers beat on the xylophone keys
13   165.1, 2: Oil preens the waters with peacock feathers.

1940–7   SALMON DROWNS EAGLE   [166.3]

The golden eagle swooped out of the sky
And flew back with a salmon in her claws,
Well-caught herself, till she could light near by
On her own rock. Meantime she heard loud caws.
5   So freighted, she could not fly fast nor far;
Nor, by God, could she let that salmon go.

Hoarse scavengers approached over the bar,
The one thing that fierce eagle hated: crow.
Now there was her rock, to stamp her prey loose
10 And crows grabbing chunks of wild fish away.
There is no argument with crows, or truce,
The eagle said, heading across the bay!
The sea is wide, black and tempestuous,
But let me disintegrate to a hook
15 Before I share with the incestuous
Daughters of some ineligible rook!
Oh, she'd have made the land easy enough,
But the fish was heavy and pulled her down.
When she lit on the bay to rest, that tough
20 Salmon turned and threshed in a way not shown
In the books. Twisting over and over,
Pulling the eagle under the water,
Till she would fly off, angry; moreover,
She was tired out. The salmon fought her:
25 And next time she lit pulled her down under.
She never came up again . . . It appears
In the mundial popular thunder
Any moral to this dins in drowned ears.

11   166.1, 2: There is no argument with crows, nor truce,

1939–40   THE CANADIAN TURNED BACK   [167.8]
                        AT THE BORDER

A singing smell of tar, of the highway,
Fills the grey Vancouver Bus Terminal,
Crowned by dreaming names, Portland, New Orleans,
Spokane, Chicago, and Los Angeles!
5 City of the angels and my luck,
Where artists labor to insult mankind
With genius coeval to the age,
And city of my love, come next Sunday.
Out of a flag-hung shop a sleeked puppet
10 Hands me a ticket and my destiny.

II

The blue exhaust speeds parting's litany.
Then, with pneumatic bounds we herd the street.
The lights, symbolic, nictitate in day.
Cautious, but with mechanic persiflage,
15 – Rolando's horn could no more strangely wind –
Past Chinatown and names like Kwong Lee Duck,
Our bus treads asphalt with the noise of bees,
By taverns mumbling of skidroad scenes,

      Then double-declutched my heart through neutral
20   And sang it into high for U.S.A.

III

      White gulls blow from the Rockies like Norway.
      High tension wires are marching in my blood.
      The bus sang o-ka-lee, sang cong-a-reee –
      That loved cry of the northwestern redwing
25   Who carries her own badge, her own fieldmark
      Of bright identity on her shoulders!
      She is her own customs official
      And crosses the wild border without let,
      To weave that lowland meadow nest, whose branch
30   No slenderer to tempest is than ours.

IV

      A pathos broods, a desolation glowers
      On an outpost of turnstiles and anguish,
      A rebuke of Labrador in the slate
      Cold grey, and striking up the mortal chill
35   Of no man's land to the soul: the Border's
      Men – badged, pistoled, polite, pitiless, – lurk
      Aware it is well named, Blaine, an itching
      On the outstretched bare hand of our country.
      A legend bird there has three eyes: indeed
40   For no tears one does not need so many.

V

      Inspectors here crunched bags on injured locks,
      Deduced a public charge from odd cowled socks,
      'A visa's not enough,' one said, and I:
      'Must man go to war, yet not say goodbye?'
45   'I didn't,' he said, without marked kinship,
      'Last time,' – Some subtle indoor Marxmanship
      Suspecting then, automatically
      Perhaps, he smiled democratically . . .
      Without me, with a trampling noise of bees
50   The bus plunged headlong toward Los Angeles.

VI

      Well, the redwing's a public charge! Over
      The border flies she: and in her choices
      Of landing rests the heart that wields the sword
      For itself too! . . . Yet, how should I praise you
55   Along the fjords by wild cat-tails going
      Or keeping watch from your mast in marshlight?
      God speed, my darling, wherever you blow,
      Each wave and tuft of your direction.

Nature far more generously supports
60 You, than we the out-of-work whistlepunk.

VII

The packed bus that brought me back glared and stunk
Of beer, chiefly mine, in vaporous quarts.
But chaos caught me in the suction
Of a roaring parallel darkness, now
65 Stabbed with landmarks in the wet night, none quite
Verified, all of a heartbreak flowing
Past lovers united on billboards, through
The crash – sigh – of juggernauts borderward,
And the grinding of hypocrites' voices,
70 And the mind jammed in reverse forever...

VIII

The helpless submarine is left aglow,
A smoking cigar on the Sargasso.
So burns the soul in this fluxion! Well,
No peace but that must pay full toll to hell.
75 But, little friendly bird, rather would I
A thousand human deaths inhuman die
That have no wings, than this which gives a song
Wherewith, to the snarled applause of the strong
Sea, in a Vancouver ashen with war,
80 Brief, to praise Oregon and Mount Tabor.

T 167.1–5: A Canadian turned back at the border
               An Englishman turned back at the border
               A Canuck turned back at the border
               A Limey turned back at the border
    167.7: The Border
1 167.1–5: A singing smell of tar and open road
2 167.1–5: The Vancouver Bus Terminal
               Fills the Vancouver Bus Terminal
3 167.1–5: Is crowded by dreaming names, New Orleans
               Crowded by dreaming names, New Orleans
               Crowned by dreaming names, New Orleans
6–8   167.1: [missing]
6 167.2–5: Great tinsel city, insult of mankind
               Mad gilt city, insult of mankind
               Mart of the gilded insult of mankind
8 167.2–5: And city of my love...
               And city of my love, – ah, my harbour!
               And city of my love I'll see Sunday
11 167.1–5: The blue exhaust seems part of the blue day
               The blue exhaust seems part of the litany
12 167.1–5: With a pneumatic bounce she springs the street
               of departure pneumatic bounce the street
               With a pneumatic bounce she fills the street
13–5   167.1: [missing]

13   167.2–5: Like the street of my love,
             So like any street in the city of my love
14   167.2–5: Slowly she treads with mechanic persiflage
15   167.2–5: Rolando's horn could no more abyssal winds,
17   167.1–5: Slowly she treads with a noise like angry bees
             She treads asphalt with a noise like bees
18   167.1–5: The sweating asphalt: these are the scenes
             The lights symbolic nictitate in day: the scenes
19   167.1–5: Slowly she went, then double declutched my heart,
             She went slow, then double declutched my heart
21   167.1–5: High tension wires are marching in my blood
             The Rockies wheel away like Norway
             The Rockies wheel away like lost Norway
22   167.1–5: Great symbols and spans of bridges the bus crosses
24   167.1–5: This is the song of the northwestern redwing
       167.6: Like that song of the northwestern redwing
25   167.1–5: Who carries its own badge, its own fieldmark
       167.6: Who carries his own badge, his own fieldmark
26   167.1–5: Of bright identity on its shoulders
       167.6: Of bright identity on his shoulders
27   167.1–6: He is his own custom's official
29   167.1–5: from lowland meadows, ponds of Columbia
             Little northwestern bird whose lowland nest
             From slough to marsh, building that nest whose branch
31   167.1–5: Gigantic democrats barred my passage
             Gigantic democrats with faces glum as tombs
             And the customs, for excuse, was unimpressed by Mars
32   167.1–5: Barred my way and read the letters
             Kindly, firmly, – albeit horribly –
             Adding: that what I'd thought was such a cinch
33   167.1–5: To my love, and opened suitcases and said
             Barred my way, most finally deterred
             wasn't: hadn't deceived him one damn bit.
34   167.1–5: and typed and said, and said again
             it. Typed and said again, what I'd guessed is
             'So far as I'm concerned, go straight to hell
       167.6: grey, evil, striking up the mortal chill
35   167.1–5: That I might be a sort of public charge
             Right. You will be a sort of public charge and that would
             But not via the U.S.' There were folders
36   167.1–5: In that city of the angels and my luck
             Let on it. In that city of the angel
             On the table, of L.A. The sealed shock
       167.6: Officials, – badged, pistoled, pitiless, – lurk,
37   167.1–5: That tinsel city, insult of mankind
             And your luck, that tinsel city of the folders,
             Of this did not unwax itself till spring
38   167.1–5: With genius co-eval to the age
             That tinsel city, insult of mankind
             But still he smiled most dramatically . . .
39   167.1–6: There is a bird here has three eyes: indeed
41   167.1–5: He crunched my suitcase on its injured lock –
             He snapped my suitcase on its injured lock.

	167.6:	He crunched my suitcase on its injured lock
42	167.1–5:	[missing]
		Likely to be a public charge. 'Visas
	167.6:	[missing]
43	167.1–5:	I'm sorry, we can't let you pass.' But I
		Are not enough.' 'But I
44	167.1–5:	Don't want to go to war without saying
		Can't go to war without saying goodbye
	167.6:	It was a plain duty to say goodbye
45	167.1–5:	Goodbye.' He said, 'I did' last time, and so
	167.6:	'I didn't,' he said, 'last time,' – no more, – so
46	167.1–5:	Like some strange eternal proctor, Kafkan
	167.6:	Like one of those mystic proctors, Kafkan
47	167.1–6:	Or, on the Russian border, Afghan,
48	167.1–6:	Who fears some subtle indoor Marxmanship,
49	167.1–6:	Uprose, between two motions of a doom
50	167.1–6:	The bus plunged over the border, toward death.
51–80	167.6:	[missing]
51–60	167.1–5:	Well, the redwing's a public charge too, – truth

51–60 167.1–5: Well, the redwing's a public charge too, – truth
Is that nature far more generously
Than we the meanest scheme
Of indigenous purpose, with a sportsmanship
That we who scorn all hopeless nidification
Such as would meet nature's edification
Completely lack, granted she gives wide powers to
The murderer, and yet we wrong
Old age and the returning soldier and leave to die
The out-of-work whistlepunk.

61–70 167.1–5: The bus that brought me back then said damn all
Save that there would be heartbreak near glendale
Which was, anyhow, unavoidable.
For the beaked freighter lay at San Pedro
The *LYKAION* from Aragon or Biscay
To take me back to Avonmouth and death
That would have struck again had I been first saved.
Yet would I have died ten thousand deaths such as these
Than this which returned me to new birth
Back to the very cradle of my soul.

71–80 167.1–5: Poor comfort, such reprieve, when in that fluxion
Our brothers bowels are skeined in each subway.
Yet would I a thousand deaths, die them all,
Than that one which returned me to old day,
Back to the very cradle of my soul.
But, little red-winged bird, our suffering
Which cannot give man wings, may give one song,
Wherewith, to the applause of the ocean,
Here, in a Vancouver grown grey with war,
To praise Oregon and Mount Tabor.

Dollarton, 1940–54: Uncollected Poems

AFTER LOWRY ASSEMBLED and sent to Albert Erskine the November 1947 selection, he and Margerie travelled until 1949; as a result their Dollarton years beak into two periods: 1940–7 and 1949–54. Lowry's major post-1940 works fall clearly into these two periods. During the first he was concerned almost exclusively with *Under the Volcano*, although after 1945 he worked also on *Dark as the Grave Wherein My Friend Is Laid;* from 1949 to 1954 Lowry established his short story canon, posthumously published as *Hear Us O Lord from Heaven Thy Dwelling Place,* and wrestled with the voluminous *October Ferry to Gabriola.* All 54 poems in the 1947 selection date from the first Dollarton period; 155 uncollected Dollarton poems are included in this section, and 26 Dollarton fragments are included in Appendix C.

Although Lowry did have a short, prolific spurt of poetry composition in the early 1950s, only 19 of the 155 uncollected poems can be definitely assigned to the 1949–54 period, and three of these poems – 'Beneath the Malebolge lies Hastings street' [178], 'Save that the optimistic ones are worse' [285], and 'Thoughts to be Erased from My Destiny' [307] – are dated '1946; 1950' because the blue 3⅛ × 4¾" paper on which they are written appears in Lowry's outgoing correspondence for both those years. The majority of poems in this section, then, date from the first Dollarton period. It is safe to estimate that Lowry composed approximately 190 poems during the 1940–7 period and that out of these he collected a volume of 54 poems in 1947. Including the 19 poems assigned to 1949–54, the Dollarton love poems, and fragments, Lowry wrote a total of approximately 266 poems while living in the shack on the beach.

The manuscripts for the uncollected poems are similar to those for the poems in the 1947 collection. For example, newsprint 8½ × 11" paper predominates, and four types of 7 × 9¼" notebook paper frequently appear. During the 1950–54 period, the Lowrys' outgoing correspondence shows an increasing use of a variety of fine white 8 × 10" letter papers, sometimes ripped from a pad perfected with red adhesive. This paper appears more frequently in the manuscripts of the uncollected poems, probably for the simple reason that the uncollected poems include the period 1950–4, while the manuscripts for the 1947 collection contain the 8 × 10" papers only when a collected poem continued to be revised into the 1950s.

The overriding feature of the uncollected poems manuscripts is their incompleteness; of the 155 poems, only 73 exist in typescript versions, and even in these cases extensive holograph corrections on the typed sheets indicate further rounds of revisions. Half of the 82 manuscript poems exist only in one draft, and these single-draft poems exhibit a disregard for line initial capitals, the extensive use of which Lowry adopted for his finished poems. Any *Lighthouse* poems revised in the 1940s, for example, use line initial capitals. The fact that drafts for some of the poems in this section first appear on discarded, recycled sheets of Lowry's Dollarton prose further heightens the incomplete or 'work in progress' tone of this section.[1]

The poems are arranged alphabetically, because no precise dating pattern emerges by which the poems can be chronologically arranged. For example, 60 of the poems can be dated only as 1940–54, because the cheap newsprint Lowry used throughout the Dollarton period poems cannot be dated to any specific year within that period. Therefore, the poems in this section require a variety of dating techniques. Some are datable through their content; most of Lowry's war poems, such as 'Dream of the Departing Soldier' [204], generally scribbled on newsprint or notebook paper, were composed between 1940 and 1945. 'A Lament – June 1944' [240], a poem about the Lowrys' burned shack, is also datable by content. The state of sheets that sustained some damage during the 1944 fire also provide dating clues. For example, the first draft of 'Oh gentle Jesus of the hymnal once' [263] appears on a sheet of charred newsprint, indicating a composition date of 1940–4. Sometimes a poem appearing in Lowry's outgoing correspondence can be precisely dated. In 1946, for instance, Lowry sent to Albert Erskine weekly batches of corrected *Volcano* manuscript; in a batch dated 15 July 1946, Lowry included the poem 'Correcting Manuscript' [194]. The previous batch had been sent 8 July 1946, so that the poem was probably composed during the week between the two letters. Three of the uncollected poems appear in published versions of Lowry's prose and can be dated with the prose manuscripts. These poems are: 'Lament in the Pacific Northwest' [241] (*October Ferry* 189), 'A Prayer' [280], and 'The Young Man from Oaxaca' as 'A Limerick' [322] ('Through the Panama' in *Hear Us O Lord* 45). Some can be dated when their drafts are on the same sheets as drafts of other poems; Lowry's poem 'My hate is as a wind that buffets me' [252] dates 'I met the spirit of tragedy in the wood' [227], because the latter's single draft shares a sheet with a draft of the former.

All textual notation in this section accords with the 'Dollarton, 1940–54: Selected Poems, 1947' format. In this case only two poems have drafts so mixed that it is impossible to order them chronologically: 'Born ailing on a hemisphere apart' [180.1–3], and 'My hate is as a wind that buffets me' [252.1–10]. When a poem exists in one draft with uncapitalized line initials, I have silently emended to capitals since Lowry usually capitalized. Although Lowry did not always use line capitals, some consistent editorial policy has to be set regarding the treatment of drafts, and, in order to reflect Lowry's poetic characteristics accurately, it seems prudent to emend towards his habitual usage.

NOTE

1 From the manuscripts of *Under the Volcano:* 'Old Blake was warm, he got down to the hub' [266], 'Poem on Gold' [277], 'The Schoolboy's Complaint' [286], 'Smell of Burning' [292]. From the manuscripts of *October Ferry to Gabriola:* 'Lament in the Pacific Northwest' [241], 'Oh, poor Mary Ann' [265]. From the manuscripts of 'The Present Estate of Pompeii': 'And yet his suffering got involved with all this' [173], 'Pines write a Chinese poem upon the white-gold sun' [271]. From the manuscripts of 'Through the Panama': 'I tried to think of something good' [230], 'Lines on the Poet Being Informed That His Epic about the Philistines, Etc. Needed Cutting' [243], 'A Prayer' [280], 'The Young Man from Oaxaca' [322]. From the manuscripts for 'Elephant and Colosseum': 'The sun was almost shining' [300].

1940–54   THE ABACUS   [168.3]

Only 3 years ago it was 4 years ago
But now it's 7 years ago.

And 4 years ago it was only 3 years ago
But now it's 7 years ago.

5   And just over a little over 4 years ago it was not even 3 years
                                                              [ago
But now it's 7 years ago.

And only 3¼ years ago it was only 3¾ years ago
But now it's 7 years ago.

Only 2¾ years ago it was only 4¼ years ago.
10   But now it's 7 years ago.

Only 1¹⁄₁₂ years ago it was only 5¹¹⁄₁₂ years ago.
But now it's 7 – seven – years ago.

T   168.1: The Mind's Abacus
            The Abacus, I Grieve
5 168.1, 2: And just a little over 4 years ago it was not even 3 years ago

1940–54   AFTER LABOUR DAY   [169.1]

Like white giraffes the fishing craft
With masts and gear braced high
Come stately round the point, while aft
Two launches, gallantly

5   Approach, and passing, reach the bay
– Ah, empty for all their steam! –
Silent, that only yesterday
Had ferried song upstream . . .

1940–54   ALTERNATIVE   [170.1]

Rather than that, I'd go down to the bar
And gulph down sixty whiskies every hour
I'd drink all that day and the next; the next
Return; and then, unmanned, if not unsexed
5   I'd watch the horrors fill the mantelshelf
And shake in impotent terror at myself.

1940   [171.1]

And now I brood on what I think I know,
But never watch intently – our stage!
Two old lamps burning with a steady flame
A dear face reading disaster, whereof
5   She reads will perish – 'love does not die'

Brightness of scissors at midnight
Objects which are not images,
Of no poetic stature.
The trudge of sea and the tramp of rain
10   The thud of the threatened unbudged boat
Snow on the mountains, and there will be snow
Here tomorrow, deep on the path to the store
And we must wheel the wood as once with care
I wheeled my life away into the dark
15   The pinprick quiet when sea and rain have ceased
Out of what is good because of no moment
With wood and the night outside, steals the knowledge of
                                         [peace.

3 171.1: Two old lamps burning with a steady glow
5   – 'love does not die'] [ms omits end quotation mark]

1940–54   [172.2]

And now the seagulls feed on the front porch
Waxwings circling the roof, precisely drop.
Even the kingfisher rests from debauch,
And contemplates me from a salt grey prop
5   That can look after itself, with kinship's eye
Thus I have humbled myself for birds,
And birds only, hating
A veritable St. Francis – was it? – I
But lick the sores of my own leprosy
10   A certain stingy adulation steams
From all this noble cloying behaviour
Nor would I put past my ego's schemes
To identify myself as some white saviour . . .

1 172.1: And now the seagulls peck on the front porch:
             And now the seagulls pack on the front porch:
3 172.2: The bloating kingfisher rests from debauch,
4 172.1: Contemplating me from a salt grey prop
5 172.1: That can look after itself with an eye
6 172.1: Of kinship, multitudinously.
7–10 172.2: [missing]
11–13 172.1: Were it not that all this strange battery
              Of love, this forcing of stalemate in retreat,
              Is but the rearguard action of my hate.
13 172.2: To identify myself Christ the saviour

1950   [173.1]

And yet his suffering got involved with all this,
Had become involved with the stringers and the posts, was
                                      [nailed

Up with the cross-braces, floated in the fog and with the gulls
Leaned up against the woodshed with the shingle bolts,
5   Was hung on the wall, walked in the wood at sundown,
Swam, and sat down, and wrote: this was his ordeal,
His penance, and light enough considering.
To order that suffering as the pines were ordered in the frame
[of the sun,
The three pines, that, with superb economy, were more than
[the forest,
10   But were the forest; light enough, you would say.
It was only because he had so much that he despaired.
Had so much, that cost nothing; had everything, that cost only
this,
To live as God had intended man to live;
Suffered because he might lose it – why should he, when we
15   Shuddered to lose what we had bought and did not want
Bought and still paid for and still did not want, and still feared
[to lose
Suffered because we had not got that which even if we had we
[wouldn't know how to use
Suffered because his house had burned down
And an evil man had built on his site
20   – Yet they had rebuilt! –
They who were Adam and Eve in a sort of overstated way
Who in their very lives might have been put there to redeem
The fall of man – God knows, Wilderness should not complain.
Yet, suffered, forgetting that nobility and the kindness of the
[other
25   Fishermen without whom they could not have rebuilt
While the whole world burned down and we suffered to be
[evicted
From what we didn't want and besides had ruined!

1939–40   [174.1]

And yet I am of England too; odi et amo –
I have known her terrible towns in peace.
Was it yet your left eye or your right was blinded
Idiot England bidding the world to anchor.
5   My faith in you as home ended
In Badajoz and Salamanca.
And the muted voice of England long asleep
Was heard then.
We may not speak of islands.
10   England is like a ship in the sea
Who's moored fore and aft. The crew changes
And the terrible boatswains yell
The derricks down her deck. Cluster lamps

At night light the hold. What's in it?
15   A few old tragedies and tales, histories
Of famous men. The deceitful picture of her past.
With bowsprits stuck into the wharf of God.
England is the ultimate blockade.
It is not a matter of war or prophecy
20   What I say.
May she disown the hypocrites who sailed her
Since this time, she's not wounded.

5 I74.I: My faith in you as home has ended

1942   ANOTHER IMMORALITY   [175.2]

ON HEARING THAT EZRA POUND WAS SINGING ON MUSSOLINI'S RADIO

Sing you for love and idleness –
Or was it an abstention

From these since that the times are high
And fraught with inattention?

5   Yet we would rather that you died
We pardonably mention

Than do low deeds in Italy
That pass man's comprehension.

ST I75.I: On reading in Vancouver that Ezra Pound was singing on the
[Rome radio
From Decision to Ezra Pound on hearing him on the radio
On Hearing that Ezra Pound was singing on Mussolini's Air
[Waves

1940–54   [176.1]

– Arise, arrogant arsemongers
Come! clashing clowns
Dare! dashing Dagwoods
Flee frightened faring
5   Thanes to tired towns.
Arise!
Come!
Where we weasels walk warily . . .

1940   [177.1]

An autopsy on this childhood then reveals:
That he was flayed at seven, crucified at eleven.
And he was blind as well and jeered at

> For his blindness. Small wonder that the man
> 5   Is embittered and full of hate, but wait.
> All this time, and always lost, he struggled
> In pain he prayed that none other
> In world should suffer so. Christ's
> Life, compared with his, was full of tumult,
> 10   Praise, excitement, final triumph.
> For him were no hosannas. He writes them now.
> No one wrote hymns for him. He writes them now.
> Matriculated into life by this,
> Remembering how
> 15   This laggard self was last in the school marathon
> But turned, to discover Clare in the poor snail
> And weave a fearful vision of its own.
> Or that he was last, last in everything,
> Devoid of all save wandering attention
> 20   Wandering is the word which defines our man.

3   177.1: And he was as good blinded as well as jeered at
4   177.1: For his blindess. And worse than that. Small wonder that the man
13   177.1: Matriculated into genius by this,

1946; 1950   [178.2]

> Beneath the Malebolge lies Hastings street
> The province of the pimp upon his beat
> Where each in his little world of drugs or crime
> Drifts hopelessly, or hopeful, begs a dime
> 5   Wherewith to purchase half-a-pint of piss
> Although he will be cheated, even in this.
> I hope, although I doubt it, that God knows
> This place where chancres blossom like the rose
> For in each face is such a hard despair
> 10   That nothing like a grief finds entrance there.
> And on this scene from all excuse exempt
> The mountains gaze in absolute contempt.
> Yet this, yet this is Canada, my friend
> Yours to absolve of ruin, or make an end.

4   178.1, 2: Moves hopelessly, or hopeful, begs a dime
10   178.1: That nothing like a grief could enter there

1940–54   BESIDE ONESELF   [179.2]

> Why should I care about drooling age
> In the years of my drivelling youth and rage
> When a whisky-and-water at eighty five
> Will bring back these half dead hours alive?

1939–40; 1945–6   [180.6]

    Born ailing on a hemisphere apart
    Now tremulous to acquire a heart
    This soul yet has its awkward music
    And will not be stayed by such contempt
5   As might have muted finer viols than I.
    No legend roots in my obscurity:
    Tradition rests not on it: nor do words
    Like electric flame ripple in its wake.
    Spawn of the doomed freighter and the ruined street
10 Spewed from the maw of the Great Hypocrite
    Into a whelm of nameless trees and birds,
    And conjurings of triumph and defeat
    Not till this year had I observed a spring.
    And yet this stone must sing.

2 180.1–3: Tremulous to acquire a heart
     180.5: But tremulous to acquire a heart
3 180.1–3: No Pocahontas blesses my obscurity:
          Eve and Magdalene mean nothing to me.
4 180.1–3: St. Pancras – ruined now perhaps – admired
          St. Pancras, the only building I have seen.
5 180.1–3: By Ruskin
          By Ruskin ended.
     180.4: It well knows the fame it chose was sick
     180.5: As might have broken finer viols than I.
          As might have unkeyed finer viols than I.
          As might have unstrung finer viols than I.
     180.6: As might have muted richer strings than I.
6 180.1–3: I took the last train from St. Pancras out
          Speak time ghosts away me the genius
   180.4, 5: No Pocahontas blesses my obscurity
7 180.1–3: Tradition rests not on it neither words
8 180.1–3: That like the wake of ships ripple in flame
          Which like the wake of ships rippling in flame
     180.4: Which like the wake of the electric
          Ripple in its wake the wake of the electric
     180.5: Like flame ripple in its wake.
9 180.1–3: Will light it for friendly condemnation
     180.4: Rippling in flame, tractable . . .
10 180.1–4: Accidental, conjured out of penance
11 180.1–3: And ignorance and lies and nameless trees
          Of ignorance and lies and nameless trees
     180.4: And ignorance and lies and nameless trees,
     180.5: Into a spate of nameless trees and birds –
          Into a hell of nameless trees and birds –
     180.6: Into a spate of nameless trees and birds,
12 180.1–4: Spawn of the jenny and the empty will
          [mss add next lines:] Spewed from the maw of the great
                               [hypocrite
          And cruelty ages of it without end

I crawled out of the subway of the past
1 80.6: I crawled out of the subway of the past.

1940–4   BRIGHT AS THE PLEIADES UPON THE SOUL   [181.1]

Wrestling with iambics in the stormy wood
I lost the joy that wind itself may bring:
And yet the wood must struggle with the form of the gale
As poets should with words from that quarter
5   Of the plains of sense
Bent by its fury
The gale is
The wood composed in peace once more the poem.

2 1 81.1: I missed what wind itself may bring:
8 1 81.1: [adds then deletes next line:] The poem, like the wood, was
[there already.

[1953]   [182.1]

The burnt pier: the last passenger: the farewells
And the gangway running up: the tall hotels
Wheeling slowly into the mist of Vancouver.
'And there,' you said once, 'That must be our street
5   Whose nights intoxicate and torment
Because we still exist!' The bone-white deck
Lifts to a leeward swell. 'That old freighter
Is still there, smashed, on that rock where we swam.'
Now we have made fast in the remembered port,
10   Unshipped our freight of iron, and iron despair,
And forced the injured window of the past
That gives on haggard streets where falls not a flake,
Though there is snow, piled high against the clock,
Where broken heart meets broken tryst in time.

12 1 82.1: That gives on haggard streets where falls no flake,
13 1 82.1: Though the snow is piled high against the tower of the clock,

1939–40; 1945–6   BYZANTIUM: OR WHERE   [183.2]
                   THE GREAT LIFE BEGINS

(OR GETTING A BIT KNOCKED OOP NOW.)

– Don't come any of that Byzantium stuff
On me, me swell young toff! Just plain Stamboul
Is good enough fer me and Lamps and Bill.
Constantibloodynople's right enough –
5   Used to be, eh? Eh? Don't give me that guff
Like that wot you said about the ideal –
In a blind eye socket! But a girl's a girl

And bobhead tigers here will treat you rough
And give you, 'ideal!' *Farewell, smoke is real –*
10   *And ukuleles mourn a ululu:*
And engine stampedes: more fool you fool you:
And aeriel says: oh whither where away:
And sea: each one-eared dog will have its day:
And stars wink: Venus first, then Mercury.

2 183.1: On me, me fine young toff! Just plain Stamboul
12 183.1: *And aerial breathes: oh whither where away:*
13 183.1: *And sea: says: every dog must have its day:*

1940–54   [184.1]

Canny Castor, Punching Pollux
Disapproved of Theseus' Βολλux
Helen, thou never shall abduct!
(Which did not stop her being øukτ) –

1 184.1: Casual Castor, Prancing Pollux
4 184.1: (This did not stop her being øukτ) –

1939–40; 1945–6   [185.2]

A child may find no words for its sorrow
But may hear at night strange presage of comfort
That injured stones know pressed to the earth
Or he may learn that stones themselves may speak
5   Flintly, their language of heartbreak
In the cloakroom is the roar of the sea
And a rebuke but even that is comfort
In that it means one less rebuke

Had I known then what I know now
10   Would I have lived?

Between himself and death
The sole recovery, perhaps –
Whereas tomorrow's unsolved problem
Will always be one mystery the more
15   And on the hearthrug gazing into hell
There is the future – the stokehold perhaps –
Who knows. – There are flames, and there
I see ablaze my doomed country
What shall happen, they will never know.
20   This was unreal time.

Only now do I see its tragedy . . .

2 185.2: But may hear at night strange presage of release
He may hear strange words of comfort

3   185.2: That injured stones know listening to the earth
5   185.2: Their language of heartbreak
7   185.2: And a rebuke but even that is good
11 185.2: Lies between oneself and death
13 185.2: Just as tomorrow's unsolved problem
18 185.2: I see my father's doomed country.
19 185.2: All what happen, they will never know.

185.1: A child may find no words for its sorrow,
        Nor loneliness.
        But with my ear close
        He may hear strange words of comfort
        From those he may not live to read,
        Or if he read, he could not understand.
        The dog, after the fifteenth hole retrieved
        The old lost golfball in the rough.
        The roar of the sea
        The one afloat, these
        Old lifeless things may give him comfort
        As madmen find in marbles or in string
        Even a rebuke is comfort, in that it
        Is expected, means one rebuke
        Less between himself and death,
        The sole recovery
        The numbed abyss between tea and dinner
        And on the hearthrug gazing straight into hell
        There is the future, – the stokehold perhaps,
        Who knows. There are the flames, and death
        Again, the only possible recovery.
                  This was unreal time.
        Only know I see it is a tragedy . . .

1951–2   CHILLIWACK   [186.1]

        This is a town of rumours. For eleven days
        Underneath the mountains
        People have been hearing planes, intercepting
        Messages, and seeing signals, flares and smoke.
5   But nothing definite is known of the fate
        The fate of the eleven flyers lost
        In the snow-choked mountains.
        One sees footprints in the mountains
        Another, a tent pitched high in Elk Mountain.
10   This was a glacier, the other his own
        Footsteps perhaps.
        Nothing definite is known.
        A red flare turns green, and then white.
        Residents pick up smatterings of messages
15   From planes, ground parties and headquarters.
        Smoke signals electrify the town.
        But no hope comes down.

1940–54   [187.2]

Christ I am tired of fruit in poetry
To hell with the semicolon technique!
I think that poetry should have bowels
In every page you hear a parrot shriek
5   In borrowed plumes its consonants and vowels.

Poetry such as this ought to have bowels.
Christ I am tired of fruit in poetry!
To hell with the semicolon technique!

1   187.2: My Christ I am tired of fruit in poetry
3   187.2: I think that poetry must have bowels
          [ms adds next line:] Why are there so many parrots in modern
                                                                    [verse

187.1: Christ I am tired of fruit in poetry
       To hell with the semi-colon technique
       I remember in an old day, Coventry
       And it was frozen in a shriek.

       It knew what was going to happen
       And so did London. And so did.
       The cathedrals stood around the great clock tower
       What is going to happen to you.

       I don't want to make your flesh creep
       No need to do that, your great notion
       Already keeps, in aftermath,
       An horripilation.

1943–7   THE CLOSED PUB   [188.1]

The Fox and Geese is shut; the Fox and Geese
Has been shut before, and that before hours
With me inside and the foxy hand that pours,
Shall pour no more nor dispense bread and cheese
5   But now it is boarded up
And what we did there that day for some wheeze
Or what another did, or left a tool of ours
The abhorrent memory that finally sours
These things are of no great matter. Time please
10   Has been called for the landlord and the Fox
And Geese is shut where I played Hare and Hounds
And with it all those wounds.

Yea, is shut and with it, how much of remorse
That now no more shall wander from its source!

2   188.1: Has been shut before, sometimes before hours
4   188.1: Shall pour no more nor scrabble bread and cheese
11 188.1: The Fox and Geese is shut where I played Hare
           Geese is shut where I played Hare

12   188.1: And Hound. And with it all those wounds.
              And Hounds. And shut are all those wounds
              The Fox and Geese
13   188.1: Is shut, and with it how much of remorse

1940–54   COMFORT   [189.2]

        You are not the first man to have the shakes
        The wheels, the horrors, to wear the scarlet
        Snowshoe, nor yet the invincible harlot
        Dogged by eyes like fishnets. Leaning, aches
5   The iron face with agate eyes, and wakes
        The guardian angel, sees the past,
        A parthenon of possibilities.
        You are not the first to be caught lying
        Nor yet to be told that you are dying

6   189.1: Your guardian angel broods, sees the past

1940–54   [190.2]

        Consider what you have lost by lack of faith
        And simplicity, the ideas
        Picked up cheap in the forest like punk.
        Consider the lives like night-scented stock
5   The laughter like porterhouse steak
        And children's laughter, like lost waterfalls,
        Or butterflies flying out to sea
        Soldered lives in rebellion only against that
        Which injures their love. And let this pathos
10   Tear you to pieces.

1940–54   CONSOLATION   [191.1]

        Mamma's got rings
        Mamma's got things
        Mamma just sings,
        For joy and pride
5   But I've got Pisces on the fifth house cusp
        And Venus, well dignified . . .

3   191.1: Mamma just sings, for joy and pride
5   191.1: But I've got Venus and the fifth house cusp

1939   CONTEMPLATION OF DEAD RECKONING   [192.3]

        Snow-freaked rocks the eagle alone questions,
        The wild geese dare them but to clang away.
        It is as though the pines marched down to the water

From that perennial headache of snow
5   As we tramp down to the valley below,
They cannot fight off the fog's hangover
Blest when it gathers some lost souls together
As now when exile calls exile brother
Saying: The only way a ship can find
10   Her course through that fjord down there in the fog
Is by the echo. It is as if you went
Ten steps in the wood now and then stopped
So you advance so many revolutions
Sometimes a period of time. The sound
15   Your whistle and listen for the echo.
And if it comes back quicker from one side
You know you're closer to which rock which quarter
And have to steer away. If an equal echo
Doubly strikes you're in midstream and safe.
20   But in a snowstorm there is no echo.
Then know – as you must! – the dread of steering
By dead reckoning. How lunacy it is;
You can't stop going. If you stop you're lost.
Nor when you travel by dead reckoning
25   May you wait for the faithful tide
That burgeons through precipices to the sea
Where Pacificward at high, clear nightfall,
You see the word of workers sailing wide.
Better be a young man going home through snow
30   Now! For all the hemlock's freezing stillness
In the fog! Better your peaked house, your light
A wink of passion in the wilderness,
Since now the snow is driving on the night
And such a storm as shall yield no echo.

2   192.1: Or the spirit, on wandering freighter!
       192.3: The wild geese dare them but to disappear away.
5   192.1: They could not fight off the fog's hangover,
           They cannot fight off the fog's hangover,
       192.2: They cannot fight off the hangover of the fog
7   192.1: Blest when it gathers some lost together
       192.3: Blest when it gathers the lost to his brother
11   192.1: Is by the echo. And if it comes back at you
12–15 192.1: [missing]
16   192.1: Quicker from one side than from t'other
17   192.1: You know you're closer to the rocks that side
       192.2: That's the side you're closer to the rocks
18 192.1, 2: And have to steer away. But if an equal echo
19   192.2 Doubly strikes, you're in midstream – you're safe.
20   192.1: But in a snowstorm there comes no echo.
21   192.1: Then you will know the horror of dead reckoning
       192.2: Then know – as you must! – the horror
22   192.1: Horror, because you can't stop going

	192.2:	Of steering by dead reckoning
		By dead reckoning. And why is it horror?
23	192.1:	And if you stop you're lost
27–34	192.1:	[missing]
27	192.2:	[missing]
	192.3:	Where seaward at high, clear nightfall,
28	192.2:	Bearing the word of worker sailing wide
29	192.2, 3:	Better be a man going home through snow

1940–7   CONVERSATIONS WITH GOETHE   [193.4]

I have two selves and one lives free in hell
The other down a well in Paradise.
Evil has made the first in evil wise,
The second, baffled, stifled in that well,
5   Battened on top, may scarce be wise at all –
Unless the knowledge he is where he is
Can be a sort of wisdom in disguise –
Since outside, he hears angel footsteps fall.

Help me, Oh God, God, God, trap that other,
10   Consume him utterly and set me free.
This well is black and dismal as the pole . . .
When shall some angel stoop and calling brother,
And peering downward like a star at me
Draw up the living waters of my soul?

1	193.1:	I have two selves, and there's one lives free in hell
11	193.1, 2:	This well is cold and dismal as the pole . . .
	193.1:	This well is dull and dismal as the pole . . .
12	193.1:	When you some angel stop and call brother
13	193.1:	And peering down like some good star at me

1946   CORRECTING MANUSCRIPT   [194.4]

How are we off for awares?
And how are we off for despairs?
How, oh Lord, for wives?
And how, oh God, for lives?
5   How are we off for not?
And how many deaths have we got?

1940–7   [195.5]

Courage is not standing on the crosstrees
Checking the topping-lift, when this demand
Though in a gale, upon the steady hand,
Is native to our practicalities.
5   Nor is it slanting to the Hebrides
Some fabulous leaky plank that might be sound,

Nor yet to salt some sacrificial wound.
A cause already grovelling on its knees
Would never thank you given strength to rise
10   Save with a falsehood honour should disown.
Such courage wakes with cowardice but to weep
And looks not courage to our simple eyes,
Which is to be a strong sheep, in our town,
Whose whiteness keeps it pure for war's Bo-peep.

1	195.2–4:	Courage is not to stand on the crosstrees
2	195.1:	To check the topping lift when this demand
3	195.1:	Though in a hurricane upon the steady hand
4	195.1, 2:	Is native to one's practicalities.
5	195.1:	Nor is it sailing to the Hebrides
		Nor is it slanting down the Hebrides
7	195.1:	Nor sprinkling into some useless wound
		Nor sprinkling into some silly witless wound
	195.2:	To shovel salt into some witless wound
	195.3:	Nor yet to shovel salt into some sacrificial wound
8	195.1, 2:	Would never thank you for strength to rise
10	195.1:	Save with some lie clear honour should disown
11	195.1:	Nor is it what is published in our town.
12	195.1:	Nor is it what it was when I first thought this
	195.2, 3:	And is not courage to our simple eyes
13	195.1:	No, courage is to be a sheep chaste and demure
		No, courage is to be a sheep chaste and wise
	195.2:	Which is to be a wise sheep in our town
	195.2, 3:	Which is to be a giant sheep in our town

1939–40; 1945–6   THE DAYS LIKE   [196.1]
                 SMITTEN CYMBALS OF BRASS

When I was young, the mildew on my soul,
Like Antiphilus, it chanced to me
Or Melville's Redburn, to take that soul to sea
And have it scoured
5   Ah! The days like rust smitten from iron decks

They were beaten into one deafening roar
Of sunlight and monotony.
I had expected the roar of the sea,
And of tempest
10   Not this sullen unremitting calm
This road of blue concrete to the Antipodes.
Where thunder was gunfire behind the hill.
When I returned I boasted of typhoons,
But to have possessed a unique anguish
15   Has been some solace throughout the years
This was not the heroic working class,
Where men live, looking to the future
But petty squabbles, jealousies,

A hatred of bosuns, of Mr Facing both ways,
20   One green eye the mate's and one the mens'
That see, it springs for mankind too, so fierce
See – it lives! Writhing terrible like Kansas whirlwind
Between myself, and what flaming ports I make.

  4 196.1: [ms adds then deletes next line:] The days like smitten cymbals
                                              [of brass
10 196.1: But not this sullen unremitting calm
12 196.1: Where war was thunder behind the hull
21 196.1: From which now's spring for men ashore, such fierce loathing
22 196.1: That see – it lives on writhing like a Kansas whirlwind
23 196.1: Between me and these panic ports I make
             Between myself, and the humble ports I make.
             Between myself, and such terrible ports I make.

1939–40; 1945–6   [197.4]

Dead men tell cryptic tales and this is one.
– Free will bends fate, to that's affixed
A signature of stars. But you have axed
The wood, slashed clean! Such is your simple task
  5 Keep God inside, infinity without
That engulfed you, whose talent could not flout
The rising sea. Who set on both his seal
Is wiser even than the slavish sun
Rolling on freedom many-winking eyes.
10 Questions there are the dead no longer ask.
But in the shed with beauty's packed the wood
The word of God, which you burn piecemeal.
For God's the only warmth against a world
That freezes spring out of the years with lies.

  4 197.2: Keep God inside, and infinity out.
  5 197.2: This engulfed you, whose genius could not stem
  7 197.2: The rising sea. He whom you got it from
8–10 197.2: [missing]
14 197.2: [adds last line:] And this is not a tale, after all
        197.1: Dead men tell cryptic tales and this is one.
              Free will bends fate, to that's affixed
              A signature of stars. The cycle
              You believe you love on earth's no loop.
              The same for the age, too. Study ellipses,
              Less false are they than circles. Though many's
              The story, could tell of wheels.
              Consider the journey of a humble trampship,
              Lone on the ocean, steering by the Great Circle,
              Sure that's a sort of circle, but the journey!
              Which doubles back upon itself, what of that,
              Before returning, perhaps not to its home port?
              The captain's less important than his crew,
              And of that crew, let us consider only you.

The line your journey traces upon heaven
May be more nearly perfect.
In London stands the Goat and Compass,
Where friends roar backward over the swimming bar,
                    Your entry there is
Your dream of homecoming.
God encompasseth us is the true name
Whose geometry is highly personal.
You see – of course you don't! – but it's no matter.

1940–54   [198.1]

The devil is a gentleman
He comes to tea at four
He treats the children like a man
And rarely is a bore
5   But this I know for certain,
Yes, this, and how much more,
That Bahomet lives at sixty three
And Saturn lives next door.

1940–54   DOGGEREL   [199.3]

Down at the bottom of a well
I lie and know I am in hell
It stinks so badly I can tell
This is the end of Malcolm L.

5   But far above he saw a star
Without much curiosity thus far
Until at dawn the star began to go
Then did our friend feel singularly low.

The star bent down next night with angel face
10   And hoisted up our slimy friend apace
Forgave him all his filth and self deceit
And give him raiment and wild plums to eat.

And now their little chimney smokes nearby
The star and our friend dwell most happily
15   When they want water to the well they go
Into which pure mountain waters flow.

Then was the world as when it first begun
And all the stars and crickets sang one . . . one . . .

17   199.1, 2: Thus was the world as when it first begun

1939–40; 1945–6   THE DOLLARTON BUS STOP   [200.3]

I fear it much as I fear death
Not over much, but still a pang.

The seats we hold, the straps that hang
The driver's back: these are our faith.
5 The station then was like our birth.
The shapes that beck, sigh past, or clang
Like hopes and years. That bell that rang
Pulled in our fate, a cross, a wraith.

It was stupid to be afraid
10 Since now we go to love and tea
All merry as a marriage bell.
And yet it might be one was dead.
It might, that halt was purgatory.
It might be now, heaven or hell.

15 It might, that view was not the sea.

T 200.1: The Bus Stop
   200.2: [missing]
1 200.1: I fear the stop as I fear death
   200.2: I fear the Bus stop like I fear my death
          I fear the stop as I fear my doom
2 200.1: Perhaps not much but still a pang
          Perhaps not overmuch but still a pang
   200.2: Not very much, for still a pang, a pang
          Perhaps not much, but still a pang, a pang
   200.3: Not much, but still a clutch, a pang.
3 200.2: The seats we lurch on and the straps that hang
4 200.2: The driver's narrow face are these like faith
          Our parcels and our place, all which
5 200.1: The station was like our birth
   200.2: We cling too, lose, exchange, give up, – our birth
6 200.1: The shapes that sigh past with a clang
   200.2: Itself, all are as years that each succeeding bang
7 200.1: Are years. I think I heard the bell that rang
   200.2: Brings closer was that the bell rang
8 200.1: Our place doom floats like a wraith
   200.2: For here our stopping place floats like a wraith
          For here our stopping place floats nearer like a wraith.
9–15 200.1: [missing]
10 200.2: Since now we go to happiness and tea
11 200.2: And home, all merry as a marriage bell
13 200.2: It might have been our halt was purgatory
   200.3: It might, our halt was purgatory
14 200.2: It might be now in heaven or in hell.
15 200.2: [missing]

1943   DONNE HE'S REGULAR   [201.2]

FOR WHOM THE LOG ROLLS

Once more thou art the rage oh good John Donne
Once more oh Donne hast thou set sail for Spain
Once more thy fame as art the Cheshire Cheese

But now a greater cheese hast sung thy fame.
5   Ah little thought'st thou, among the Anabaptist Germans
That plump shadow boxers would quote thy sermons
Puffing down the Boulevard Saint Germain saying
'son of a bitch'...

2   201.1: [adds then deletes next line:] But little thoughtest though thou
5–7   201.1: [missing]

1940–54   DON'T, HAVE ONE FOR THE ROAD   [202.2]

Moons I have lost and suns unwept and gone
And stars that stalled along the eastern sky –
But drunk in the rumble seat I passed them by
Into another alcoholic dawn –
5   Clash in one thunder bidding me atone!

T̲]   [missing] {202.1}

1940–5   DRAFT BOARD   [203.3]

Back broad and straight from crop to hocks:
Legs short and straight and squarely placed.
The chest wide and deep and also round:
Poll well defined and jaws clean.
5   Tail fine, coming neatly out of the body
On a line with the back and hanging at
Right angles to it.
Add 25 counts for progeny.
See you in Le Havre.

9   203.1: See you in Berlin.
          See you at Dieppe.
          See you in Liverpool.

1940–5   DREAM OF THE DEPARTING SOLDIER   [204.2]

The midtown pyromaniac, sunset,
Has set flame to all the aerieled roofs,
And you and I, talking, wait the onset
Of the last night, meek as eight standing hooves.
5   Or penned plump beeves loved not beyond slaughter.
Here is a thought – read when the journey palls –
Nor turn from corridor trees or laughter:
The horror is, the curtain never falls
On the dull interminable murder,
10   Nor will eyes rest in death's democracy;
Delirium's there, and there the girder
Is set, the house raised to hypocrisy.

Good bye, old comrade, of your death I pray
It prove sweet marjoram nor turn caraway.

T 204.1: [missing]
2–4 204.1: Has set his torch to the steep rooves
    And you and I in hand await the onset
    Of the night, meek as doomed beeves.
4 204.2: Of the last night, meek in doom's oiled grooves.

1940–54   THE DRUNKARDS   [205.3]

The noise of death is in this desolate bar
Where tranquility sits bowed over its prayer
And music shells the dream of the lover
But when no nickel buys this harsh despair
5   Into this loneliest of homes
And of all dooms the loneliest yet
Where no electric music breaks the beat
Of hearts to be doubly broken but now set
By the surgeon of peace in the splint of woe
10   Pierces more deeply than trumpets do
The motion of the mind into that web
Where disorders are as simple as the tomb
And the spider of life sits, sleep.

T 205.2: The Lovers
4 205.2: But when no nickel brings this quaint despair
7 205.2: When no electric music breaks the beat

205.1: Two lovers sitting at bar, half asleep, music shelling
    Their dream perhaps they have been married before:
    Tranquility gives a picture of despair:
    But when there is silence, where no nickel purchases this music,
    The motion of the mind pierces more deeply than trumpets do
    Into the web of sleep.

1940–54   EELS   [206.3]

Eels seem to spawn in the deep dark water:
Nobody has seen them apparently;
No one has seen their eggs, only later
The larva rise, knife-like, transparently.
5   Open sea young eels turn into glass eels
Moving only by day to the far shores.
But nobody knows it, nobody reels
Them in as they breast even Niagaras.
But by night they swim back to their great grave
10   In the abysses of the Hebrides –
Their shape is like their life and like the wave
That breaks over them is the death of these.

The will of the eel is its destiny.
No eel ever comes back from the dark sea.

T 206.2: Eels – On Reading Thomson
2 206.1: [adds then deletes next line:] Only, like a blade, rising
                                          [transparently
3 206.1: [adds then deletes next line:] The knife blade larva rising
                                          [transparently,
4 206.1: Larva like a knife rises transparently
6 206.1: Moving towards the distant rivers and shores
9 206.1: Then they travel back by night to their great grave
         Then they swim back by night to their great grave
         [adds then deletes next line:] Eels seem to spawn in the deep
                                          [dark water
10 206.1: Their shape is their life as with the curved wave.
11 206.1: In the abysses of the Hebrides.
12 206.1: [missing]
13 206.1: The will of the eel finds its destiny

1940–54   EPITAPH   [207.2]

        Dear Scipio Sprague
        sans plague sans blague
        (if I seem vague)
        I'm extremely beholden
5   for your words golden
        as bourbon olden
        in which prosit to you
        as you sail toward the blue
        on some Pequod gaily
10   or Behemoth sprightly
        from Malcolm Lowry
        late of the Bowery
        whose prose was flowery
        if somewhat glowery
15   who worked nightly
        and sometimes daily
        and died, playing the ukulele . . .

T]   [missing] {207.1}
15–17 207.1: He lived, nightly, and, (sometimes), daily:
              And died playing the ukulele

1940   EPITAPH ON OUR GARDENER,   [208.3]
                 DEAD NEAR LIVERPOOL

        Here lies George Edward Cook, a man
        Who to the world's wickedness added naught.
        Can you say the same? May God guide my pen
        To do him justice, Who in earth has sown

5   Him where he laboured . . . Good folk of Wirral,
Empty the sky one instant of evil
And then look far to sea — you did not know
Lycidas died out there, beyond Hilbre
But so it was — whose harsh salt smell resists
10 The tears. His eyes had often thus followed
Those hills, which darkening gave presage of storm
Not such as blasts you now, not for what you sought.
But in Flintshire still great furnaces glow
And now the world one garden is, of iron,
15 Remember him to whom it was not so.
For there are ambiguous angers in our blood
Nor do we know at what we shake our fists
Although we give it name. Here lies our friend.
He's dead but ancient lawns remember him.
20 And though these words have a hard sound of doom,
Let hatred pause a moment. Rest your gun
Against this stone in heart, or fact, and say:
— Or say it not, if it be without courage —
Here lies more than a man — here lies an age.

T 208.1: On our Old Gardener, Dead near Liverpool
I 208.1: Here lies George Edward Cook, here lies a man
7–10 208.1: Then look to the sea whose harsh salt smell resists
        The tears . . . (The sea-gazing mourner did not know
        Lycidas died out there beyond Hilbre, —
        But so it was —). And his eyes often followed
11 208.1: Those hills, which evening gave presage of storm
12 208.1: Not such as flails you now, not for what you sought.

1940–54   EXILE'S RETURN   [209.1]

      The Prodigal speaks:

      I have no forgiveness in my soul
      And I want to get out of this hell hole.

1940–54   THE EX-POET   [210.3]

      Timber floats in the water. The trees
      Arch over, it is green there, the shadow.
      A child is walking on the meadow,
      There is a sawmill, through the window.
5   I knew a poet once who came to this:
      Love has not gone, only the words of love,
      He said. The words have gone
      Which would have painted that ship
      Colours red lead never took upon
10   In sunsets livid at the Cape.

I said it was a good thing too.
He smiled and said: Someday
I shall have left this place as words left me.

1953   EYE-OPENER   [211.5]

How like a man, is Man, who rises late
And gazes on his unwashed dinner plate
And gazes on the bottles, empty too,
All gulphed in last night's loud long how-do-you-do,
5   – Although one glass yet holds a gruesome bait –
How like to Man is this man and his fate –
Still drunk and stumbling through the rusty trees
To breakfast on stale rum sardines and peas.

T   211.1: [missing]
     211.2: A Passing Phase
     211.3: No, No
            Like Me, Too
1   211.1: How like a man is this man rising late
            How like a man is Man, that rises late
     211.2: How like to man is man that rises late
     211.3: How like a man, is Man, that rises late
2   211.2: To gaze upon his unwashed dinner plate
3   211.1: And wonder at the bottles, empty too
4   211.1: All gulphed down in last night's loud long how-do-you-do.
            All emptied in last night's loud long how-do-you-do.
5   211.1: Although one glass still holds a gruesome bait
7   211.1: Half drunk and stumbling through the rusty trees.

1939–40; 1945–6   [212.1]

Faking was three times married to Faking
First and second the child: and third the child.
In short dedicated self to self, to hold
And have in glee or in heartbreaking.
5   Said as he died, Faking mischievously
In all in all we have not had a wild
Time. I was not a good fellow, not hailed
As a genius. Not me not painstaking.
We learned nothing ordinary souls learn.
10   Nor did we burn what others ought not burn.
Our virtue was: we had no good ideas,
We had no hope but neither had we fears.
Long in life we Fakings have abided
And in death we are not divided.

5   212.1: Said as he died one evening, Faking mischievously

1940–6   [213.1]

I

Fear ringed by doubt is my eternal moon
Risen to bring us madness none to soon.
My moon, thy moon, is fear all ringed by doubt
Though every day (they say) the sun comes out.

II

5   Terror will pay your way through strange bazaars
Through strange bazaars, terror will pay your way
Through strange bazaars it will pay your way today
But to-morrow you must be sober and count the hours.

T   213.1: [possibilities listed:] Him Gwine Wax
            Gastown Gruesomes
            In a Mist
            Plenty off Center
            Wild Bleeding Heart
            Ukulele
            Huge 5c Scribbler
            Aged in Wood

1940–54   FIESTA   [214.3]

The gulls are baaing in the creek
And night is whetting up its beak
Church bells are chiming on the rail
And wheels the stormy killer whale . . .

T   214.1: Nocturne in Burrard Inlet

    214.1: Church bells are chiming on the rail
            And wheels the frightened killer whale
            The gulls are baaing in the creek
            And night is whetting up its beak . . .

            With a moon in a blue sky at evening
            And Venus alone burning hard in daylight . . .

1940–54   FRENCH PRONUNCIATION SIMPLIFIED   [215.2]
                 FOR JULIAN TREVELYAN

nine egg sister better weeps little flower
lamp so much to dance without drum large field
money child thought customer entering slowly
to climb end inclusive impossible stamp came wine.

[1940–5]   FROM THIS ACCEPTANCE, SIR,   [216.2]
                WE MIGHT PROCEED

        I feel an unvintageable contempt
        For those who make the cause of right seem plain
        And who catastrophically preempt
        Our souls for their own faces' sake, our pain
5   For their feeble names'. Pious precentors
        Freckled foul jowled blowers of last no trumps
        And wicked psalmody, hollow mentors
        I would not snub your noses in our stumps.
        Tossing moose-heads, voice of the idiot son
10   Praising your brother's drunkard's rigadoon
        As if your sober-bloody pleas had won
        Him already to the two-faced cartoon
        Its blatant truth of one day's seeming scorn.
        Condemned are we all, nor should have been born.

    T   216.2: War Politicians
    8   216.2: I would not snub your noses with our stumps

1940–54   [217.5]

                    Give me a poem
                    To wring the hearts of men
                    Sheer as blades
                    As the stroke of a clock
5   Over the fen.
                    Tell me the meaning, ghost,
                    And tell me the hour
                    At which I am lost,
                    And in what room found again.
10   Give my hand power
                    That my words may be sane
                    And strong as flight.
                    Guide my pen,
                    Help me to write,
15   Show me the gates
                    Where the orders are;
                    And the cage
                    My soul stares at,
                    Where my courage
20   Roars through the grates.

    3   217.1: As sheer as blades
    5   217.1: Striking over the fen.
    9   217.1–3: And found again.
    13   217.1–3: [missing]
    13   217.1–4: [adds next line:] Rilke and Yeats,
    15   217.1: Where are the gates

1952–4   GOLDENEYE AND GOLDFISH   [218.4][470]

The goldeneye swam on the goldfish pond,
The goldfishes swam in the pond as well.
(The wild duck thought: 'They're kind of blond')
– While the goldfishpond's owner came shouting like hell
5   ('Gold sort of things, might taste good, come to that.')
– While the fishpond's owner waved his midday hat
The goldeneye duck on his goldfishpond at. . .
'Shoo!' cried he. – 'Quack.' The wild duck hove
To. – 'Shoo!' clapped he. The goldeneye clapped,
10   Clapped her wings, then sagely dove
As 'Alas for my goldfish,' the owner cried –
While against the stones the water lapped
And beneath the stones glided goldfish serene
And ourselves watched the wonderful, ludicrous scene –
15   'Alack my poor goldfish!' – that had not died
As we pointed out – while the goldeneyed
Sweet clanging marauder soared afar
To her mate in the slew near the wild harbour bar.
– For though that pond was artificial
20   Those goldfishes' instinct was initial. . .

T   218.1: The Wild Duck and the Goldfish
              The Goldeneye and the Resourceful Goldfish
      218.2: The Goldeneye and the Goldfish
1   218.1, 2: The wild duck swam on the goldfishes pond.
2   218.1, 2: The gold fish swam in the pond as well.
4   218.1: While the gold-fish pond's owner coming running pell mell.
5   218.1: ('Gold sort of things, might taste good, at that.')
9   218.1, 2: To. – 'Shoo!' clapped he. The wild duck clapped,
11   218.1: [adds then deletes next line:] 'For that, vile duck, I should
                                              [get my gat
13   218.1, 2: And beneath the stones slid those goldfish serene
14   218.1: [adds then deletes next line:] 'For that, vile duck, I shall
                                              [get my gat.
15   218.1–3: 'Alack my poor goldfish! – which did but hide,
16   218.1: Which we pointed out as the goldeneyed
      218.2, 3: As we pointed out – as the goldeneyed
17   218.1: Wild clanging marauder soared afar
      218.2: Sweet whistling marauder whistled afar
      218.3: Sweet clanging marauder whistled afar
20   218.1: That old goldfish instinct, was initial

1940–54   A HANGOVER – READING RILKE,   [219.1]
                SCHNITZLER OR SOMEONE

The worst has happened: nothing ever was worse
You have been betrayed but not before
Betraying much that you loved well. The hearse

Draws up before the bereaved door
5   To take away your happiness with a curse.
Horns sound no triumph in the yard of your heart.
The driver wears no towering hat, the horse
Nods no plumes, no bridles burn in the sun
(The horse will die too, before the day is done.)
10   The grip of sorrow holds you at the lead window
Looking with lidless eyes into the past
The coachman shakes compassion of memory...
The hearse sighs down iron avenues of remorse
To dissolution's wedding, life's divorce.

4   219.1: Draws up before the black door
9   219.1: (The horse is old and, his day too is done.)
13   219.1: The hearse sighs down the avenues of remorse

1940–54   HEAT WAVE   [220.3]

The day was not, the morning died of heat
And black clouds threatened rain at half past two
Rain fell, we fell, between the sheets
Then there was nothing more to do.

5   Tea was a round survived a moment only
Knocked out the house lay flat till half past ten
Only at midnight do we rouse and manly
Pursue our work like men.

T]   [missing] {220.1}
4   220.1: And there was nothing more to do.

1940–54   HOSPITALITY   [221.1]

Fiend fallen are the rich from dives
And dulcet are the poor.
Though never a man among you lives.
Good bye. And shut the door.

1940–54   HOSTAGE   [222.2]

A day of sunlight and swallows...
And saw the fireman by the fidley wave
And laughed. And went on digging my own grave.

1940   [223.2]

I sing the joy of poverty, not such
As war insults with ruin of its own
Evil. But such as the soul enjoys when much
Of its domain is lost. Here is a town

5   Of which one's sudden mayoralty
     Prize of long kinship with disaster,
     Qualifies, to readjust the dead.
     Ideas stampede here, and here's encamped
     The hypocrites, and undertakers, and yet, lo
10   They are pitiable and in different guise
     With hanging heads, melancholy.
     And shall I tell them every one
     Of the good of the soul scrubbed to the bone.
     The walls bare of learning, as the trees
15   Of leaves, good too, and the sea, less bounded
     The freer for being innocent of ships
     Ah, to see, to touch, smell out the pages of a book
     Whose lying words cannot so parry the sense
     Is end of poetry. And learning too.
20   Who knows what I'll not say by that last rush
     But none will heed my song nor have ever.

3   223.2: Evil. But such as the soul enjoys when much
6   223.2: Won by long kinship with disaster
14 223.1: Of leaves; and the sea, – beyond – less bounded
17–21 223.1: What voices have they now, what shapes of hopes?
          Will gather there, no nearer to the truth,
          And what is the reckoning for having cheated death
          The Cross knows what I'll not say by that last never
          But no one shall heed my song, nor have they ever
18 223.2: Whose empty words cannot so parry the sense
          Whose ancient words cannot so parry the sense

1940–54   HYPOCRITE! OXFORD GROUPER! YAHOO!   [224.3]

     Six demons came and cut down three tall trees
     Next to our shack, one windy Saturday
     With neither damn your eyes nor if you please.
     I asked them if our float was in the way.
5   They laughed without replying, cleared the brush,
     Tore our path into a chaos of skewed planks
     And in the midst of all this strange onrush
     Inconsistent, borrowed our boat with thanks.
     – Well, that was disarming about the boat
10   As it was maddening about the path.
     When they had gone I stood upon our float
     Beyond the ruined steps, forcing my wrath
     To hate less these rough neighbours, casting my pride
     With pines face downward in the flooding tide.

T   224.1: [missing]
     224.2: Hypocrite!
            People Building a House Next Door
1   224.1: Six ravagers came and cut down five tall trees
2   224.1: Next to our house, one fine Saturday

3   224.1: With neither by your leave nor if your please.
5   224.1: They giggled, hated me, cleared out the brush,
      [adds then deletes next line:] With no respect for our stake,
      [and smashed our steps
6   224.1: They smashed our steps into unidentifiable plank,
     224.2: Smashing our steps into chaos and senseless planks.
7   224.1: With no respect for our stake, – and in their onrush,
8   224.1: Quite regardless, they borrowed our boat without thanks
9–10 224.1: Their swim over, they set the foundations
      With the stumps, wined and dined
      And went
      The young builder
      Standing on my float beyond the ruined steps
      And pines face downward in the rising tide
      For two full hours, I hated them passionately
      Now the land was government owned, we had no case
      Save to hate
12   224.1: Beyond our ruined steps, and made up my mind
13   224.1, 2: To love these rough neighbours

1940–54   [225.2]

             I do not wish to live
             I do not wish to die
             I do not wish to strive
             To extirpate this I

5   I do not wish to work
             I do not wish to play
             I do not wish to shrink
             I do not wish to say

             I do not wish to live
10   I do not wish to strive
             I do not wish to fish
             I do not wish to wish

   T 225.1: So What
 6–7 225.1: I do not wish to shrink
             I do not wish to play

1940   [226.2]

          I met a man who had got drunk with Christ.
          And this is what he told me Christ said.
          'Trust no man who is not always drunk.
          And always ready to be drunk.
5   There is no excuse for sobriety.
          But one. That is war
                    And I who say that, envy
          The knocking knees of the years,
          Get off my cross, return to my hotel.'

10   That was in Oberammergau, before the war, –
      Before the fires came spirit cleft again.

9   ... to my hate.'] [omits end quotation marks]
10   Oberammergau] Obergammerau

226.1: I met a man who had been drunk with Christ
      He was sure that it was Christ, and he said this
      This former man was my friend, and his friend
      Was Christ man too, not so literally –
      This Christman not Christ was a drunk too,
      At Jesus the three of us talked drunkenly of Christ.
      Now
      Each night, he said, I get down from my cross
      And return to my hotel

1940   [227.1]

     I met the spirit of tragedy in the wood
     Where he lives. 'And I don't like
     You,' he said. 'I've done my weeping best
     Slaughtered your parents east and west,
5   And scattered your home.' A flake
     Of snow fell, like a tear. 'Yes, and I sent winter
     Of terror to freeze and fire you.' 'And still you laugh.
     I would like to know what is so damned funny
     About all I've done to you.' 'Why don't you really
10   Try', I said 'to be funny. Then I might weep.'

2 227.1: Who lives there. 'And I don't like
4 227.1: Slaughtered your parents and brothers east and west,
5 227.1: Have scattered your home to the winds.' A flake
8   is] [missing]

1939–40; 1945–6   [228.1]

     I set this down as humble prayer
     Please let my hand write something
     That may be used by the humble
     And the mad and the abused
5   When long words and excuses fail.
     Too much deliberate simplicity
     Will call down such savagery
     As: 'Why do you not draw cartoons?'

     I would but make the obvious beautiful.

1940–54   [229.1]

     I think that I shall never see
     A tree that's half so good as me

>   – Trees are made by poets in pod –
> But only man can make up God.

2 229.1: A tree that's like my poetry
4 229.1: But it takes man to make up God

1939–40; 1945–6   [230.3]

> I tried to think of something good
> That I had thought or done or said
> But in my life seemed only food
> For such thoughts as awake the dead
5   To send them howling down a gulf
> Of their own selfishness and dread
> Each hunted soul its Beowulf:
> For the grave is but a drumming bed
> Of nightmares I had understood
10   From spirits who had been misled.
> In life by self, for such as they
> That threw in life their death away.
> And thus I thought had I too sunk
> Although I was not dead, but drunk.
15   But at this point I heard a voice
> Which said 'My boy you have a choice:
> Tomorrow there is left and right
> To-morrow there is day and night
> To-morrow there is right and wrong
20   And death-filled silence, life-filled song.
> So get down on your drunken knees
> And thank God for the choice of these
> And after that, get up, I think
> Your father needs another drink'
25   – Miraculous such nights as these
> Should be survived, how no one knows
> Much less, how one reached finer air
> That never breathed on such despair.

1   230.1: I'd try to think of something good
5 230.1, 2: And send them howling down a gulf
6   230.1: Of their own selfishness instead
7   230.2: Each soul its hunter, Beowulf.
8 230.1–3: For the grave was but a drumming bed
12 230.1, 2: Who threw in life their death away.
13   230.2: And thus I think have I too sunk
14   230.2: Although I am not dead, but drunk.
16   230.2: That said 'My boy you have a choice:
20   230.2: And likewise silence, lifefilled song.
                 And deathly silence, lifefilled song.
                 [adds then deletes next line:] And you may chose the right
                                            [of these
22   230.2: [adds then deletes next line:] That is your imagination
23   230.2: [adds then deletes next line:] And mix one up another drink
25–28   230.2: [missing]

15–24   230.1: Indeed I hear a voice which says
           Doubt. I hear a voice that I should say I was delirious.
           Or drunk enough to hear a voice
           Which says my son you have a choice
           But days come and one's still alive

1946–54   [231.3]

     I wrote: In the dark cavern of our birth,
     The printer had it tavern, which seems better:
     But herein lies the subject of our mirth
     Since on the next page death appears as dearth
5   So it may be that God's word was distraction
     Which to our strange type appears destruction:
     Which is better...

7   231.1: Which is bitter...

1940–54   THE ILLEGAL HEART   [232.2]

When the man in the plane is a man I could shoot him on
                                  sight –
Though alas for the thought and alas for these treacherous
                                qualms:
When the man in the plane is a man I could kill him outright:
But not when the man is a man with a girl in his arms.

1940–54   [233.2]

     Imprisoned in a Liverpool of self
     I haunt the gutted arcades of the past.
     Where it lies on some high forgotten shelf
     I find what I was looking for at last.
5   But now the shelf has turned into a mast
     And now the mast into an uptorn tree
     Where one sways crucified twixt two of me.

6   233.2: And now the mast has turned into a tree
7 233.1, 2: Where one hangs crucified twixt two of me
       233.2: Where one is crucified twixt two of me.

1940   [234.3]

   *Translation of a letter written somewhere in the North Atlantic and
sent to the Government of Canada by Inspector Ovide Hubert of Cap-
aux-meules, Magdelen Islands. The letter was written in Norwegian and
had been found in a bottle by the sea near l'Etang du Nord by Hubert
Duclos, a fisherman, on November 25, 1940. The letter was addressed to
Lovise Stigen, Kalandeenet (?) Fana.*

IN MEMORIAM: INGVALD BJORNDAL AND HIS COMRADE

FOR NORDAHL GRIEG

While we sail and laugh, joke and fight, comes death
And it is the end. A man toils on board;
His life blows away like a puff of breath:
Who will know his dreams now when the sea roared:
5   I loved you, my dear, but now I am dead,
So take somebody else and forget me.
My brothers, I was foolish, as you said;
So are most who place their fate in the sea.
Many tears have you shed for me, in vain.
10   Take my pay. Mother, Father, I have come
A long way to die in the blood and rain.
Buy me some earth in the graveyard at home.
Goodbye. Please remember me with these words
To the green meadows and the blue fjords.

Note   Kalandeenet] Dalandeenet {234.1, 2}
ST   [missing] {234.2}
ST 234.1: [missing]
3 234.1: His life blows away like a gust of breath:
    234.2: His life drifts away like a gust of breath

1949–50   IN PRAISE OF AN UNDERSTUDY   [235.5]

Goodheart I beat years of Sundays ago at golf
In a hundred stormy sunset battles at Deal,
Both of us actors, in Rosmersholm, Little Eyolf,
Kaiser and Strindberg: and one whole summer, O'Neill.

5   And drink his bestriding demon of club or cue
– One down on the boards and dormie on the tee –
And, late of Aldwych, the Old Vic – or the New –
In Liverpool, the Playboy, and Riders to the Dee . . .

Yet one good shot James lofted over the abyss
10   One green has gained while my foozling mashies went wide
One part has learned whose lines are more surely his
While I still stand in the wings: my old friend died.

And scarcely unique though this achievement is
Its tragic dignity is not to be denied.

1 235.1, 2: Travers I beat all those Sundays ago at golf
4 235.1, 2: Ibsen and Strindberg: and one whole summer, O'Neill
5   235.1: And drink was the demon that missed both putt and cue
          And drunk the bestriding demon that missed his putts
    235.2: And drink our bestriding demon of club and cue
          And drink the bestriding demon of club and cue
    235.3: And drink that bestriding demon of club or cue

7   235.1, 2: As once at the Aldwych, the Old Vic – or the New! –
    235.2, 3: Ah late of the Aldwych, the old Vic – or the New! –
9   235.1, 2: Yet one shot he has lofted over the abyss
             Yet one shot Travers has lofted over the abyss
    235.2: Yet a single shot he has lofted over the abyss
    235.3, 4: Yet one hit good James lofted over the abyss
10   235.1: One green has reached, while my foozling mashies went wide
11   235.2: One part has learned whose lines are most surely his
12   235.2: While I yet stand in the wings. My old friend died –

1940–7   IPHIGENIA IN AULIS. AGAMEMNON SPEAKS: [236.2]

    Sacrificed – and still no sound from the sea,
    Sacrificed, and the birds are still silent,
    And the sails still, and the wind
    Hushed over Euripus.

T   236.1: [adds:] Something Wrong
    236.2: [adds:] A Mistake
2   236.1: [adds then deletes next line:] And the wind dead hushed in the
                                         [Gulf of [?Euboea]
4   236.1: Dead over Euripus

1939–40; 1945–6   [237.4]

    Is there no song that I can sing
    Who never understand
    Just what the various bells that ring
    Suggest, mean or command?

5   For you who run and you who stroll, –
    With wisdom on your heads
    To duties that same ugsome toll,
    That hoisted you from beds

    Where all night long you dreamed dry dreams
10   Of bourgeois usefulness,
    Now calls you to discharge in reams
    Of high resourcefulness –

    May never hear nor read such songs
    All written in detention.
15   As mine that right the private wrongs
    Of wandering attention.

    And you will answer other calls
    And bells and trumpets doubtless
    Whilst I limp sour by prison walls
20   Rheumatic if not goutless.

    And scrawl thereon as you march by –
    With morale undefilable

> With strapped and chinless chins held high –
> Something quite indescribable.

4	237.3:	Suggest or else command?
7–8	237.3:	To duties, which that same toll
		Which hoisted from your beds
11	237.3:	Which you discharge in reams
	237.3, 4:	Calls you to discharge in reams
12	237.3, 4:	Your high resourcefulness
13	237.3:	Will never sing or read my songs
		Will never sing nor read my songs
	237.4:	Can never hear nor read such songs
18	237.3, 4:	And other trumpets doubtless
19	237.3:	While I limp sour by prison walls
21	237.3:	And thereon as you march by –
		And write thereon as you march by –
22	237.3:	With morale indescribable
		With morale unimbribable
24	237.3:	Something quite unimbribable.

237.1, 2: Is there no song that I can sing
Oh, not to thee, assured ones
I would not touch your hearts for anything
But to the bored ones?

There is no song that I can sing today
Oh striped one with pockets bulging
Go happy and loathsome on your way
And undivulging.

But you who pass with bowed disgusting look
I might tell you
You will not find your suffering in a book:
I might fell you.

And you who lurch on spiritual all fours
Erect but tragic
I have a word like rain that swiftly cures
The thirst like magic.

I would some grotesque thing that I had said
Might move the bloated and incurious dead.

1943–4   ISLE OF MAN WILDFLOWERS   [238.2]

Eringo root in the north,
Samphire at St Annes Head,
Pennyroyal in the marlpits of Ballaugh
Lenbane near Derbyhaven,
And seakale near Peel.

1940–54   THE LADDER   [239.2]

Like a rotten old ladder
cast adrift from a dismantled sawmill

```
        to float, shoulders awash, the rest
        waterlogged, taken by teredos
 5      barnacle encrusted shellfish
        clinging in blue gravelottes
        stinking, heavy with weeds and the strange life
        of death, and low tide, vermiculated,
        helminthiatic
10      seems my conscience
        hauled out now to dry in the sun
        leaning against nothing
        leading nowhere
        but to the past to use perhaps,
15      salvageable, to be graved,
        up and down which
        each night my
        mind meaninglessly
        climbs.
```

T   239.1: The Poem Shaped Like a Ladder
8   239.1: and life, seems my conscience
          of death and low tide, vermiculated, helminthiatic
9–1 239.1: [missing]

1944   LAMENT – JUNE 1944   [240.6]

```
        Our house is dead
        It burned to the ground
        On a morning in June
        With a wind from the Sound
 5      The fire that fed
        On our marriage bed
        Left a bottle of gin.
        Black under the moon
        Our house is dead.
10      We shall build it again.
        But our poor house is gone
        And the world still burns on.
```

T   240.3: Lament for a Little Cabin on a Beach in British Columbia –
                                                  [June 1944
     240.4: [missing]
     240.5: Lament for a Little Shack on a Beach in British Columbia –
                                                  [June 1944
1   240.1, 2: Our poor house is dead
3   240.5: One morning in June
4   240.1: [adds next line:] With a wind out of tune, –
       240.1, 2: [adds next line:] A dread sight for the moon
5   240.1, 2: Of a fire that has fed
       240.5: In a fire that fed
6   240.1, 2: On our poor marriage bed
7–10 240.1, 2: But Thy will be done

10   240.3: Dare we build it again?
11 240.1–3: Our poor house is gone.
      240.4, 5: But our house is gone
        240.5: But our home is gone

1949–50   LAMENT IN THE PACIFIC NORTHWEST   [241.2]

They are taking down the beautiful houses once built with
                                                  [loving hands
But still the old bandstand stands where no band stands
With clawbars they have gone to work on the poor lovely
                                           [houses above the sands
At their callous work of eviction that no human law
                                                  [countermands
5   Callously at their work of heartbreak that no civic heart
                                                  [understands
In this pompous and joyless city of police moral perfection and
                                                  [one man stands
Where you are brutally thrown out of beer parlors for standing
                                               [where no man stands
Where the pigeons roam free and the police listen to each
                                               [pigeon's demands
And they are taking down the beautiful homes once with
                                                  [loving hands
10   But still the old bandstand stands where no band stands.

1   241.1: They are taking down the beautiful houses cared for with
                                                  [living hands
9   241.1: And they are taking down the beautiful homes once cared for
                                               [with loving hands

1940–54   [242.1]

Like the black iron steps
leading from some aerial footway
flung over road and lines down at the dockside
crowded with holiday makers
5   is the past

and evermore my mind climbs down that stair
to find, below, the selfsame wharf, despair.

But one day a new ship is waiting there.

1946–54   LINES ON THE POET BEING INFORMED   [243.5]
      THAT HIS EPIC ABOUT THE PHILISTINES ETC.
                 NEEDED CUTTING
                    David
                  (Rave-id)

```
        Goliath
        Defieth
5       Sling –
        Bing!
        And Goliath
        Dieth.
```

1940–54   LOOK OUT! THE BLOODY BOSUN   [244.4]

A ship long laid up is a filthy thing,
Cabled with rust, debris of the shore gang,
Filters gangrened, only a homesick tang
Reminds us of our longed-for suffering
5   The sea! the watches pass; the hours take wing
Like seagulls stuffed with bread. Tin-tin; pang-pang.
And this monotony is our sturm und drang
Of which few sailors have the heart to sing.

I like to think we're scaling the old world
10   Down for a dose of red lead, as hammers snap
And ever grindstones wait to whet their lust.
Splendid to think so, yet in dreaming whirled
To abstract hulls, one falls into the trap
Set by that two-faced man who sees mere rust.

3   244.1: Filters gangrened, only a soapy tang
5   244.1: The sea! Days pass, the hours take wing
6   244.1: Like seagulls stuffed with bread, – each one a pang
7   244.1: And this monotony is our sturm und drang
8 244.1, 2: Of which few poets have the heart to sing.
9   244.1: I like to think we're chipping the old world
     244.2: I like to think we're scaling down the old world
10   244.1: Down for a dose of fresh lead, as the hammers snap
14   244.1: Of him to whom though two faced rust's just rust.

1939–40; 1945–6   [245.1]

Love and wisdom have no home
Over the world they wander
Love and wisdom have no end.

Love is tired and wisdom lame.
They are driven like gander.
5   Love and wisdom have no home.

But were there any saw them come?
Was none then their defender?
Love and wisdom have no end.

Wisdom has a simple arm
10   It lies in love's heart tender.
Love and wisdom have no home.

Though angels lament our shame
And god's wrath we engender
15   Love and wisdom have no end

Though driven of the false storm
Into the false world's threats
Love and wisdom have no end –
Love and wisdom have no home.

4   245.1: Love is sick and wisdom lame
13   245.1: Save where angels weep our shame
14   245.1: And god's rage we engender

1940–54   LOVE OF A SEAGULL   [246.1]

Beautiful, tame, and wild
Sad, pathetic, eating starfish on the windrow.
The map of Russia, floating in the storm.
I'd dreamed they shot the seagull...

1940   MAD POEM: WIND BLOWING   [247.4]
                  THROUGH THE SHACK

One two three four five, six and one, seven
And one is dawn, better late than never
Door bangs; wood snaps; be awake forever
Old corpse flower that should be in heaven
5   Full of wool and honey, wake...

The bacon smells go singing down the gale
Wind blows ragged coffee smoke –
One two three four five six seven eight nine ten
Set out into the day's sting and roar
10   To seek that Calthian violet where it dwells,
Its rich royal deep sea blue open bells!

T   247.1: Mad Song
      247.3: Wind Blowing Through the House
10   247.1, 2: To seek that Caethian violet where it dwells,

1940–54   [248.1]

a marathon of gulls,
a chiming of chickadees,
an ecstasy of swallows
a tintabulation of titmice
5   a scapaflow of grebes
a caucus of crows
an unavoidability of vultures

a Phalacrocorax of capitalists
a proletariat of Peacock (sing)
10   a gobbledegookery of critics
a leprosy of letter writers
a minority of man

and a close of this correspondence.

1940   MARINA –   [249.4]

When she was born the wind was north
And the various planets were where they were
And her mother was buried after her birth
And the sea was her mother's bier.
5   Oh, she could endure the sea at first,
Her infant blood was not aged for its thirst
And the bosun's whistle was the worst
And would she had died with her mother then
And been buried within the humming sea
10   In the humming sea with its simple shells
With its simple shells and belching whales
And aye remaining lamps and when
The storm did not whirr her away from her friends
As on this voyage which never ends.

T   249.2: Marina — A Refugee
13   249.1, 2: The storm did not whirr her from her friends

1939–40; 1945–6   A MINSTREL IN LABRADOR   [250.1]

The seasons have plunged past my destiny
With only the terror of the passing lorry.
The palpitant relief, that still, miraculously,
One has summer. And is it spring or autumn
5   Spurs these words? It is a strange Labrador
My life My [?parts]
That I have haunted for many a year.
It has always been winter.
In the tall mirror I see a strange
Innocent of minstrelsy, who suggests
10   It was not for nothing that your life was writ
In a perpetual springtime of spirit
Now of summers as others see them,
Though none shall heed your cry nor have ever.

7   250.1: [adds then deletes next line:] I have known nobody,
                                     [even vaguely [?]
8   250.1: In my steep mirror I see the voice
13 250.1: Though none will heed your cry nor have ever

[at foot of sheet:] it is a pilgrimage of innocent minstrelsy
[?a lone quest]

1940–1   MORE IMPATIENCE   [251.2]

Albeit you're a set book these days oh Keats,
I shall not read you till I'm thirty one:
And so my essay is but half begun
And so I shall not reason out your beats
5   Nor follow through your mountaineering feats
Nor ponder the Miltonic inversion
In the first version of Hyperion
Though others cleave at lectures to their seats.
Such immersion is for others not for you
10   I tell myself, hubris or not, and odd
Let it sound in one from favours far.
But share you with these pimply oafs from Crewe
And Marlborough, that I will not, by God,
Whose only meaning is another war.

 1   251.1: Thou art a set book these days, Oh Keats
 3   251.1: [adds then deletes:] Nor shall I understand thee, oh John Donne
 4   251.1: And so I shall not measure out thy beats
 5   251.1: Nor pondered on your mountaineering feats
 6   251.1: Nor ponder yet the Miltonic inversion
 7   251.1: Of the first version of Hyperion
12   251.1: But share you with these scrofulous oafs from Stowe
          But to share you with these pimply oafs from Stowe
13   251.1: And Marlborough, that I will not though Pindar law

1939–40; 1945–6   [252.10]

My hate is as a wind that buffets me
All blind to need, deaf to supplication
Scattering my words, inchoately,
The only orders which will save the ship, –
5   Lost! From all this I found sanctuary
Where wine congratulates compassion
Chuckling: that shilling you once gave a tramp
Bought you both but the skies you coveted.
So might Saturn have given gold for chaos!
10   That weeping child whose misery you hated,
And subtly gave false hope, but saved you for another song
Of fretful tenderness, in a life of wrong.
What knots of self in all abnegation
– No other solution save the cross! –

 1   252.1–9: My hate is like a wind which buffets me
 2   252.1–9: Blinding me to pleas, dumb to supplication

 3 252.1–9: And dumb, save for my inchoate words, pleas
              Scattering my prayers inchoately
 4 252.1–9: Like orders shouted in a gale of wind
              The only orders that will save the ship
 5 252.1–9: The only orders which will save the ship
              Drifting away, lost in the storm. From this I took
              Lost! From all this I took refuge in a house
              Lost. From this I took refuge in your inn,
              Lost. From this I took refuge in your arms
 6 252.1–9: Refuge in your arms, recalled five good things I had done.
              Where wine first congratulates compassion
              Where wine congratulates compassion,
              And recalled only three good things I had done.
              In wine revived two instances of compassion
              In wine recalled with tears two good things I'd done
 7 252.1–9: Two shillings I once gave a tramp.
              Then wheedling; 'That Saturnian shilling
              Warning: That last shilling you once gave the tramp
              The last two centavos I once gave a tramp
              My last two shillings I once gave a tramp
              Wheezing: 'That shilling you once gave a tramp
              Gloating: that last coin you gave the tramp
 8 252.1–9: And insect I once rescued, a scorpion,
              You gave that tramp, but bought him your chaos
              Bought him but skies you coveted
              Bought him but the skies yourself had coveted
              Rescuing an injured scorpion
              Bought the tramp but the skies you coveted
              Bought him but chaos you coveted
 9 252.1–9: So might Saturn have traded gold for chaos
              Yet, am like the grim vinegaroon and of
              You coveted.' 'Or that weeping child whose misery
              That weeping child whose misery was yours
              A weeping child whose misery was mine
              Succouring an injured scorpion
              A screeching child whose misery was mine
10 252.1–9: And so staunched, but rescued one more song
              To whom I gave cautious, false hope
              You gave false hope to, knowing there was none
              I gave hope to, knowing there was none.
              Knowing there was none, I gave false hope
              More than you loved, to whom you gave false hope
              More than you loved, to whom you have false hope
              To whom you subtly gave false hope, remarked
              You bought for a false hope
              These five against a lifetime of wrong
11 252.1–9: How I congratulated my compassion.
              Yet was I too that grim vinegaroon
              And thereby saved yourself for another song
              Yet was I too, that grim vinegaroon
              And did but save myself for another song
              But saved yourself, for another song

But rescued you, for another song
And yet what I hate is hypocrisy, and yet hypocrites are
Famine, rescued you for another song.

12   252.1–9: These few against a lifetime of wrong
That stings itself to death beneath the stone,
Where no message is, on the mescal plain.
Both wind and blaze to my loathing.

13   252.1–9: What evil in all self-abnegation
So did but save myself, for another song
These three against a lifetime of wrong
Would that I had left it under the stone

14   252.1–9: Where no messages are, on Oaxacan plain.
Where no messages are, on Cortes plain.

1940   [253.2]

The names of Mexican rivers I forget
– Or on memory's smudged map may not mark
Xochimilco, – Xochitepec –
These are not rivers either: and yet
5   All I conjure of names from oblivion.
But Styx, Acheron, Cocytus, Phlegeton,
Will do, for Guardalquivir – , and such
But better than these too classical drinks
Do I remember Lethe, surnamed tequila
10   All I know is, Mexico is death, which shares with love
The only passion mankind can respect
Whereof who drinks forgets not only
Joy and grief, pleasure and pain
But else but that which is symbolic:
15   United you see your life float down on that stream
Swifter than Hebrus, to no Lesbian doom
You have not known what a real thing sadness is –
Or understood of what symbolic gloom.

253.1: The names of Mexican rivers I forget
But that Mexico is death, I know
– Or on the map of memory may not mark –
But Styx, and Acheron, Cocytus, Phlegeton
Will do, for Guadalquivir, and such
But most of all, far better than these classical drinks
Do I remember, Lethe, river of oblivion,
Surnamed tequila: or mescal
Whereof who drinks, forgets not only
Joy and grief, pleasure and pain
But all else but that which is symbolic:
In each state, in each town
The swinging door will lead you a path
Where you may drink her rum
Until you die again
Into a strange world where serpents are wise

1939–40; 1945–6   [254.1]

    Need it be so niggardly of meaning too?
    The world at best is bloody: its cadaver,
    Is bestrode by men whose words are heard
    Which reek with falseness but at least reek.
    From the blank face of this rock of the world's doom
5   Strike out a stream of water that man at least may drink
    And though there still are those who reek and think.

    And yet this conspiracy of poets and critics to
    The tyranny of the printed page admits only where treason
    Of those who do not love poetry, the poetasters
10 Who think the artist really thinks
    Picasso's nose is purple?

1940   [255.2]

    Never in a comedian's life have I laughed till then!
    ... Wherefore the legend grew that there were ghosts
    Somewhere between Dead Tree and Merry Island,
    And from our love revived an Indian slaughter.
    Oh you who something something something land
    May you too be blessed by such enormous laughter
    As even God and whales might not approve.

1940–54   THE NEW GUINEA GARDENER BIRD   [256.3]

    There is a bird who builds his mate a bower
    With slender rafters, and delicate twigs between,
    And woven mosses, a kind of Orchid-tower
    With a porte cochere, through a graceful carpet, green,
5   Of soft moss, all free from stones or grass or weeds
    And objects not in harmony with its design
    Transported thither and kept smooth and clean,
    Then on the ground he scatters fruit and flowers
    Shining fruit pods and toadstools and silvery leaves
10 Everything that withers is removed
    And everything unsound, replaced by fresh, so he weaves
    In this elegant garden house to worship his beloved.
    So dear could not my bower for thee be made
    Yet so by thee it was with love entwined
15 That love itself within that forest shack enshrined
    Never undreamed our dream it was built by God.

T   256.1: The New Guinea Gardener
      256.2: [missing]
1   256.3: There is a bird who builds its mate a town
2   256.1: With slender rafters, and delicate mosses green
3   256.1: An interwoven mosses, an orchid-tower

An interwoven orchidaceous tower
256.2: Interwoven mosses, an Orchid Tower
256.3: And interwoven mosses, an Orchid-tower
4　256.1: With a graceful carpet, sort of porte-cochere between
5　256.1, 2: Of soft mosses freed from stones dead weeds or grass
256.3: Of soft moss, set free from stones or grass or weeds
6　256.1, 2: And objects not in harmony with his design
7　256.1: [adds next line:] In honour of the adored one, should she pass
In honour of the adored should she pass
In honour of the adored feet, should she pass
For the feet of the adored, should she pass
256.2: [adds next line:] In honour of the adored, should she pass
10　256.1: While everything that withers is removed
11　256.1, 2: And moved, replaced by fresh: and so he weaves
12　256.1, 2: An elegant house, to worship his beloved
[adds next line:] Something like Yeats, though written by
[a bird
14　256.1, 2: Yet so for thee it was with love entwined
15　256.1: That love once within our forest home enshrined
256.2: That love within our forest home enshrined
256.3: That love itself within that bower enshrined
That love itself within that little house once enshrined
That love itself within that little cabin once enshrined
16　256.1: We never believed it had not been built by God.
256.2: As never could undream it built by God.
256.3: Never once dreamed it was not prepared by God.
Never dared dream it was not built by God.
Never once dreamed it had not been built by God.

1939–40; 1945–6　　NO KRAKEN SHALL BE　　[257.1]
FOUND TILL SOUGHT BY NAME

Here is the ship then, with decks all holy white
Pure as the stone that scrubbed them to the bone.
Scuppers cleansed: and red lead shining where it
Would be, the blood all carefully swept from the deck
5　The poop an arc makes on the Indian sky
Cabined and perfect, with flag flying
And bosun reading the bible, while with t'other hand
He gropes for Ahab's solution. And at the wheel
Another Ahab, whose rhetoric's however not his own.
10　Ah, who shall say that this is not the noblest of all ships
Whose cargo's underwritten by heaven.
The dirt's all neatly stowed beneath the hatch,
The stokers are dropped overboard at night
And sure her virtues do not lack acclaim
15　As, certain of salvage, she steers toward the rocks
. . . Never so proud as in her hour of doom.

T　257.1: Ship

1940–54   NOBLE CITY FULL OF PIGEONS OR   [258.1]
            EVERYONE A HYPOCRITE INCLUDING ME

            Vancouver is a place of fears
            Her taverns have no place for beers
            Vancouver is a place of weirs
            (Were all as good as Harold; cheers!)
5   Though he had trouble with his gears
            Alas, not so, for so one hears
            Her conscience is in sad arrears
            Repression rules with ugly leers
            (The censors really are the queers)
10   Authoritarianism sneers
            Hypocrisy is that which steers
            As the rock of gaunt Neurosis nears
            And Judas rules and all his peers
            From all of which it much appears
15   My damned ferocious little lears
            The fates are waiting with their shears
            She soon will be a place of biers
            She soon will be a place of tears
            Or, once again, a place of beers.
20   (More happily, a place of beers.)

     2   258.1: Her tables have no place for beers
     7   258.1: Her maturity is in sad arrears
    12   258.1: As the gaunt rock of neurosis nears
    17   258.1: She soon could be a place of bears
    18   258.1: She soon could be a place of tears
19, 20   beers] bears

1940   [259.1]

            Not all of us were heroes said my brother wit
            Corporal Animus, by a damned sight
            He went on. Which one of us has not
            Cried out, give me the war, my mother.
5   A headline far more welcome than the score
                            Which one of us has not
            Cried out, the war, give me the war, my mother
            Which told us to believe Gloucester beat Kent,
            Or England and Australia collapse
10   When Warsaw burns to Joe Venuti's swing
            Or with Kipling take the wings of the morning
            And flop around the world until we're dead
            Or rot upon a rusty wire instead
            A vexing bathroom Armada having
15   The bias on the distaff side,
            At Plymouth Hoe or at the Hare and Hounds in Devon.
                He's played woods too long

On dark unshaven greens.

Cried out, the war, give me the war my mother,
20   Let sunlight flood my wounds
And melt my conscience like a pan of ice.

13 259.1: Or rot upon a gusty wire instead
17 259.1: He has skimmed woods too long

1940–54   NOTE   [260.2]

Poems should be made out of cedar, axe
bowsaw, clawbar, shakes
and between the wheelbarrow and the watering can
the whimpering whale's revolving fin
5   the iron stove repaired by tea-time
with tin, tin snips
woodashes, salt, asbestos and salt-water.

T 260.1: [missing]
3 260.1: [adds next line:] cross of the gull, the plane
4 260.1: the passing whale's one revolving fin
5 260.1: the stove repaired by tea-time

1940–54   NOTE FOR A POEM   [261.1]

Study the irregular verb
Mourir, to die.

1940–54   OCTOBER SUNSET   [262.4]

The sun that never rose has now gone down.
The lamps are shining on the road to town
And wind along the coast the slow grey hulls
Beneath a straggling marathon of gulls...

T   262.1: [missing]
2 262.1–3: And lamps are shining on the road to town

1940–44   [263.2]

Oh gentle Jesus of the hymnal once
Jesus of evening prayers, the mariners hymn
Fierce raged the tempest o'er the deep; and grim
The storm that swept me from the church door hence
5   How often have I in hate blasphemed Thy name
Not knowing that I cried out to Thee in shame!

6 263.1: Not knowing I cried out to Thee in shame

1939–40; 1945–6   [264.1]

      Oh my dear good lost schoolmates, no comrades
      Of mine, thank god. What you have not
      Some fairies may have claimed for you in verse –
      But I don't see it.
5   Triumphant choirboy in the ruined church
      Shaking your fist at – whom?
      Heroic sheep of unimpeachable wool
      Oh most indescribable morale –

1 264.1: Oh my dear good lost comrades, no comrades

1950–4   [265.1]

      Oh, poor Mary Ann
      When she got to the top
      Her heart went flipperty-flop
      As the wheel began to stop
5   The man in the moon began to laugh
      Oh, Mary began to squeal
      She lost her situation
      Through the great – big – wheel –

1941–2   [266.2]

      Old Blake was warm, he got down to the hub
      When he said we should worship in the pub
      Save only in Canada, where I'm told
      The tavern and the churches both are cold.

1940–54   [267.2]

      On board the Matsue Maru.
      Two bells
      From the focsle
      Head . . . Two o'clock. And the
5   Afternoon stretches endlessly
      Ahead.

      There is no pity
      There is no pity at sea.
      The sea is the sea.

10   Seven bells
      Is twenty past three
      That is a long way away
      But the flying fish abaft the beam
      Know no time.

1940–54   A PASSING IMPATIENCE   [268.2]
                        WITH A NOBLE COUNTRY

Undone, it seems are we, if to old woes fresh ones we add ere
we have drained the former to the dregs.

The nurse in Medea
Had the right idea?
I ordered a beer.
But four Finns
5   In the corner
Have fourteen.
Alone among men
I detest the Finns
Who boil themselves
10   Instead of swim
Who win the mile
Without a smile
And pay their debts
On time for their sins.
15   And choke on their second war
Before their first is drained.
And mine the fish
Out of the inlet
And never spratling leave for their sons.

T 268.1: [Note precedes title]
          A Fisherman's Lament
1 268.1: Was it the nurse in Medea
9–14 268.1: With their useless way
          Who pay their debts
          And mine the fish
          Out of the inlet
          And never spratling leave for their sons.

1949–52   A PICTURE   [269.2]

A grey ship with yellow red lights
like a little grey town, lying at the
oil wharf, three miles away,
oblique...

5   grey green hills, and silver grey oil-refinery.
and the smoke from a train going Eastward
to meet the smoke of a shingle mill
and the grey smoke of the shingle mill
hanging in the air mingled
10   with the smoke of the train, and reflected
in the black-green water...

– then the wash of a ship like a great wheel

the vast spokes of the wheel
whirling across the bay!

T 269.1: Study in Green
3 269.1: oil wharf, and grey green hills three miles away
　　　　[adds then deletes next line:] silver grey oil refinery three miles
　　　　　　　　　　　　　　　　　　　　　　　　　　　　　　　　　[away,
6 269.1: and the smoke of the train going Eastward
7 269.1: to meet the smoke of the single mill

1940–54　　　　　　　　　PIGS – FOR T.H.　　　　　　　　　[270.3]

　　　　　Pig is a young sow or boar,
　　　　　A mass of molten metal
　　　　　To bring forth pigs to live like
　　　　　Pigs.

5　　　　Pigging is pigged pigiron
　　　　　Is iron in pigs on rough bars
　　　　　Pigtail is hair in the form
　　　　　Of a tail hanging down the
　　　　　Back: a queue of twisted
10　　　 Tobacco...
　　　　　And more, than this in Oceania.

T 270.1: [missing]
2 270.1: A mass of twisted metal
4 270.1: To live like pigs
6 270.1: Pig iron is iron in pigs or rough bars
　　　　　[adds next line:] Or rough bars.
10 270.1: Twisted tobacco...
11 270.1: [missing]

1950　　　　　　　　　　　　　　　　　　　　　　　　　　　[271.1]

　　　Pines write a Chinese poem upon the white-gold sun
　　　Rising over the mountains,
　　　Gigantic, the pines against the Chinese sun
　　　Illumined and embodied by light, the pines are real
5　　That were broken bottles guarding the hill.
　　　The three pines slip out of the sun's grasp,
　　　Out of the grasp of the form of the sun;
　　　The golden reflected Chinese lantern of the sun
　　　Reflected in the calm slate ebb.
10　 And into this, for it is deep, one dives, troubling
　　　All, to emerge reborn. The smells
　　　Of bacon and coffee sing through
　　　The window, where love waits.
　　　Grey gulls, reversed, go to towns beneath the sea.
15　 The two suns burst through the fog and sea in double brilliance.

Sun in the sky, haze of mountains, a wrinkled golden scroll of
        [wave, and reflected sun, perpendicular.
The mountains and sea bisect the suns – look and it is the form
        [of a cross!
The hunchbacked fisherman, wrestling with his Evinrude,
        [floats out to work.
A kindly silent figure who came at Christmas with rum.
20   Through the window, a crab stake and its reflection
Hangs like a ghostly arrowless bow in mid-air
In the mid-air of sky and sea
Or love, upon a wall, of fog and sea:
Forks into the fog: the Evinrude hums, growls, grows fainter,
        [falls. Has gone.
25   Schoolbells toll from the invisible coastwise railway across the
        [bay;
And other sounds, diatonic, of fog; a muffled cosmopolitan hum.
Other bells and explosions strike on the rail:
Gone too: circles of water spread: spider's web, like frosted
Symbols of tenuous order, the same order as the circles of
        [water:
30   The fog comes rolling in before the sun that will drive it
        [away again.
And behind, the huge green trees, guard the little house with
        [friendly arms of benediction.
And in this paradise, one loves, swims, eats and works
And pays, nothing, save in tribute to God, ordering past
        [suffering.
– Is this the marvellous death writers are supposed to die?
35   While I toiled in the smoking city once known as Gastown
Cramming algebra into ungrateful youth
Cramming the history that was their ruin down their
        [ungrateful gullets.
How could one live a day, a moment, and not give thanks?

  5 271.1: That were broken bottles yesterday guarding the hill.

1939–40; 1945–6   THE PLAGIARIST   [272.1]

The fake poet sat down in his gilt
Took borrowed plume and wrote this humble verse.
'Oh Great Articulate, everywhere abroad,
To whom the soaring bridge and symbol road
5   Are attestation, and to whom the ship is
As a poem man wrote to the sea
Dedicated to man's trade and foundering,
As a poem and – multitudinously inscribed –
To the ubiquitous foundering of man
10   And if my heart refused to freeze in a rhyme,

At least my suffering was not more fake than iron.
                  Some oblique and unique greatness yield
                  To him who plagiarised a book on stealing.'
Who exhausted not its usefulness at once
15   In that it serves us as a symbol of life and death.

See the wound the upturned stone has left
In the earth! How doubly tragic is the shape
Swarming with anguish the eye can't see nor hear.
It is a miracle that I may use such words
20   As shape. But the analogy has escaped.
Crawling on hands and sinews to the grave
I found certain pamphlets on the way.
Said they were mine. For they explained a pilgrimage
That otherwise was meaningless as day.

2   272.1: Took borrowed plume and wrote unborrowed words,
4   272.1: You whose talents ten are
             To whom the soaring symbol of bridge and road
6   272.1: Is like a poem God's written on the sea
10 272.1: And if my heart won't freeze in my own rhyme,
11 272.1: At least my suffering's no more fake than iron.
17 272.1: In the earth. How doubly awful is the hollowed shape
21 272.1: Crawling on my hands and elbows to the grave
24 272.1: That otherwise was not much more meaningless as day.

1940–54   [273.5]

              Plingen plangen auf gefangen
              Swingen swangen at my side
              Pootle swootle off to Bootle
              Nemesis: a pleasant ride.

1   273.1: Klingen klangen auf gefangen

1946–54   POEM   [274.1]

              Wet street in Liverpool
              Wet streets in Hartlepool
              And frightful viaducts at night
              Whence are seen strange pillows of life
              Weep for me . . .

1946–54   POEM   [275.2]

              When drunk he crawled home on his knees
              His wife, they sent to fetch her
              But now he's sober, if you please,
              He drives home on a stretcher.

1940–54   POEM INSPIRED BY AUDEN   [276.3]
                     AND CLARE'S SNAIL

The best were last in the school marathon
Turning with stitch and misery, outrun

To weave a lonely vision of their own
To weave a wining vision all alone,

5   And were bad at maths: nor was it the sun
     Rising on the smart ruler back had won

Them away; lonely, often despairing,
These lives that once may have seemed past bearing

Demonstrate now a strange will to be whole
10   A sort of schoolboy prowess of the soul.

T 276.1: [missing]
6 276.1: Rising on the grim ruler back had won

1941–2   POEM ON GOLD   [277.1]
                         See Dictionary

Gold – ah, that most beautiful of words
Most malleable and ductile of metals, most
Lovely of colours, – bright epithet –
The golden grain, age, eye, glow, goose, fleece, mean:
5   The goldeneye, for instance, Glaucionetta
Clangula, and gild in all its goldenness
Gold beats to brick goldbeaters skin
Goldfinch and goldsmith goldenrod goldthread
And gold of pleasure – ah malleable –
10   Ah that all golden days that never grow old
Should dedicated be to blood and gold.

1   277.1: Gold – golden – ah most beautiful of words
3   277.1: Lovely of colours – and bright epithet –
5   277.1: The goldeneye, the whistling duck, for instance, Glaucionetta
9   277.1: [adds then deletes next line:] and ever new but oh so old
10 277.1: That all golden days which never grow old

1940–54   PRAYER   [278.1]

I pray that I may form a prayer, oh Lord,
Who lie here wakeful, silent, without word,
With tumult in my heart and round my head
The spectres of the unforgiving dead.

5   Our Father, thus it was we learned to pray
But first forgot the word and then the way
And then in useless striving lies, and gall,
Forgot the need to pray to thee at all.

10   Then pray for those who lie in dungeons deep
        Who keep no faith with your world but yet keep
        The truth alive you did your best to maim
        And if you know none such, pray just the same.

        And pray for those imprisoned by their lies,
        The famous boastful men that men call wise
15   The hypocrites for whom death holds no cure
        But merely confirmation they are pure.

1939–40; 1945–6   PRAYER   [279.2]

        Oh thou who art not above.
        Oh thou who art not below.
        Teach me how to love.

        Since heart last saw the dove,
5   Since heart leapt with the doe
        Oh thou who art not above

        Is measured by the groove
        Worn in the soul by 'No';
        Teach me how to love,

10   My selfish thoughts unglove
        From their rotten fur of woe
        Oh thou who are not above

        Let not those arsons rove
        From my conscience, its hard pillow
15   Ah, teach me how to love.

        And do thou to me prove,
        Inedible, my sorrow.
        Teach me how to love
        Oh thou who art not above.

T   279.1: [missing]
3   279.1: I pray, teach me how to love.
4   279.1: Since now has flown the dove,
                For fled forever was the dove
        279.2: Since last heart saw the dove,
                Since last heart flew the dove,
                Since last heart launched the dove,
5   279.1: Since now has run the doe,
6   279.1: Oh thou art not above
7   279.1: I pray, teach me how to move,
8   279.1: My selfish mind from woe
                Worn selfishly by woe
                Worn in the soul by woe
9   279.1: I pray teach me how to love.

279.1, 2: Oh teach me how to love.
    279.2: Pray teach me how to love,
10   279.1: My selfish soul unglove
11   279.1: From its rotten fur of woe
13   279.1: Let my thoughts, that swiftly rove
             Lest my thoughts, that swiftly rove
15 279.1, 2: Teach me how to love.
16   279.1: And lastly, to me prove
17   279.1: The evil of my inedible sorrow.
19 279.1, 2: Oh thou art not above.

1940–52   A PRAYER   [280.8]

God give those drunkards drink who wake at dawn
Gibbering on Beelzebub's bosom, all outworn
As once more through the windows they espy
Looming, the dreadful Pontefract of day.

T 280.1, 2: [missing]
    280.3–6: A Prayer for Drunks
2   280.1: South of the Tropic of Capricorn
3 280.2, 3: As once more through their windows, stark and grey
4 280.2, 3: Looms up the dreadful Pontefract of day
    280.3: They see the dreadful Pontefract of day.
    280.4: Looming, the frightful Pontefract of day.

1941   PRAYER FROM THE WICKET GATE   [281.2]
              FOR FORTY ONE DOORS
                 FOR FORTY TWO

           A PRAYER FOR THIS NEW YEAR

A trillion moons the thimbleberries: coral
The thickets of diamonded frost flowers blazing:
Banked mephitic sawmill glow, and razing
The Rockies, Mars: a spun glass tinsel ball,
5 High on the dead year's Christmas tree, the real
The multiflected, moon rides high, dazing
Orion, and the steel cat who, grazing
The bound of the path, becomes stiff laurel.

Reaching the cliff we kiss and look to sea,
10 The tide is coming in, and so is fear,
– Not so, old clockwork year! – You light without heat,
Oh abstract cold, but yet light, but yet me,
Prick hearts ablaze with warmth this nighted year
Be kind to two simple people, one cat.

ST]   [precedes main title; pencilled in available space]
ST 281.1: [missing]
1   281.1: A million moons the thimbleberries: coral

2   281.1: The bush of diamonded frost flowers blazing:
11   281.1, 2: – Not so, old clockwork year – Ah, light sans heat

1940–54   [282.1]

Promises made drunk should be kept drunk.
Or sober, all save this, a promise
To keep sober, all save this –
– Herr Ober!

1   282.1: Promises made when drunk should be kept drunk.
2   282.1: Or sober; do not try to keep sober
         [adds then deletes next line:] – Oh – Herr Ober!

1940–7   QUEER POEM   [283.2]

I knew a man without a heart,
Boys tore it out, they said,
And gave it to a hungry wolf
Who picked it up and fled.

5   And fled the boys, their master too,
All distant fled the brute,
And after it, in quaint pursuit,
The heartless man reeled on.

I met this man the other day,
10   Walking in grotesque pride.
His heart restored, his mien gay,
The meek wolf by his side.

T]   [missing] {283.1}

1949   R. USHER   [284.3]

Roderick Usher rose at six
And found his house in a hell of a fix.
He made the coffee and locked the door,
And then said, what have I done that for?
5   But had poured himself a hell of a snort
Before he could find any kind of retort,
And poured himself a jigger of rum
Before he heard the familiar hum
Of his matutinal delirium
10   Whose voices, imperious as a rule,
Were sharper today, as if at school:
Today, young Usher, you're going to vote.
Said Roderick, that's a hell of a note.
So he packed his bag full of vintage rare,
15   His house fell down but he didn't care,

And took the nine-thirty to Baltimore
And was murdered, promptly, at half past four.

T   284.1: [missing]
5   284.1: And poured himself a liberal snort
6   284.1, 2: Before he could make any kind of retort,
7   284.1: And had another damn good jigger of rum
8   284.1: And studied himself in delirium
10   284.1: Were colder today, as if at school:

1946; 1950   [285.2]

Save that the optimistic ones are worse
Who'd have no trees at all in their ideal wood
But who with model factories enhearse
God's green and man and nature's neighbourhood
5   I'd set some mournful poets of our pride
I mean the great ones, princes of anthologies
The one who had ten but buried nine beside
Of ten they buried nine with useless sighs

On this strange unleaven
10   What passion do they on this hopelessness
What power, what energy expend
To cut down all our hopes that lead to heaven
Like loutish loggers, who to the fire and wind
Leave nothing but this vicious slash behind.

1   285.1: But that the optimistic ones are worse
8   285.1: [deleted]

1941–2   THE SCHOOLBOY'S COMPLAINT   [286.2]

Milton, we like thee not, forgive us, please
Perhaps Il Penseroso bores us most,
(And we could do without, sir, Paradise Lost.)
We do not quite see what the critic sees
5   Even in Lycidas, though on our knees
Honestly we've grappled with the host,
– Nor do we say this as an idle boast –
We mean the works, including Samson Agonistes.
Yet Wordsworth said your soul was like a star,
10   And God knows Dryden thought that you were hot,
While as for Blake, the dear old boy outflanks
Them both in praise – still, damn it, here we are.
Though all this impresses us a lot,
Milton, we like thee not, forgive us. Thanks.

4   286.1: We do not see quite what the critic sees
11   286.1: While as for Blake, he probably outflanks

1 940–54   THE SEARCH   [287.3]

> In Dante, no, in Shakespeare, no,
> Nor yet in any library you go.
> And in His book nor scarcely may you dare
> To hope you'll find your agony there.

1 944–54   [288.2]

> Shakespeare's house is safe and sound
> And curses on his tomb are found
> And if Rip Van Winkle rose to stare
> At least some kind of a house was there
> 5   Though gravestones sink yet time does keep
> Some faith with people while they sleep.
> And Stonehenge stands and even war
> May leave a roof, a wall, a door.
> Yea, Shakespeare's house is safe and sound.
> 1 0   Our house burned to the ground.

3   288.1, 2: And if Van Winkle rose to stare
4   288.1, 2: At least some kind of house was there.
5   288.2: Though graveyards sink yet time does keep
1 1   288.1: But ours burned to the ground

1 940–7   SHIP   [289.4]

> The ship lies black against the wharf,
> And now a speck, far out to sea,
> While all along the coast a scarf
> Of smoke floats languorously.
>
> 5   Hull down she goes: as with despair
> We see her fade or faint discern:
> The ship is bound for God knows where
> And God knows when she will return.

4   289.1: Of smoke floats leisurely
5   289.1: Hull down she goes, without despair

1 940–7   [290.1]

> A ship stands drawn like a jewelled dagger
> From the dark scabbard of the town, lost now
> On the seaboard of the night, whereon she
> Moves silently,
> 5   She gives one last wild hungry cry
> The portholes quiet, she is a moving town
> Herself, that dagger! No, though she has
> Stabbed many a man to the heart with her
> Drab beauty.

10   I remember Jules who loathed the sea –
        Dreaming of the metro
        Porte Maillot Direction Porte de Clignancourt!
        Direction!
        Jammed on the crosstrees by the [?] storm
15   Crucified, beneath the wild Southern cross.

15   290.1: Crucified there, beneath the Southern cross.

1940–54   [291.1]

        The ship will sail again, the watches sing
        The seamen pace the poop again, and bells
        Ring out, and shovels, hammers ring and sting
        The coast of Sokotra stormy between spells
5   And quartermasters ever at his beck
        The mate will stride and whistle, will pass.
        And morning and blue water drench the deck.

        Yea, though the heart itself be docked and broken
        Bilged forever in some dread Hoboken...

10   Ah, the felling of morning, of morning
        On a ship...–

1944–54   SMELL OF BURNING   [292.1]

        There's something burning, you said, when we were hammering
        Up the ceiling, nailing the trough with three ply wood
        But down the ladder, we started stammering.
        To let it burn and this was understood.
5   Nor was what we said at once understood.
        And not till the little house we oversearched
        The damp closets full of written frustration
        Into the damp woodshed we lurched
        For possible spontaneous combustion
10   The woodbox sacked for sparks, the chimney and roof
        Bed and the roofrack contemplated.
        Thus we quenched our mutual fire discerning
        That no longer was there smell of burning.

3   292.1: Bang down the ladder, you started stammering.
5   292.1: Nor was your meaning at once understood.
7   292.1: The cold closets full of written frustration
8   292.1: And the damp woodshed we lurched

1940–54   SONG FOR MY WIFE   [293.2]

        I know of one without compare
        Passionate, lovely, brave and fair
        And fair as herself is she –

Oh poets may talk of beauty rare
5   Yet never their loves they see
But I go singing home aloud
Through our woods that are far from the town and the crowd
To our home by the western sea,
Singing passionate, lovely, brave and proud
10   And fair as herself is she.

9   293.2: Oh passionate, lovely, brave and proud

1943–5   THE SOUL   [294.4]

(On November 13th I was brought down here from London. From two o'clock till half past two on that day I had to stand on the centre platform of Clapham Junction in convict dress, handcuffed, for the world to look at. Of all possible objects I was the most grotesque. When people saw me they laughed. Each train as it came up swelled the audience. Nothing could exceed their amusement. That was, of course, before they had been informed who I was. As soon as they had been informed they laughed still more. For half an hour I stood there in the grey November rain...
    De Profundis.)

Naked you saw the soul endure those blows
That life inflicts as with a rubber hose
Toughening its fibre for the spiritual crows.
While the executioner admired your demise
5   Not naked. Clad in prison garb it goes
Nor goes, but handcuffed, waits, nor waits, but dies,
Shivering, in an extremity of compunction,
With Wilde, on platform 3, at Clapham Junction...

T   294.1: [quote missing]
3   294.1: [adds then deletes next line:] While lightning flashes,
    [thunder follows.
4   294.1: [adds then deletes next lines:] Not naked, but clad in
    [prison clothes
    Mentally going on the [?]
    But on a day of [?]
    Clad in prison garb, not
    [naked, for know
    It waits among its barrier
    [crowding foes
5   294.1: Not naked. But in prison clothes
    in]it{294.1}

1943–5   THE SOUL'S PENTONVILLE   [295.1]

1500 crimes have you committed
And not been brought to book for one:
And if for one why not another one
And if another one why not for one
5   Or others unadmitted?

To buck remorse,
You need a conscience strong as a horse.
It might be worse, it might be worse
But that the poet means himself of course...

6   295.1: To buck remorse, to buck remorse

1940–54   [296.3]

The stars have simple paradigms
But cabbalistic are their signs
The sea is rough and blue and pure
The ships that sail it are obscure
5   Yet we shall endure.

2   296.1: Yet cabbalistic are their signs.
3   296.1: The seas are rough and blue and pure
4   296.1: The ships that sail them are obscure.

1940–7   THE STOWAWAY   [297.1]

The captain paces the bridge in lofty scorn
The mates and bosuns all have hooked their door
Some other bloody deckboy swabs the floor
Wishing to Christ he never had been born
5   Ignorant that this is called a deck
For which the mate will wring his neck.

T   297.1: Memory of the Sea
2   297.1: The mates and bosuns all have locked their door
          The mates and bosuns all have shut their door
6   297.1: And that at then the mate will wring his neck.
          [at foot of page:] But all [?this nothing]
          But worst of all it is the rhymless self
          Wishes the bloody little man were dead.

1945–6 [1947]   [298.1]

Success is like some horrible disastar
Worse than your house burning, the sounds of ruination
As the roof tree falls succeeding each other faster
While you stand, the helpless witness of your damnation.

5   Fame like a drunkard consumes the house of the soul
Exposing that you have worked for only this –
Ah, that I had never known such a treacherous kiss
And had been left in darkness forever to work and fail.

1   298.1: Fame is like some horrible disaster
3   298.1: As the roof tree falls following each other faster
7   298.1: Ah, that I had never suffered this treacherous kiss
8   298.1: And had been left in solitude forever to flounder and fail.

1944–7   SUN, AEROPLANE, LOVERS   [299.1]

When the sun goes in a shadow flies over.
When the sun goes in, a shadow flies over.
When the sun goes in a shadow, flies over.

When it comes out again it is fiery.
5   When it comes out again, it is fiery.
When it comes out, again it is fiery.

1950   [300.2]

The sun was almost shining
The sky was almost blue
There was a silver lining, almost,
In that cloud of leaden hue –
5   The birds were almost singing
The bells were almost ringing
When upon the mattress springing
I fell half in bed with you.

3 300.1: And almost, there was a silver lining
4 300.1: In those clouds of leaden hue –
7 300.1: When, on that mattress springing

1939–40; 1945–6   [301.1]

There is a sort of conspiracy about the great,
Johnson said none die sans affectation.
What I mean is that their fate,
I read of unknown warriors, and feel
5   Of heroes, of indescribable morale.
Too publicised are you, oh unknown wool,
What heroism can this be
Which hypocrites and vultures so commend,
Self-immolation for an eternity of publicity.
10   No saint is there, but
Was haunted by himself, imprisoned in the dull window
What renunciation of the world is this
Turned to scarlet fire.
Martyrs who will burn at unknown pyres
15   Their triumph is to be unremembered
In glass or monument
Their cause, to live in no legend.
Save in the unimaginable library of the dead.

6 301.1: Too publicised are you, oh great unknown wool,
14 301.1: Martyrs who will burn at scorned pyres
          Martyrs who will burn at unseen pyres

1939–40; 1945–6   [302.3]

They will be ashamed after they are dead
Not of what was casually said before death
To make a vexed heart glad
With the false sustaining pride of the hour
5   But of the mouths which, watering, voice your lies
Oh ghouls of the microphone and pulpit,
Poltergeists of the ether – disinterrer,
Oh fine and bowler-hatted at the bar
No word for you save the contempt of love
10   We need enlightened scorn to wither up
The seed of your infamy.
               Yet, well do I know,
Were these my last words, how they would be used.
I call on the ghost of Shelley to rise up
15   And haunt those who have abused him.

  2 302.1: Not so much of what was honestly said
           Not so much of what was excusably said
      302.2: Not of what was excusably said
  3 302.1: At the moment, to make a mother's heart glad,
           At the moment, to make a beloved heart glad
      302.2: Before death, to make a vexed heart glad
  5 302.1: But of the use to which the words are put
           But of the mouths which voice your dying words.
      302.2: But of the mouths which voice your noble lies.
6–11 302.1: By those who . . .
           We need enlightened scorn to wither up
           These hypocrites; to shrivel them at the root.
           I am speaking of you, ghoul of the microphone,
           And lest you be deceived that I think I speak of someone else,
           I, your rival, am speaking of you, too.
  7 302.2: Poltergeists of heaven –
  8 302.2: [missing]
11 302.2: [missing]
13 302.3: Were these my last words, how they would be abused.

1940–54   [303.2]

This business of evil
Like brokers the weevil
I find hard to solve,
The more, as a factor
5   In one who's an actor
In our good resolve;
But I think for the present
It highly unpleasant
Such thoughts to revolve

10   So they go on the shelf,
          That our kind benefactor
          Is the devil himself.

7   303.1: I think of the present

1940–54   [304.3]

          Those were the days,
          And never again
          Will those days come back.
          Though the wind and the rain
5   Are the wind and the rain
          They have always been,
          Those were the days,
          Shall be no more seen,
          Though the sun turn black
10   And the moon turn green.
          Though the wish is conceit
          And the cry itself vain,
          Those were the days,
          And never again.

7–8   304.2: [missing]
8   304.3: Shall be never more seen,
9   304.2: Though the sun should turn black
        304.3: Though the moon should turn black
10   304.2, 3: And the moon should go green
13   304.2: Those were the days, and never again!

        304.1: Those were the days and never again, –
               Will those days come back though the wind and the rain
               Is the wind and the rain it has always been
               Though the sun should turn black and the moon should turn
                                                              [green
               Those were the days shall be never more seen
               Though the wish is conceit and the cry be vain
               Those were the days, and never again.

1940–54   [305.1]

          Those who die young will look forever young
          Whatever that means. Chatterton, Brooke
          Will never wear a god-forsaken look.
          For better or worse, those who sung
5   And got it all over in some early book
          And died, those fellows will not age
          While Doughty, Melville, crabbed, glower from the page.

1940–7   THOUGH I HAVE MORE   [306.3]

Who holds the flag while I hole out in three?
Who hunts my silver king along the shore,
And who, when it is proven in the sea,
Remarks that that was better than before?
5   Ah, who upon that last and final green,
Though I have taken ninety-five or more,
A round of divots, futile and obscene,
Accepts my ten and three score?
– Though I have more.

1946; 1950   THOUGHTS TO BE ERASED   [307.1]
                  FROM MY DESTINY

He reads and reads, this poet to be,
Perhaps in this very anthology

Revised that is, ten years from now
Which gives our poet ample time to grow

5   He reads and reads, but does not understand
'Set at a tangent' even in his own land

Reads more as if writing between their lines
In which scant sense or fury he divines

To their aggregate daemon
10   His forces stand as firemen to seamen

He reads but does not understand.

Save where, in some fragment of biography
Is written 'Perished by his own hand.'

T 307.1: The Poet To Be

1940–54   [308.1]

The two streams came from a different source
To come down to the water together....

Your fight no whit more noble
Than I, victorious and humble, knew.

5   That long has been a positive in my dreams

Under his burning wheels.

And, out of that cold thought
May not compare juniper, with dog violet,
The thought, the drumming things at night.
10   The mutterings and lamentations

The chaos, the noise! Imaginary orchestras

Telegraph woes, the purple hills.

1940–7   [309.2]

Very dark and clear with an onshore wind
And the sound of surf you couldn't see
The summer stars in spring were overhead
Presage of summer, and the stars bright.
5   Very clear and dark
A beautiful strong clean wind
And the moon, waning, rising...

Very dark and clear with an onshore wind
A wild sky full of summer stars and bright
10   The summer stars in spring were overhead

5–7 309.1: Clear and dark, and the moon had not risen.
A beautiful shiny clean onshore wind
And the moon, waning, but rising, rose.

1940–54   VILLANELLE, AN INTERVIEW ON MORALE   [310.1]

– Grey day, but the heart is not grey?
– Grey ship, grey, grey, and greyer yet
The ship is a long way away.

It was just such a Saturday
5   We had her bastard keel first set.
– Grey day, but the heart is not grey?

– I don't think it our job to say
Too much what we think about it
The ship is a long way away.

10   We do our work, we get our pay
And you, you get yours too: I bet.
– Grey day, but the heart is not grey?

– Well, she's standing out in the bay
She looks as if she were all set.

15   The ship is a long way away.

Disaster chaos and decay
And drains to you.
I'm glad we met.
– Grey day, but the heart is not, eh?

20   The ship is a long way away.

1940–54 VIRGO [311.2]

Since you are in your element of fire
Or soon will be, such being my desire
I do not think that you should seem to me
As frightened as a kitten at the sea.

T 311.1: Leo

1945–54 VISITING THE WRECK: [312.1]
AN ABLE SEAMAN EXPLAINS

The bosun is a pimp as white as snow.
Pox came with those grey hairs and worse than pox
Drop on them. When this ship ran on the rocks
Of course he was sleeping like a stick below.
5 And him with his 'where are we men?' at eight bells.
I never knew him utter a kind word.
He would have broke every man's heart aboard.
Then they've stories the chief steward tells
I wouldn't want to go into them now.
10 But the carpenter said he'd like to know
If there's a dirty trick he hasn't mastered.
Nothing remains to add about the man,
Seeing as how you're ladies; only swine
Bugger, thief, and at the last, a bastard.

7 312.1: He would have broke each man's heart aboard

1940–54 [313.1]

The volcano is dark and suddenly thunder
– Engulfs the haciendas
In this darkness, I think of men in the act of conception
Winged, stooping, kneeling, sitting down, standing up,
[sprawling
5 Millions of trillions of billions of men moaning
And the hand of the eternal woman flung aside
I see their organ frozen into a gigantic rock
Shattered now . . .
And the cries which might be the groans of the dying
10 Or the groans of love –

2 haciendas] haciender

3 313.1: In this darkness, I think of men in the act of procreating

1939–40; 1945–6 WALK IN CANADA [314.3]

The diving board trembles
Beneath a weight of snow; and snow

Crusted on shacks, white sycamores behind;
Snow on the mountains, snowlight on the Sound.

5   And silver timber burnished on the beach.

– The road out of the mountains bent away
To wild strawberries in the snow, laurel,
And different kinds of moss: some frozen,
Some not touched: and blackberry bushes,
10   Strange deodars that sweep out in the spring
Their lower branches skirting the ground
Silvery-grey-green, with fine tufted needles.
And spruce, fir, juniper, arbor vitae.
('We'll hack ourselves a Christmas tree,' you said.)
15   And pine and hemlock. Maples and birch were bare.
Sweet fern (whose seed makes us invisible)
You who are my eyes and seeing heart
Showed me! And leaves on which the fallen snow
Had melted, but not before another frost
20   Nipped snow and leaf together in such conjunction
As only those poets know whose hearts
Have broken twice before supporting song.
And orange lichen, not of the sea,
And frost like rock candy makes fine crunching
25   Under the feet . . .
See how the frost makes ferns of the moss
And traces out each filament!

Always under the bracken goes the corduroy road.

Ways built by man must have some purpose –
30   A ruined sawmill, with frozen sawdust
And cylinders of wood, frosted: where are the timber wolves
That pay no bounty any more? But the rabbit trails
And deer trails go over the bridge.

A bridge that, built by man, yet leads us nowhere!
35   The day was drawing in, we lost our way.
Two trees had fallen; their fall broken
By a blasted stump, and as they fell had clasped
Another nameless tree. So perhaps the
Dead help the living. We called then to the dead.
40   'For these roads you have built all lead to death.'
Not quite as Wolfe remembered Gray.
No footsteps answered of the melting frost
For frost was hard upon us and black frost
Hard over the world in a grip of lies –
45   What joy it was to find the way at last
That led us back to light and good kindling!

1   314.1: A weight of snow trembles on the diving board,

2	3 I 4.I:	Snow on the diving board and mountains, snow
3	3 I 4.I:	Crusted on shacks, and sycamores behind. Snow
4	3 I 4.I:	The silver timber burnished on the beach.
5	3 I 4.I:	The snowlight on the Sound is maniacal

           [adds then deletes next line:] That day in war I struggled
                                   [blind to school.

8	3 I 4.I:	And different kinds of moss, some of it frozen,
9	3 I 4.I, 2:	Some not hit: and blackberry bushes
I0	3 I 4.I:	Where were those that sweep out in the spring

           [adds next line:] The deodars symmetrically shaped

I8	3 I 4.I:	Showed me! And leaves on which the snow had fallen
I9	3 I 4.I:	Then melted, but before it had done, came another heavy frost
20	3 I 4.I:	Freezing snow and nipped leaf together, in such conjunction
2 I	3 I 4.I:	In such conjunction only those poets know whose hearts
22	3 I 4.I:	Whose hearts have been broken twice before their prime
27	3 I 4.I:	[adds next line:] This beauty which you see I feel in words
3 I–3	3 I 4.I:	The cylinders of wood, frosted: where are the timber

           Wolves who pay no bounty any more?
           Rabbit trails and deer go over the bridge.
           [adds next line:] The Indian Trail! Oh blood, battles
                               [fought here . . .

34	3 I 4.I:	This bridge was built by man but leads nowhere.

           [adds next lines:] And elsewhere, vitaller bridges are down.
                    The bridge by which man crossed the sea to
                                       [God

36	3 I 4.I:	Two trees had fallen; their fall was broken
4 I	Gray]	Grey
44	3 I 4.I:	[adds next lines:] And hard upon this unobserved country

                    Whose heart is England and whose soul is
                                   [Labrador,
                    Whose men roam free, or hunt in packs like
                                     [wolves:

I940–54   WE SIT UNHACKLED DRUNK   [3 I 5.I]
                       AND MAD TO EDIT

           Notions of freedom are tied up with drink
           Our ideal life contains a tavern
           Where man may sit and talk of or just think
           All without fear of the nighted wyvern,
5   Or yet another tavern where it appears.
           There are no no trusts signs no no credit
           And apart from the unlimited beers
           We sit unhackled drunk and mad to edit
           Tracts of a really better land where man
I0   May drink a finer, ah, an undistilled wine,
           That subtley intoxicates without pain,
           Weaving the vision of the unassimilable inn
           Where we may drink forever,
           With the door open, and the wind blowing.

2   315.1: [adds then deletes next line:] Where, without thought of the
                                              [nighted wyvern
4   315.1: And without fear of the nighted wyvern,
8   315.1: Free men sit unafraid to edit
              I may sit unhampered there
13 315.1: Where we shall drink forever, sans cash, sans owing

1939–40; 1945–6   [316.1]

When I was young I broke all drinking records,
But not a quart of this do I regret.
The sober of all things I hate –
Since drinkless now, intoxicated yet.
5   A different kind of drunkness rolls me yet
Into and out of beds, across, and under the world.
Perhaps some ghost of older wine heaves my heart,
With one foot upon the rail of God's snug bar
Distrust the sober, the columnist, the Oxford Grouper.
10   Drunk on credit the livelong day
Shun the face that closeted sees God
And shoots it off outside.

2   316.1: And not a quart of this do I regret.
3   316.1: [adds then deletes next lines:] Their miserable white worms'
                                              [souls across the world.
                            Oh foul and bowler-hatted at
                                              [the bar –
                            Cruel
                            When I start, breaking records
                                              [once again
                            And to the strongest curse yet
                                              [uttered, add mine.
8   316.1: I have one foot on the rail of God's snug bar
12 316.1: But shoots it off outside.

1939   WHERE DID THAT ONE GO TO, 'ERBERT?   [317.1]

(A.P.H., author of the lampoon, 'Where is Lance?' reprinted from Lon-
don's Punch in a recent *Daily Province*, is A. P. Herbert, also author of
'The Water Gipsies,' 'Holy Deadlock,' etc., and a member of Parliament,
which institution has itself been shaken by his emancipatory opinions.)

So what, if Lance the Leftist, did shout once for 'Arms for
                                              [Spain'?
For other valid reasons, so did J.B.S. Haldane.
And so did Mann and Hemingway, good democrats and true,
And many others I could mention: even, perhaps, you.
5   Come, come, weren't you a 'rebel' A. P. H., despite your looks,
And all the beer and skittles of your admirable books?
You've had radical moments, sir: admit it, they weren't warm,

Those agitations were red-hot, for marital reform!
And if Russia seemed to Steve a mystical solution
10   He's not the only one two-timed by 'Comes the Revolution.'
Weren't you yourself quite startled, since this latest war began,
To discover that the vaunted Bear can't even *walk* like man?
Modern Mervyn may be mawkish, and Ermyntrude a tramp,
But since we do not put them in a concentration camp,
15   And since the fight's for freedom, and since, after the war,
With brains blown out they may behave exactly as before,
Why not tell our Know-all Nesta now, our poor old Percy Pink,
The fact that this fight's for the right to say just what they
                                                     [think?
Else when Stalin dines on dachshunds, and Molotov on Hess,
20   And Goebbels gobbles rush funds intended for the mess,
When vodka is verboten, when sauerkraut's but a dream,
And the last iron cross is eaten and there's shrapnel in the
                                                     [cream,
All the parlor Bolsheviki will be pinking once again.
(Still, where would be the Empire if we'd no one to complain?)
25   But apart from that it's boring, they ought to have the tip
There's really no objection to their indoor Marxmanship.
And now each man's a Left and Right within him, as it were.
And age may swing the coalition just as well as war,
When all of us must emulate, each fellow in his way.
30   The celebrated Vicar lately domiciled at Bray.
Now Left is Right and Right is Left and ever the twain shall
                                                     [meet.
And your lampoon which raps the Left might be a right defeat –
A worthier target for your wit! The more especially,
Since Lance has upped and ruddy joined the bleeding infantry.

1940–7   WINDOWS FROM A MACHINE SHOP   [318.3]

Nine-light windows that never saw the sun
Now face the dawn in a house that's scarce begun.
Ah who can tell though this were all forseen
That once lent grudging joy to a machine
5   What joys and agonies they will light within?

T   318.1: [missing]
2   318.1: Now face the dawn.
3   318.1: Who can tell (though this much is certain)
       318.2: Ah who can tell what might have been
              Ah who can tell to whom all is forseen
4   318.1, 2: that once gave grudging joy to a machine
5   318.1: What joys and agonies they will know within.

1939–40; 1945–6   WORDS ON A GRAVE   [319.2]

Do not presume to bury me with them
I did not die for what they died for.
I shall insist on this – this poem
Is the measure of my insistence. Or
5   Else you will be haunted by a fiend
Oh foul and bowler-hatted at the bar –
Who for one hour pretends to be a friend.
It was for no freedom other than from
This corrupt world and you! Can damn
10   It and you with impunity now. And yet
Oh you my solitary reader who reads this,
I wish you well,
And ponder it, less long than the wildflowers and wilder wind
When bells toll out where Lycidas was drowned
15   I wish you well, would guard you, if you ask, from harm
If you must mourn for me let it be drunk,
                    I loved the sea,
Out where it goes, beyond the bermudas
Taking the surges now a long way. I loved the sea
20   And as I say the dead are haunted too
By shadows of the world like birds.

9   319.1: This foul world and you! Can damn

1945–6   THE WOUNDED BAT   [320.2]

On a summer's afternoon, hot
And in the dusty path a bat,
With injured membrane and little hands
A contact that would have knocked young Aeschylus flat
5   She looked to the twig...
Its red mouth, helpless, like a mouse or a cat
A buzzing, like a buzzer, electric
Pathetic crepitation in the path
She hooked to the twig, I laid her in the shade
10   With compassion, yet with blind terror
            Praying that not too soon
Death might care to do for me as much.

9   320.1: It hooked to the twig, I laid it in the shade
12   320.1: Death might have to do for me as much
            Death would even do for me as much
            Death might some day do for me as much
            Death might one day do for me as much
       [also, see Appendix G]

1940–52   A YOUNG FELLOW NAMED CRANE   [321.3]

            There was a young fellow named Crane
            Who stood on a bridge in the rain
            It wasn't at midnight
            He wasn't a bit tight
    5   Nor was he awaiting a Jane.

T   321.1, 2: [missing]
1   321.1: There was a young poet named Crane
5   321.1: But tight in a manner insane
              Just then: still, the guy went insane.

1940–52   THE YOUNG MAN FROM OAXACA   [322.6]

            There was a young man from Oaxaca
            Who dreamed that he went to Mintaka
            And lived in Orion
            (And not in the Lion
    5   The pub where he drank, which was darker.)

3   322.1: And dwelt in Orion

Explanatory Annotation

Explanatory Annotation

PREPARED BY CHRIS ACKERLEY

IN A LETTER to Robert Giroux, Lowry paid tribute to Jay Leyda's *The Melville Log* (1952), which he had been sent as a Christmas present, defining its method as a 'technique of cross-references spatially divided' (SL 285). The following notes are of necessity more divided and have fewer cross-references, but if they can do for Lowry's poetry what the *Log* did for Melville, they will serve their purpose. Like Melville's later works, Lowry's poems are not without difficulties or limitations; but they have been too long neglected and often contemptuously dismissed. A typical view is that expressed by Douglas Day: that most have not been published and ought not to be; that Lowry thought of himself as a poet primarily, but that his poetry is prosaic in the extreme; and that the selection edited by Earle Birney in 1962 shows Lowry at his best (Day 282–3). To which one can only reply: that many of the poems are unpolished, and a few unfortunate, but others are simply magnificent; that the impulse behind the poetry also shaped *Under the Volcano* (Lowry's finest poem); and that the 1962 *Selected Poems* is but a partial and unrepresentative sample of his work as a whole. This is not to claim that Lowry is an undiscovered Yeats, but rather to suggest that a considered reading of his poetry may reveal a talent and an achievement more substantial than hitherto imagined.

Yet an unaided 'considered' reading of the poems is no easy matter. The difficulties the poems contain are not always of the kind cherished by the New Critics – ironies, ambiguities, and paradoxes built into the well-wrought urn. Rather, Lowry looks inward, and his poetry may strive for (and attain) effects that cannot be fully appreciated until significant details, often of a personal kind, are taken into account. He is widely recognized as an allusive writer, whose works are encyclopaedic, autobiographical, and (by his own admission) heavily indebted to other writers – often to works beyond the pale of common understanding. He rarely creates *ex nihilo*, and his specific sources are frequently an important part of the effect: see, for instance, Poem 68, where an intimate knowledge of Edmund Wilson's essay on Rimbaud in *Axel's Castle* is a prerequisite for comprehending Lowry's intention; or Poem 79, where an apparent allusion to Byron turns out to be to *Moby Dick* and that fact alone makes it imperative to read the words 'fatal sound' with reference to whaling. Some would take the position that poetry ought not to depend upon such external references, but Lowry's does, and time and again the appreciation of esoteric detail transforms a poem from common verbiage into a miracle of meaning. Hence, the notes and annotations need to be more comprehensive than usual.

These notes are intended for both the general reader and for the Lowry specialist. They are meant to offer a complete factual account of the material necessary for the proper appreciation of the poetry – biographical details, literary allusions, historical and geographical references, explanations of unusual words and things – and the weighting of detail and the emphasis given to it are roughly in keeping with the topic's significance within the poem. In addition, they incorporate marginalia that may be of interest, comments upon the choice of metrical and stanzaic forms, and explanations of the way that the contents of the poems derive from or are subsequently fed into Lowry's other works. While he was writing *Under the Volcano,* Lowry tended at first to keep poetry and prose apart, but in his later revisions of the novel (and in particular, following the failure of the *Lighthouse* poems to find a publisher), he increasingly borrowed extensively from the poetry for the prose (see, for instance, Poem 51: 'Love which comes too late,' almost all of which was worked into *Under the Volcano* as an expression of Laruelle's remorse). Much of the novel is in fact composed in units that might reasonably be called prose poems, and a consideration of the compositional method of the poetry will explain much about that of the novel. Occasionally, too, a detail in the poetry will unfold an enigma in the novel: the association of floribunda with the death of Eddie Lang (see **16:59**) accounts, as does nothing else, for what the Consul feels in 'the agony of the roses' in Chapter Three. Nor are such echoes confined to *Under the Volcano:* having once traced the origin of the word 'rigadoon' to Zola's *L'Assomoir* (see **39:3**), the reader of *Dark as the Grave* can no longer respond neutrally to the pain of *Drunkard's Rigadoon.*

The notes also testify to the rich variety of Lowry's reading and sources. While the early poems reflect the direct influence of such poets as Blake, Whitman, Tennyson, Masefield, Eliot, Yeats, and, above all, Conrad Aiken, the main body of his work also incorporates lesser known writers such as Henrik Ibsen, Nordahl Grieg, B. Traven, R.B. Dana, Wallace Stevens, and Herman Melville (then not widely read), and a host of other figures. His reading was 'selective' (i.e., eclectic and erratic), and poem after poem is built up from details articulated by others. Lowry's heavy dependence on his sources has often been criticized, but we cannot begin to understand his creative method until we appreciate what might be called his sense of *order:* as in Eliot's 'Tradition and the Individual Talent,' where the works of the past are said to form an 'ideal' order, one modified by the introduction of the really new work of art, so too in Lowry's imaginative universe there is asserted a mystical continuity between his own writings and those to which he alludes. This is summed up by the phrase, 'the unimaginable library of the dead' (see **301:18**), and it is something very different from plagiarism. Yet Lowry, being Lowry, was also paranoid about stealing and afraid of being regarded as a plagiarist (see **272:T**). He took some care not to borrow too obviously from canonized authors (see **127:2,** where he is unnecessarily apologetic about borrowing the word 'jonquil' from Faulkner); but the compulsion to work from written sources, be they newspapers, menus, or inscriptions on cenotaphs, was an instrinsic part of his method. Aiken's *Blue Voyage* is the work in which the mystical bond is most obvious: in Poem 21, for instance, where the theme is the perversity of Acapulco, the reference to 'Dean Donne,' even if known to be a reference to John Donne's 'Communitie,' will remain opaque for most readers until they appreciate the perverted irony of the line, 'Chang'd loves are but chang'd sorts of meat' (what really did go on with Bousfield?); an irony that can be comprehended only when Aiken's novel is kept in mind. That no reasonable reader can be expected to notice such subtleties is in the end less important than that they should be there.

Yet Lowry often gets things wrong. Despite a marginal comment to the effect that to forget a fact is to lose a foothold on reality (he characteristically adds, 'Who said that?'), he makes a number of slips: Chatterton did not vent his fury upon Chesterfield, but on Walpole (see 52:2); Potato Jones was not the master of the *Seven Seas Spray* (see 90:15); Oregon is not the US state adjacent to British Columbia (see 167:80); and Melville's 'last address' was not on 28th Street (see 93:3). It is an open question how much such errors matter in literature; I can only point them out and wonder privately about a novella entitled *The Last Address*, the very point of which is an imagined identification with the dying Melville, based upon such a misapprehension. Lowry shared with Joyce an obsessive fascination with trivial detail, but he sometimes lacked Joyce's intellectual rigour in applying it.

The sources for a number of details have so far proved impossible to find. Some, presumably, do not matter too much (the identity of Peter Gink, 15:52); but others do (that of Ingvald Bjorndal, 234:T). Poem 234 (the translation of a message in a bottle) has proved particularly frustrating because the detail given with the poem is apparently so precise (Lowry is usually reliable with this kind of information), specifying a date of 25 November 1940; if this is accurate, then the poem must have been written almost immediately thereafter, for it is included with a letter sent to Conrad Aiken and dated 11 December 1940. Lowry is obviously working with a written source, but the details cited do not seem to appear in any likely Canadian newspaper of that period. We have only to compare a similar poem, Poem 155, 'The Deserter,' where the written source has been found, to see how closely word and phrasing in the poem follow the newspaper report. There is a similar problem with Poem 256, 'The New Guinea Gardener Bird,' which is presumably based on a written account (compare Poem 157, 'The Dodder'), but in this instance there is no clue to suggest even where to begin to look. Some might argue that there is no need to look at all, that the poem should be appreciated for what it is in and of itself; given the 'selective' nature of Lowry's reading this might seem like good advice, but with Lowry a fuller understanding of background and context invariably leads to an enhanced understanding (and, perhaps, appreciation) of the poetry (again, see 'The Dodder').

Even so, a major problem in this kind of annotation is knowing where, precisely, to draw the line. So much *could* be noted; how much *should* be? It is not simply that Lowry is so allusive that virtually every phrase seems to be half an echo of something, but rather that, paradoxically, the closer one gets to tracking down the sources, the more evasive many of the details seem to become. His own marginalia often give valuable hints about his intention or refer to books that he had been reading; but these are sometimes tantalizingly incomplete, or deliberately misleading: Lowry has a tendency to steal, and to feel guilty about it, and consequently to raise a cloud of dust as he tries to cover his tracks (see, for example, 219:T).

Many of the following notes are based upon privileged information, derived from the manuscripts in UBC's Special Collections, from the books of Lowry's personal library, and from letters and cards between Lowry and others. This raises a special problem in relation to balance and uniformity from note to note. For instance, Poem 108, that written on the El Popo menu mentioned in Chapter Eleven of *Under the Volcano*, is in the collection and can be examined, so the material for a complete evaluation is at hand. However, a letter to Gerald Noxon suggests that Poem 238 ('Isle of Man Wildflowers') is a response to a specific folder sent to the Lowrys by Noxon in 1944 (and presumably destroyed in the burning of their shack); in the interests of a balanced appraisal, should not that unattainable source also be taken into account? In other words, pertinent background material is sometimes available, but often it is not; and a comprehensive theory of annotation must make allowance for such unevenness. My guiding principles have been essentially decorum and a tendency to take advantage of such details as are available in the hope that documented instances will give some insight into the more general processes of Lowry's intention and working methods (for instance, the note upon *Soma* in Poem 25 gives a unique insight into the way that he would go back to his earlier drafts, perhaps of some years earlier, and tinker with them). I have also tried to suggest the approximate amount of doubt and tentativeness in my commentary by using gradations from 'probably' to 'perhaps' and 'possibly' when certainty is impossible but speculation seems warranted; and I have used the word 'elsewhere' (in reference to Lowry's other writings) to suggest either that there are a number of instances of the same detail or that something is buried so deeply among the manuscripts that a more exact reference is either impossible or too cumbersome; the reader will have to take such instances on trust.

A related difficulty concerns the choice of what *needs* to be annotated. I have avoided pedantic definitions of what may reasonably be said to lie within the realm of common understanding and excluded definitions and such words and things as can be readily looked up in a dictionary or an encyclopaedia, save for genuine rarities (where did he find 'feverfew' and 'agatha,' 71:5, 6?) and usages that are associated with nuances of meaning not readily apparent (see the note on 'Timbuctoo,' 16:29). When in doubt, my usual approach has been to insinuate the common meaning, but at the same time to direct the reader to the specific sense of word or phrase implicit in Lowry's usage. Inevitably, this method will frustrate some readers, who will want a factual explanation, and annoy others, to whom it seems obvious; but a commentator's lot is not a happy one, since what seems to him worthy of annotation may not be deemed so by others.

Deciding on the amount of detail necessary was particularly hard in metrical and formal matters. In the final analysis, Lowry may not have had total command of technique and prosody, and it is sadly true that he often spoils his effect by straining too hard for one last flying line or by adopting a rhythm not entirely appropriate to the subject (the anapaestic pentameter of Poem 232, 'The Illegal Heart') or by overdoing the sonnet form (Aiken once felt compelled to remind him that freedom comes *after* mastery, not before, and that the sonnet consists of fourteen lines of five-beat iambics, with a distinctive rhyming scheme). Even so, there are a number of shorter poems that on first glance seem quite casual, but that turn out to be exercises in a specific stanzaic form: the *rondelet* (Poem 125); the *sestina* (Poem 127); the *villanelle* (Poem 132); the *triolet* (Poem 137); *terza rima* (Poem 164); and *Rhyme Royal* (Poem 233). Some of these are most proficient; in particular, Poem 143, where the forms of *haiku, cinquain,* and *tanka* are combined exquisitely to simulate the flight of a kingfisher. In such instances I have drawn attention to the form used, since it is unfortunately true that Lowry's command of versification has been underestimated by many, including Aiken.

I have endeavoured to avoid interpretation; however, it will be evident to any reader that some of the poems are more equal than others and that some are more obviously incomplete. With respect to the Uncollected Poems (98 to 113, 168 to 322, and most of the Fragments) it is impossible to ascertain which are approximately finished and which are simply rough drafts. Some of the latter are most interesting: Poem 99, in which a mystical state of mind reverts to reality; and Poem 259, a bathtub meditation upon the War, for example. Both are almost indecipherable scraps, unshaped and unpolished, yet they are fascinating in their intent and may be classed as poems rather than fragments (the distinction is not always easy to maintain) even though they have not reached a final form. In other words, even the rougher poems may be of interest for what they reveal of Lowry's preoccupations, his potential, his mode of composition, and his changes of mind.

In the end, Lowry was not a Great Poet, but in the sense, perhaps, that Puccini was not a Great Composer; that is, he lacked an essential quality of genius, he had to work too hard at his compositions, and his all-too-human frailties show. Yet those very frailties, when combined with wit and melody and self-deprecation, may be in the end more attractive than genius can ever be. In Lowry's poetry there is much to be loved, and if these notes can help make that possible, then the old bastard would probably be happy.

NOTE: references to Lowry's poems are matched by number and line to the edited text; those to his other works to editions specified at the beginning of this study; and those to the works of others to either the standard editions (I have tended to refer to chapter and verse, rather than page) or to the specific text read by Lowry. An exception is Conrad Aiken, where for reasons of convenience I have chosen to refer to the *Collected Novels* (1964), the *Collected Poems* (1953), and the *Selected Letters* (ed. Joseph Killorin, 1978).

Juvenilia

1:T   *Der Tag:* Ger. 'The Day.'

1:1   *every Friday afternoon:* Mr. Balgarnie, master at The Leys and the original of James Hilton's Mr. Chips, would set a weekly test on Friday afternoons; any boy failing it would have to re-sit on the Saturday afternoon when others would be sitting around in their studies, cooking a tea of sausages and beans (hence, l. 20, 'Pork and Bean').

1:4, 9   *Postgate...Rutherford:* J.P. Postgate's *The New Latin Primer* (London 1888) and W.G. Rutherford's *First Greek Grammar* (London 1878), texts used at The Leys in Lowry's time.

1:5–8   *sibi...capiat...alvus...carbasus:* L. 'himself' (dative); 'he may take' (subjunctive); 'belly'; and 'linen.' The two nouns are feminine but follow the masculine second declension, 'carbasus' being further distinguished by an irregular neuter plural.

1:11   *My kingdom for a San-excuse:* echoing Richard III's 'My kingdom for a horse' (5.4.7); with reference to the school sick-bay as a means of evading the Friday test.

1:18   *on paper green:* boys obliged to re-sit the test were required to write on green paper, which they had to buy at ½d a sheet.

1:32   *Colney warders:* those of Colney Hatch, a London lunatic asylum.

1:33–4   *Ah! me putes amentem:* L. 'Ah! you think me crazy'; a phrase illustrating the 'potential subjunctive,' i.e., the use of that mood following the indefinite second person singular of verbs of saying, thinking, or imputing.

1:35   *a dromedary:* i.e., a 'Camel'; Lowry's penname, derived from his initials C.M.L., which he used as a school reporter in the *Leys Fortnightly;* it apparently had been suggested by Mr. Balgarnie, then president of the magazine.

2:1   *Jones:* a name used by Lowry for the little man often designated as 'Smith'; later defined in Conrad Aiken's *King Coffin* (341) as 'The anonymous one, the abstract one, the mere Specimen Man.'

2:2   *Kruschen:* Kruschen Salts, a patent laxative popular in the 1920s to promote 'that Kruschen feeling' of vigorous health.

2:3   *Pepsodent:* the ubiquitous dentifrice, with its tasteless jingle: 'You'll wonder where the yellow went / When you brush your teeth with Pepsodent.' Advertisements of the 1920s were full of the terrors of *film:* 'clinging film, a dangerous glue-like film.'

2:11   *a sixpenny bit:* the recommended dose of Kruschen Salts was 'enough to cover a sixpenny piece'; Jones's willingness to substitute six brown pennies is likely to bring on the 'thruppennies.'

2:14–15   *Liver Oil and malt:* Cod Liver Oil and Extract of Malt, commonly regarded as wonder-workers; the one taken after the other to mollify the nastiness.

2:16   *'Andrews' Liver Salt':* a popular bicarbonate, for 'inner cleanliness.'

3:16   MISS GWEN FARRAR: a British actress (1897?–1944), best known at the time for her flamboyant public behaviour (fast driving and assaulting a policeman in The Strand) and for a musical hall turn in which she played the cello (to which, presumably, the old woman's wail is likened).

3:19   *a Robert:* a 'Bobby' or constable (after Sir Robert Peel, who in 1805 established the Bow Street Runners).

3:36   *Pope and Bradley:* then a tailor's shop in the King's Parade, Cambridge.

4:13–19   *When I am dead:* a verse derivative of any number of Elizabethan lyricists or their pre-Raphaelite imitators; yet charmingly placed within a poem otherwise using conventional graveyard imagery and an abba stanzaic form perhaps too reminiscent of Tennyson's *In Memoriam.* The second stanza of the poem may deliberately imitate part of Conrad Aiken's *Punch* (*Collected Poems* 311): 'The night was thick. No moon there was. / The wind made whickerings in the grass. / The willows tapped at the churchyard wall / And we saw, like ghosts, the dead leaves fall.'

5:10   *'By crimes . . .':* an oath used in John Masefield's 'The Widow in the Bye Street' (1912), the language of which had caused some scandal in its day.

5:11   *an Annamite:* then the usual form of *Anamese,* i.e., one from *Anam* (that area of French Indochina near Hue). In *Ultramarine* (173), one of the seamen reflects: 'Those Annamite fellows are all right – give you all the samshaw you want for a little soap.'

5:15   *Tin-Sing:* an anticipation of Tsjang-Tsjang, the fictive Eastern destination of the voyage in *Ultramarine* graced by a ghastly anatomical museum of venereal diseases.

5:20   *samshaw:* otherwise *samshoo,* a Chinese spirit distilled from rice or sorghum.

5:21   *ling-fish:* 'stock-fish'; various kinds of coarse sea-fish related to cod, split and dried.

5:33   *eight bells:* at sea, rung to indicate the end of a watch (a four-hour turn of duty).

5:34   *Kobe trout:* a delicacy from Japan.

5:45   *Ephraim:* a typically Jewish name; thus, conventional anti-Semitism.

5:47   *Biarritz:* a resort for the affluent, on the southwest coast of France.

6:16   *the scouse:* otherwise, *lobscouse,* a dish of meat stewed with vegetables and ship's biscuit; mentioned without enthusiasm by one of the sailors in *Ultramarine* (177).

6:16   *Sunday's duff:* in R.H. Dana's *Two Years before the Mast* (1840), such plum-puddings, lovingly described, are the highlight of the week!

6:17   *tabnabs:* small pastry delicacies, usually reserved for officers and passengers (thus, to be 'nabbed' from the 'table').

7:8   *Klio:* invariably used by Lowry for the cry of a gull, as if to suggest the scavenger muse of History. The cry, and most of the imagery of the next few lines (notably, the fiddler crabs and red sponges), is taken from Aiken's *Blue Voyage,* Chapter 4, where the noise of the seagull forms a harsh chorus to thoughts of love and pity.

7:18   *I have no father:* in rhythm and diction, an imitation of one of Blake's *Songs of Experience,* e.g., 'The Chimney Sweeper.'

7:26   *The Board of Trade:* a British government department, established in 1786, with responsibility for trade and commerce and for the laws relating to merchant shipping.

8:6   *pitch and toss:* a game in which coins are thrown at a mark, he who pitches closest having first right to toss for the others; and a pun used in Thomas Hood's 'Sea-Spell' iv: 'The bounding pinnace played a game / Of dreary pitch and toss, / A game that, on the good dry land, / Is apt to bring a loss.'

9:1   *dart of gold:* traditionally, the shaft of Apollo, god of Poetry and of the Sun.

9:4   *through dead volcanoes:* as in Jules Verne's *Journey to the Centre of the Earth* (1864), which Lowry may have had distantly in mind.

9:8   *burning, burning, burning Lord:* echoing Book 4 of St. Augustine's *Confessions,* where Carthage is described as a cauldron of unholy desires: though Lowry's source would be T.S. Eliot's *The Waste Land,* where, at the end of Part 3, a prayer is uttered for deliverance from such fires.

10:12   *the moon:* the imagery of tower and stairs, moon and poor blind queen, imitates that of Yeats in such poems as 'The Tower' and 'Blood and the Moon.'

11:1–2   *like a webbed bridge:* suggesting Whitman's image of the isolated soul in 'A Noiseless, Patient Spider' (l. 19): 'Till the bridge you will need, be form'd – till the ductile anchor hold.' Lowry sent this poem, with the three preceding ones, to Conrad Aiken for appraisal, and in the accompanying unpublished letter (March/April 1929), he commented: 'I have been told by some that I have a tendency to rely on Whitman. I think not.'

12:T   *Nordahl Grieg:* Norwegian writer and journalist (1902–43), with whom Lowry felt an obscure identity and whose 1924 novel *Skibet gaar videre* (trans. 1927 by A.G. Chater as *The Ship Sails On*) was a lasting influence upon him. The incident described here occurs in Chapter Twelve of the novel, the two friends being the central character Benjamin Hall (who has been working as a fireman) and Sivert (who dreams of home).

12:2   *an iron moloch:* Moloch, god of the Ammonites (1 Kings 11:7), a man with the face of a bull, in whose fiery bowels children were sacrificed. In *The Ship Sails On* (2), the *Mignon* is described as 'a Moloch that crushes the lives of men between its iron jaws, and then calmly turns its face to the solitudes as though nothing had happened.' In the same paragraph Grieg notes that it also visits lands of beauty.

12:13   *girls laughing in linked quintets:* a vision repeated in *Ultramarine,* as Dana Hilliot's ship enters Tsjang-Tsjang and he must face the fearful choice of whether or not to find his first prostitute. The image recurs in Poems 95 and 114.

12:14   *spirochaetes:* twisted spiral bacteria of syphilis, the disease that claims Benjamin Hall in Grieg's novel and one that terrified Lowry all his life. Lowry's direct source is Aiken's *Blue Voyage* (74): 'The blessed spirochete. Swarms. The blood boiling with hook-nosed spirochetes. MISERY. Horror, the maggot, hatches and quarries in the very pulse of love.'

12:19–20   *Trondhjem . . . Tvedestrand:* Norwegian towns mentioned in *The Ship Sails On* and *Ultramarine,* where they are associated with dreams of home (in Grieg's novel [61], Sivert is told by the mate that he will never see Tvedestrand again).

12:21   *Iphigenia:* daughter of Agamemnon and Clytemnestra, sacrificed on the shore of Aulis that the gods might bring fair winds to the departing Greeks (see 236:T). In an extension of the myth she was rescued by Artemis and taken to Tauris, where she dreamed of home.

12:41   *the life of the chicken:* the description blends images from Grieg with others from Sherwood Anderson's short story, 'The Triumph of the Egg' (1921), where the miracle of new life is equally the triumph of futility.

12:49   *a white dream of a girl's face:* a motif from *The Ship Sails On,* also appearing in *Ultramarine.* Lowry uses the words 'white dream' to signify an unattainable vision (see 15:56–7).

12:57   *as though the very ship itself has given birth:* quoted directly from *The Ship Sails On* (111).

13:T   *Cape Cod . . . Conrad Aiken:* in August 1929 Lowry stayed with the American writer Conrad Aiken (1889–1973) at his South Yarmouth home on Cape Cod, Massachusetts. Aiken was acting at the time *in loco parentis* for Lowry, and his writings (in particular *Blue Voyage,* 1925) were to have an immediate effect upon the younger man. (Aiken once observed, a little acerbically, that Lowry's poems were riddled with borrowings from his works.)

13:4   *I have discovered a language:* Lowry's poem gently mocks Aiken's 'Landscape West of Eden,' Part 10, which is based upon a dream by Aiken of two sages, the first of whom had discovered a language in which meaning had been so fragmented into particles and surds that it would require a thousand years to assemble enough of them to constitute a single statement; to which the other replied that this was nothing, for he had discovered a language in which meaning was so concentrated that a single syllable, a single sound, was itself the equivalent of a thousand years. The dream is recounted in *Ushant* (167) and in a letter dated 22 July 1929, in which Aiken also anticipates Lowry's coming (*Selected Letters* 153).

13:15   *I tell you this young man:* the voice of Aiken (cf. 47:9). The phrase 'snoring volcanoes' is used in *Ultramarine* (30), and 'shawled islets' in a later poem (see **105:16**).

14:T *Coke to Newcastle:* referring to the adage about carrying coals; and suggesting by 'coke' not only the non-alcoholic drink but also Joyce's 'Gas from a Burner,' which this poem resembles in tone and, partly, in form.

14:NOTE *J.L. Morison:* 1875–1952; professor of Modern History at King's College (formerly Armstrong), Newcastle, 1922–40; who wrote on Indian and Commonwealth history but had in 1902 edited *Reginald Pecock's Book of Faith.* His outburst was published in the *Sunday Times* in the issue of 28 September 1930 (17) under the heading of 'Modern Authors,' and it is cited accurately though with a few omissions.

14:4 *Flaherty:* Robert J. Flaherty, explorer, writer, and film-maker, whose *Nanook of the North* (1922) had become legend for its frank description of sexual behaviour ('Nanook loves his nookie'); but apparently cited here because of a current film, *Tabu,* which he was codirecting with the German, F.W. Murnau, whose *Sonnenaufgang* ('Sunrise') was later described by Lowry as a lasting influence upon his own writing.

14:10 *Gertrude Stein:* American novelist and poet (1874–1946) and centre of a celebrated web of writers in Paris during the 1920s; also notorious for her lesbian association with Alice B. Toklas.

14:20 *Crome Yellow:* Aldous Huxley's first novel (1922); a witty, irreverent satire of contemporary moeurs. The association of saffron with decadence is an ancient one: the streets of Rome were sprinkled with it when Nero made his entry, and the herb was used as an aromatic in halls and theatres and in the Roman baths; it was particularly associated with a scented salve used by the *hetaerae,* or professional female entertainers, and as a pomatum for painted ladies then and later.

14:31 *boll-weevil:* a small destructive insect that destroys the cotton-boll; but also a phrase used by D.H. Lawrence to describe the human insects around him.

14:42 *Douglas the dimpled:* Douglas Haig (1861–1928), Commander-in-Chief of the British forces in WWI and thereafter President of the British Legion; here singled out as the representative of the establishment for the simple reason that his name suggests Haig's Whisky, celebrated for its dimpled bottle.

14:26 *the grey ones:* again, a phrase used by Lawrence, most notably in his 1929 essay 'Pornography and Obscenity' (which Aiken and Lowry seem to have in mind), to describe those not of his persuasion. The phrase derives from Swinburne's 'Hymn to Proserpine' (35): 'Thou hast conquered, O pale Galilean; the world has grown grey from thy breath.'

14:48 *sever the strings:* in imagery and rhythm, an echo of Poe's 'Annabel Lee' (30–33): 'And neither the angels in Heaven above / Nor the demons down under the sea / Can ever dissever my soul from the soul / Of the beautiful Annabel Lee.'

The Lighthouse Invites the Storm

Title: an image derived in part from Henryk Sienkiewicz's *The Lighthouse-Keeper* (1882) and associated in *UV* (203) with the Consul's self-destructive longing for the Farolito.

Epigraph: unidentified; however, the words 'September – remember October – all over' are cited as an epigraph to Hart Crane's 'Eternity' and identified there as a 'Barbadian adage.'

I. PETER GAUNT AND THE CANALS

15:1   *De Lesseps:* Ferdinand Maria de Lesseps (1805–94), French diplomat and designer of the Suez Canal; invoked here as one whose vision was translated into progress.

15:2   *Peer Gynt:* title character of the 1867 verse drama by Henrik Ibsen (1828–1906); invoked here as one whose visions are grandiose but self-serving.

15:3   *dunes in the desert:* in *Peer Gynt* (4.6) Peer is in the Moroccan desert, where he has a vision of building a canal to bring the desert to life. Most of the details of Lowry's poem, as well as the reflections on the Almighty's purpose, are taken from this part of the play, Lowry's precise source being the 1902 translation by William and Charles Archer.

15:4   *rings and a watch:* Peer reflects (4.4) that to base one's life upon such trappings is to found one's house upon the sands.

15:25   *frigates:* punning upon 'frigate-birds.' Ibsen has 'sailing ships . . . like stray birds on the wing.'

15:30   *Habes:* otherwise *Habesch,* the Arabian word for Abbysinia; mentioned in Peer's vision in reference to a journey down the Nile.

15:31   *Cape:* the ambition of Cecil Rhodes was to extend the British Empire from Cairo to the Cape; Lowry's *Ultramarine* (1933) had been published by Jonathan Cape; both were dreams of the Self.

15:31   *Peeropolis:* Peer's vision raises from the desert a vast capital, a monument to the magnificence of himself. The vision is like that of Marlowe's Tamburlaine the Great, who dreams of riding in triumph through Persepolis.

15:33   *another Petersburg:* St. Petersburg (now Leningrad) rose in the early eighteenth century from the Neva marshes because another Peter, Peter the Great, had a vision of the new city that would open a window to the West.

15:34   *peopled with Norsemen:* Peer envisages replanting the Norwegian race in Gyntiana, his virgin land – had he but the 'capital.'

15:37   *khedive:* the title of Turkish viceroys in Egypt from 1867 to 1914. In 1869 Ibsen had been invited, as a guest of the Khedive, to the opening of the Suez Canal; before the ceremony he took a trip up the Nile and into Nubia.

15:40   *Ab esse ad possess:* L. 'From being to possibility.' In *Peer Gynt* (4.5) the quotation adds 'et cetera' and refers to the logical principle 'ab esse ad posse valet, ab posse ad esse non valet consequential' – i.e., it is possible to argue from fact to possibility, but it does not follow that the reverse is true. Lowry's puns ('possess' and 'capital') accentuate the materialism behind the dream.

15:43   *'Hall of the Mountain King':* the home of the Troll-King, whose daughter Peer had seduced and abandoned and whose motto – to thine own self be sufficient – he has adopted as his own.

15:44   *Noah's donkey:* an old riddle: Q: what ass brayed so loudly that everyone in the world could hear it? A: the ass in Noah's Ark.

15:50   *Grieg:* the Norwegian composer Edvard Grieg (1843–1907), who wrote the incidental music to *Peer Gynt;* also, remotely, his collateral relative, Nordahl Grieg (see 12:T), whose middle name was 'Brun.'

15:51–2   *the six Brown brothers:* Lowry's invention; the desert equivalent of a 'Blues' band.

15:51   *the riffs:* in jazz, a melodic phrase constantly repeated; but also the desert tribesmen of Spanish Morocco, in the 1920s engaged in a protracted uprising against Spain; hence, the passing pun.

15:52   *Peter Gink:* unidentified.

15:54   *an older dream:* as in Ignatius Donnelly's *Atlantis* (1882), where the Biblical account of the Flood is considered but another retelling of a more ancient Chaldean legend.

15:56–7   *a dry world washed white:* a complex image reiterated throughout Lowry's writings (in UV [303–4] the Consul has a similar vision of Tlaxcala as a sepulchral city). In its simplest terms it refers to the unattainable vision, the impossible dream (see 12:49); but it rises out of a more esoteric tradition of a Hyperborean Atlantis (see 69:14), perhaps implicit in the strange ending of Poe's 'The Narrative of Arthur Gordon Pym' (1838). Lowry's most immediate source is *Moby Dick*, Chapter 42, 'The Whiteness of the Whale,' where Melville associates the 'certain nameless terror' of white, the mystical intensity, with 'the knowledge of demonism in the world.' In a famous passage he comments: 'Is it by its indefiniteness it shadows forth the heartless voids and immensities of the universe, and thus stabs us from behind with the thought of annihilation, when beholding the white depths of the milky way? Or is it, that as in essence whiteness is not so much a color as the visible absence of color, and at the same time the concrete of all colors; is it for these reasons that there is such a dumb blankness, full of meaning, in a wide landscape of snows – a colorless, all-color of atheism from which we all shrink?'

15:64   *solid:* i.e., unlike the onion that Peer peels in the final act of the play, trying to reach the central core of his being.

15:67–8   *'Automat'* ... *Tamotua:* reality (a stool in a coin-operated restaurant) turned into dream (a fictive tropical isle).

15:74(var)   *rats live on no evil evil star:* almost a palindrome, and one as traditional as the other: 'A man, a plan, a canal: Panama.'

15:75   *a cigarette:* in *Peer Gynt*, a cigar; but here a more personal pun on the 'Camel' brand.

15:76   *ostrich:* mentioned in *Peer Gynt* (4.4), but the 'reflection' that follows is Lowry's own. The eyes are 'sand-filled' because the ostrich traditionally buries its head in the sand.

15:79 *Peter:* from Gk. *petros,* 'a rock'; as in Matthew 16:18: 'thou art Peter, and upon this rock I will build my church.'

15:90 *Myers:* F.W.H. Myers (1843–1901), English essayist and poet, whose later life was devoted to the work of the Psychical Research Society and whose major works were *Science and a Future Life* (1883); *Phantasms of the Living* (1886); and *Human Personality and Its Survival of Bodily Death* (1903). He had also edited his father's lectures as *Great Men* (1890), and these, like his own writings, assert a trust in 'progressive moral evolution' and spiritual discovery.

15:94 *bitter lakes:* two lakes, Great and Little Bitter, in the isthmus of Suez, linked and utilized by the Suez Canal.

15:95 *from Casino-Palace to Bab-el-Mandeb:* from the Suez Canal to the narrow straits (Ar. 'Gate of Tears') at the entrance to the Red Sea. 'Casino-Palace' seems to be Lowry's understanding of the *Kasr-el-Nil Palace,* in Cairo, where the Khedive hosted a reception on 2 December 1869 to honour de Lesseps following the opening of the canal.

15:96 *Caribees to Tehuantepec:* from the Caribbean Sea (Lowry is echoing O'Neill's *The Moon of the Caribbees*) to the Pacific, via the isthmus of Tehuantepec, in southern Mexico – a route contemplated for the Canal, but rejected in favour of Panama.

15:97 *Liverpool to Canaan via Manchester:* an ironic reflection on the Manchester Ship Canal (opened 1894) in terms of the Promised Land.

15:98 *Runcorn:* a port on the Mersey estuary, where the Ship Canal begins.

15:99 *Archangel to Kattegat and Sound:* from Archangel, the Russian port on the White Sea, via the narrows of the Danish Kattegat, to Sound, i.e., the Danish Øresund, the strait between Zealand and Skane separating Denmark from Sweden; in the words of Ibsen's Great Boyg, the long way round. A network of canals linking the White Sea to the Baltic, at Leningrad, was then being built.

15:101 *many coloured meanings:* in Eckermann's *Conversations with Goethe* (entry for 21 February 1827), Goethe tells of the 'innumerable benefits' to mankind if such plans as the Panama Canal and one to link the Danube to the Rhine were to be realized; and in *Faust* (Part 2) canals feature among the many great works wrought for humanity. The phrase 'many coloured meanings,' which might seem to imply Shelley's vision of life being like a many-coloured dome of glass staining the white radiance of eternity ('Adonais,' st. 52), thus has its origins equally in Goethe's various experiments with light and colour, as discussed extensively by Eckermann.

15:107 *the White Sea:* a sea of northwest Russia, beyond the Murmansk Peninsula, kept virtually ice-free by the Gulf Stream. The title of Lowry's burnt manuscript, *In Ballast to the White Sea,* implies a voyage thither, but with something of the mystery and terror of *Moby Dick,* Chapter 42, where Melville asks: 'why, irrespective of all latitudes and longitudes, does the name of the White Sea exert such a spectralness over the fancy?'

15:110   *sea-changed:* cf. *The Tempest* (1.2.390), where Ariel's song, 'Full Fathom Five,' concludes with a vision of sea-change 'into something rich and strange.'

15:124   *Solveig and Aase:* respectively, Peer's sweetheart (whom he leaves waiting for him) and mother (whom he sets upon a millhouse roof to prevent her interfering in his mischief); the love of these two women may be the only thing to save Peer from the Button-Moulder.

15:129   *Madrid:* in the Battle of Madrid (November 1936) during the Spanish Civil War, the Republican populace, aided by the International Brigades (the point of the allusion), held out against a vastly superior Fascist force.

15:135   *the four horsemen:* the Four Horsemen of the Apocalypse in the vision of St. John the Divine (Revelation 6:1–8).

15:139   *Jones:* 'Potato' Jones, a breezy sea-dog who made a name for himself by trying to run Franco's blockade of Bilbao, bringing to the Republicans munitions concealed beneath a cargo of potatoes (see, however, 90:15).

15:143   *a loyalist column:* a Republican brigade; but, metaphorically, the making of the self a monument to life.

15:147   *Lorbrulgrub:* an apparent variation on Swift's 'Glubdrubdrib,' in Book 3 of *Gulliver's Travels.*

15:148   *Ithaca:* the home of Odysseus, where his faithful Penelope awaited him; the town in New York State was named after the Greek island.

15:149   *Georgia:* three Georgias: that in the southern US, that in the Russian Caucasus, and South Georgia in the Southern Ocean. The three are linked by a mystical triangulation of the kind that attracts the distant star Aldeberan (in the constellation of Taurus) to the Scottish Aberdeen.

II. LETTER FROM OAXACA TO NORTH AFRICA, 1936

16:T   *Oaxaca:* Oaxaca de Juárez, capital of Oaxaca state and later to be Lowry's personal City of Dreadful Night (see **24:1**) Despite the given date of 1936, it seems that Lowry and his first wife Jan visited Oaxaca in February 1937, at which point the poem was probably completed.

16:1   *Martin:* Dr. Martin Case (1905–78), a friend of Lowry's from their Cambridge days, who spent much of his later life in Kenya.

16:3   *over a wayward sea:* echoing the opening lines of Poe's 'To Helen': 'Helen, thy beauty is to me / Like those Nicean barks of yore, / That gently, o'er a perfumed sea, / The weary, wayworn wanderer bore / To his own native shore.'

16:8   *whiffenpoof:* 'The Whiffenpoof Song' first appeared in a 1918 Yale songbook, though it was composed by a Harvard man, Guy H. Scull, to the words of Kipling's 'Gentlemen-Rankers.' It was popularized in 1935 by Rudy Vallee, the chorus beginning 'We're poor little lambs who have lost our way' and ending 'God have mercy on such as we.' Lowry's beast may be related to the Greater Horned Kudu, but it is also to be found in Aiken's *Blue Voyage* (93).

16:9   *Selah:* in Hebraic music and liturgy, a pause; associated in particular with the Psalms.

16:11, 13   *Vigil Forget...Peter Gaunt:* respectively, spy and dreamer; two figures recurring throughout the *Lighthouse* poems.

16:15   *Nyasaland:* a former British Protectorate, now Malawi. It had not by 1936 issued any stamps depicting giraffes. Lowry seems to have confused Nyasaland with Nyassa, a district of Portuguese Mozambique administered by the Nyassa Company; it issued stamps from 1897 to 1929, a number of which portrayed giraffes.

16:16   *Spain:* several of Lowry's friends and Cambridge contemporaries (among them John Sommerfield and John Cornford) were then serving in Spain with the International Brigades, and Lowry's guilt about not doing his bit is a recurrent theme.

16:22   *longitude:* a pun on 'latitude,' initiating the absurd image (exerting a speckledness over the fancy?) of giraffes making love.

16:22   *Tehuantepec:* an isthmus in the south of Mexico (see **15:96**); likened elsewhere by Lowry to the neck of a giraffe and alluded to with some awareness of Wallace Stevens's 'wonderful poem,' 'Sea Surface Full of Clouds,' set in November, off Tehuantepec (see 'Through the Panama,' entry for 22 November).

16:25   *the Nubian three-horned:* an apocryphal rhinoceros from the Nubian desert of northeast Sudan, with a freakish endowment promising enormous aphrodisiacal power (hence, the need to be 'four-armed').

16:29   *beans:* i.e., Mexican jumping beans.

16:29   *Timbuctoo:* an antibaccius meaning 'I love you,' and a way of evading direct statement of the sentiment. The tradition of wit associated with the word goes back at least to 1829, when Tennyson won the Chancellor's medal at Cambridge for a poem on 'Timbuctoo,' the subject assigned because there was said to be no rhyme for it; thus, the parody; 'If I were a cassowary / On the plain of Timbuctoo / I would eat a missionary / Prayerbook, Bible, and hymn-book too').

16:30   *Harrow:* referring to the striped blazers of the public school boys.

16:31   *the Aldershot tatoo:* a colourful display held annually in June at the large military base in Aldershot, Hampshire; with a pun on 'tattoo.'

16:34   *annex:* in Mexico, an administrative district.

16:37   *Americans who want to get divorced:* Conrad Aiken may have been about to leave to stay with Lowry in Cuernavaca, there to await his Mexican divorce.

16:40   *Lawrence:* D.H. Lawrence (1885–1930) spent some time in Oaxaca and wrote *The Plumed Serpent* from what he thought was his Mexican experience. Lowry alludes to Lawrence's reputation for sexual freedom ('licence'), and means by 'pouncing' what he calls elsewhere 'the great primeval consciousness.'

16:41   *chingarn:* from Sp. *chingar,* 'to rape,' 'to fuck'; a common obscenity.

16:42   *my bawdy tune:* a phrase perhaps suggested by the 'bawdy strings' of Wallace Stevens's 'The Comedian as the Letter C,' which may have been (in a very general way) Lowry's model for his own poem.

16:45   *too badgery:* literally, exhibiting too many armorial bearings; with a pun on the Boy Scout earning of merit badges.

16:50   *Wasserman turnips:* from A. von Wassermann (1866–1925), German bacteriologist and discoverer of a diagnostic test for syphilis using blood serum and spinal fluid. 'Turnips' may allude to the shape of the spirochaete (see **12:14**).

16:52   *How long...oh Lord:* an echo of Revelation 6:10. 'How long, O Lord, holy and true, dost thou not judge and avenge our blood on them that dwell on the earth?'

16:58   *Ed Lang:* Eddie Lang (1902–33), real name Salvatore Massaro; guitarist friend and accompanist of Joe Venuti. He died of complications following a tonsillectomy (hence, l. 59, 'gall and lung').

16:59   *floribundia:* floribunda, a hybrid of polyantha and tea-rose, growing in clusters without fragrance. In UV (70–71), the Consul also considers 'the agony of the roses' in relation to 'floribundia.'

16:62   *duns upon my pen:* echoing a complaint by Melville, as recorded in Lewis Mumford's 1929 biography, *Herman Melville* (72): 'When a poor devil writes with duns all around him, and looking over the back of his chair, and perching on his pen, and dancing in his inkstand – like the Devils about St. Anthony – what can you expect of that poor devil?'

16:64   *Beiderbecke:* Leon Bismarck ('Bix') Beiderbecke (1903–31), cornet and jazz trumpet, who died an alcoholic at the age of twenty-eight and became a cult figure after his death; one of Lowry's favourite composers.

16:64   *'In a Mist':* a piano solo recorded by Beiderbecke in New York on 9 September 1927; played by Plantagenet in the City Hospital (*Lunar Caustic*, Chapter 8).

16:65   *Singing the Blues:* a Trumbauer-Beiderbecke composition, recorded in New York, 4 February 1927; the narrator of 'Forest Path,' on his way back from the spring, thinks of a break in the recording that seems 'to express a moment of the most pure spontaneous happiness.'

16:66   *'Walking the Dog':* a recording cut in New York, 5 October 1929, featuring Hoagy Carmichael but with Eddie Lang on guitar.

16:67   *Frankie Trumbauer:* jazz musician (1900–56), C-melody saxophone. By seventeen he had formed his own band and worked with many leading musicians, including a lasting association with Bix Beiderbecke. Lowry's Martin Trumbaugh, the lead of 'Through the Panama,' owes much to this original.

16:67   *'Imagination':* not a Trumbauer composition; Lowry may be thinking of the New York (1 June 1928) recording by Red Nichols and his Five Pennies, including Eddie Lang on guitar.

16:67   *Gogol:* Nikolai Gogol (1809–52), Russian novelist, whose masterpiece *Dead Souls* (1842) is hinted at here.

16:68 *Birmingham...edgbaston:* the home of Martin Case, in the Birmingham suburb of Edgbaston, where Lowry had visited over the Christmas vacations of 1930–32. 'Gillot Street' (l. 74) in the unrhyming world is more properly Gillot Road.

16:69 *Grantchester:* a small village near Cambridge, nostalgically associated with Rupert Brooke's 1912 poem of that name.

16:73 *Ralph and Bob and Margaret:* Martin Case's two brothers, Ralph and Robert, and his first wife, Margaret.

III. THE CANTINAS

17:3 *Papegaai:* presumably a mispelt variation of Ger. *papagei,* 'parrot'; i.e., a kind of gaudy *aguardiente,* or cheap brandy.

17.3 *Mezcal:* a variety of tequila, distilled from the *piña* or heart of the agave maguey cactus; associated in UV with the Consul's damnation.

17.3 *Hennessey:* a variety of cognac.

17.3 *Cerveza:* Sp. 'beer.'

17:10 *flowers that know the sun:* so to reject the sunflower, in terms of Blake and Swedenborg, is to ally oneself wilfully with the forces of darkness.

18:2 *Swedenborg:* Emanuel Swedenborg (1688–1772), Swedish scientist and mystical philosopher, whose 'half wisdom' is the knowledge of Hell (he wrote equally of Heaven).

18:3 *Lawrence thought backward:* i.e., to attain a primitive consciousness.

18:4 *the dark abysm:* from *The Tempest* (1.2.49–50), where Prospero asks Miranda what she can remember of the time before she came to the island: 'What seest thou else / In the dark backward and abysm of time?' 'Time's maidenhead' is before even the innocence of Eden, when the deep was a vast abyss of chaos; Shakespeare (Lowry implies) had an intuitive knowledge of that dark.

18:5, 6 *Maidenhead...Richmond...Maida Vale:* districts of London. Lowry, using the Biblical 'know,' thinks backward to more innocent times.

18:6 *Baker Street:* London, in which Madame Tussaud's waxworks (with its Chamber of Horrors) is located and where (at 221B) Sherlock Holmes might have been sought.

18:9 *Charlotte Street:* in Soho, London; the location of a favourite Lowry tavern, the Fitzroy.

19:9 *bully the cabbage:* cryptic; possibly, not to answer back, from the old proverb about not boiling the cabbage twice (not repeating oneself), associated here with bull-beef.

19:10 *In God we trust:* a repeated cynical reference to the inscription on US currency (see **66:5**).

20:2 *Fernandez Passilique:* unidentified; in an early short story, 'Goya the Obscure,' the narrator is Joe Passilique, late trimmer on the *Dimitrios N. Bogliazides,* who suffers from venereal disease.

20:6 *inhibitory:* Lowry elsewhere puns upon 'inbibitory.'

20:7   *Trujillo:* a city in Spain, and hence the reference to the Inquisition and the contemporary agony of the Spanish Civil War; but also *Ciudad Trujillo,* otherwise San Domingo, capital of the Dominican Republic on Hispaniola (see **20:13**).

20:7–8   *Ring out, you bleeding bells:* the bells of Tennyson's *In Memoriam* (106): 'Ring out the old, ring in the new' but with an inquisitorial glance at the rack as well.

20:10   *Mint Springs:* in the 1930s, a popular brand of cheap, rotgut Bourbon whiskey.

20:11   *my corn king assassin:* associating bad Bourbon with Sir James Frazer's myths of the corn gods in *The Golden Bough* (the opening image of which is the slaying of the priest-king at Nemi by his designated successor).

20:12   *Tortu:* Fr. 'tortured'; but also the *Ile de la Tortue,* off the Hispaniola coast; and Lowry's consistent spelling for Tartu University, Estonia, described by the Consul (*UV* 61) as the place where nothing interferes with the business of drinking.

20:13   *San Domingo:* an oath; but also a pun linking the capital of the Dominican Republic to the Cathedral of Santo Domingo in Oaxaca and thus bringing together the major images of the poem (church and pub, bells and the tortures of drinking).

21:1   *Acapulco:* the resort city on the Pacific coast, through which Lowry first entered Mexico in 1936 (according to him, on the Day of the Dead).

21:3   *Dean Donne:* John Donne (1573–1631), poet and dean of St. Paul's. The lines referred to are from one of his religious poems, 'Communitie' ('Good wee must love'); but Lowry has taken them, not from Donne, but from Aiken's *Blue Voyage* (122), where Demarest perverts them to a meditation upon the final lines: 'Chang'd loves are but chang'd sorts of meat.' He likens his 'Samson Complex,' i.e., the attraction he feels towards the flashy Faubion as opposed to his other choices, to the difference between poetry and prose and cites Donne in support: 'For they are ours as fruits are ours. / He that but tastes, he that devours, / And he that leaves all, doth as well.' To which Silberstein replies: 'Take all the lyrics you want, but leave me the legs.'

21:8   *Wells Fargo:* the American express delivery service, established in 1852, which Lowry used frequently for *poste restante* purposes.

21:9   *Paraiso de Caleta:* Sp. 'Paradise of the inlet,' an Acapulco morning beach and also (according to Margerie's later marginal note) the hotel in Acapulco where Malcolm had stayed with his dubious friend Bousfield.

21:10   *held no horses:* alluding to the tradition that Shakespeare's first job in London was to hold the horses of the gentlemen who came to the playhouse.

21:12   *Globe:* the Globe Theatre, in London, where Shakespeare's plays were acted.

21:13   *Marston:* John Marston (1575–1634), playwright, whose *Antonio's Revenge* (5.4.3) is here effectively misquoted: 'Rich happiness that such a son is drowned.' The line, as cited by Marston, is twice quoted in Aiken's *Blue Voyage* (138, 139).

22:2   *Melville:* Herman Melville (1819–91), American whaler and writer of massive novels, whose *Moby Dick* was ever at hand on Lowry's voyage. Chapter 97, 'The Lamp,' tells of the changed aspect of the forecastle when oil for the lamps is suddenly plentiful, for instead of stumbling in darkness to his pallet the whaleman may make of his berth an Aladdin's cavern and lay him down in it, 'so that in the pitchiest night the ship's black hull houses an illumination.' Lowry seems conscious of this passage, but his specific allusion is to the poem 'The Enthusiast,' written in Melville's darker days, with its motto 'Though He slay me, yet will I trust in Him.' The poem is an exhortation to be true to the light and concludes: 'Nor cringe if come the night: / Walk through the cloud to meet the pall, / Though light forsake thee, never fall / From fealty to light.' The poem is quoted in Lewis Mumford's 1929 biography, *Herman Melville,* and it, rather than Melville's works, seems to be Lowry's immediate source.

22:4   *well met:* an ironic echo of Oberon's words, *A Midsummer Night's Dream* (2.1.60): 'Ill met by moonlight, proud Titania.'

23:6   *Tequila of Jalisco:* a cheap tequila from the Mexican state of Jalisco, a bottle of which the Consul has hidden in his garden (*uv* 131).

23:10   *salty jest:* tequila is traditionally drunk with lemon and salt.

23:18   *the heart's next recession:* from de Quincey's 1923 essay, 'On the Knocking on the Gate in Macbeth,' which analyses such retiring of the human heart in terms of the suspension of earthly passion.

24:1   *a city of dreadful night:* combining James Thomson's poem, 'The City of Dreadful Night' (1874) and Kipling's tale of the same name (1885) with Lowry's personal memories of Christmas 1937, when he spent some time in a Oaxaca jail for having drawn, he claimed, a map in tequila on the bar (more probably for drunken behaviour).

24:5   *In the dungeon:* in various letters elaborating his experience, Lowry likened himself to the Count of Monte Cristo, imprisoned in the dungeons of the Château d'If.

24:8   *from the garden:* Lowry is citing the sign he saw in a public garden in Oaxaca: '¿Le gusta este jardin que es suyo? ¡Evite que sus hijos lo destruyan!' ('Do you like this garden which is yours? See that your children do not destroy it!'). In *uv* it is a sign of a paradise about to be lost, and the Consul, like Lowry here, misinterprets it to mean: 'we evict those who destroy.'

24:11   *the cathedral:* the military headquarters in Oaxaca, as in the fictional Parián, are in what used to be a monastery adjacent to the Cathedral of Santo Domingo.

24:14   *oh multitudinous:* plaintively blending Sir Thomas Browne's 'o altitudo' (*Religio Medici,* 1:10) with Macbeth's expression of guilt and horror (*Macbeth,* 2.2.63).

24:15   *sloans liniment:* Sloan's liniment, a common household embrocation.

25:T   *Cuautla:* the second city of Morelos, some forty km southwest of

Cuernavaca and historically significant as the centre of Zapatista activity during the Revolution. A manuscript note by Lowry claims that the poem was begun in Cuautla, July 1937, but Conrad Aiken also notes that it was written in and sent to him (as an imitation of one of his own Preludes) from Charlie's Bar in Cuernavaca.

25:1   *This ticking:* this imagery of a soul awaiting death is used several times in *UV*. Lowry seems to have in mind Aiken's 'Three Preludes,' where the ticking of an alarm-clock is like 'the sound of an abyss / Dedicated to death'; Poe's short story, 'The Tell-Tale Heart,' where the ticking is a sign of guilt; and Frances Cornford's 'The Watch,' which concludes: 'I thought it said in every tick: / I am so sick, so sick, so sick. / O death, come quick, come quick, come quick, / Come quick, come quick, come quick, come quick.'

25:5   *wainscot:* the late addition of this word may be in response to T.S. Eliot's similar vision of disintegration in *East Coker* (l. 12); if so (as with the *Soma* reference, **25:Note**), it shows Lowry still revising the poem well into the 1940s.

25:5(var)   *the death-watch beetle:* one of the family of *Anobiidae* that makes a ticking sound as it bores through wood, commonly considered an omen of death. In Aiken's *Great Circle* (249), Andrew Cather reflects that this beetle will 'precede him on his march to the frontiers of consciousness.'

25:19(var)   *thunder...towers:* obvious echoes of Eliot's *The Waste Land,* Part 5, presumably discarded as being too conspicuous.

25:25   *jalousie:* the horizontal metal slats making up the outer door of a cantina.

25:36   *the pictured calendar:* in his later revisions of *UV*, Lowry added this picture of Canada to the calendar of saints seen by the Consul in the Farolito (352) as he completes his 'hideously mismanaged' act of intercourse with Maria.

25:NOTE   *Soma:* in Vedic literature, the nectar of immortality, conveying vitality and transcendent vision to all who drank it. The note, taken verbatim from H.G. Rawlinson's *India: A Short Cultural History* (1937) (30), was a later (1943?) addition to the text and had first formed part of the Consul's cerebral chaos (*UV*, Chapter 10); its (pencilled) presence in the two early versions of the poem can be explained only as retrospective additions to the manuscripts.

26:2   *Derelicts do not dream of being ships:* yet in *Lunar Caustic* 'Bill Plantagenet' does precisely that, even to the extent of admitting himself to hospital as the S.S. *Lawhill.*

26:8   *Ben Jonson:* Jacobean poet and dramatist (1573?–1637), who is buried upright in Westminster Abbey in what later became Poet's Corner; he had bargained with Charles I for one square foot of the abbey, and at his death he was granted exactly that. According to Aubrey's *Brief Lives,* Jonson's epitaph, 'O rare Ben Jonson,' was 'donne at the charge of Jack Young, afterwards knighted, who, walking there when the grave was covering, gave the fellow eighteen pence to cutt it.'

26:10   *Tarquin:* cf. *Macbeth* (2.1.55), where Tarquin, with ravishing stride, 'moves like a ghost' towards his design. Shakespeare is referring to his own poem, 'The Rape of Lucrece,' which tells how Sextus Tarquinius, son of the king of Rome, steals into the chamber of the innocent Lucrece, rapes her, and flees; the resulting outcry moves the populace to rise up against the Tarquins and overthrow their rule.

27:T   *Vera Cruz:* Sp. 'True Cross'; the port and city founded by Cortés in 1 5 1 9 before he set off into the interior to seek and destroy the Aztec civilization.

27:2   *the Biltmore:* a relatively expensive hotel, near the Vera Cruz waterfront; but, as a deleted original title indicates, the initial delirium was in the Biltmore of Mexico City (Lowry may have not ever visited Vera Cruz). 'Cuarto' is Spanish for 'room.'

27:9   *that forked rashed image:* an ironic neo-Platonic reflection of the traditional definition of man as a forked radish (in *Blue Voyage* [1 3 8], Demarest describes himself as such).

27:8   *error:* alluding to the Gnostic notion that the material world is the creation of inferior demiurges and therefore imperfect; man, being a microcosm of that greater whole, shares its imperfection.

27:1 2   *Sodium perborate:* an oxidizing agent ($NaBo_2\ H_2O_2$) used in the preparation of hydrogen peroxide; Lowry surely means *boric acid* (i.e., sodium borate, H_3Bo_3), a mild antiseptic used in gargles and mouthwash (the 'per' added as a catalyst to the scansion).

27:1 3   *telephone disconnected:* throughout uv Lowry makes similar use of disconnected telephones to suggest imperfect or interrupted communication with the spiritual world.

27:1 4   *smashed all the glass:* an act of physical violence triggered by metaphysical terrors and, as such, a demiurgic reaction against the Light; the $50 bill ('dollars' rhyming with 'dirty collars') reaffirming the realities of the material world.

28:T   *Usquebaugh:* Gaelic 'water of life,' from which 'whisky' is derived.

28:7   *worms:* in context, the cactus worms included in every good bottle of mescal; allusively, those of Marvell's 'Coy Mistress' (ll. 27–8): 'then worms shall try / That long preserved virginity.' The word 'sabbatical' may have the sense of a witches' Sabbath.

28:1 2   *nescient:* i.e., 'non-knowing,' in the sense of an experience beyond the comprehension of the rational faculties. Lowry is probably responding to Aiken's *Great Circle* (2 5 7), where 'nescience' is used in free association with cold Arctic airs, the interstellar current of the soul, and the wings of birds.

28:1 3   *unsheathed:* i.e., without a condom.

28:1 3–1 5   *Tarquin . . . Lucrece:* see **26:1 0**; Lucrece is here described as 'plattered,' or laid out, in oblique reference to Eliot's Prufrock, who sees his head (like that of John the Baptist) brought in upon a platter, to satisfy the unnatural desires of a woman.

29:T   *the Dôme:* the *Café du Dôme,* a legendary Parisian café of the 1 920s, open to all hours and very much at the heart of the literary and artistic scene; it was located at the *Carrefour de l'Observatorie,* where the Boulevard Montparnasse meets Raspail and Vavin (an area featured in Hemingway's *The Sun Also Rises* and recalled by the Consul, *UV* 283).

29:7(var)   *the Battery:* on the southern tip of Manhattan Island, at Battery Point, an old fort, conspicuous from the sea and often referred to by Melville.

29:9–10   *boots to lick...the Pope's toe:* Decadent desolation: misery and humiliation, then a turning to Catholicism – the path followed by so many of the Tragic Generation, of whom Lowry here imagines himself the sole survivor.

IV. SONGS FOR SECOND CHILDHOOD

30:4   *Wesleyan:* Methodist, with connotations of joyless discipline and the fear of God. The Methodist Church was founded by John Wesley (1703–91) as a non-conformist breakaway from the Church of England.

32:1   *The dead man:* compare Aiken's *Preludes for Memnon*, 45: 'The dead man spoke to me and begged a penny.' In an unpublished letter to Aiken (12 March 1931) Lowry claimed that this work increasingly seemed to him 'one of the greatest poems ever written.'

33:1   *paying the savage piper:* an image of resented privilege; in the popular adage, he who pays the piper calls the tune.

33:4   *your frailty or your sex:* Lowry cultivated memories of having been bullied as a child, and he was conscious of his small penis; but a note in the typescript ('too Spender') suggests he may have been aware of overdoing the pathos: the reference is to Stephen Spender's poem which begins: 'My parents kept me from children who were rough.'

33:6   *be prepared:* the motto of the Boy Scout movement.

33:8   *tiger, wolf, lion:* unlike 'stoat' and 'dove,' typical names for Boy Scout patrols.

33:11   *the whirring of the chapel bell:* in *UV* (140), the Consul experiences a similar sense of vertigo (see **23:18**).

33:19   *the oath:* that taken by a Boy Scout, promising among other things to honour God, to obey the king, and to be clean in thought, word, and deed.

33:20   *Pathfinder:* in scouting terms, one who has gained his explorer's badge.

33:21   *like Adams:* perhaps a reference to Genesis 2:20, where Adam gives names to every beast of the field, but has no helpmate for himself.

34:1   *The stone:* that at the entrance to Christ's sepulchre, to be removed by divine agency on the day of Resurrection.

34:2   *Jones:* the anonymous little man; here, the poet himself.

34:3   *Pelican:* an emblem of the self-sacrifice of Christ; when food was short, the pelican was said to plunge its beak into its breast for blood to feed its young.

35:3   *Rupert Brooke:* the English poet (1887–1915), best remembered for his patriotic war sonnets and his poem 'Grantchester.' He was described by Frances Cornford as a 'young Apollo,' for the long littleness of life 'magnificently unprepared'; and his death at the Dardanelles epitomized the loss of the best of his generation.

36:4   *Oswald:* at the end of Ibsen's *Ghosts* (1881), Oswald Alving, reduced by venereal disease to blindness and imbecility, calls out to his mother for the sun.

37:2   *Shelley's elided fragment:* a reference to Shelley's 'Rain' (1821): 'when / The gentleness of rain is in the wind, / But all the earth and all the leaves are dry.' Brief as it is, only the line cited by Lowry was published in William Michael Rossetti's 1870 edition of Shelley's poems.

37:4   *the Castle:* the English title (1930) of *Das Schloss* (1926), the posthumously published novel by Franz Kafka (1883–1924). It tells of one K., newly arrived in the village, who tries to get entry to the castle above, but (just as in human relationships) in vain. Like the smithereens of Shakespeare, the Shelley fragment, and God's black manuscript, Kafka's novel is unfinished.

37:6   *James or Jones:* perhaps, the exquisite dubieties of a Henry James or the anxious uncertainties of a nobody.

37:13   *one flying line:* i.e., the Shelley fragment, likened to the New Guinea Bird of Paradise, celebrated for the beauty of its plumage (there are legends of its flying to the sun).

38:1   *Hatteras:* Cape Hatteras, off the North Carolina coast, noted for the violence of its storms, and overlooking 'the graveyard of the Atlantic' where more than five hundred ships have perished. Also, a reference to Hart Crane's poem, 'Cape Hatteras' (Part 4 of *The Bridge*), which takes as its theme: 'we, who round the capes . . . return home to our own hearths.'

38:3   *a stuffed mattress:* i.e., a sailor's palliase in the forecastle, before the mast. In Grieg's *The Ship Sails On* (9), Benjamin Hall lays claim to 'a foul and ragged mattress, shedding its hay in all directions'; and in *Ultramarine* (43), Dana Hilliot terms his a 'donkey's breakfast.'

38:5   *Tierra del Fuego:* Sp. 'Land of Fire'; a large island at the tip of South America, and associated here (as in R.H. Dana's *Two Years before the Mast*) with the rite of passage of rounding the Horn.

38:11   *Which is the cape and which the horn?:* Cape Horn is the southernmost tip of Horn Island, south of Tierra del Fuego; but sailors attempting to round it may be deceived by False Cape Horn (see 163:T).

38:26   *eight bells:* see 5:33.

38:28   *veronica:* in bull-fighting, an elegant pass with cape and sword in which the body of the matador bends (hence the phrasing, ll. 37–8) while his feet do not move, as the horns of the bull pass dangerously by. Lowry may be thinking of Hemingway's advocacy of the purity of the line with the maximum of exposure.

39:3   *a rigadoon:* a quick gay dance for two, originating in Provence; also, the beat of the drum in the French army as culprits are marched to punishment. In the manuscript of *Dark as the Grave* Lowry notes 'Zola' beside the word; his reference is to the unique citation in

L'Assomoir ('Drunkard'), the amazing ending of which depicts the drunkard Coupeau, in the hospital-asylum of Sainte-Anne, dancing in a delirious convulsion. Even when he collapses (after four days of horror), his feet continue to dance in a spastic rhythm that is terminated only by his death. See also **54:7**.

39:4   *Sweeney Todd:* in Victorian melodrama, the Demon Barber of Fleet Street, who would slit the throats of his customers then swing them through a trapdoor to the pie-shop next door.

39:9   *who dwelt with Cyclops:* like the crew of Odysseus, trapped in the cave of the one-eyed monster, with every prospect of being devoured.

39:10   *perfumed seas:* inappropriately echoing Poe's 'To Helen,' with its wayworn wanderer (see **16:3**).

40:T   *The Devil was a Gentleman:* in Chapter 63 of *Moby Dick*, Stubb observes to Flask that the devil is a curious chap, who 'went a saunter-ing into the old flag-ship once, switching his tail about devilishly easy and gentlemanlike.'

40:7   *Dantesquely:* as Dante loved his Beatrice, with an idealized adora-tion.

40:18   *gehennaed:* obviously, a diabolical compound of henna and mer-capatan, for those devilishly good looks (see **47:2**).

41:1   *ubiquitous:* used in the specialized sense of having the power (since physical laws are in abeyance) to be in more than one place at the same time; in *Moby Dick* (Chapter 41), the White Whale is said to be ubiquitous in this manner.

41:3   *polygonous:* Lowry's preference for the more usual 'polygonal,' 'many-sided,' and invariably associated by him with the compound eyes of insects.

42:1   *Bierce.* Ambrose Bierce (1842–1914?), the Old Gringo. A news-paperman, writer of short stories, and compiler of *The Devil's Dic-tionary*, Bierce went to Mexico to take part in the Revolution and disappeared without trace.

42:1   *Hart Crane:* American writer (1899–1932), whose long mystical poem *The Bridge* fascinated Lowry, as did his suicide by jumping from a ship, the *Orizaba*, into the Gulf of Mexico (see also **321:T**).

43:8   *vetch:* a plant of the genus *vicia*, related to the bean, with a climb-ing stem and violet-purple flowers; Lowry may have in mind John Masefield's 'The Dead Knight,': 'The vetches have twined about his bones (l. 18).

43:11   *merdurinous:* compounded of dung and urine.

43:13   *houghs . . . cataplasm:* for twisted ankles ('hough' is Scots dialect for 'hock'), a poultice or plaster (Gk. *cataplassein*, 'to plaster over').

44:11   *ashes:* this imagery of Dead Sea Fruit or the Apples of Sodom may be drawn from W.J. Turner's 1929 play, *The Man Who Ate the Popomack;* according to the Consul in an early draft of *uv*, he was 'a cithernhead who ate some kind of forbidden fruit and stank so badly ever after nobody wanted to come near him.'

45:1   *Another than Wordsworth:* by implication, Ernest Dowson, who is invoked at the end of the poem (see **45:14**). The literary rage of 1936 had been Margaret Mitchell's *Gone with the Wind,* alluded to indirectly here; its title is taken from Dowson's poem 'Cynara.'

45:4   *Rydal:* Rydal Mount, Wordsworth's Cumberland home.

45:5   *The Ohio:* the manuscripts indicate that the original of this ship was the *Pennsylvania,* on which Lowry left San Francisco for Mexico in September 1936.

45:7   *God's mad dog:* imagery evocative of Francis Thompson's poem, 'The Hound of Heaven' (1893).

45:11   *gules:* in heraldry, the tincture red. Aggressively imitating Keats's 'The Eve of St Agnes,' st. 25: 'And threw warm gules on Madeleine's sweet breast'; though 'gules,' an emblem of the scarlet A embroidered on Hester Prynne's gown and branded on the minister's flesh, is the last word in Hawthorne's *The Scarlet Letter.*

45:14   *Aeolus Dowson:* Ernest Dowson (1867–1900), Decadent poet of the 1890s; here likened to the Keeper of the Winds. Lowry alludes to l. 19 of Dowson's 'Cynara' *('Non sum qualis eram bonae sub regno Cynarae'):* 'I cried for madder music and for stronger wine'; and he imitates, intermittently, Dowson's use of the alexandrine line.

46:2   *'Informal'. . . infernal:* some of these misapprehensions were later to be worked into Chapter 9 of *uv,* where is also mentioned the Zebra Room and the clock proclaiming man's 'public inquiry of the hour' (266).

46:4   *'Virgil'. . . Vermont:* streets of Los Angeles, the former suggesting Lowry's spy, Vigil Forget and anticipating the reference to Dante (l. 13).

46:5   *St. Vitus:* i.e., St. Vitus Dance, or *chorea;* a disease marked by un-co-ordinated muscular twitching.

46:6   *wurlitzer. . . howitzer:* the first, a mighty organ; the second, a mighty cannon.

47:2   *Hinnom:* otherwise, *Gehenna,* a deep valley south of Jerusalem, associated in the Old Testament with sacrifices to Moloch and Baal; and later with the fiery torments of Hell.

47:3   *Nantucket:* an island near Cape Cod, once the centre of an important whaling industry (the allusion implies an education based on Melville, as Melville's had been on whaling).

47:3   *Bellevue:* a New York City hospital to which Lowry was briefly committed for alcoholism in 1935 and which forms the setting of *Lunar Caustic.*

47:4   *my first murder:* a reference to Conrad Aiken, at whose Cape Cod home Lowry had stayed in 1929 (see 13:T); whose head he had cracked open the first night there; and from whose works he had 'borrowed' liberally. In *Ultramarine* (93), Dana Hilliot admits to the same crime.

47:5   *In a windmill:* an apt description of the small two-storied houses on the Cape Cod peninsula and one used by Aiken in *Great Circle,* when Andrew Cather recalls his childhood there. Lowry often referred to Aiken's house thus, and in *uv* (113), *La Sepultura* is said to have on its roof 'a toy windmill, of the kind one saw in Cape Cod, Massachusetts.'

47:6   *a planchette:* a small heart-shaped board supported by castors, with a vertical pencil; believed to produce automatic writing when moved lightly across a surface.

47:7 *a raspail:* a café-bar on the boulevard of that name, in the Montparnasse area of Paris (see **29:T**).

47:7 *a bal musette:* after the celebrated Parisian dance-hall, in the Rue de la Montagen, Sainte Geneviève, with its celebrated accordion band; in Hemingway's *The Sun Also Rises* (Chapter 3), the place where Jake Barnes meets Brett Ashley.

47:9 *If I am dead:* in reply, the voice of Aiken, the Master (cf. **13:15–18**). The words mock Rupert Brooke's 'If I should die, think only this of me; / That there's some corner of a foreign field / That is forever England.'

47:12 *Herford:* a town in Westphalia, Germany, the location of an ancient nunnery. Beyond its contribution to a Rhineland mindscape, the point of the reference is obscure.

47:13 *lazarene:* i.e., 'leprous' (rather than 'resurrected'?); the word is not recorded in any major dictionary.

47:14 *Hebephrene:* abstracted from *hebephrenia*, a variety of schizophrenia resulting in adolescent emotional response, bizarre behaviour, and delusion; hence, an atmosphere of delirium. Aiken uses the word in *Great Circle* (**240**).

48:1 *Pigling, pigling, burning bland:* an incongruous mating of Blake's Tyger and Beatrix Potter's Pigling Bland.

V. THE COMEDIAN

TITLE: an echo of Wallace Stevens's 'The Comedian as the Letter C.'

50:T *Uruapan:* Uruapan del Progreso, in Michoácan State. The title was added later, and there is no record of Lowry having visited there.

50:1 *I met a man:* Lowry's poem is a close imitation of Baudelaire's 'Les sept viellards' ('Fourmillante cité, cité plein de rêves, / Où le spectre en plein jour raccroche le passant'), which tells how the poet on a dismal morning meets with a decrepit old man, then another and yet others, seemingly in conspiracy against him – until sick with fear and self-loathing he turns to go home. Lowry's imitation may have been encouraged by that of Rilke in *The Notebooks of Malte Laurids Brigge* (see **219:T**) as much as by the allusion in *The Waste Land* (l. 60).

51:1 *Love which comes too late:* from *All's Well That Ends Well* (5.3.57–60): 'But love that comes too late, / Like a remorseful pardon slowly carried, / To the great sender turns a sour offence, / Crying, "That's good that's gone."' Most of the sonnet was worked into *UV* (16) to define Laruelle's remorse.

51:1 *that black storm:* suggesting the darkness over the earth at the time of Christ's death; but also a Swedenborgian image of a world and a soul denied God's love.

51:6 *a surprised land:* as in *The Waste Land* (ll. 8–9): 'Summer surprised us, coming over the Starnbergersee / With a shower of rain.'

51:13 *It slakes no thirst:* an echo of Marvell's 'Clorinda and Damon' (ll. 15–16): 'Might a soul bathe there and be clean, / Or slake its Drought?'; lines cited in Eliot's 1921 essay 'Andrew Marvell' as an image of spiritual purgation and repeated as such by the Consul in UV.

52:2   *Chatterton to Chesterfield:* Thomas Chatterton (1752–70), poet and forger of the mediaeval Rowley manuscripts; admired by Wordsworth as 'the marvelous boy,' his early suicide left his promise tragically unfulfilled. Philip Stanhope, Earl of Chesterfield (1694–1773), statesman, wit, and essayist; friend of Pope and patron of letters. There was no connection between the two. Chatterton's fury at being denied patronage was directed at Walpole, in a poem beginning 'Walpole! I thought not I should ever see / So mean a Heart as thine has proved to be' and ending: 'But I shall live and Stand / By Rowley's side – when Thou art dead and damned.' Lowry seems to have confused the event with the more celebrated account of Samuel Johnson's rejection of Chesterfield's patronage, which came too late.

52:4   *evening land:* Ger. *Abendland,* a stock Romantic phrase for death.

52:9   *My love is dead:* the refrain of Chatterton's 'Mynstrelles Song': 'mie love ys dedde, / Gon to hys death-bedde, / Al under the wyllowe tree.'

53:6   *hartseye:* also, *hart-thorne,* both obsolete terms for the shrub *buckthorn,* the berries of which make a powerful carthartic.

54:1–2   *There is a tide...fortune:* an exact quotation from *Julius Caesar* (5.3.218–19), the words of Brutus to Cassius, the next two lines being: 'Omitted, all the voyage of this life / Is bound in shallows and in miseries.' Lowry is here self-critical (in relation to the Spanish Civil War) of his failure to have taken such a moment.

54:4–5   *ten feet...by fourteen:* the dimensions of the sonnet (fourteen lines of pentameter).

54:6–7   *out of tune with his time:* an echo of the opening lines of Ezra Pound's *Hugh Selwyn Mauberley* (1920): 'For three years, out of key with his time, / He strove to recuscitate the dead art / Of poetry.' Pound contemplates in HSM a similar choice of action or aestheticism.

54:7   *drunkard's rigadoon:* see **39:3**; hence, a drunken dance. Lowry later used the phrase in *Dark as the Grave* to stand for Charles Jackson's *The Lost Week End* (1944) – a novel about drinking that had stolen much of his thunder.

54:12   *a great poet:* Federico García Lorca (1898–1936), Spanish poet noted for his affirmation of life amidst the rhythms of blood and death. He had offended many Catholics with his unorthodox 'Ode to the Holy Sacrament' and by his claim that the fall of Moorish Granada to the Catholic Isabella and Ferdinand was a disaster; while his 'Ballad of the Civil Guard,' with their 'skulls of lead' and 'souls of patent leather,' was deeply resented by those so scorned. His brutal death without trial in the *madrugada* of 20 August 1936, on the outskirts of Granada, was thus the inevitable and tragic fulfilment of all he had written.

57:5   *poppies:* i.e., the poppies of Morpheus, for oblivion.

57:14   *host...haunted:* an etymological pun relating 'host' to 'ghost.'

57:14   *that whirlpool:* Lowry's poem is self-consciously written in the

'Dreamland' tradition of Poe, with whirlpool and chasm perhaps taken specifically from 'A Descent into the Maelström.'

58:2   *Marvell:* i.e., Andrew Marvell might have laughed because the prognostications of 'To His Coy Mistress' seem to have come to pass.

58:3   *Shakespeare:* no specific allusion seems intended, yet Lowry is punning on the Bard's typical use of 'physic' (i.e., 'medicine') and using the common obscenity, 'A fig!' (cf. *Othello* 1.3.322: 'Virtue! a fig!').

58:5   *the virgin Dante:* i.e., because his love for Beatrice remained metaphysical.

58:6   *My third best bed:* In his will, Shakespeare left to his wife his second-best bed, provoking much speculation about the first.

60:15   *out of Gogol:* the image is that of a Dead Soul.

61:11   *the Strauss song:* 'Allerseelen' (1882), by Richard Strauss; the eighth and final song of the Opus 10 cycle, to words by Hermann von Gilm. The song refers to the belief that on All Souls' Day (2 November, the Day of the Dead) the souls of the departed may communicate with the living and, as in Lowry's poem, depicts one trying to use this opportunity to revive a dead love affair. The poignant refrain ('as once in May') is used by the Consul in his letter to Yvonne (*UV* 45) and sets the feeling of much of the novel.

VI. THE MOON IN SCANDINAVIA

62:1   *Hikopale,* etc: a pseudo-Hawaiian accompaniment to the taropatch (Lowry's term for his ukelele), with flickers of sense thrown out: 'mokuaweoweo' is a crater of the volcano Mauna-Loa; 'Hilo' a town, also on the Big Island; while 'Oolahi' and 'walawalaki' may suggest stomach upset and seasickness – but the major chord is 'hikapale,' i.e., 'gibberish.'

64:1   *that man:* Lowry's father, a staunch Methodist, whose hopes for his son were continually disappointed. On the manuscript Lowry added some semi-fictionalized notes (he calls himself 'Martin') in which he tries to define further the ambiguous feelings of the poem, explicitly calling himself the youngest abortive beauty and saying that his father was perhaps not such a blight after all.

64:6   *the great guns:* unlike Malcolm, his three brothers had 'done their bit' in one or the other of the Great Wars.

64:7   *Morro Castle:* an American liner destroyed by fire off the New Jersey coast, 8 September 1934, with the loss of 136 lives. It was named after the *Castillo del Morro* of Havana Harbour and is invoked here because of the familiar saying that an Englishman's home is his castle; in the manuscript notes 'Martin' points out that the *Morro Castle,* as well as being a ship, was also a prison, built upon a rock.

65:T   *Redburn:* Melville's 1849 novel on the theme of a boy's first going to sea and being deeply hurt by the sustained hostility of his fellow sailors.

65:9   *de Maupassant:* Guy de Maupassant (1850–93), French writer of short stories, whose syphilis led to insanity in the last years of his life;

his 'Qui sait?' records the ecstasies and the horrors of that state.

65:15   *unvintageable:* a word used a number of times in Aiken's *Blue Voyage* as an epithet for the wine-dark sea.

65:16   *the mildew still upon its soul:* from *Redburn* (Chapter 2): 'Talk not of the bitterness of middle-age and after-life; a boy can feel all that, and much more, when upon his young soul the mildew has fallen: and the fruit, which with others is only blasted after ripeness, with him is nipped in the first blossom and bud. And never again can such blight be made good; they strike in too deep, and leave such a scar that the air of Paradise might not erase it.'

66:3   *N.B.C.:* the National Broadcasting Corporation, then the major American radio network.

66:5   *if in God you do trust:* referring to the inscription on the nickel (and all US currency) – a sentiment apparently as hollow as the pointless tune tapped with it to fill out the time. The 'tipi-tipi-tin' is the tune played by Sigbjørn's disreputable friend Stanford (Bousfield) in the *El Petate* restaurant bar, 'until it nearly drove him mad' (*Dark as the Grave* 101).

66:7   *Wrecker of gardens:* see **24:8**. He has been evicted. He is bored. But (suggests the Consul) so was Adam in his garden (*UV* 137).

66:7   *Yale yell:* to encourage the 'Bulldogs,' a pointless song of support in which the words 'Boola boola' are the most evident.

66:8   *Everest:* then unclimbed, so an unassailable challenge.

66:9   *Ixtaccihuatl, Popocatapetl:* snow-capped volcanoes dominating the Vale of Mexico; invested here (as in *UV* and Aztec mythology) with a majesty and wonder conspicuously absent from the 6-par-T-pak ginger ale.

66:10   *Quetzalcoatl:* the plumed serpent of mesoamerican mythology, the most powerful yet beneficent of the gods of Teotihuacán and, as such, epitomizing the Magic and Mysteries of Mexico.

66:10   *jail:* see **24:1**; that side of the Mexican experience was at least not boring.

66:10   *Xicotancatl:* Xicohtencatl Axayacatzin, national hero of Tlaxcala, who led the initial opposition of his people against Cortés, and though he later helped the Spaniards against the Aztecs, he never really accepted the alliance (for which distrust Cortés had him hanged in 1521).

66:11   *whaleship's blubbery education:* alluding to Ishmael's celebrated claim (*Moby Dick*, Chapter 24) that a whale-ship was his Yale College and his Harvard.

66:12   *they have all gone:* echoing Henry Vaughan's *Silex Scintillans* Part 2 (S-81): 'They are all gone into the world of light / And I alone sit lingring here; / Their very memory is fair and bright, / And my sad thoughts doth clear.'

66:13   *Xanadu:* the stately pleasure dome of Coleridge's 'Kubla Khan.'

66:13   *Belawan:* a small Indonesian town on the Straits of Malacca.

66:14   *Saigon:* now Ho Chi Minh City, then the largest and most beautiful city of French Indochina.

67:T   *Blepharipappus Glandulosis:* as defined in Margaret Armstrong's

1915 *Field Book of Western Wild Flowers* (a copy of which Lowry owned), the botanical name of the White Tidy Tips: 'A beautiful kind, eight or nine inches tall, with pale green, hairy leaves, the lower ones toothed, and a slender stem, bearing a charming flower, nearly an inch and a half across, with neat pure white rays and a bright yellow centre. This grows in mountain canyons and is widely distributed as far north as British Columbia.'

67:2   *the daisy:* Lowry's tribute to Chaucer's praise of that simple flower in his Prologue to *The Legend of Good Women.* The poem appears to have been written some years before the title was added to it.

68:T   *Edmund Wilson...Rimbaud:* Edmund Wilson (1895–1972), American literary critic; Arthur Rimbaud (1854–91), French symbolist poet, whose dramatic and chaotic career is the subject of the final chapter, 'Axel and Rimbaud,' of Wilson's *Axel's Castle* (NY 1931). Most of the detail of Lowry's poem is taken from Wilson's account of Rimbaud's erratic attempts to reach Africa (279–81).

68:1   *quarries in Cyprus:* in the spring of 1878 Rimbaud reached Cyprus and got a job as foreman in a quarry, but he caught typhoid and returned home.

68:3   *Stevedore of Marseilles:* Rimbaud had previously tried to raise the money for a trip to Alexandria by unloading cargo at Marseilles.

68:4   *the whuling Cyclades:* Rimbaud had a friend who owned a soap factory in the Cyclades, the Greek islands in the Aegean Sea. 'Whuling,' i.e., 'whirling,' is Lowry's addition, taken from p. 132 of Aiken's *Blue Voyage,* where Smith reflects on history and immortality: 'It is ourselves whose bones lie unclaimed in the deep water that washes the Icarian Rocks; or beside the Needles; or at the "whuling Cyclades." The sea is the sea – this we know – but also were not our prayers answered? for we had, after all, or we have, our "safe passage home."'

68:5   *No son:* once in Africa Rimbaud conceived the ambition of making enough money to marry a French girl and have a son who would become a famous engineer (though 'bridge' is Lowry's addition, to suggest Hart Crane's unrealized dream).

68:6   *Carlist:* Rimbaud had once enlisted in the Carlist army, i.e., in the ranks of the Spanish contenders who had originally supported the claims of Don Carlos to succeed his brother Ferdinand in 1833 and who between 1872 and 1876 were engaged in a series of wars on behalf of the former's successor.

68:6   *communist:* Rimbaud was not a Communist, but he was both a peasant and a visionary who despised the bourgeois world. The word relates Wilson's essay to more contemporary events in Spain (the Socialist opposition in the early 1930s to the Carlist Alfonso XIII, leading to the latter's exile).

68:6   *dutch soldier:* to get passage to Java, Rimbaud enlisted in the Dutch army and landed at Batavia, but he deserted at once and went home.

68:7   *David...black forest:* once when walking through the Black Forest, Rimbaud knocked Verlaine down with a club and left him unconscious.

68:8 *Livid sleeper:* contrasting Rimbaud's colourful dreams with his sordid existence (he had written a 'Sonnet des voyelles,' equating different sounds with colours). Wilson tells how Rimbaud and Verlaine were once arrested at a railway station for discussing imaginary crimes; and he frequently notes that symbolist poets tended to work by night and sleep by day.

68:9 *Absinthe mangue:* obscure; possibly Lowry's response to Wilson's remark about Rimbaud carrying Verlaine off on a vagabondage of adventure through Belgium and England. A 'Yorkshire Grey' is a kind of shepherd's thick coat, but the phrasing seems to imply an absinthe derelict at, perhaps, a Yorkshire hunt.

68:10 *Seller of key-rings:* after being robbed in Vienna, Rimbaud was obliged to sell keyrings and shoelaces in the street. On another occasion, in Germany, he sold his trunk to get to Italy.

68:11 *'Springboart & Tumplingakt':* a name taken from *Ultramarine* (69), where Dana Hilliot recalls (in bad Norwegian) a circus featuring 'Hand balances from a Springboart and Tumpling act' (i.e., springboard and tumbling); Wilson states, more simply, that Rimbaud fell in with a circus, with which he travelled as an interpreter and barker on a tour of the Scandinavian countries.

68:12 *railways to Addis Ababa:* Rimbaud traced for the first time the itinerary later taken by the Ethiopian railway to the capital.

68:13 *Ahab:* because, like the sea-captain in *Moby Dick,* Rimbaud had to have his leg amputated.

68:14 *No Onan:* in Genesis 38:8–10 Onan, married reluctantly to his brother's wife, spills his seed upon the ground, thus displeasing the Lord, who slays him also.

68:16 *fiend of the family:* Rimbaud completely disrupted Verlaine's household and family life, seduced him, was responsible for his being imprisoned, made him drunk enough to blaspheme his faith, and did him physical damage.

68:17 *balls between your shoulders:* Wilson cites an outburst from Rimbaud, in response to a friend buying books: 'You've got a ball between your shoulders that ought to take the place of books. When you put books on your shelves, the only thing to do is cover up the leprosies of old walls.'

68:19 *Harrar:* in Ethiopia, where Rimbaud in 1880 successfully set up a trading post of his own, trafficking in goods and arms and intriguing with the local kings.

68:21 *wives from Obangui-Tchari-Tchad:* Rimbaud maintained a harem of native women, carefully selected from different parts of the country, to teach him their languages. Lowry's locations, apparently remote and fanciful, issue stamps with terrible tigers on them (*Lunar Caustic,* Part 11).

68:22–3 *camels ... Sokotra:* similar details appear in the early drafts of *UV,* as part of Hugh's dream; they apparently arise from something said to Lowry when he travelled east on the *Pyrrhus* in 1927 and passed by the mysterious island of Sokotra in the Arabian Sea – in legend, an island of bliss, but guarded by fearsome scorpion-men. For the 'islands of the damned,' see 105:15.

68:24   *canals:* as in 'Peter Gaunt and the Canals,' signifying the dream in the mind of man.

68:27   *Isabelle:* the poet's sister, who had not known till he died of his poetry, but who heard him 'end his life in a sort of continual dream, saying strange things very gently.'

68:28   *Dying far from home at harvest time:* Rimbaud died in Marseilles, tended by his sister, whose absence from the family home at harvest time was bitterly resented by their mother.

69:4   *Hinnom:* Gehenna (see 47:2).

69:5–7   *Upper Slaughter... Morocco:* places chosen more or less at random, but suggestive of exile or gloom: *Upper Slaughter:* in Gloucestershire, near Bourton-on-the-water, perhaps a pun on 'Upper Volta'; *Aberdeen:* hinting at the song of exile, 'The Northern Lights of Aberdeen'; *Xochimilco:* a suburb of Mexico City, famous for its *chinampas,* or floating gardens (those of a civilization long destroyed); *Bodo:* Bodö, a Norwegian port north of the Arctic Circle, which in Grieg's *The Ship Sails On* is home for fireman Anton and his sister; *Chester-le-Street:* a depressed mining town of North Durham, also mentioned in UV (135); *Worms:* a city in Germany, associated through its paronomastic Diet with thoughts of death; *New Brighton:* on the Wirral Peninsula, a home thought from abroad; *Morocco:* both Redburn's 'Old Morocco' (his guide book to Liverpool) and Peer Gynt's desert of exile.

69:10   *pewter Timon:* Timon of Athens, in Shakespeare's play of that name, who became a total misanthropist when exiled from Athens (Lowry's hatred cannot be so unalloyed). The phrase derives from Aiken's *Great Circle* (267): 'Our little pewter Christ is now ready for the great betrayal.'

69:11   *Leander:* in Greek mythology, the youth who falls in love with Hero, priestess of Aphrodite at Sestos, and who must swim the Hellespont each night to be with her. He finally drowns in the endeavour (there is a notoriously cold current in the Bosphorus).

69:14   *Invite the soul:* a phrase given to Jacques Laruelle in the early drafts of UV; it derives from Walt Whitman's celebration of himself (1855): 'I loaf and invite my soul.'

69:14   *Borealian:* from Boreas, the Greek god of the North Wind; hence, pertaining to the Borealis or Northern Lights. Again, the theme of bare, alien exile and the Hyperborean longing for the White Dream (see 15:56–7).

70:1   *the fable:* as in Aesop, the story of the boy who cried 'Wolf!' so many times that when the wolf did come nobody would believe him.

70:8   *Tortu:* Tartu, Estonia (see 20:12). Here, perhaps, a way of concealing any direct reference to Hermann Hesse's *Steppenwolf* that may lurk behind the final lines.

71:1   *King Lear... Sophocles:* Shakespeare's *King Lear* (1604) and the *Oedipus Rex* of Sophocles (496–405 BC); the two are often associated because of the common themes of cruelty and blindness.

71:3   *Cordelia:* Lear's rejected but loyal daughter; the type of goodness.

71:5, 6   *feverfew…agatha: feverfew:* a corruption of 'feather-foil,' a feathery-leaved plant *(pyrethrum parthenium)* used to cure an upset stomach; *agatha:* more correctly, *agathosma* (Gk. 'good smell'), a shrub of the rue family. When Lear goes mad he runs about crowned with weeds and flowers.

71:7   *Priam:* King of Troy during the Trojan wars. An elliptical allusion, likening the restoration of his shepherd son, Paris (who had been exposed as a child), to the similar sparing of the infant Oedipus by the shepherd ordered to kill him; both acts were to have disastrous consequences in later years.

71:9   *Each hour a tinker:* i.e., bringing nearer the inevitable *damn*ation (a somewhat hermetic pun) as the Greek ships cross the sea, coming to the kingdom of Troy (with intimations of disaster in the phrase 'kingdom come').

71:11   *Jocasta:* wife and mother of Oedipus, who unwittingly fulfilled the Pythonic prediction that he would kill his father and marry his mother.

71:13   *Four thousand yards of incandescent pain:* i.e., the distance from the palace of Thebes, where Oedipus blinded himself, to the refuge of Colonus, to which, guided by his daughter Antigone, he must painfully make his way.

71:14   *Smell your way to Dover:* Regan's cruel words to Gloucester, following his blinding (*King Lear* 3.7.93–4).

71:15   *bobelin:* otherwise 'bobolyne,' a rare form of 'bobolink' (a blithe songbird), with the meaning (as defined by the OED) of 'a fool, a gaby.'

71:16   *No more sing:* cf. the words of Lear to Cordelia (5.2.8–9): 'Come, let's away to prison. / We two alone will sing like birds i' the cage.'

71:17   *from the great bison's bung:* a phrase repeated in the first edition of *Ultramarine* (1933) in the surreal context of animals defecating all over the deck; the revised text (184) ruins the effect by changing 'bung' to 'dung.'

71:18   *Cannot you hear the beach:* cf. Edgar's words to Gloucester, when his father, who wishes to fling himself from the cliffs, doubts if they have reached the shore: 'Hark, do you hear the sea?' (4.5.4).

72:1(var)   *for Nordahl Grieg:* see **12:T**; the sentiment, as well as the imagery of Lowry's poem, as related to the sailors' nostalgia for home in *The Ship Sails On;* and the 'white house' resemble that of Benjamin's friend Sivert, near Christiania.

72:9   *Pandemonium:* in Milton's *Paradise Lost* (1:756), the capital of Hell.

73:2   *University City:* the *ciudad universitaria,* or university area, on a hilltop in northwest Madrid, which was in November 1936 the scene of fierce fighting between the attacking Nationalists and entrenched Republicans during the Battle of Madrid.

73:5   *Sommerfield:* John Sommerfield (b. 1908), author of *Volunteer in Spain* (1937), which tells of the battle for University City.

73:5 *John Cornford:* Rupert John Cornford (1915–36), Communist and poet, who took part in the battle for University City and was shortly afterwards killed in action. *Volunteer in Spain* is dedicated to his memory.

73:6 *hashish in the library:* John Sommerfield tells how he and others (including John Cornford) were holed up in the *Philosophy and Letters* section of the library, behind bulletproof barricades of Indian metaphysics and German philosophy, incongruously reading de Quincey (the *Lake Poets* rather than *The Opium Eater,* but hence the reference to hashish).

73:8 *Grecian Urn:* John Keats's 'Ode on a Grecian Urn' celebrates action caught in art and thus rendered timeless and immortal.

73:9 *twelfth street . . . rags:* allusion to the 'Twelfth Street Rag,' a 1916 jazz composition by Euday L. Bowman, best known in the 1927 version by Louis Armstrong.

73:12 *plumed serpent:* i.e., serpentine; but remembering the hearts sacrificed to the gods of Mexico and Spain.

73:15 *Michigan 1915:* uncertain; perhaps, a call to Margerie, who was born in Michigan.

74:2 *Neoshe:* the *Neosho,* a river running through Kansas from Oklahoma to Missouri.

74:2 *Wabash:* a river in Indiana.

74:2 *Wormwood:* the star of Revelation 8:11, which, falling upon the third part of the rivers and the fountains of waters, turned them bitter.

74:4 *Narkeeta:* uncertain; perhaps the *Narkita,* an Algonquin tribe of the Massachusetts area.

74:4 *Barnegat:* not an Indian tribe, but an Indian word for a bay on the New Jersey coastline.

74:4 *Massasoit:* a name meaning 'Big Chief'; specifically, the leader of the Wampanoag Indians, an Algonquin tribe of the Plymouth area, whose friendliness towards the new settlers in the mid-seventeenth century did little for his people's chances of survival.

74:5(var) *lobelia syphilitica:* the largest of the lobelias, with a crowded spike of blue flowers and light green leaves, flourishing on clayey soil near water; it is mentioned elsewhere by Lowry, who was obscurely terrified by the name.

74:9 *Homeric errors:* an ugly *Helen;* a *Menelaus* nearby; an *Agamemnon* bereft of all majesty; a proud *Paris* reduced (like Lord Jim's *Patna*) to carrying pilgrims; a *Pandarus* together with a *Troilus* and *Cressida* . . . in locations, such as *Kow-loon* (mainland Hong Kong) and *Perim* (a barren island at the entrance to the Red Sea), deprived of any class or classical dignity. The names of the ships (though the last three are invented and the *Paris* an intruder) are those of the Blue Funnel Line (Alfred Holt & Co., Liverpool), to which Lowry's *Pyrrus* was kin; and Lowry's poem seems to be an ironic imitation of John Masefield's 'Ships,' which mentions 'the *Alfred Holt*'s blue smoke-stacks, down the stream' and concludes: 'They mark our passage as a race of men, / Earth will not see such ships as these again.'

75:4   *The Devil's Kitchen:* Pen-y-Pass, a well-known climb in the Welsh Mountains.

75:14   *at the end of a rope:* behind these lines lies the remorse that haunted Lowry for much of his life following the suicide of his friend Paul Fitte on 15 November 1929 (hence, perhaps, the reference to 'lost Novembers'). Fitte died by gas rather than hanging, but the latter is the motif recurrent in Lowry's writing when he alludes to the incident (notably, in the 'Peter Cordwainer' memories of *October Ferry*).

VII. THE ROAR OF THE SEA AND THE DARKNESS

TITLE: the final words of Chapter 2 of Grieg's *The Ship Sails On,* as the *Mignon* sets out to sea. Lowry also uses the phrase at the end of Chapter 5 of *Ultramarine.*

76:T   *Iron Thoughts:* Lowry noted on the manuscript: 'Iron City – pun on title for a long short story by Lowell Thomas.' Thomas, an editor for *Scribner's Commentator*, 1937–42, was better known as a teller of Great True Adventures, such as *With Lawrence in Arabia* (1924), *Count Luckner, the Sea-Devil* (1927), and *Woodfill of the Regulars* (1929).

76:11   *Yet ships themselves are iron:* a selfconscious echo of the earlier poem to Nordahl Grieg (see **12:2**).

77:2   *Dimitrios N. Bogliazides:* the name (a perfect pentameter) obviously fascinated Lowry, for he refers to it elsewhere a number of times. In *Ultramarine* (72), she is described as 'an old Greek bastard of a tramp steamer, that piled up on Lundy in the end, but which had sailed in 1923 bringing a cargo of timber from Archangel to Garston' (the Helsinki point of departure seems more probable).

77:3   *Lloyds:* Lloyd's of London, international bankers and insurers, whose Registry of Shipping (established 1760) is the world's largest and sets standards of basic seaworthiness and conditions of loading. According to the registry, vessels laden with buoyant timber may be loaded deeper than other vessels.

77:12   *No sweet wood:* a vision of Masefield's Quinquireme of Nineveh, with its cargo of 'Sandalwood, cedarwood, and sweet white wine' ('Cargoes,' l. 5).

78:1   *camion:* Sp. 'truck'; but in Mexico more commonly a bus.

78:9   *sampan:* a Chinese riverboat with sails and oars.

78:10   *Stalin's Samarkand:* Samarkand, in the Uzbek Republic of Soviet Russia, is a romantic city of turrets and tiles on the Old Silk Road; Joseph Stalin (1879–1953), born in Georgia (remotely nearby), had instituted a reign of terror throughout Russia; thus, a grim romance.

78:13   *Columbus . . . Cuba:* on his first voyage to the Americas (1492), Columbus reached Cuba but thought it an outlying promontory of China. He did not reach the North American mainland, and Lowry sees this as an irony inescapably part of the triumph. In the drafts of *Dark as the Grave* Sigbjørn uses the image and adds: 'and like Columbus also it is possible I am leaving a heritage of destruction.'

79:1   *The Harkness Light!:* unidentified; not listed in the definitive *Lights and Tides of the World,* so surely invented for the sake of the final pun (see **79:31**).

79:2   *unction:* sanctimonious compunction; but the suggestion of *extreme unction* is not absent from what follows. The word 'unctious' is used frequently in *Moby Dick* in its literal sense of 'oily.'

79:3   *a man is killed:* cf. l. 30, for the fatal interval between the blow and the sound.

79:4   *four bells:* i.e., half-way through the watch.

79:15   *Jonah:* in the Book of Jonah, after the whale has swallowed the reluctant prophet and spewed him out upon the shore (hence, l. 14, 'vomitless'), Jonah finally obeys God and preaches to the Ninevites; but is angry when God forgives them. He leaves the city and sits under a gourd plant, in which the Lord has placed a worm; and his pity for the gourd lets him understand how he must feel towards the Ninevites. In Chapter 9 of *Moby Dick,* Father Mapple takes for his text the Book of Jonah.

79:18   *crowned:* i.e., drowned (see the Marston pun, **21:13**); making reference to the traditional belief that drowning men, who also clutch at straws, find their entire lives flashing before them as they sink for the third time.

79:24   *plangency:* sadness and melancholy (a favourite Lowry word). In Aiken's *Blue Voyage* (85), Demarest reflects: 'All language therefore must develop out of the sound of crying – it is probably most affecting when *plangent* for that reason.'

79:27   *Roll on:* apparently alluding to Byron's *Childe Harolde* 179; but in fact closely echoing Chapter 35 of *Moby Dick:* 'Childe Harolde not unfrequently perches himself upon the mast-head of some luckless disappointed ship, and in moody phrase ejaculates: – "Roll on, thou deep and dark blue ocean, roll! / Ten thousand blubber-hunters sweep over thee in vain."' Melville's point is that such romantic melancholy while at the masthead (in Lowry's instance, the wheel) leads the absent-minded youth to lose his identity in the deep and mystic ocean but catches no whales.

79:30   *the fated sight and fatal sound:* clearly, the Harkness light and then the noise of the rocks or reef (the interim insufficient to avoid the danger); but in terms of Melville's masthead (and the earlier reference to Jonah), the brief but fatal lapse of time between the sighting and death of a whale ('sound' having here, as in Chapter 61 of *Moby Dick,* implications of the whale's final bloody agony).

79:31   *Now leave the world to Harkness and to me:* an echo of the final line of Thomas Gray's 'Elegy Written in a Country Churchyard' (1750): 'And leave the world to darkness and to me.'

80:T   *a Metallurgy:* in an unpublished letter to Conrad Aiken (9 April 1940), Lowry likens the act of poetical conception to the processes of metallurgy.

81:1   *Christ, slashed with an axe:* literally, a crude wooden statue of Christ, of the kind often found in small Mexican churches (often described by Lowry as 'humped,' with the Hunchback of Notre Dame distantly in mind); figuratively, an allusion to Christ's wounds and agony.

81:12 *vicarious exculpator:* i.e., offering forgiveness in the name of God, even as Christ advocated (Matthew 18:22): 'I say not unto thee, Until seven times: but, Until seventy times seven.'

82:2 *Popocatepetl:* see **66:9**; as in *uv*, the snowy peak and burning heart symbolizing man's aspiring and destructive capacities.

82:12–13 *white birds...Tchechov:* the white birds suggest, in neo-Platonic terms, the escape of the soul from the material world; the reference to Chekhov combines the destruction of innocence in *The Seagull* (1896) with Sonia's last speech in *Uncle Vanya* (1899): 'We shall rejoice and look back on our present misfortune with a feeling of tenderness, with a smile – and we shall rest.'

83:5 *Archangel:* a Russian city on the Dvina River and White Sea; frequently used by Lowry (notably, in the fragments of *In Ballast to the White Sea*) as a destination of the frozen soul (see **15:107**).

83:5 *Gomorrah:* in Genesis 13:10, one of the Cities of the Plain, destroyed by the Lord for its iniquities.

83:8 *Canberra:* the federal capital of Australia; here, a fixed point in an empty desert (the use of 'archipelago' is, as it were, singularly inappropriate).

84:1 *he:* James Wolfe (1727–59), commander of the British army that captured Quebec from the Marquis de Montcalm in 1759 on the Plains of Abraham next to the citadel. Both commanders died.

84:1 *those lines:* Thomas Gray's 'Elegy Written in a Country Churchyard' (1750). Wolfe is reported as having made this remark the night before the battle as he was reading Gray's poem (his personal copy of which is now at the University of Toronto).

84:2 *Trumpington Street:* alluding to Gray's Cambridge background. Trumpington Street, which runs past The Leys and Lowry's St. Catharine's College, also goes by Peterhouse, where Gray wrote the poem.

84:5 *Cortes:* Hernando Cortés (1485–1547), Spanish conquistador, who, with a small band of adventurers greedy for gold, reduced to rubble the Aztec civilization at Tenochtitlán, thereby ruthlessly carving his name into the annals of history.

84:10 *The path led to the grave?:* Gray's melancholy conclusion (l. 36) to the boast of heraldry and the pomp of power: 'The paths of glory lead but to the grave.' Hugh comes to a similar conclusion (*uv* 108).

84:11 *Abram Heights:* the Plains of Abraham, see **84:1**. To scale the bluff a path had to be found; and Lowry imagines Wolfe, inspired by Gray, climbing it by night, towards his death.

84:11 *lupine scavenger:* i.e., the Gray Wolfe.

85:14 *no titanic case:* referring to the sinking of the 'unsinkable' *Titanic,* on the memorable night of 14–15 April 1912, following its collision with an iceberg in the North Atlantic.

86:1 *Orpheus:* in Greek mythology, the poet and minstrel who lost his

wife Eurydice to the sting of an adder and descended into the under-
world to find her. Hades agreed to let Eurydice follow her husband
out, provided he refrain from looking back at her till she was in the
sunlight, but at the critical moment he glanced around and had to re-
turn to the world alone.

87:1   *The Lighthouse:* see the **Title** note to this volume; other images of
destruction are here drawn to it.

87:10   *Chang:* the image of 'kites' (planes) leads to that of a Chinese air-
man pursued by his enemy (the Chinese Civil War was then taking
place).

87:12   *polygonous:* with multiple eyes (see **41:3**). The variant, 'epicene
Whangpoo,' with its overtones of the degenerate Chinese Imperial
Court, may have been deleted as historically unsound.

87:14   *the unshot albatross:* the Ancient Mariner did not have to shoot
the bird, but once he had done so, the curse was irrevocable. For
Lowry, a recurrent image of 'the abrogation of responsibility and wis-
dom' (SL 281). Such birds are said to embody the souls of dead sailors.

87:15   *Icarus:* in Greek mythology, the son of the craftsman Dedalus,
who with his father flew to freedom on waxen wings, but invited self-
destruction by flying too close to the sun.

89:T   *Tashtego:* In *Moby Dick,* an American Indian harpooner, whose
final defiant act as the *Pequod* sinks into the watery abyss is to nail a
red banner to the top of its mast.

89:2   *a world that sinks:* alluding to the traditional notion of the ship as
a microcosm of (here) a world that sinks like Atlantis beneath the wa-
ters of the Deep.

89:14   – *Yet regard, regard:* an imitation of Melville's impassioned
prose, as Ishmael draws attention to Tashtego's symbolic act.

90:6   *Forlorn:* ironically echoing Keats's 'Ode to a Nightingale' (ll.
81–2): 'Forlorn! the very word is like a bell, / To toll me back from
thee to my sole self!'

90:15   *The 'Seven Sea's spray':* the imagined ship of 'Potato' Jones (see
15:139), running the Bilbao blockade. In real life Jones's ship was the
Marie Llewellyn and did not break through, whereas the *Seven Seas
Spray,* under one Captain Roberts, did reach Bilbao. In one of Lowry's
Mexican notebooks the two events are conflated.

90:33   *Saturn:* wrongly identified by the Romans with the Greek god
Kronos and associated with the Saturnalia as Lord of Misrule; later
identified in astronomy and esoteric thought as the ruler of the death
planet, under whose auspices evil is born.

90:39   *sophistry:* Lowry may intend the logical term 'maieutic,' derived
from the Greek word for midwife and applied to the Socratic method.

91:8(var)   *the teeth of death:* here, an allusion to the myth of Cadmus,
in which dragons' teeth were sown and armed men sprang up.

91:9   *Nor shall death pass:* echoing the cry of *no paserán,* 'they shall not
pass,' the Republican cry of defiance made famous by Dolores Ibarruri
('la Pasionaria') during the Spanish Civil War.

91:12   *the dead ride hard:* a phrase used in the early drafts of UV, where it is associated with Nathaniel Hawthorne's short story, 'The Grey Champion,' which asserts the need for vigilance in defence of democracy.

91:14(var)   *Fist clenched:* i.e., in the Republican salute.

92:3   *lamptrimmer:* 'Lamps,' the officer responsible for tending and trimming the oil-fuelled lamps for the correct navigational lighting at night.

92:3   *thrums:* Lowry's ubiquitous word for the noise of a ship's engines, borrowed from Aiken's *Blue Voyage.*

92:12   *wormwood:* see **72:2**; hence, the star of personal bitterness.

93:1   *Cain shall not slay Abel:* the first murder (Genesis 4:8), for which, in popular legend and in Dante, Cain was banished to the moon. Lowry's phrasing is taken from Grieg's *The Ship Sails On* (146), where Benjamin Hall, wishing to be bitter, is put to shame by his friend's smile: 'Cain could not slay Abel today.'

93:2   *Nor Adam stagger:* i.e., Fall.

93:3   *Ishmael:* the narrator of *Moby Dick,* named for the son of Abram by the Egyptian maid Hagar, a wild man with every man's hand against him (Genesis 16:12), who is cast out into the wilderness (21:14). In New Bedford, where Ishmael goes when he decides to ship out, he is obliged to share a bed with the cannibal harpooner, Queequeg.

93:3   *28th Street:* in New York City. All the evidence suggests that Lowry has in mind Melville's 'last address' (that phrase, and its intended reference to Melville's death, being the working title of what was posthumously published as *Lunar Caustic*). Melville in fact lived (and died) at 104 26th Street.

93:5   *a Hoboken garboon:* Hoboken is a city on the New Jersey side of the Hudson River, opposite Lower Manhattan; invariably associated by Lowry with dirt and dinginess. The word 'garboon,' not recorded in any dictionary, appears at the beginning of Aiken's *Great Circle:* 'The familiar smell of soot and tobacco smoke, of stuffy plush and foul spittoons – garboons!' It recurs at the end of Chapter 1, again with spittoons, and in approximate range (on the page) of 'the Hoboken gambit.'

93:10   *the forsaken one:* a reference to Christ's parable of the lost sheep (Matthew 18:10–14); referred to again at l. 26, where it is said that the Good Shepherd rejoices more over the one lost sheep saved than the ninety-nine that did not stray.

93:16   *Loki:* in Scandinavian mythology, the god of fire and mischief; not usually associated so explicitly with dragons. Hence, a likely pillaging from John Masefield's 'Badon Hill' (ll. 1–2): 'Loki the Dragon killer mustered men / To harry through the western isles agen' (where 'Loki' is a Viking raider, and the 'Dragon' his ship).

93:17   *the lonely trimmer:* a coal-passer, the least prestigous member of a ship's crew, whose duties include bringing coal to the furnaces, hauling and dumping ashes, and chipping the scale from the boilers. For Lowry, explicitly, a Dante-like image of the estranged soul.

93:18   *one bell:* the first half-hour of a miserable four.

93:24   *Pentecost:* in the Christian calendar, the commemoration of the time (Acts 2:1–5) that the spirit of God descended to earth and invested with Pentecostal fire the tongues of the living. In reply to Lowry's wondering what he could have meant by 'recommemorate' (SL 412), Ralph Gustafson told him that the poem was a plea for compassion for this wrung world, a recommendation for a renewal of Pentecost for the oppressed on the part of the poets of God's mercy, who cry out to the word of non-compassion that there is no time – but more than a plea, an assertion that there must be compassion lest anguish be all (SL 452).

93:27   *a warm overcoat:* alluding to Gogol's short story, 'The Overcoat' (1841), the tale of a poor government clerk who nurses the ambition to save enough out of his meagre salary for a new overcoat to replace his tattered old one, only to be relieved of it by thieves on the first evening he wears it out.

93:28   *city of dreadful night:* see **24:1**.

93:30   *the reckoning:* i.e., the hour of execution. The word is used in UV (330) for the addition of a drinker's bill.

94:T   *Fyrbøterer:* Nor. 'firemen' (pl. of 'fyrbøter'); with specific reference to Nordahl Grieg's ship's firemen (see **12:T**).

94:5   *the twelve to four:* the loneliest watch of the night.

94:10   *the Magellan:* the Straits of Magellan, between the South American mainland and Tierra del Fuego.

94:12   *'I have worn my jacknife...':* Lowry notes on the manuscripts that this was reported true of John Masefield, and in *Ultramarine* (94), Dana Hilliot makes the same comment of himself, adding: 'what my ship-mates called being on the horns of a Demelia.' The quotation has not been more precisely identified, but in tone and sentiment it is not dissimilar to others in Masefield's *Salt-Water Ballads.*

94:13   *hull-down:* sufficiently distant that only the superstructure of the ship is visible, the rest being below the declivity of the horizon.

94:14(var)   *Saint Pierre...Monserrat:* Monserrat is a rugged volcanic island in the Leeward group of the West Indies, apparently visited by Lowry in 1929 on his way to stay with Conrad Aiken; it is described in *Ultramarine* (174) as 'a God-damned place' where a hurricane blows everything down each year. Saint Pierre would be the town in nearby Martinique; here evoked in the name of St. Peter, patron saint of fishermen and those who go down to the sea in ships.

94:16   *Hatteras...Ararat...Cedric...Cobh: Hatteras:* the dangerous cape off North Carolina (see **38:1**).

94:16   *Mount Ararat:* an extinct volcano in northeast Turkey, traditionally the final resting place of Noah's Ark.

94:16(var)   *the Cedric lies at Cobh:* the *Cedric* was the White Star Cunard liner on which Lowry sailed in 1929 from Boston back to England and on which some years earlier Conrad Aiken had written a chapter of *Blue Voyage* (Day 108). *Cobh* is a port in Ireland's County Cork with an excellent anchorage and docking facilities, which by special agreement was to be garrisoned by the British until 1938.

95:T *R.L.S.:* Robert Louis Stevenson (1850–94), Scottish author of *Treasure Island, Kidnapped,* and other tales of adventure, who spent his last years in distant Samoa. The romance is here sadly lacking.

95:3 *girls, laughing in linked quintets:* a vision not entirely without its terrors (see 12:13).

95:7 *lineaments:* literally, outlines; but used in a Blake-like manner, as in the *Gnomic Verses* (17:4): 'What is it men in women do require? / The lineaments of gratified desire.'

95:12 *Christian from Despond:* in John Bunyan's *Pilgrim's Progress* (1678), Christian must pass through the Slough of Despond before he can continue to the Celestial City.

95:13 *Friday's print:* in Daniel Defoe's *Robinson Crusoe* (1719), the marooned Crusoe discovers the footprint of the native Friday upon the sands and is suddenly conscious that he is not alone in his world.

96:T *Dostoievski:* Feodor Mikhailovitch Dostoevsky (1821–81), whose *Crime and Punishment* shapes the feeling (rather than any specific detail) of Lowry's poem.

96:1 *The world of ghosts:* i.e., Raskolnikov's sense, having murdered the old woman, of living in a spectral world. As manuscript evidence suggests, the fairground scene of *UV*, Chapter 7, was written to create precisely this sense of unreality.

96:5 *life on the short wave:* used in a sense similar to the 'poltergeists of the ether' (*UV* 157) and hence implying in the spectrum imperceptible to ordinary senses the existence of other forces;but also anticipating the imagery of the sea ('Life on the Ocean Wave') in the lines to follow.

96:6 *aching for Caesar:* i.e., wishing to be one of the conspirators who murdered Julius Caesar.

96:6 *trundled cedar:* i.e., coffins (Japan being then at war with China).

96:8 *Child bride:* enormities taking place in an atmosphere of childlike fantasy, as in the dream world of Debussy's *Pelleas and Mélisande* (1902), where the child Mélisande is taken by Golaud from forest to castle. Arkel comments at the end of 4.1: 'si j'étais Dieu j'aurais pité du coeur des hommes.'

97:T *The roar of the Sea and the Darkness:* see **Title** note to Section VII.

97:6 *Gaunt Forget:* Lowry's two personae in one compound ghost.

97:12 *sweet timber:* see 77:12.

97:14 *Climbed on board and was seen no more:* a fate intentionally reminiscent of that of the anonymous protagonist in B. Traven's *The Death Ship* (1926): a New Orleans sailor stranded in Antwerp, he is further stripped of possessions and identity before signing on the *Yorikke* – a death ship that the owners intend to sink for the insurance money – and entering a world where his name and being are wiped out and lost forever.

Uncollected Poems, 1933–9

98:4 *an aspen:* a type of poplar, especially *populus tremula,* the leaves of which flutter in the slightest wind. In Christian tradition the cross was made of aspen wood, and the aspen trembled thereafter.

98:8   *a horned curve:* Venus, star of the morning, may in its crescent phase be darkened on the side away from the rising sun so that its illuminated side appears as a crescent, thinning out to two 'horns.' In an unpublished letter to Conrad Aiken (3 May 1940) Lowry admitted taking the Venus notes from one of Margerie's astronomy books.

98:14   *To keep the sun between ourselves and love:* in *Dark as the Grave* (45) Sigbjørn comments on this image: 'He reflected that she was his wife and one aspect of that gloom could come from love itself, should he allow himself to brood upon its awful seriousness. For it was with love, as with the phases of Venus. When Venus stands between the sun and ourselves upon earth she is dark. It is only beyond the sun that she is brightest and at the full. Thus it follows that we should attempt anyhow, when well we may, to keep the sun between ourselves and love.'

99:2   *the great circle:* the shortest distance between two global points, but because of the earth's curvature not a straight line on a map; to sail the route it is necessary to change compass points constantly. Also, the novel *Great Circle* (1933) by Conrad Aiken, in which Andrew Cather, drunk and reeling, seeks the way back to his heart.

99:4   *widows in Nantucket:* in Chapter 132 of *Moby Dick,* Ahab in a rare moment of emotion regrets the desolation of solitude that this life has been and his absence from the sweet young girl he wedded: 'wife? wife? – rather a widow with her husband alive! Ay, I widowed that poor girl when I married her, Starbuck.'

99:9   *well-deck:* a space of lower elevation on the main deck between either the forecastle and bridge or bridge and poop deck.

99:10   *the disjointed derrick:* a recurrent image (see **105:20** and **118:8**), deriving in part from Grieg's *The Ship Sails On* (120), where a derrick comes adrift and plunges back and forward with terrific force in the well; but also to be found in *Blue Voyage* (112), where there is a similar recollection of a falling derrick.

99:14   *Judas, swinging in masthead:* the nautical equivalent of the suicide of Judas, by hanging from the yardarm (the fate of Melville's Billy Budd).

99:16   *drogher:* from a Dutch word meaning 'a drier,' originally a small vessel in which herrings were dried; most commonly, a West Indian coastal vessel, mentioned a number of times in Melville's *Redburn,* bringing goods out to a larger vessel; here, more simply, the small boats of the pearlfishers.

99:16   *in reverse the philosopher's stone:* the goal of the ancient alchemists was to achieve the Stone, by agency of which base metals might be transmuted to gold and imperfect man made spiritually whole. Here, transmutation in reverse, as the magical scene of lights and circles and pearl fishers gives way to childhood fears and memories: the pearl fishers circle the square (instead of, impossibly, squaring the circle), and the mystery of the stone is revealed to be only the rock of a foundering reality. For a similar return to reality, see **27:14**.

100:T   *For Under the Volcano:* a title which, like the final line, was apparently added to the manuscript some time after the rest of the poem had been written, and suggesting thus a tenuous relationship to the novel. In the manuscripts of *Dark as the Grave,* where another version is given, it is described as 'A fragment of a poem – apparently written in Mexico City, in a seafood restaurant and bar.'

100:1   *A dead lemon:* in the manuscript of *Dark as the Grave* (210), Sigbjørn defines 'the extraordinary concentration of those lines, the amazing narrowing down to a single point of thought, so that on one occasion a dead lemon in an ashtray had taken on the aspect of a cowled old woman shivering sitting in the cold rain snow.'

100:6   *Hoboken:* the New Jersey garboon (see 93:5); the exile's vision of a girl's face is an image recurrent in the early poetry and *Ultramarine.*

100:10   *teredos:* i.e., 'ship-worms,' worm-like molluscs that bore into and infest submerged wood. Lowry probably took the word from the OED, where one citation compares the body's infirmities to those of the soul, 'which being a better piece of timber, hath the more teredines breeding in it.'

100:13   *mole:* in Mexican cooking, a black and bitter chocolate-based sauce, sometimes spiced with nuts and chilis, and served on top of enchiladas and other dishes.

100:15   *mariachis:* originally, musicians from Jalisco; more usually, itinerant musicians who play popular music, typically in cafés.

100:15–16   *the beaked bird of maguey:* i.e., the effects of tequila.

100:19   *horripilation:* from L. *horripilare,* 'to bristle with hairs'; another word borrowed from Aiken's *Blue Voyage* (121), where it is defined as 'when your hair walks backward on cold feet,' i.e., as one has a sudden and unlovely intimation of the future.

100:20   *half-buried men:* see 26:8 for the echo of Ben Jonson; more directly, suggesting the huge Olmec statues of southern Mexico, which invariably depict only the upper parts of their anthropomorphic gods.

100:21   *live with Canute:* i.e., unable to keep time (and tide) at bay.

100:30   *stuffed Leopardis:* punning upon the name of Giacomo Leopardi (1795–1837), Italian Romantic poet, whose works were imbued with a chronic pessimism. James Thomson's 'The City of Dreadful Night' is dedicated to the memory of Leopardi, 'A Spirit as Lofty, / A Genius as Intense / With a yet more tragic doom.'

100:31   *Pyre of Bierce and springboard of Hart Crane:* see 42:1; he numbers himself here among those authors who have died in Mexico.

100:36   *'A Corpse should be transported by express':* the opening words of Chapter 2 of *UV,* overheard by Yvonne as she approaches the Bella Vista on the morning of the Day of the Dead.

101:6   *'brutal':* the spiky maguey cactus (from which tequila is distilled) is throughout *UV* a constant reminder of Mexican history; in the drafts of *Dark as the Grave* Sigbjørn has a vision of a crucified Christ with maguey at the foot of the cross.

101:8   *Bonn...Bootle: Bonn:* in 1928 Lowry spent some time at

Weber's School of Modern German in Bonn, where he avoided contagion by the language; *Bootle:* a depressed dockside area of north Liverpool, celebrated in the Consul's rhyme (*UV* 192): 'Plingen, plangen, aufgefangen' (see 273:1). The irony ('Nemesis, a pleasant ride') may be pertinent here.

101:20 *vanished along the Rhine:* since the first scribblings of this poem date from Lowry's early Mexican period (he seems to have visited Oaxaca by train in February 1937), the reference is likely to have been to Hitler's remilitarization of the Rhineland (1936); but the line was to prove prophetic when on 22 September 1938, at Bad Gödesburg near Bonn, a pact was made between Hitler and Chamberlain, ratifying the subjugation of Czechoslovakia and allowing the Fascist troops to stay in Spain (hence Hugh's bitterness, *UV* 106).

102:1 *poursuivant:* a follower or attendant (used here in verbal form). The term is heraldic, with the sense of Midnight denying a boon.

102:13 *the white whale:* i.e., Moby Dick, as a destructive obsession.

102:19 *Zenith:* an American manufacturer of electrical and other appliances; but also referring back to l. 2: 'finality of twelve.'

102:22 *dived for moons:* the Chinese poet Li Po (701–62) is supposed to have drowned one night while trying to embrace the reflection of the moon. He figures in a number of Aiken's poems.

103:8 *sans coat . . . sans hat:* echoing Jaques's conclusion, *As You Like It* (2.7.139), that all the world's a stage, whereon the seven ages of man lead but to second childishness and oblivion: 'Sans teeth, sans eyes, sans taste, sans everything.'

103:11 *through customs:* placing the poem into the context of Melville's life: as his reputation declined and poverty mounted, he was obliged to seek other means of support, and in 1866, aged forty-seven, he found a place as inspector (No. 75) in the Customs House of New York, a post described earlier in *Redburn* as 'a most inglorious one; indeed worse than driving geese to water' (Lewis Mumford, *Herman Melville*, 212).

104:T *Herr Toller:* Ernst Toller (1883–1939), a Jewish pacifist and radical, who was associated (as was B. Traven) with the short-lived Communist government in Bavaria, November 1918; he was imprisoned in 1919 for five years, during which time he wrote *Der Swalbenbuch* (1924), inspired by the efforts of swallows to nest in his cell. He resented the brutality of the Nazi regime and, a few weeks after the German invasion of Czechoslovakia, committed suicide.

104:2 *aspen:* see 98:4.

104:16 *Hoppla, wir leben!:* Ger. 'Hurray, we are alive!' (or, in the 1935 translation, 'Hoppla, Such is Life!'); the title of a play by Toller, first performed in Hamburg in 1927.

105:1 *the roar of the sea and the darkness:* from Grieg's *The Ship Sails On* (see **Note** to Section VII); but acknowledging such 'poets' as Conrad (whose *Typhoon* is alluded to, l. 7), and Melville (poet of the bloody harpoon and the sperm whale, l. 10).

105.5 *Inchcape Rock:* alluding to Robert Southey's poem, 'The Inchcape Rock' (1803), which tells of a bell placed by the good Abbot at a hidden rock and how it was cut loose and thrown away by the wicked Sir Ralph the Rover, who later came to grief, 'in the righteous judgement of God,' upon that very rock.

105:5 *Harkness:* see 79:1; again, the echo of 'darkness.'

105:6 *Start Point:* a headland on the Devon coast, known affectionately as 'The Start,' since it is often the last point of England visible.

105:9 *tarpon:* the Jewfish, *megalops atlanticus,* a giant herring (up to six feet and two hundred pounds) found in the warmer waters of the western Atlantic, and noted as a game fish.

105:11 *Good Hope:* the Cape of Good Hope, in South Africa; the name was given by Bartolemeu Dias when he rounded it in 1488.

105:13 *Mazatlan:* the city of Mazatlán in the state of Sinaloa; the largest Mexican port on the Pacific coast.

105:15 *Formosa:* i.e., the Formosa Straits, separating Taiwan from China, where Conrad's Captain MacWhirr does battle with the typhoon.

105:15 *the island of the damned:* Lowry's inversion of the Hesperides, the Fortunate Isles, and associated for him particularly with Sokotra (see 68:22–3), though he was not unaware of the images of damnation in *The Encantadas* (Melville's sketches of the Galapagos Islands).

105:16 *shawled islets:* cf. 13:18: 'And dismal islands shawled in snow.'

105:18 *huarache:* a kind of Mexican sandal with a slinged back and woven upper.

105:19 *dhow:* a lateen-rigged Arabian sailing vessel of the Indian Ocean.

105:20 *the plunging derrick:* an image derived from Grieg's *The Ship Sails On* (see 99:10).

105:21 *the Indian Ocean:* suggesting the deceptive calm just before the *Patna* inexplicably hits something in mid-ocean and Jim must make his critical decision.

105:22 *asphodel:* a kind of lily; in classical mythology, the flower that grows eternally in the fields of the dead.

105:25 *Samarkand:* see 78:10; again, the dereliction of romanticism.

105:31 *canvassed:* in deference to the 'poets of the storm' (see 105:1), who both sailed and sought.

105:33 *forked-radish Neptune:* see 27:9; here, the God of the Sea, flourishing his trident.

105:34 *the oxy-eye daisy:* the *chrysanthemum leucanthemum,* also known as the *marguerite;* often mentioned by Lowry and here used as an apparent pun on the alternative name ('marguerita,' the tequila-based cocktail).

106:1 *Is this an airplane:* in a letter to W.S. Simpson (12 December 1960), Aiken said that in 1937, in an attempt to keep Lowry sober, he set him a series of exercises in blank verse, extremely difficult, with emphasis on vowel and consonant control and caesura, 'and it was out of this came the line I quote, "Airplane or aeroplane or just plain plane"' (SL 306). The other three poems of the series are numbers 25, 29, and 107.

106:11, 12   *Avro . . . Sopwith:* British fighter planes of WWI; the Avro seaplane or biplane; and the Sopwith Camel, Pup, or Scout.

107:1   *Mammon:* the demon of cupidity, as in Matthew 6:24: 'You cannot serve God and Mammon.' The poem was written for Aiken in Cuernavaca, and its title alludes to Aiken's *Preludes for Memnon* (the Egyptian deity, 'who sang the day before the daybreak came'); but Lowry has deliberately invoked Mammon in the oblique Freudian sense of anal retention.

107:4   *hebephrene:* delirium (see 47:14).

107:5   *lumbago:* in *Ushant* (348), Aiken writes of Lowry's having lumbago when he saw him in Mexico; Lowry claimed he had contracted it from his swimming-pool.

107:6   *brass ferrule:* usually, a metal ring or cap placed round a cane or stick to prevent its splitting; here, the stick itself.

108:5   *Hounded by eyes:* the poem, essentially that written on the back of the El Popo menu in UV (330), bears some resemblance in diction and imagery to Francis Thompson's 'The Hound of Heaven' (1893), a poem that describes the flight from God, the pursuit, and the overtaking. The use of 'preterite,' which also has the theological sense of 'those passed over,' the non-elect, supports the comparison.

109:1   *S.O.S. Sinking fast:* these lines, part of a despairing yet selfconscious letter (1937) to John Davenport, are in response to Lowry's Oaxaca nightmare following his separation from Jan Gabrial (see 24:1); Lowry seems genuinely to have believed that Davenport was the only one who could help him out. For references to the *Morro Castle* and *Titanic,* see 67:4 and 85:14. 'C.Q.D.' ('Come Quick Davenport'?? 'Cash On Delivery'?) is perhaps an ironic reflection that not all is lost.

110:12   *having known the corpse:* in an early draft of UV, the Consul at one point likens his vision of the insect world to a crashed aeroplane he once saw dragged in at low tide by about a thousand holiday makers, all of whom wanted to make themselves feel important. A manuscript note reads: 'Hart Crane again'; presumably alluding to that poet's thoughts while drowning (see 42:1 and 321:T).

111:4   *Franco:* Generalissimo Francisco Franco y Bahamonde (1892–1975), commander of the Fascist forces during the Spanish Civil War and thereafter dictator of Spain until his death. The Catholic Church gave open support to Franco; and Lowry uses another Catholic, an Irishman fighting for the Republicans, to ponder the significance of that.

111:10   *our myth ancestral land:* alluding to the tradition that the Milesians, the earliest inhabitants of Ireland, came originally from the Iberian peninsula.

112:3   *back to Pier Head:* i.e., back to the point of departure, the metaphor implying the ship of the soul returning to its Liverpool. Pier Head, also romanticized in the *Salt-Water Ballads* of John Masefield (himself an out-of-work sailor turned writer), is described in Lowry's 'Goya the Obscure,' with its brown fenders 'hanging in a shaggy row, like heads at Tyburn.' The 'salt gray prop,' l. 10, is presumably the end of the pier.

I I 2:I 2   *the remotest shelf:* a pun combining the outlying declivities of Dante's Mount of Purgatory and distant continental sea-shelves with the bookshelves of the poet and his reader(s).

I I 3:I   *this suicide pact of love:* that between Malcolm Lowry and Jan Gabrial (though Andrew Cather in Aiken's *Great Circle* uses the phrase of his own marriage); the metaphor inverting the usual 'Treu bis zum Tod' sentiment into the terms of a Faustian compact.

Dollarton, 1940–54: Selected Poems, 1947

POEMS OF THE SEA

I I 4:T   *Old Freighter:* essentially the same poem as that earlier entitled 'On Reading R.L.S.' (See notes for Poem 95.)

I I 5:6   *the second fret:* the second ridge across the fingerwork of a ukelele; with a pun on 'fret.'

I I 5:9   *Each snapping string a hawser:* a similar image of breaking strings as cables of the heart is found in UV (I 59), as Hugh recalls the pangs of youth and fading of hope. According to Martin Case, Lowry's tenor ukelele was tuned to A, D, F#, and B (Day I 29).

I I 6:2   *the twirling log:* originally, a ship's log was a wooden board attached to a log-line and hove from the stern of a vessel; it was allowed to run out for a specified time, so the speed of the ship could be calculated from the length of line.

I I 6:5–6   *old Mr. Facing Bloody Both Ways:* Janus-like, because the Bosun is neither Full Officer nor Ordinary Seaman and hence may be despised by the one and resented by the other. Masefield's glossary to his *Salt-Water Ballads* gives one point of view: 'A supernumerary or idler, generally attached to the mate's watch, and holding considerable authority over the crew.'

I I 7:T   *The Western Ocean:* earlier entitled 'The Roar of the Sea and the Darkness' (see Poem 97); the 'Western Ocean' being a mildly romantic term for the Atlantic.

I I 8:T   *Joseph   Conrad:*   Teodor   Josef   Konrad   Korzeniowski (I 857–I 924), Polish-born seaman and novelist who became a British subject after twenty years at sea. Those of his works that most influenced Lowry were *The Nigger of the Narcissus* (I 897), *Lord Jim* (I 900), *Heart of Darkness* (I 902), *Typhoon* (I 902), and *Nostromo* (I 904). He is invoked here as the type of the writer that one part of Lowry aspired to be. The poem, for all its storm and stress, is a disciplined Petrarchan sonnet.

I I 8:I   *This wrestling:* Lowry enclosed this poem in an unpublished letter to the other Conrad, Aiken, admitting: 'An article of yours I discovered in a yellowed New Republic in the Vancouver Library inspired this, in which there ought not to be more than ninety-four plagiarisms.' If the article is 'Gigantic Dreams' (27 June I 928, I 46–7), the direct borrowings are imperceptible, though the theme of a struggle towards consciousness is perhaps shared.

118:8   *derricks of the soul:* forces of destruction (see **99:10**).

120:T   *Danish Sailor's Song:* the original has not been identified.

121:T   *Jokes Amidships:* for all its apparent simplicity, this poem (like the one following) is a villanelle (see **138:T**).

123:T   *Choriant or Paeonic:* a *choriamb* is a metrical foot comprising a trochee followed by an iamb (/xx/) and associated with the dance and chorus of Greek drama; a *paeon* is a variable combination of four syllables, one long and three short (e.g., /xxx/). It is difficult to see either, however injured, as the basis of Lowry's beat.

124:T   *Dimitrios N. Bogliazides:* a rusty Greek tramp steamer (see **77:2**), the wanderings of which form an unvintageable travesty of those of Odysseus. In a note to his anticipated editor, Albert Erskine, Lowry commented: 'This little love song takes place in the Mediterranean. I thought northward should be homeward; but Margerie thought it should be northward, so that's the result.' The final compromise, 'seaward,' equally mutes the echo of the Homeric Homecoming.

124:5   *ships:* Erskine queried the sense of this verb: 'Is the "bastard lot" the water "shipped" into the foc'sle – or the crew? I hope it's the former.'

124:7   *Venus:* the Greek Aphrodite, goddess of love and beauty, who according to Hesiod sprang from the foam (Gk. *aphros*) of the sea that gathered about the severed member of Uranus when mutilated by Cronos. Erskine's comment, 'I don't like "bloody" – the color's wrong for a "grey day,"' rather misses the point.

125:T(**var**)   *rondelet:* from *rondel,* a poem of three stanzas (ab)ab ab(ab) abab(ab), with the first two lines repeated as the two last lines of the second and third stanzas (this is the definition noted by Lowry in his drafts of the poem); a *rondelet* (a rare form) is a shortened instance of that, seven lines (a)b(a)baa(a) (again, Lowry's note).

125:T(**var**)   *Jaunty Song:* i.e., a *shanty,* or lively sailors' song; but perhaps an ominous one, as a *jaunty* is a master-at-arms, or ship's policeman.

125:3   *they'll wash your clothes:* i.e., as a preliminary to sharing them out among the crew; the washing, like the terrible oaths, a means of avoiding the dead man's curse.

126:18   *The Pillars of Hercules:* the Rock of Gibraltar and Mount Abyla, parted by the arm of Heracles to open the way to the Western Ocean; hence, 'beyond the Pillars of Hercules' to signify into the unknown.

POEMS FROM MEXICO

127:T   *Sestina:* a poem of six six-line stanzas, plus an envoy, in which the final words of the first stanza are repeated in varied order in the other five. Here, a double sestina, one of the very few in the language; Lowry exactly duplicates the classical pattern: 123456, 615423, 364125, 532614, 451362, 246531, and the envoy 123456.

127:T(var) *veterio vestigia flammare:* an impossible transcription: Lowry's writing is here indecipherable, and the words do not make up a recognizable quotation. The intended meaning seems to be something to the effect of remnants of the past flaring up in the old man.

127:SCENE *Vera Cruz:* a Mexican port (see **27:T**); Lowry here plays on the sense of 'True Cross.'

127:0/1 *Legion:* see Mark 5:9: 'My name is Legion, for we are many'; said by the man of unclean spirit from whom Christ releases the devils (see **127:72/3**). Also, Kipling's 'Gentlemen-Rankers', st. 1: 'To the legion of the lost ones, to the cohort of the damned.'

127:2 *Jonquil-colored:* in a letter to his editor, Albert Erskine (*SL* 116), Lowry seems a little too anxious to point out that 'jonquil' in relation to dawn is one of Faulkner's favourite adjectives too (it is borrowed from 'The Hamlet').

127:12/13 *St. Luke:* there is a popular tradition that Luke was a doctor (from the words of St. Paul [Colossians 4:14], who describes him as 'the beloved physician').

127:15 *that sparkling greenhouse ocean:* an identical image of sunlight on a greenhouse roof is used in *UV* (281) as a mirage; and in one of the early drafts of *UV*, it is described as 'Maeterlinck's greenhouse in the forest.'

127:18 *Bengal:* the Bay of Bengal, between India and the Malay Peninsula, where (in one of Lowry's fantasies) his maternal grandfather Captain Boden had gone down with his ship.

127:18/19 *Sir Philip Sidney:* the Elizabethan poet and courtier (1554–86), whose exemplary life and death (dying, he gave his water-bottle to another) made him a figure of the perfect man. The author of the sonnet sequence *Astrophel and Stella* and the pastoral *Arcadia,* he is here invoked for the poem 'Strephon to Klaius' in Book 1 of the latter, possibly the only other instance of a 'doble sestine' in the language and, as such, surely Lowry's model.

127:39 *jalousies:* see **25:25** for a similar vision of cantina doors.

127:42 *hall of mirrors:* a distortion of the magnificent gallery in the Palace of Versailles, built to reflect the glory of *le roi soleil*, Louis XIV.

127:48/9 *Richard III:* as barman, Regent of the Dark. The opening lines of *Richard III* refer to the winter of discontent made glorious summer by this sun of York.

127:60/61 *El Universal:* in the 1930s, the most important newspaper in Mexico City.

127:72/3 *The Swine:* i.e., the drunks exiting from the tavern, described in terms of the Gadarene swine (Mark 5:11–13): when Christ met the man of unclean spirit, whose name was Legion, he sent the devils into a herd of swine, which ran violently down a steep place into the sea and were drowned.

128:6 *surcingleless:* i.e., unrestricted; a 'surcingle' (from L. *cingulum*, 'a band') is a wide belt under the belly of a horse used to hold its load in place.

128:14 *Whose eyes are lidless:* in **106:17–20** Lowry's God watches him with eyes that do not move; while throughout *uv* the horse is a similar agent of the psychological forces of destruction.

1 29:T   *Xochitepec:* small town, some fifteen miles south of Cuernavaca; perhaps to be associated with sacrifices to the flower goddess Xochiquetzal at the Aztec pyramid there.

1 29:T(var)   *Lupus in fabula:* L. 'the wolf in the fable' (see 70:1). In a letter to Ralph Gustafson (*SL* 4 1 2) Lowry noted that this alternative title 'was suggested by an article by J.B. Priestley on being followed in a dream by some beastie perhaps of the fifth dimension!'

1 29:T(var)   *mescalitos:* in Oaxaca, a potent colourless liquor (distinct from mescal) that is a straight distillation of the agave cactus without the addition of the usual sugars.

1 29:1   *Those animals that follow us in dreams:* in *uv*, the Consul is thus dogged by his familiar, and at the end of Chapter 5 he has a fearful vision of the invasion of the insect world (the variant 'kingdom' is used with such a sense of psychic dominion).

1 29:7   *Tlampam:* a suburb in the south of Mexico City; then as now the bus terminal for Cuernavaca and other destinations south.

1 29:7(var)   *The goat:* the image of the charging goat may have been taken from the poem because it was needed for *uv*, Chapter 4 (Lowry then tending, as he later did not, to keep prose and poetry apart). As he noted in a letter (*SL* 1 98): 'The goat means tragedy (tragedy – goat song) but goat – *cabron*-cuckold (the horns).'

1 29:8   *our cats:* in *uv* (93), Oedipuss and Pathos have met with a similar fate.

1 29:16   *the very last day:* recollections of Lowry's parting from Jan Gabrial, in early December 1 937. In *uv* (93), on the morning of Yvonne's departure, the Consul had likewise sat drinking chilled mescal and listening to the sounds of two little fawns being dragged in, shrieking, to be slaughtered.

1 30:T   *Under a Real Cactus:* a peculiar hybrid of Jonah's gourd plant and the prickly pear of Eliot's 'The Hollow Men'; the honorific 'Mr. Lowry' acknowledging, in the tone of Mr. Lear, the 'Mr. Eliot' whose Sunday Morning Service had more recently become an Ash Wednesday.

1 30:T(var)   *Genet:* Jean Genet (1 9 1 0–86), thief and poet, whose *Notre-Dame des Fleurs* (1 944) Lowry may not then have known, but whose reputation he obviously did.

1 30:T(var)   *The Cashier:* i.e., one aspect of the Redeemer.

1 30:T(var)   *The Thief at Sunset:* i.e., St. Dismas, to whom Christ's offer of salvation was extended at the hour of his death, in Luke 23:43: 'Verily, I say unto thee, Today shalt thou be with me in paradise.'

1 3 1:T   *Delirium in Vera Cruz:* identical to Poem 27.

1 32:T   *Death of a Oaxaquenian:* a response to the shattering news, as recorded at the end of *Dark as the Grave,* of the death of Lowry's Zapotecan friend, Juan Fernando Márquez, who had been shot in a barroom brawl in Villahermosa. The poem is a villanelle (see 1 38:T), the formal intricacy of which belies the simplicity of apparent direct

expression in the face of such unspeakable enormity.

132:17   *New Spain:* i.e., *Nueva España,* the name for the Spanish Americas, with especial application to Mexico; but one that since the War of Independence (1821) had largely fallen into disuse.

133:1   *Pity the blind:* an apparent echo of Aiken's poem 'The Nameless Ones,' which begins: 'Pity the nameless, and the unknown, where / bitter in heart they wait on the stonebuilt stair.' The problem (physical and psychological) depicted here was for Lowry now and again a very real one as he tried to cash the remittance sent from home.

POEMS FROM VANCOUVER

134:9   *the pale:* literally, the faded sky; but also with the sense of a restricted area (not 'beyond the Pale'), thus anticipating the magnipotent image of policemen glistening in the trees.

135:2   *a pillar:* i.e., a mail box.

136:T   *The Glaucous Winged Gull:* Lowry is working in part from the various entries on gulls *(laridae)* in Peterson's *A Field Guide to Western Birds,* where the glaucous-winged gull *(larus glaucescens)* is described as a pink-footed full with a pale grey mantle. Peterson earlier describes the bills of gulls as 'slightly hooked' and comments on the change of plumage after the first year. The 'edible stars' are, prosaically, starfish.

136:3   *catsbane:* i.e., killer of cats.

136:4   *finial:* in architecture, having the pointed form of a bud about to open and used of an ornament on top of a spire; hence its appearance in Aiken's *Blue Voyage* (111): 'and one sea gull perched on the foremast like a gilded finial.'

136:7   *the Mauretania:* the famous Cunard Liner, brought into service in 1907 and, before she was scrapped in 1935, the holder of the Blue Riband for twenty-two years.

136:8   *snowblinded once, I saved:* echoing Aiken's 'A dog, I saved once,' in *Blue Voyage* (76). The episode of the seagull was worked into UV (155), where Hugh recalls rescuing it, 'blinded with snow.' The action of 'hoving' it back at heaven, however, reverses the last act of Tashtego in *Moby Dick,* when he pulls down a sky-hawk, a 'living part of heaven,' with himself and the ship.

137:T   *No Time to Stop and Think:* in syntax and rhythm, a passage similar to the opening of Part 5 of Eliot's *The Waste Land,* describing a journey across a very dry land; but in form (as the title variant suggests) a *triolet,* i.e., a verse form with eight lines and two rhymes, in which the fourth line repeats the first and the eighth repeats the second (here, the seventh also repeats the first, and an ambiguity is created, in some variants, by the accentuation of the final *you*).

138:T   *Villaknell:* i.e., a *villanelle* (but with a ring of doom); a French form of verse in nineteen lines with two rhymes, arranged in five tercets with a concluding quatrain; the first and third lines of each tercet are repeated as the final lines of the others and to conclude the quatrain (Lowry observes the form).

1 38:5   *Tiger Bay:* the dock of Cardiff; apart from its name, no more exotic than the Mersey or Liverpool's Pier Head.

1 38:1 3   *Stamboul:* the old romantic name for Constantinople (as was *Cathay* for the Celestial Kingdom, otherwise China); in particular, the older part of the city near the Golden Horn. The name had been changed to 'Istanbul' in 1 9 3 0, and a popular song of the time advised: 'So, if you've a date in Constantinople, / She'll be waiting in Istanbul' ('Constantinople,' by Harry Carleton).

1 39:T   *Sigbjørn:* in a number of his later short stories and unpublished works Lowry uses the name 'Sigbjørn Wilderness' for his artist-hero.

1 39:3   *Skjellerup:* a small town in Jutland, Denmark; the name perhaps chosen by Lowry for its modern and unromantic association with the rubber manufacturers. In a letter to Priscilla Woolfan (SL 1 87), Lowry refers wryly to an imagined half-revue of *UV* in the 'Skjellerup Schnappstasters Annual.'

1 39:8   *the maelstrom ... the Kattegat:* the *maelström* is a fearsome whirlpool off the Norwegian coast, popularly supposed to suck in all vessels passing nearby and to be the entrance to the abyss beneath; the *Kattegat* is the strait between Denmark and Norway; it is thus associated here with the safe passage home.

1 40:T   *Kraken:* a fabulous sea-monster, a 'frightful poulp' most famously described in Bishop Pontopiddan's *Norges Naturlige Historie* (1 7 5 2) as a mile and half in size and often mistaken by deluded sailors for an island; it supposedly lived off the Norwegian coast and caused the *maelström* when it plunged.

1 40:8   *crabs:* in the drafts of *Dark as the Grave,* Sigbjørn Wilderness offers some background to this poem by telling of a visit to an Englishman living nearby in his house with fresh shingles and scarlet sills: ' "Aye, and the inside's good too. On the shore," he added, " 'ave you seen them? they're *crabs wot jump.*" His speech was such (thought Sigbjørn) as Wordsworth dreamed to record, humble and good as plates on a farmhouse shelf.'

1 4 1:1   *live ice:* for the deep-sea fishermen, whose boats were not refrigerated, the distinction between white and blue ice was crucial. They would set off with artificial white ice from the Cold Storage Depot, but before reaching the outer grounds, they would need to replace it by chipping from the rocks the 'blue' or glacial ice, which (being more compacted) would stay frozen much longer.

1 42:2   *Bored Prosperos:* in *The Tempest,* Prospero, erstwhile duke of Milan, lives on an island with his daughter Miranda and devotes himself to magic and secret learning; a mage in the Platonic tradition, he represents the combination of wisdom with virtue, which perhaps makes life even more boring.

1 42:6   *tilth:* from O.E. *tilian,* 'to plough'; hence, old-fashioned downto-earth honest labour.

1 43:T   *Kingfishers:* on the manuscript, Lowry notes that the first section of the poem is a *haiku* (a three-line imagist poem in seventeen syllables; five, seven, and five); followed by a *cinquain* (an unrhymed

stanza of five lines of respectively two, four, six, eight, and two syllables); then a *tanka* (similar to the haiku, but with thirty-one syllables in five lines; the first and third are of five, and the other three of seven).

143:9–10 *a left wing threequarter:* in rugby football, an outside back. Rosslyn Park (not to be confused with the 'Roslyn' near Dollarton) is in the Hampstead area of London and was in the 1930s the name and home grounds of one of the major club sides.

143:13 *halcyon days:* in fable the halcyon, or kingfisher, was reputed to breed at the time of the winter solstice in a nest floating upon the sea and to have charmed the wind and waves so that the sea was calm; hence, days of perfect tranquillity.

144:T *Twenty-five:* in rugby, the line twenty-five yards (now, twenty-two metres) out from the try-line, marking off a quarter of the field. Lowry likens the writing of his poem to a defensive scrum ('scrimmage') on his twenty-five, with the poet as half-back ('scrum-half') waiting for the ball to come from the ruck, to set up a kingfisher-like movement along the flying back line, leading to a try (but fearing that the ball will come out flat).

144:9 *Poet:* as the following lines intimate, there is a Poe in every Poet.

144:12 *wappened:* an obsolete rare word, meaning old and stale and useless; the OED offers one citation, from *Timon of Athens* (4.3.38): 'this is it / That makes wappened widows wed again.'

145:1(var) *Union suits:* undergarments with shirt and drawers as one.

147:T *Scribner's Sons:* the New York publishing firm of Charles Scribner's Sons, who took an unconscionable time to reply to the Lowrys in respect to the proofs of Margerie's mystery novel, *The Shapes That Creep;* and who then, with *The Last Twist of the Knife*, omitted to print the final chapter. The poem is a villanelle of sorts (see **138:T**).

148:3 *the gibbous moon:* the moon between three-quarters and full, when more than half the visible surface is sunlit; thus, the opposite of 'crescent.'

148:8 *Eagles:* happiness for golfers; hole played in two strokes under par.

151:14 *Ilium:* the city of Troy; here, an iliupersic image of the poet's mind.

153:T *Harpies:* in classical mythology, loathsome winged monsters with the head and trunk of a woman and the lower extremities of a bird.

154:6 *Lycidas:* a grotesque reference to Milton's pastoral elegy of that name (1637), in which the poet laments the premature death of his college friend Edward King, who was drowned at sea just off the Cheshire coast, not far from the Lowry home.

154:12 *Burtons:* bottles of bitter beer from the breweries of Burton-on-Trent, England.

155:T *Deserter:* a tale that wrung Lowry's heart: of a young conscript, Paul Reynolds Scott, who had gone AWOL in England and had worked his passage on the ss *Barrwhin* from Glasgow to be back with his family at Christmas. His body, and that of another young man, was found on 21 November 1940, trapped in a refrigerator car. Lowry worked over his poem many times, using a regular sonnet form but taking care that every rhyme should be oblique and harsh; he worked closely from a report in *The Vancouver Sun* of 9 December 1940, 9, under the heading 'Gov't Must Probe Death of My Son': 'A demand for an official inquiry into the death of Corporal Paul Reynolds Scott, 20, who died with Roger Scully, 17 . . . who was found dead on Nov. 2 [*sic*] in a refrigerator car at Empress, Alta., near Medicine Hat, was made today by his father, Frederick W. Scott, Port Coquitlam. "There must be an investigation into this," he said bitterly as he prepared to attend funeral services today in Paterson Funeral Home at New Westminster . . . "I have received no assistance or advice from responsible authorities since I first heard of my boy's death," he said. "I paid my own way to Empress and identified the body. It was in a small room, lying on bare boards. There wasn't even a sheet over him." Mr Scott said he wanted an explanation of why his son was in the refrigerator car and why there had been no investigation by military authorities as young Scott wore an army greatcoat and carried military papers with him when he was found.' Lowry also jotted these notes on the manuscript: 'It would have been simple to identify him by mail. He had some scars and a birth mark on his ear which the police never mentioned when they wrote us' . . . 'he worked his way back' . . . 'The elder Scott said he had to take the body from Empress to Medicine Hat by truck and then to obtain permission to bury it without an inquest.'

155:8   *Category B:* in a later report in *The Daily Province* (11 December 1944, 11), it was pointed out that Scott had not been officially discharged, but a letter to his parents was cited in which he said that he had been reduced from Medical Category 'A' to 'C'; this, however, would not have required his return to Canada on medical grounds.

155:10   *New Westminster:* a municipality east of Vancouver on the Fraser River; the citation of 'old' incriminates the Westminster government of London, who had wanted this man.

155:11   *back for Christmas day:* Scott had not in fact told his parents that he was coming to Canada, but a subheading in the *Sun* of 7 December 1940, 19, read: 'Home For Christmas' and was followed by the comment that his family expected his arrival.

156:T   *Mrs. Traill:* Catherine Parr Traill (1802–99), naturalist and writer, a copy of whose *Studies in Plant Life in Canada* (1885) Lowry had once owned and which he consulted regularly for his naming of plants. He took extensive notes from the book, including the following account of what the gardener said (70): 'Oh! madam, in these days they turn poor Poetry out of doors, but in the olden times it was not so, for it was the language in which God spake to man through the tongues of angels and prophets. Aye, and it was the language in which even sinful man spake in prayer to his Maker: but now they only use hard words for simple things, such as the flowers of the field and the garden; or the talk is about gold, and the things that gold purchases!'

1 56:6   *dwarf oaks:* varieties of scrub oaks, praised by Mrs. Traill (101) for their bright frosted foliage and described in detail (177–80) where their role in antiquity and Biblical times is mentioned.

1 56:7   *love-lies-bleeding:* referred to by Mrs. Traill (95) as the drooping amaranth, closely resembling the Indian strawberry.

1 56:11   *Gayfeather:* otherwise 'Button Snake-root' *(liatris cylindracea),* described by Mrs. Traill (92–3) as growing on dry hills and water-courses; with a slender upright stem, dark green leaves, and a long spike of densely flowered purple heads.

1 56:11   *blazing star:* according to Mrs. Traill (93), one of the same family *(liatris scariosa);* 'a handsome flower of the North western prairies.'

1 56:11(var)   *tansy:* a plant of the genus *tanacetum,* with a strong aromatic odour and a bitter taste; mentioned briefly by Mrs. Traill (80) and praised for its resinous properties and medicinal qualities.

1 57:T   *The Dodder:* according to Mrs. Traill (75): 'This singular parasitical plant occurs on the rocky shores of our inland lakes. There seems to be two species, one with bright, orange-coloured coils, and greenish white flowers; the other with green, rusty wing stems, and smaller blossoms. This last occurs on the rocky shores of Stoney Lake, where in the month of August it may be found twining around the slender stems of the lesser Golden-rod, a small, narrow-leaved Solidago.' She adds (76) that it is never associated with any other plant, that it seems leafless and rootless, and that the golden-stemmed species forms a pretty contrast with the dark foliage around it.

1 57:2   *The hooded violet:* the *viola cucullata;* a blue violet that, according to Mrs. Traill (7), is so called from the involute habit of the leaves, which are folded inwardly as if to shield the tender buds of the flowers from the chilling winds.

1 57:2–3   *the branching white wood violet:* the *viola Canadensis,* or Canada violet, with slender leafy-bracted branches, many buds, and pure milk-white flowers. Mrs. Traill comments (8) that the plant continues to send forth blossoms all through the summer and even late into September (this, and most of the detail following, was noted by Lowry into one of his working booklets).

1 57:5(var)   *the arum's drunken tasting:* Mrs. Traill discusses (21) the various concoctions distilled from the root of the arum plants.

1 57:6   *cowled cuckoo-pint, jack in the pulpit:* according to Mrs. Traill (22) names for the old English arum; the first one no doubt suggested from the appearance of the plant about the time of the coming of that herald of spring, the cuckoo; the second from the hooded spathe shrouding the spadix like a monkish cowl.

1 57:8   *Katchewanook:* in her 'Introductory Pages' (1–3), Mrs. Traill tells how she first settled in the unbroken backwoods on the borders of Lake Katchawanook [*sic*], some distance from Peterborough, Ontario, where she taught herself to observe and study the native flora around her.

1 57:10   *goldenrod:* the *solidago latifolia,* discussed by Mrs. Traill (93);

a hardy flower, varying in colour from gorgeous orange to pale straw and making the grassy banks of inland streams and the rocky cliffs of islands gay with their bright colours.

158:2   *cigarettes:* a reiterated motif in Lowry's writings for the brevity of human existence (see **187:71**).

159:T   *John Davenport:* 1908–66; poet and drinker and friend of Lowry's from their Cambridge days. Lowry had visited Davenport in Los Angeles in 1936 and was in turn visited in Cuernavaca. In a letter from Oaxaca (see **109:1**) Lowry had called Davenport his closest friend.

159:T   *Cervantes:* Miguel de Cervantes Saavedra (1547–1616), creator of *Don Quixote* (1605 and 1615); hence the sense of the 'quixotic' that infiltrates the following poem.

159:5   *Sierra Leone:* a republic in West Africa, bounded by Guinea and Liberia; invoked here in the sense of 'the white man's grave.'

159:14   *Surabaya:* a large city in east Java, Indonesia. For *Archangel,* see **83:5**; and for *Tlampan,* **129:7**. The Far East, the White Sea, and Mexico were all part of Lowry's romantic world.

160:10   *O.C:* here, 'Officer Commanding.'

162:1   *Birkenhead:* a borough on the Wirral Peninsula, Cheshire, linked by a road and rail tunnel (see l. 10) to Liverpool, of which it forms an important industrial annex.

162:6   *Charon:* in classical mythology, the son of Erebus and Nox, who ferries the souls of the dead across the River Styx to Hades.

163:T   *False Cape Horn:* a headland of Tierra del Fuego, at the tip of the Hardy Peninsula and a hazard for seamen since it resembles Cape Horn (see **38:11**).

163:T(var)   *Maximilian's Palace:* the ruined palace of UV (18), based on Cuernavaca's Borda Gardens, in which Laruelle hears voices of the royal couple, Maximilian and Carlota, fading into those of the Consul and Yvonne.

163:10   *The blatant beast:* from Spenser's *The Fairie Queene* (5.7.37–8): 'A monster which the blatant beast men call / A dreadful feend of gods and men ydrad.' There, the epithet of a thousand-tongued terror, begotten of Cerebus and Chimera, the quest for which is similar to Ahab's 'sounding' of the White Whale. The word 'hackle' usually implies 'to hack,' 'to cut roughly'; but as used of this beast may imply its fur being 'hackled,' or combed down.

163:13   *Kraken:* the Norwegian sea-monster (see **140:T**, and SL 278).

163:14   *No peace but must pay full toll to hell:* an echo of James Thomson's 'The City of Dreadful Night,' 6: 'He snarled, What thing is this which apes a soul, / And would find entrance to our gulf of dole / Without the payment of the settled toll?'

164:T   *Indian Arm:* a long northern continuation of Burrard Inlet, northeast of Vancouver; Lowry's Dollarton shack was at the point where the inlet meets the arm.

164:1   *Mill-wheel reflections:* much of this poem, including some of the variants, was to be worked into Yvonne's vision of the Northern Paradise (UV 271); the use of *terza rima* is thus appropriate.

165:T *Port Moody:* a port towards the end of Burrard Inlet, directly opposite Lowry's home. The Shellburn oil refinery there constituted a vision that constantly threatened his paradise (in *October Ferry* [159], the 'S' of the brightly-lit 'SHELL' has gone out, leaving the other letters to blaze forth ominously).

165:8 *loveliest of oil refineries:* echoing Housman's 'Loveliest of trees' ('A Shropshire Lad,' 2) but invested with an irony that lends disenchantment to the view.

166:T *Salmon Drowns Eagle:* a story told to Lowry by his fisherman friend, Sam Miller.

167:T *The Canadian Turned Back at the Border:* in September 1939, a month or so after arriving in Vancouver, Lowry decided to visit Margerie, who was still in Los Angeles, but he was refused admittance to the US at Blaine (see 167.37) 'as a person liable to be a public charge.' The incident contributed to his already considerable fears of authority, adding another theme ('Turned back at the border') to his litany of woes (Day 254); and since it meant a year before he could re-apply for admission, it may have been a major factor in his subsequent self-definition as a 'Canadian' (see the variant forms). In *Dark as the Grave* (34–5), Sigbjørn thinks of the poem he has written about the experience: 'What kind of a poem, though, had he been trying to write? A kind of sestina, though more elaborate than a sestina, of eight verses, of ten lines each with, to begin with instead of the end words being repeated, the last line of the second verse rhyming, or rhyming falsely, or striking an assonance with the first line of the first. But what had been his general purpose in choosing such a form? Sigbjørn remembered that he had wanted to give the impression of the bus going one way, towards the border and into the future, and, at the same time, of the shop windows and streets flashing by into the past.'

167:2 *the grey Vancouver Bus Terminal:* the Motor Transport Building, on Dunsmuir Street (not far from Chinatown).

167:9 *a sleeked puppet:* in a version of this poem sent to Albert Erskine, Lowry noted some of his sources: 'H. Crane last two lines of V.1: a poet named Wainwright early influence of T.S. Eliot (V.11) had a car *herding* flies: imperceptible echo of Crane end of V.2: the bird – the redwing a bit obvious & even Vachel Lindsayish: but God, what a wierd [*sic*] form – a kind of canon or Webernian sestina, caused by the dragging backward of the theme: the thought may not be profound, but if you *get* it, it *is moving* ["Bees" & "Los Angeles," likewise a bit like Stevens Byzantines & tambourines.]' The echoes are oblique: the 'H. Crane' in 'V.1' is probably 'the terrible puppet of my dreams' ('The Visible, the Untrue,' l. 2), issuing a ticket for 'The Tunnel' (*The Bridge*, Part 7): 'That last night on the ballot round, did you / Shaking, did you deny the ticket, Poe?'; the 'poet named Wainwright' is perhaps Philip Wheelwright (though the line is not identified); and the 'influence of T.S. Eliot' may be equally the promise of 'pneumatic bliss' ('Whispers of Immortality,' l. 20). For other remote echoes of this kind (more indicative of Lowry's fears than plagiarized sources), see **167:22**, **167:24**, and **167:49**.

167:13 *nictitate:* i.e., wink. In the drafts of *Dark as the Grave* Sigbjørn agonizes: 'Could the lights nictitate? And what were they symbolic of? Night in day? the war? the underlying anxiety *there,* despite the joy? No matter.'

167:15 *Rolando's horn:* Roland is the hero of the early twelfth century *La chanson de Roland,* which tells of the treachery of the Saracen king, Marsile, against Charlemagne. Roland, commanding the rearguard as the army crosses the Pyrenees, is suddenly surrounded by 400,000 Saracens, but when urged by his friend Olivier to sound his horn and recall the army, he refuses until it is too late. Aiken uses a similar image in *Great Circle* (187): 'One ringing word like Roland's horn, winding among the wind-worn Pyrenees.'

167:22 *High tension wires:* in an early draft of *Dark as the Grave* Sigbjørn says: 'That was a bit like Stephen Spender, but never mind, he wouldn't see.' The allusion is, presumably, to Spender's poem 'The Pylons.'

167:24 *cry of the northwestern redwing:* Lowry is using Peterson's *A Field Guide to Western Birds,* where the redwinged blackbird *(Agelaius phoeniceus),* distinguished by its red epaulets and found freely from Alaska to Costa Rica, is said to sing with a gurgling 'o-ka-lay' or 'o-ka-lee-onk.' Its other sound, 'cong-a-ree' (as the drafts of *Dark as the Grave* confirm) is 'rather like Vachel Lindsay'; i.e., an echo of his appalling poem, 'The Congo,' which has, admittedly, a certain rhythmic vitality. The conceit that the bird is its own customs official and can cross the wild border without let is repeated in 'The Bravest Boat.'

167:31(var) *unimpressed by Mars:* Lowry appears to have told the authorities that he was off to join up for the war (see **167:66(var)**).

167:33 *Labrador:* an image of the frozen soul (see also Poem 250).

167:37 *Blaine:* the US city at the International Border, where all buses are stopped for passport scrutiny. As Lowry intimates, a 'blain' is an irritated sore, or pustule.

167:39 *A legend bird has there three eyes:* although the mystical third eye is an attribute of many mythological beings (all-seeing, all wise), there seems to be no reference to such a bird among the myths of the Indians of the Northwest Pacific. However, the raven is the bird most frequently depicted in their art, and it is also the bird of Odin, who surrendered one of his eyes as the price of wisdom. Lowry's legendary bird is thus a composite of several traditions.

167:41–2 *locks...socks:* in the draft of *Dark as the Grave* Sigbjørn comments: 'And now, here he was at the border itself, the bus had stopped for the time being, so the single detached verse that followed called simply for an aa, bb, treatment.' In the final stanza, isolated in Vancouver, Lowry repeats the pattern.

167:46 *indoor Marxmanship:* mocking any potential comradeship between them; the phrase had been used by Conrad Aiken in a letter dated 15 December 1939 in which he criticized the naivety of Lowry's politics, and it was repeated by Lowry in 'Where did that one go to, 'Erbert' (see **317:Note**), published in *The Vancouver Province* of 29 December 1939.

167:46(var)   *proctor, Kafkan:* the border officials described in terms of Cambridge proctors (responsible for discipline), as if out of a nightmare by Kafka.

167:49   *a trampling noise of bees:* see **167:9**. Lowry also admits in the drafts of *Dark as the Grave* that: 'It was possible that the bees bore some resemblance to Wallace Stevens' tambourines'; i.e., to 'Peter Quince at the Clavier,' 3, where, having revealed Susanna in her shame, the simpering Byzantines 'Fled, with a noise like tambourines.' The echo is so distant that one is tempted to see Lowry as mocking, through his character, his own mode of composition.

167:55   *wild cat-tails:* an angry pun using a detail of Peterson's *Field Guide,* where the tricolored blackbird (similar to the redwing) is said to nest among the reeds and cattails (catkins). The 'cat-tail' on a ship is the inner part of the 'cathead,' which keeps the anchor clear of the side of the ship; hence, the nautical imagery of the following line.

167:55(var)   *nidification:* a marginal note in the manuscript says 'process of building a nest'; a pun upon 'identification' in terms of Peterson's recognition of the redwing by its distinctive woven nest.

167:56   *marshlight:* i.e., *ignis fatuus,* a phosphorescent light caused by the spontaneous combustion of marsh-gas (methane); but referring also to the masthead light of a sailing ship.

167:60   *whistlepunk:* in logging, a workman who operates the signal line running to the donkey engine whistle (not an exacting occupation); thus, a term of abuse.

167:66(var)   *the LYKAION:* i.e., the *Lycaeon,* a liner working the Yokohama to Philadelphia route; in context, a ship to take him from the Californian port of San Pedro back to Avonmouth (Bristol) for wartime service. Perhaps deleted as improbable, though Lowry was to repeat the story to Margerie's mother (*SL* 17).

167:71   *the helpless submarine:* an image used in UV (38), in the context of the Consul's guilty recollections. The *Sargasso Sea* is in the western Atlantic; a powerful eddy causes the Sargasso weed to collect on the surface; hence an area traditionally fraught with danger.

167:74   *No peace:* see **163:14,** where the identical image is used for a soul denied entrance even to Hell.

167:80   *Oregon and Mount Tabor:* ironically to compare his failure at the border (the bus imagined as having by now reached Oregon) with the epic events at Mount Tabor, east of Nazareth – the stronghold of Israel against the Canaanites and later the Romans and reputed to be the place of Christ's transfiguration. However, Lowry's explanation was a little different: in the drafts of *Dark as the Grave* Sigbjørn admits to having thought all the time that Oregon was the American border state next to British Columbia and says that the last note was to be one of pity – so lacking in the border guards that they would need the three eyes of the legendary bird (see **167:39**) to look towards Mount Tabor. However, Sigbjørn also adds: 'My God, what brackish bilge is this?'

Dollarton, 1940–54: Uncollected Poems

169:1   *Like white giraffes:* as in UV (43), the reference is to the local fishing boats with their exceptionally tall masts, one of which (the *Caileag Gheal,* or White Lady) was built and owned by Lowry's fisherman friend Jimmy Craige.

171:12   *the store:* the nearby general store, owned by Percy Cummins, and the focal point of the Dollarton community, where they went to shop, to collect their mail, to catch the bus, and to hear the latest gossip.

172:4   *a salt gray prop:* part of Lowry's pier, the phrasing linking it to Pier Head, Liverpool (see **112:3**).

172:8   *St. Francis:* Francis of Assisi (1182–1226), founder of the Franciscan Order, who set out to follow the example of his Saviour in every step of his life by living a life of poverty and self-denial and calling all creatures his brothers and sisters. He signalled his conversion by kissing the hand of a leper but is best known for the apocryphal legend of his talking to the birds.

173:2   *stringers:* long horizontal timbers used to connect uprights in a frame or to support a floor. The poem commemorates the ordeal of rebuilding the Lowry shack after the disastrous fire of 7 June 1944.

179:9   *The three pines:* in the context of an ordeal, suggesting the three crosses of Golgotha; but the image of such pines framed by the sun is to be found elsewhere in Lowry's writings (see **271:1**).

173:23   *Wilderness:* Sigbjørn Wilderness, a persona often used by Lowry in his later writings, notably in *Dark as the Grave* and the unpublished typescript, *The Ordeal of Sigbjørn Wilderness.*

173:26   *While the whole world burnt down:* the theme of a Northern Paradise followed by an inevitable eviction and finally a world in apocalyptic flames is a recurrent one in Lowry's Dollarton writings (see **240:T** and **288:1**).

174:1   *odi et amo:* from Catullus, *Carmen* 85: 1–2: 'Odi et amo: quare id faciam, fortasses requiris. / Nescio, sed fieri sentio et excrucior' ('I hate and I love: why I do so you may well ask. I do not know, but I feel it happen and am in agony').

174:3   *your left eye or your right:* Horatio Nelson (1758–1805), British naval hero, lost his right eye in 1794 at the taking of Calvi; Lowry's theme, however, turns more on the famous signal at Trafalgar (fought off Cadiz, Spain, on 21 October 1805): 'England expects that every man will this day do his duty.' Nelson died in the battle, having (he thanked God) done his duty, and by so doing set an example conspicuously lacking in the determination of the British government of Lowry's time to turn a blind eye towards what was happening in Spain.

174:6 *Bajadoz and Salamanca:* centres of fierce fighting during the Spanish Civil War. *Bajadoz,* in Estremadura, western Spain, had been captured by the Nationalists in August 1936, and the victory was marked by atrocities and mass executions of the populace in the local bull-ring. *Salamanca,* in León, 110 miles northwest of Madrid, was the capital for the Nationalists during 1937–8.

174:7 *the muted voice of England long asleep:* a specific reference to England's failure to intervene in Spain, probably derived from the end of George Orwell's *Homage to Catalonia* (1938), with its vision of Englishmen 'all sleeping the deep, deep sleep of England, from which I sometimes fear that we shall never awake till we are jerked out of it by the roar of bombs.' The sentiment recurs in *UV* (102), in Hugh's implied criticism of his brother's lack of responsibility.

174:13 *Cluster lamps:* large lamps attached to the end of a rope and lowered into a ship's hold to facilitate unloading at night; commonly used by Lowry (as in *UV* 54) to look into the soul.

174:18 *blockade:* Franco's maritime blockade of Spanish waters to prevent aid reaching the Republicans, as agreed to by France and England as part of the policy of non-intervention (compare l. 4: 'bidding the world to anchor'); and thus to Lowry a betrayal of the Republican cause.

174:22 *not wounded:* unlike Nelson, who lost an eye, an arm, and finally his life.

175:T *Ezra Pound...Mussolini's radio:* Ezra Loomis Pound (1885–1972), American poet, who prior to WWII professed to find the heritage of Jefferson in Mussolini's Italy; after war broke out, he broadcast Fascist propaganda on the Rome radio. After the war he was returned to the US to face trial for treason. He was found to be of unsound mind, and after some years in St. Elizabeth's Hospital, he was released and he returned to Italy. Lowry's poem is a close imitation of Pound's 'An Immorality': 'Sing we for love and idleness, / Naught else is worth the having. / Though I have been in many a land, / There is naught else in living. / And I would rather have my sweet, / Though rose-leaves die of grieving / Than do high deeds in Hungary / To pass all men's believing.'

177:2 *flayed at seven:* as Day points out (62), Lowry had suffered as a child from a neglected eye infection, and in later life he tended to exaggerate the trauma in terms of childhood terrors and his mother's rejection of him.

177:16 *Clare:* John Clare (1792–1864), poet and madman, best known for his rural and pastoral verse. Lowry refers to his 'Summer Images' (ll. 106–12). 'And note on hedgerow baulks, in moisture sprent, / The jetty snail creep from the mossy thorn, / With earnest heed and tremulous intent, / Frail brother of the morn, / That from the tiny bents and misted leaves / Withdraws his timid horn, / And fearful vision weaves.'

178:1 *the Maleboge:* from It. 'evil ditches'; in Dante's *Inferno* the name given to the eighth circle of Hell, consisting of ten circular trenches, or *bolge,* in which are placed seducers and panderers, simoniacs and barrators, thieves and sowers of discord; to each of whom is meted an appropriate affliction. *Hastings Street,* in downtown Vancouver, is in the heart of the city's poorer area, the domain of drunks and drug addicts, pimps and prostitutes.

178:8   *chancres:* specifically, the initial lesions of syphilis.

179:1   *Why should I care:* a response to Yeats's 'The Spur': 'You think it horrible that lust and rage / Should dance attention upon my old age; / They were not such a plague when I was young; / What else have I to spur me into song?'

180:1   *Born ailing:* a manuscript note attributes the following to Robert Frost: 'A complete poem is one where an emotion has found its thought, & the thought has found its words.' Lowry's poem went through many subsequent revisions.

180:3(var)   *Pocahontas:* the Powhatan Indian maiden (1595–1617) who saved the life of Captain John Smith by flinging herself down upon him and imploring her father to spare his life.

180:3(var)   *Magdalene:* Mary Magdalene, like Eve a fallen woman (see Luke 7:37 for this debated attribution), who yet followed Christ to Jerusalem and was the first to see the empty tomb on the day of the Resurrection.

180:4(var)   *St. Pancras:* a parish and borough of central London, known for its impressive Victorian railway station (the major terminus for Scotland and the North).

180:5(var)   *Ruskin:* John Ruskin (1819–1900), critic and artist, who did much to shape the aesthetic taste of his age and whose *The Stones of Venice* (1851) helped create a vogue for architecture very different from the massive grandeur of St. Pancras.

180:12(var)   *Spawn of the jenny:* i.e., offspring of an ass.

181:T   *the Pleiades:* a group of seven stars in the constellation of Taurus, said by the ancients to have been seven sisters (the seventh, Merope, hiding herself in shame for having loved the mortal, Sisyphus). Specifically, in Vancouver's Stanley Park, 'a constellation of seven noble red cedars,' mentioned in Lowry's short story, 'The Bravest Boat.'

183:T   *Byzantium:* the ancient name of Constantinople, later Istanbul, capital of the Eastern Roman Empire and centre of the Greek Orthodox Church until its capture by the Turks in 1453. The 'ideal' of l. 6 mocks Yeats's vision of Byzantium as a City of the Imagination.

183:T   *Knocked oop:* Lowry is echoing Conrad Aiken in a letter to him dated 29 October 1939, in reply to a request for financial aid: 'I'm a bit knocked oop meself' (SL 234).

183:3   *Lamps:* the lamptrimmer (see 92:3).

183:7   *a blind eye socket:* in an unpublished letter to Conrad Aiken (16 July 1934), Lowry recalls the Suez Canal and 'a sowsow woman whose blind eye socket could be procured for a mere song.'

183:8   *bobhead tigers:* the ladies in waiting at the Miki and Baikine bars of Tsjang-Tsjang (*Ultramarine* 81).

183:10   *ululu:* from Gael. *uileliugh,* 'a wail of lamentation.'

183:12   *aeriel:* Ariel, the etherial spirit of *The Tempest,* translated into the radio aerial of a ship.

183:14   *Venus first, then Mercury:* i.e., love first, then the mercury treatment for syphilis.

184:1   *Castor . . . Pollux:* the Dioscuri, twin sons of Zeus and Leda later constellated as Gemini; they rescued their sister Helen when, as a child, she was carried off by Theseus (legendary King of Athens and slayer of the Minotaur).

185:16   *the stokehold:* the confined space in a ship's lower depths, from whence the furnaces are fed.

186:1   *Chilliwack:* a town in the Lower Fraser Valley, east of Vancouver and not too distant from the area (in what is now Manning Park) of a tragic plane crash in 1941; Lowry has in mind, however, the crash of a US Navy twin-engined Neptune on 23 December 1950, on McCreight Mountain, Vancouver Island. The wreckage was not located for some time, and it was not until September 1951 that the bodies of the eleven dead airmen were recovered.

186:9   *Elk Mountain:* i.e., Elkhorn Mountain, at the head of the Elk River, close to McCreight Mountain.

187:1   *fruit:* the poetic equivalent of still-life in painting.

187:3(var)   *Coventry:* during the violent German air-raids of November 1940 and April 1941 the centre of that town was laid waste, and St. Michael's Cathedral was destroyed save for its 295-foot tower and spire. In like manner, Big Ben, atop the Houses of Parliament and near Westminster Abbey, escaped any direct damage.

187:16   *horripilation:* see 100:18; here the word is used explicitly with Aiken's sense of prescience.

188:1   *The Fox and Geese:* not a Vancouver pub but an imagined English one, its name referring to the board game in which pegs representing the geese can only be moved forward to corner the fox, while the piece representing the fox can remove geese from the board by jumping over them.

188:11   *Hare and Hounds:* a game in which two people set out, leaving behind them a trail of confetti, and try to keep ahead of their pursuers before reaching a designated place.

189:2   *The wheels:* for Lowry, the seaman's equivalent of 'the shakes,' or D.T.s (presumably, because everything goes round). The 'scarlet snowshoe' seems to be Lowry's own symptom of a similar cabin fever.

189:5   *agate eyes:* Poe's Helen stands at the window niche, an agate lamp within her hand ('To Helen,' l. 13); an image taken up by Hart Crane in 'The Tunnel' (Part 7 of *The Bridge*), when he confronts the visage of Poe, with 'eyes like agate lanterns.'

189:7   *A parthenon of possibilities:* the word 'parthenon,' suggesting the Temple of Athena on the Acropolis, is used in conscious opposition to 'scarlet' and 'harlot' and with a sense of its etymology as *virgin.*

190:3   *punk:* wood so dry that it is on the point of crumbling into dust.

191:5   *Pisces on the fifth house cusp:* in astrology, a *cusp* is the beginning or first entrance into a House (one of the twelve divisions of the Zodiac); and persons born under the first or last week of a sign fall under the cusp of that sign, and thus have hybrid characteristics. Lowry's 'science' does not seem exact; the choice of Pisces is unexplained (he was born in June), and Venus enters rather wilfully, but the general idea is that when one's sign enters into the fifth House, it presages good fortune, particularly in matters of love.

193:T   *Goethe:* Johann Wolfgang von Goethe (1749–1832), the greatest of German poets. The title alludes to Eckermann's celebrated *Conversations with Goethe* (1836), but the imagery derives directly from *Faust* 764–9, where Faust tells Wagner of his divided being: 'Two souls, alas! are lodged within my breast, / Which struggle there for undivided reign: / One to the world, with obstinate desire, / And closely-cleaving organs, still adheres; / Above the mist, the other doth aspire, / With sacred vehemence, to purer spheres.'

195:1, 2   *the crosstrees...the topping-lift:* on a sailing ship, the *crosstrees* are the light timbers at the topmast head, supporting the 'top,' or upper mast, and spreading the rigging; a *topping-lift* is the tackle by which the outer end of a boom is 'topped,' or hoisted.

195:13   *a strong sheep:* a complex breed of Christian and coward. In the drafts of *Dark as the Grave* Sigbjørn is explicit about 'His sense of guilt about not participating in the war, but his loathing of the sheep-like complacence with which everyone went to it.'

196:T   *smitten cymbals of brass:* see Corinthians 13:1: 'Though I speak with the tongues of men and of angels, and have not charity, I am become as sounding brass, or a tinkling cymbal.'

196:2   *Antiphilus:* Antiphilus of Byzantium, in the early years of the Christian era a writer of epigrams, many of which are ingenious paradoxes or descriptions of freak accidents but which reflect a genuine love of ships and the sea.

196:3   *Melville's Redburn:* for the image of mildew on the soul, see 65:16.

197:5   *Keep God inside:* alluding to the traditional tales of gods and spirits (e.g., Silenus) trapped within wood, then 'slashed' free.

197:5(var)   *ellipses:* ellipses may be 'less false' than circles, because the figure traced by a moving wheel, and the movement of the entire planetary system, is elliptical rather than circular; and the *Great Circle* route itself (see 99:2), the shortest distance between two global points, is more truly part of an ellipse.

197:17(var)   *the Goat and Compass:* there are a number of public houses by this name, which is popularly supposed to have arisen (as the next lines intimate) from the phrase 'God encompasseth us.' Faintly behind Lowry's lines may be the circle traced by Donne's more famous compasses in his 'A Valediction: Forbidding Mourning.'

198:1   *The devil is a gentleman:* for further evidence of this, see Poem 40.

198:7–8   *Bahomet...Saturn: Bahomet* is a corruption of 'Mahomet' and in esoteric lore one of the major demonic powers; *Saturn* is a figure of Time, the devourer of life, under whose auspices occur works of malediction and death; thus *sixty-three,* which ought to be of favourable omen (6 + 3 = 9, a trinity of threes), is shadowed by evil. Lowry lifted the phrasing from Frater Achad's QBL (1922), where the precise significance is equally mysterious.

199:9   *The star:* Margerie Lowry had acted in some minor Hollywood roles.

201:T   *Donne:* John Donne (1572–1631), poet and Dean of St. Paul's Cathedral, whose star had been somewhat occluded until T.S. Eliot's essay 'The Metaphysical Poets' (1921) led to a reappraisal; but which swam further into public view in 1940 with the success of Ernest Hemingway's great novel of the Spanish Civil War, *For Whom the Bell Tolls* (see next entry), alluded to in Lowry's sub-title. 'Regular' is a term of approbation; in 'Through the Panama' (entry for 11 December), Martin Trumbaugh considers the division of humanity into those who are regular and the sons of bitches.

201:T   *For whom the log rolls:* from Donne's *Meditation* 17 (1623): 'No Man is an *Iland*... Any Mans *death* diminishes *me,* because I am involved in *Mankinde;* And therefore never send to know for whom the *bell* tolls; It tolls for *thee.*' The expression 'to roll a log' also means to use the efforts of one to promote the fortune of another, as those of Hemingway had for that of Donne (in 'The Ordeal of Sigbjørn Wilderness' (132), Lowry notes: 'Donne – whose new popularity thanks more to Hemingway that Eliot').

201:2   *Spain:* the setting of Hemingway's novel; but also an allusion to Donne's travels as a gentleman-volunteer with Essex to sack Cadiz (1596) and with Raleigh hunting Spanish treasure ships off the Azores (1597).

201:4   *the Cheshire Cheese:* an ancient hostelry in London's Fleet Street, since the days of Johnson associated with the literary arts and in the 1880s and 1890s the meeting-place of Yeats, Dowson, Symons, and other members of the Rhymers' Club.

201:5   *among the Anabaptist Germans:* in his *Sermons* (2.3.633–49) Donne tells of a visit to Aix-la-Chapelle (1612? 1619?) during which he lodged in a house of Anabaptists who 'for the exercise of their religion' never met, for though they were all Anabaptists yet they detested (and excommunicated) one another.

201:6   *plump shadow-boxers:* Hemingway was a passionate advocate of physical activity of any kind and took up shadow-boxing shortly after arriving in Europe (though after visiting Spain he would sometimes substitute shadow-bullfighting).

202:3   *the rumble seat:* a folding seat in the back of an automobile, not covered by the canopy; for another 'alcoholic dawn,' see Poem 128.

204:2   *aerieled roofs:* spiritually receptive (see 183:12).

204:14   *sweet marjoram... caraway: sweet marjoram* is an aromatic herb, related to oregano, and associated with the madness of King Lear: 'Give the word – sweet marjoram – pass' (4.6.94). *Caraway* is an aromatic seed used in cookery, but also chewed to disguise the liquor on the breath (Lowry's pun turns on the popular etymology, 'care away').

205:1   *The noise of death:* on the manuscript Lowry appends this 'explanation': 'This must mean: the antithesis is: While the music is going the trumpets pierce the web of deep sleep which the mind is trying to pierce, but it is comparatively tranquil: while there is silence the mind pierces the web more deeply, but there is nothing but disorder, & a sleep symbolised by horror.'

205:4   *nickel:* i.e., to feed the 'Nickelodeon.'

206:T   *Eels:* referring to the belief that eels spawn in the mysterious depths of the Sargasso Sea and to the popular assumption that nobody has ever proved this to be so. The variant reference to 'Thomson' and details of the darkness and the abyss may imply an elveric equivalent to 'The City of Dreadful Night.'

206:5   *glass eels:* the transitional and semi-transparent stage in the evolution from elver to eel.

207:1   *Scipio Sprague:* identified in SL (372), as one Arthur A. Sprague, a friend of David Markson's, to whom this poem, in the form of a letter, was addressed on 1 June 1954; designated as 'Scipio' in reference to Scipio Africanus Minor (185–129 BC), Roman consul, orator, and man of letters, who was later praised by Cicero as the greatest of Romans.

207:9   *Pequod:* Captain Ahab's fated whaling ship in *Moby Dick,* named after the Pequots, 'a celebrated tribe of Massachusetts Indians, now extinct as the ancient Medes' (Chapter 16).

207:10   *Behemoth:* in Job 40:15–24, a great monster, assumed to be the hippopotamus; hence, anything of great bulk or unwieldy size.

207:12   *the Bowery:* from D. *bouewerij,* 'a colonial farm'; in New York City, a street and the nearby area notorious for cheap saloons and homeless derelicts.

208:1   *George Edward Cook:* identified by Russell Lowry as indeed the family's gardener; of local farming stock, he was one of the considerable team employed to lay out and plant the Inglewood gardens of the Lowry home at Caldy on the Wirral Peninsula (Cheshire); and he stayed on for life, living in the picturesque village shop cum post-office nearby.

208:8   *Lycidas:* see **154:6**; here, a tribute to George Edward Cook as Milton's poem was to Edward King, drowned in that very area while crossing from Chester Bay to Dublin.

208:8   *Hilbre:* 'Hildeburg's Island,' off the Wirral Peninsula in Cheshire and easily visible from near the Lowry home.

208:13   *Flintshire:* a county of northeast Wales, across the Dee estuary from the Wirral, and poetically appropriate for the stony connotations of its name.

210:4   *a sawmill:* Dollarton originated as a sawmilling centre in 1916, when the Robert Dollar Company built and operated a mill there and set up a village with a post-office and school for its employees. The mill declined in the Depression, but it remained operative until 1943.

210:5   *I knew a poet once:* the poet is unspecified and may be Lowry himself, but tone and phrasing suggest Thoreau talking to Emerson at Walden Pond.

213:T(var)   *Gastown Gruesomes:* a jazz tune taking its provenance from Vancouver's Gastown, an older part of the city named for 'Gassy Jack' Deighton, who opened a saloon near the Hastings sawmills on Burrard Inlet and attracted around it a small community.

213:T(var)   *In a Mist:* after the Bix Beiderbecke piano solo (see **16:64**).

213:2   *Risen to bring us madness:* see **25:36** for the calendar with its picture of Canada and the brilliant full moon.

214:T(var)   *Burrard Inlet:* an extensive inlet off the Strait of Georgia, continuing past Vancouver and extending north of Dollarton as Indian Arm; named by Captain Vancouver for his friend Sir Harry Burrard (1765–1840).

215:T   *Julian Trevelyan:* an artist friend from Lowry's Cambridge and Paris days. Though a year younger, he had acted as guardian in 1933 when Lowry spent three months in Paris and as best man at his marriage to Jan Gabrial. Lowry had renewed contact with him when visiting Paris again in 1948. The 'poem' makes better sense when translated into simplified French ('neuf, oeuf...', etc.).

216:10   *drunkard's rigadoon:* a drunken dance (see **39:3** and **54:7**); here, with general reference to WWII.

216:14   *Condemned... born:* although a common enough sentiment, it is perhaps best known from Calderón's *La vida es sueño:* 'El major delito del hombre es haber nacido' ('the worst crime of man is having been born'). The play had been translated into English in 1923 by Lowry's tutor at St. Catharine's, H.J. Chaytor.

218:T   *Goldeneye:* a large-headed diving duck (*Bucephala clangula* or *Glaucionetta clangula,* and (according to Peterson's *Field Guide*) so-called for the large round spot before the eye; a white duck with a black back and puffy green-glossed head.

219:T   *Rilke:* Rainer Maria Rilke (1875–1926), German poet known for the *Duino Elegies* (1922) and *Sonnets to Orpheus* (1923); though Lowry may have in mind *The Notebooks of Malte Laurids Brigge* (1910; trans. 1930), in which the twenty-eight-year-old Brigge (like Rilke himself) gives vent to the feverish anxiety that afflicts his soul and tries to write the despair out of his system by making things out of fear. Lowry alludes to this work elsewhere, notably in 'Through the Panama' (entry for 10 December), where he almost admits that his reference is not to Rilke directly but to an article in the *Kenyon Review* 10, 4 (1947): 511–31 (a translation of some letters).

219:T   *Schnitzler:* Arthur Schnitzler (1862–1931), Austrian dramatist known for his ruthless analyses of the human psyche; his plays often deal with the theme of illicit love. In *Dark as the Grave* (63), Lowry refers to Schnitzler's *Flight into Darkness,* given to 'Sigbjørn' by 'Ruth' just prior to the first journey to Mexico, and which takes as its theme the gathering forces of darkness in the human mind.

219:1   *The worst:* echoing the words of Edgar on seeing his blind father: 'The worst is not / So long as we can say "This is the worst"' (*King Lear* 4.1.29–30). The following lines bring together allusions such as Shakespeare's 'To love that well that thou must leave ere long' (Sonnet 73); Wilde's 'Yet each man kills the thing he loves' ('The Ballad of Reading Gaol'); the desolate bleak house of Tennyson's *In Memoriam;* and the lidless eyes and remorseful memories of Eliot's *The Waste Land* – to form a composite image of despair.

221:1   *dives:* punning on the New Testament story of Dives and Lazarus (Luke 16:19–31), in which the rich man, Dives, suffers the torments of Hell, while the beggar, Lazarus, is comforted in Abraham's bosom. Melville discusses the episode in some detail in Chapter 2 of *Moby Dick.*

222:2   *fidley:* in nautical idiom, the 'fiddley' is the iron framework around the deck opening leading to the stoke-hole of a steamer, or the hole itself; in *Ultramarine* (24), the entrance to Hell.

224:T   *Oxford Grouper!:* the Oxford Movement, or Oxford Group, was a religious revivalist movement, committed to moral rearmament, brought to England from America in 1921 by Frank Buchman, an owl-faced pastor from Pennsylvania, and characterized by the 'sharing' of personal problems in groups. The Canadian attorney, A.B. Carey, who acted as Lowry's guardian when he first arrived in Vancouver, was an Oxford Grouper, and the phrase for Lowry always expressed the utmost hypocrisy.

224:T   *Yahoo!:* in Book 4 of Swift's *Gulliver's Travels,* a degenerate species of brute with many of the characteristics of man; hence, human beings of degraded or bestial nature. In the drafts of *Dark as the Grave* the vandals are named 'the Macritchies.'

224:9–10(var)   *the land was government owned:* in 1944 the Dollar Mill property was assessed for a proposed Roslyn Park Subdivision, and a number of lots were sold, the buyers tending to fell trees, build ugly new houses, and put pressure on the local authorities to get rid of the shacks. Lowry's short story 'Gin and Goldenrod' is set against the background of threatened eviction, the hideous slash of felled trees, and the destruction of the forest.

226:10   *Oberammergau:* the Oberammergau Passion Play, given once every ten years in the small Bavarian village, forty-five miles southwest of Munich. The play was first performed in 1634, to fulfil a vow made by one of the villagers during an outbreak of plague; and it tells in eighteen acts the story of Christ from the entry into Jerusalem until the Resurrection. In *Dark as the Grave* (94) and *UV* (185), Lowry refers to the story of the actor playing Christ who gets down off his cross to get drunk on Pilsener and/or return to his hotel room for the night.

229:2   *A tree:* a fitting response to Joyce Kilmer's sentiments about 'Trees': 'I think that I shall never see / A poem lovely as a tree' and: 'Poems are made by fools like me, / But only God can make a tree.'

229:3   *poets in pod:* i.e., as like as two whales.

230:7   *Beowulf:* the hero of the Old English poem by that name and as such embodying its old Germanic ethic of inevitable defeat; hence, an image of the soul fated to meet its dragon.

231:1   *In the dark cavern of our birth:* a poem evocative of John Masefield's tribute to his mother, which begins: 'In the dark womb where I began / My Mother's life made me a man'; part of the point for Lowry being Masefield's title 'C.L.M.,' almost his initials (he had earlier responded in this way to Aiken's *Blue Voyage,* which had been dedicated to 'C.M.L.,' i.e., Clarissa Lorenz, Aiken's second wife).

233:1   *a Liverpool of self:* the imagery of the opening lines may derive from Melville's *Redburn,* where, having landed in Liverpool, young Redburn uses his 'Old Morocco,' or guide-book, that he might identify himself with the town. For the imagery of crucifixion at the masthead, see **290:15.** The poem is written in *Rhyme Royal,* the Chaucerian measure favoured by John Masefield in 'Dauber.'

234:Note   *Translation of a letter:* despite the apparent precision of date and name, the details and Lowry's source of them have not been identified. The poem was one of Lowry's favourites, and in the last year of his life he recalled it as such (*SL* 408).

234:T   *Ingvald Bjorndal:* unidentified.

234:T   *For Nordahl Grieg:* the Norwegian writer (see **12:T**). When the poem was published in the *Atlantic Monthly* 168 (4 October 1941), this dedication was omitted, but the poem was attributed to 'Malcolm Boden Lowry,' the middle name being that of his mother's family and in Lowry's imaginative scheme of things affirming a Norwegian identity.

235:1   *Goodheart:* a common Elizabethan salutation, as in *Love's Labours Lost* (4.3.153–4): 'Good heart, what grace hast thou, thus to reprove / These worms for loving, that art most in love?' As the variant confirms, Lowry has in mind his friend from Cambridge days, James Travers, who had died in a blazing tank in the Western Desert in 1942. He is invoked in 'The Ordeal of Sigbjørn Wilderness' and remembered with affection as 'Historian and silver fox farmer, writer and iconoclast, beer drinker and wit, seven years dead, but as live as a barrel full of monkeys.'

235:2   *Deal:* a town in Kent, reputedly the landing place of Julius Caesar and later one of the Cinque Ports. Lowry is recalling the summer of 1930 or 1931, when he was staying with Conrad Aiken in nearby Rye.

235:3   *Rosmersholm, Little Eyolf:* two plays by Henrik Ibsen, from the later part of his career: *Rosmersholm* (1886), with its complex heroine Rebecca West, is a penetrating study of deception and guilt; *Little Eyolf* (1894) looks into the interior of a soul in which love has died. There is no clear record of Lowry or Travers acting in either play, but Lowry was sporadically associated with the Cambridge 'Footlights' players and composed lyrics for at least one of their productions.

235:4   *Kaiser:* Georg Kaiser (1878–1945), dramatist and expressionist writer, who was in 1933 expelled by Nazi pressure from the Prussian Academy of Arts and who lived from 1938 in exile in Switzerland. In a letter to Clemens ten Holder (his German translator), Lowry said that he had once seen Claude Rains playing in *From Morn to Midnight* in England, 'as I was later to have a minor hand in the production of the same at Cambridge' (*SL* 239).

235:4   *Strindberg:* August Strindberg (1849–1912), Swedish dramatist and author of such plays as *The Father* (1887) and *The Ghost Sonata* (1907), as well as the better-known *Miss Julie,* which has been performed at Cambridge during Lowry's time.

235:4   *O'Neill:* Eugene O'Neill (1888–1953), American dramatist, all of whose works Lowry admired, but whose early dramas of the sea were of particular importance in shaping his younger sense of his self (in 'Through the Panama,' entry for 8 November, Martin Trumbaugh defines himself as the man who went to sea because he read *The Hairy Ape* and *The Moon of the Caribbees*). In the letter to ten Holder (above), Lowry suggests that the best of O'Neill's plays ('Der Gross Gott Braun') could not have been written without the influence of Kaiser.

235:6   *dormie:* more often, 'dormy'; in golf, the condition of being as many holes ahead of one's opponent as there are holes left to play.

235:7   *Aldwych, the old Vic – or the New:* well-known theatres of the London West End.

235:8   *the Playboy:* since Liverpool is not far from the Dee estuary (on the other side of the Wirral Peninsula), the name of its theatre suggests (because of *The Playboy of the Western World*) J.M. Synge's *Riders to the Sea* (1904).

235:10   *mashies:* antiquated irons, used for short lofted pitches to the green.

236:T   *Iphigenia in Aulis:* in the play of that name by Euripides, Iphigenia, daughter of Agamemnon and Clytemnestra, is sacrificed in atonement for a crime against Artemis so that the gods might send winds to take the invading Greeks to Troy. Each of the drafts has one note in pencil added to it: 'A mistake' and 'Something wrong'; Lowry is perhaps in doubt as to the desirability of including the phrase as part of Agamemnon's thoughts.

236:4   *Euripus:* the name of the channel at its narrowest point between the island of Euboea and mainland Greece and a strait remarkable for the fierceness of its current and variability of its tide; it was here, at Aulis, that Iphigenia was sacrificed.

237:9(var)   *But you who pass:* see Lamentations 1:12: 'Is it nothing to you, all ye who pass by? behold, and see if there be any sorrow like unto my sorrow, which is done unto me, wherewith the Lord hath afflicted me in the day of his fierce anger.' The first sentence is inscribed on the War Memorial on Hastings Street, Vancouver.

238:T   *Isle of Man:* small island in the Irish Sea, 'not parcel of the realm but of the possession of the Crown of England,' with the world's longest enduring parliament and a strong sense of its own identity; in Lowry's day linked by regular packet sailings to Liverpool. In a letter dated 3 January 1944, the Lowrys thank Gerald Noxon for the 'Isle of Man folder' that he had recently sent them.

238:1   *Eringo root:* the candied root of the sea holly, formerly used as a sweetmeat and regarded as an aphrodisiac.

238:2   *Samphire:* the plant *Crithmum maritimum,* which grows on rocks near the sea, the aromatic leaves of which are used in pickles; often associated with the Sea Holly.

238:2 *St Annes Head:* a small promontory about two miles southeast of the village of St. Anne ('Santon'), itself some six miles southwest of the village of Douglas.

238:3 *Pennyroyal:* a species of mint, formerly much cultivated and esteemed for its medicinal properties. The 'marlpits' are pits out of which is dug *marl*, a clay rich in calcium and used as a fertilizer.

238:3 *Ballaugh:* a small inland town, a little north of Peel and west of Douglas.

238:4 *Henbane:* an annual found often on waste land, with dull yellow flowers streaked with purple, an unpleasant smell, and narcotic qualities; sometimes associated with despair.

238:4 *Derbyhaven:* a fishing village on the southeast coast of the island.

238:5 *seakale:* the plant *Crambe maritima,* of the mustard family, with a fleshy branching root-stock and long ovate leaves; cultivated for its young shoots.

238:5 *Peel:* a fishing port and resort town on the west coast of the Isle; known for its castle and its ruined thirteenth-century cathedral.

239:4 *teredos:* shipworms (see **109:9**); hence, l. 8, 'vermiculated,' or 'worm-eaten.'

239:6 *gravelottes:* clusters of marine detritus; to 'grave' a ship (l. 15) is to cleanse its bottom by burning off such accretions and then paving the timbers with tar.

239:9 *helminthiatic:* the Helminth is a maw-worm, or intestinal parasite; hence, 'riddled with worms.'

240:T *June 1944:* lamenting the destruction by fire, on the morning of 7 June 1944 (*SL* 45: it 'had to be the 7th') of the Lowry shack, the antiquated local fire-truck being unable to reach or cope with the blaze. Although the manuscripts of *UV* and many of the poems were saved, those of *In Ballast to the White Sea* were almost totally burnt, and virtually all the Lowrys' personal possessions were lost.

240:7 *a bottle of gin:* quite possibly saved and, hence, perhaps, the ironic ending of 'Gin and Goldenrod,' where the unexpected survival of a bottle of gin after a different sort of disaster allows the blooming again of a wry kind of hope.

240:12 *And the world still burns on:* their fire as a microcosm of universal conflagration; but retaining an ironic perspective – what is such a sorrow in the context of global affliction and the D-Day landings in Normandy only one day before.

241:4 *work of eviction:* see **224:9–10(var)**; the North Vancouver city fathers disapproved of squatters who paid no taxes, and over the years a number of notices of eviction were served, though it was not until the late 1950s that the last shacks were finally bulldozed.

241:2 *the old bandstand:* an imposing wooden rotunda, originally built in 1914, at English Bay in Vancouver's West End; since Lowry's day it has been restored and is back in use.

241:7   *where no man stands:* compare Poem 26. One of the barbarisms of Canadian beer parlours for Lowry, apart from beer so weak that no self-respecting drunkard could enjoy it, was the thought of waiting to be served while sitting at small tables rather than standing at the bar.

243:T   *Philistines:* the inhabitants of Philistia and, in the Biblical story of David and Goliath, at war with the Chosen People; hence, aesthetically, those deficient in the finer sensitivities.

244:6   *Tin-tin:* the insistent sound of the ship's bells in Aiken's *Blue Voyage*.

244:7   *sturm und drang:* Ger. 'Storm and stress'; a term used of the Romantic movement of the late eighteenth century, as characterized by the exaltation of nature and the sense of the individual in revolt against the constraints of his world.

244:10   *red lead:* otherwise *minium*, red oxide of lead, used as the basis of an anti-corrosive paint. The *hammers* are chipping-hammers, small hammers with triangular heads used for removing rust.

244:14   *that two-faced man:* i.e., the bosun (see **116:5–6**).

245:1   *Love and wisdom:* in form a villanelle (see **138:T**).

245:5   *gander:* as in Mother Goose, an imperfect rhyme with 'wander.'

246:3   *the map of Russia:* a reference to Chekhov's *The Seagull* (1896), which ends with the death of Constantine Treplev, who, having failed as artist and lover, identifies himself with a dead seagull and shoots himself.

247:4   *corpse flower:* according to Mrs. Traill's *Studies in Plant Life in Canada* (97), a name for Indian pipe, a plant perfectly colourless from root to flower, 'of a pellucid texture and semi-transparent whiteness' but which turns black and unsightly within a few minutes of being gathered; Lowry took extensive notes upon the plant from Mrs. Traill, adding in his margin that it was 'the Moby Dick perhaps of the plant world.'

247:10   *the Calthian violet:* more correctly, the Calathian violet *(Gentiana Saponaria)*, as praised by Mrs. Traill (98): 'On sandy knolls, among fading grasses and withered herbage of our Oak-plains, we see the royal deep blue, open, bells of this lovely flower, its rich colour reminding one of a Queen's coronation robes.'

248:3   *an ecstasy of swallows:* the usual 'correspondence' is 'an ecstasy of larks,' but in Peterson's *A Field Guide to Western Birds* the two species are related and described on the same page.

248:4   *a tintabulation:* a diminished 'tintinnabulation,' suggesting the musical chiming of little bells (the word was invented by Poe in 'The Bells' (l. 11): 'The tintinnabulation that so musically wells').

248:5   *a scapaflow of grebes:* because they go under, like the German fleet interned and scuttled at the Orkney Island anchorage after the surrender of 1918.

248:6   *a caucus of crows:* 'cause they caw.

248:8   *a Phalacrocorax of capitalists:* in Peterson's *Field Guide* (18), the term is used of the double-crested (breasted?) comorants *(phalacrocoracidae)*.

248:9   *a proletariat of Peacock:* tempting as it is to see a reference to the singular Mr. Glowry of *Nightmare Abbey,* the phrase as used by Lowry in a letter to David Markson (*SL* 260) refers to the reluctance of poets and writers to give away anything that would harm their 'bloody little conception of their own uniqueness.'

249:T   *Marina:* a manuscript note states: 'lines written reading Pericles in 1940.' Virtually every word in the poem is drawn from Shakespeare's *Pericles,* emphasizing not so much the restoration of Marina to her father as the pathos of the daughter, born in a storm and believing herself bereft of father and mother.

249:1   *When she was born the wind was north:* Marina is born at sea in a terrible storm: 'the grizzled north / Disgorges such a tempest forth / That, as duck for life that dives, / So up and down the poor ship drives' (*Pericles* 3.1.47–50). Marina herself says more simply: 'When I was born the wind was north' (4.1.53).

249:2   *the various planets:* cf. *Pericles* 3.1.31–3: 'Thou hast as chiding a nativity / As fire, air, water, earth and heaven, can make, / To herald thee from the womb.'

249:3   *And her mother was buried:* Thaisa, mother of Marina, is believed to have died in giving birth; she is placed in a chest, calk'd and bitumed, and set upon the waves, whence she is cast up at Ephesus and revived.

249:5   *she could endure the sea:* Marina, named so for she was born at sea, is raised at the house of Cleon in Tharsus, but her beauty enrages Cleon's wife, who plots her death. At the critical moment she is rescued by pirates, who sell her to a brothel, from which she is delivered (intact) and restored to her father.

249:7   *the bosun's whistle:* echoing *Pericles* 4.1.64–5: 'The boatswain whistles, and / The master calls, and trebles their confusion.'

249:10–12   *the humming sea...shells...belching whales...lamps:* see *Pericles* 3.1.61–4: 'where for a monument upon they bones, / And aye-remaining lamps, the belching whale / And humming water must o'erwhelm thy corpse, / Lying with simple shells.'

249:13   *The storm did not whirr her away from her friends:* see *Pericles* 4.4.18–21: 'Ay me! poor maid, / Born in a tempest, when my mother died, / This world to me is like a lasting storm / Whirring me from my friends.'

249:14   *this voyage that never ends:* Lowry's intended title for his greater masterpiece was to be *The Voyage That Never Ends,* originally conceived as a trilogy, with *Under the Volcano* as its Inferno, an expanded *Lunar Caustic* as Purgatorio, and *In Ballast to the White Sea* as Paradiso; but it developed into a much larger and more intricate structure (*SL* 267), which could not have been realized. The phrase was his variant of Grieg's *The Ship Sails On* and epitomizes a quest in marked contrast to the final words of Pericles, home from the sea after long and troubled voyaging: 'Our play now is ended.'

250.2   *the terror of the passing lorry:* it has become something of a game among contemporary novelists (Cabrera Infante, Anthony Burgess, among others) to try and work in an allusion to Malcolm Volcano's *Under the Lorry.*

251:2 *thirty one:* the age, presumably, which Lowry was approaching as he wrote the poem (Keats had died in 1821, at the age of twenty-five). As Lowry may or may not have known from Villon, thirty-one is the age to write one's *Testament.*

251:5 *your mountaineering feats:* fantastic as it may seem, the drafts of *Dark as the Grave* reveal just how much Lowry was impressed by the fact that Keats had put a vulture in the first part of *Hyperion.*

251:7 *the first version of Hyperion:* Keats's *Hyperion: A Fragment* was first written in 1818, then revised as *The Fall of Hyperion: A Dream* in 1819. Remarkable for its bold attempts to match the weighty inversions of Milton with Keats's Romantic sensibilities, the 1818 version tells the story, in three parts, of the Titan Hyperion, son of Uranus and Gaea, who is called upon by the fallen Titans to help Saturn regain his kingdom from Jove. The fragment concludes at the point where Apollo, having spoken to the goddess Mnemosyne of his anguish, attains his deification; it would presumably have gone on to tell of the dethronement of Hyperion by Apollo.

251:9 *immersion:* just possibly, an allusion to Keats's chosen epitaph: 'Here lies One Whose Name was writ on Water.'

251:10 *hubris:* in classical Greek drama, an overwhelming pride or confidence that constitutes a fatal flaw.

251:12–13 *Crewe and Marlborough: Crewe* is a major railway junction in south central Cheshire, and the view of its chemical works and machine shops is conspicuously devoid of magic; *Marlborough,* in Wiltshire, is a marketing town best known as the seat of the original Duke of Marlborough, who at the Battle of Blenheim (in Southey's words) achieved a famous victory.

252:9 *Saturn:* god of the leaden planet and harbinger of chaos (see 90:33).

252:9(var) *vinegaroon:* more precisely, 'vinegarone,' a whip-tailed scorpion so named from its secreting, when alarmed, an acid substance with the odour of vinegar.

252:14(var) *Cortes plain:* for his efforts in conquering Mexico, Cortés was awarded the title of Marquis of the Valley of Oaxaca (though not that of Viceroy, which he felt he deserved), and his lands extended from his palace in Cuernavaca some three hundred miles south to Oaxaca.

253:3 *Xochimilco . . . Xochitepec:* not rivers, but towns: *Xochimilco,* now a southern suburb of Mexico City, is celebrated for its *chinampas,* or floating gardens; *Xochitepec,* a small town near Cuernavaca, is the site of an Aztec pyramid (see 129:T).

253:6 *Styx, Acheron, Cocytus, Phlegethon:* four of the five rivers of Hades: the *Styx,* over which Charon must row the souls of the dead; *Acheron,* where the dead souls bathe; *Cocytus,* or the wailing river; and *Phlegethon,* the river of fire.

253:7 *Guadalquivir:* the major river of Andalusia, flowing towards the

Atlantic through the Moorish cities of Cordova and Seville.

253:9   *Lethe:* the other river of Hades, whose waters of oblivion cause the dead to forget their previous existence.

253:16   *Hebrus...Lesbian doom:* referring to the legend of Orpheus after his return from Hades; disconsolate at the loss of Eurydice, he returned to Thrace and eschewed the company of the other sex. He was set on by the Ciconian women, followers of Dionysius, who tore him apart and flung his head and lyre into the Hebrus River, whence they floated, still singing, to the island of Lesbos. Lowry is probably echoing Milton's *Lycidas*, l.68: 'Down the Swift Hebrus to the Lesbian shore.'

254:5   *Strike out a stream of water:* as did Moses in the wilderness (Exodus 17:1–7), when the people murmured that there was no water to drink.

254:11   *Picasso:* Pablo Picasso (1881–1973), Spanish artist and creator of Cubism, whose innovative use of colour and powerful dislocations of style offended the aesthetic senses of many, but who became recognized increasingly as perhaps the most influential artist of the century.

255:3   *Dead Tree and Merry Island:* small islands off the Sechelt Peninsula, north of Vancouver. The names conform to what Lowry, in an unpublished letter to Aiken (22 November 1940), called a 'pleasing Rabelasian whimsy,' of which this was intended to be the ending, but for which he hadn't yet the beginning.

255:4   *an Indian slaughter:* the islands were between the lands of the Squamish Indians and the more northerly tribes and were the subject of territorial dispute in pre-European times.

255:7   *whales:* the islands are close to one of the regular migratory paths of the killer whales.

256:T   *The New Guinea Gardener Bird:* the bower bird *(Ambylornis inornata)* of New Guinea, one of a number of small and plainly coloured birds that build an ornate nest for their mates in much the way celebrated here, then make in front of the bower a garden of moss, which they adorn with fresh flowers. Lowry appears to be working from an unidentified written description.

256:4   *porte cochere:* literally, a doorway under which a carriage or coach may be drawn; more commonly, a door leading through the wall of a building into a small courtyard within.

256:12(var)   *Something like Yeats:* W.B. Yeats, who bought and restored an old Norman tower at Ballylee for his wife George and dedicated it to her in his verse.

257:T   *Kraken:* a fabulous sea-monster (see **140:T**).

257:2   *the stone:* the holy-stone, a large piece of sandstone used for scrubbing wooden decks, which turn sparkling white when sluiced with salt water; so called because to use them seamen must get down on their knees. Large holy-stones were known as 'Bibles,' and smaller ones (for use in tight corners) as 'Prayer-books.'

257:3   *scuppers:* drainage holes cut through a ship's bulwarks to allow any water on deck to drain away down the side.

257:8   *Ahab's solution:* in Chapter 36 of *Moby Dick*, Captain Ahab has the entire ship's company assemble on the deck and tells them of his determination to raise his great enemy; the agreement between him and the crew is then ratified by drawing a great measure of grog which is quaffed from the sockets of harpoons to cries and maledictions against the White Whale. Such a 'solution' is not available to Lowry's bosun, presiding over a funeral at sea.

258:1   *Everyone a Hypocrite, Including Me:* echoing the name of the cantina in UV at the end of Chapter 8: 'Todos Contentos y Yo También' ('Everybody happy, including me'). Chapter 8 also refers to the bus driver's 'aerial pigeons,' closely related to the stool-pigeons here.

258:4   *Harold:* a waiter at the Lynnwood Inn (1515 Barrow, North Vancouver), near the old railway bridge on the North Shore and then the pub closest to Dollarton; he is remembered clearly by William McConnell, who recalls Lowry talking of him; he is not to be confused with the 'Harold' of *Ultramarine* (180), in the obscure anecdote about the customer coming back to the same bar through another door.

259:2   *Corporal Animus:* i.e., Soul of the Body, though not without a sense of animosity in the conjunction.

259:8   *Gloucester beat Kent:* a reference not to *King Lear*, but to English County Cricket; the following reference takes its point from the trophy, played for by England and Australia, called 'The Ashes' (Lowry elsewhere uses the phrase, taken from Grieg's *The Ship Sails On* (163) 'to collapse like a heap of ashes').

259:10   *Warsaw:* alluding to the destruction of the Polish capital in WWII; but also, perhaps, to the 'Warsaw Concerto,' a popular jazz classic.

259:10   *Joe Venuti:* 'Joe' Guiseppe Venuti, 1898–1978, born in mid-Atlantic, jazz violinist and accompanist to Eddie Lang (see **16:58**).

259:11   *Kipling:* Rudyard Kipling (1865–1936), poet and story-teller; Lowry cites here 'The Widow of Windsor' (ll. 36–9): 'Take 'old o' the Wings o' the Mornin', / An' flop round the world till you're dead; / But you won't get away from the tune that they play / To the bloomin' old rag over 'ead.'

259:14   *vexing bathroom Armada:* the manuscript has a tentative gloss: 'a battle in God's bathroom long since fought'; and the image of playing with toy boats (even, perhaps, at 'Ducks and Drakes'), followed by the reference to the 'distaff' or womanly side, is barely a manly one.

259:16   *Plymouth Hoe:* alluding to the famous (if apocryphal) incident of Sir Francis Drake and his commanders playing bowls upon the Hoe (an elevated terrace on the Plymouth sea-front) on 19 July 1588 when the Spanish Armada was first sighted; Drake is reputed to have said there was time to finish the game before first and beat the Spaniards after.

259:16   *the Hare and Hounds:* the pub is unidentified, but its name acts as a metaphor of evasion (see **188:11**).

259:19–20   *mother...sunlight:* the cry of Oswald Alving in Ibsen's *Ghosts* (see **36:4**).

260:3   *between the wheelbarrow and the watering can:* as in Beatrix Potter's *The Tale of Peter Rabbit,* where Peter is hiding in the tool-shed from the angry Mr. McGregor.

262:4   *a marathon of gulls:* see **248:1**.

263:1   *gentle Jesus:* a common enough piety, best known from Charles Wesley's 1742 hymn, 'A Child's Prayer': 'Gentle Jesus, meek and mild'; also used by fireman Gustav on the death of Anton in Grieg's *The Ship Sails On* (82).

263:2   *the mariners hymn:* Hymn 561 of *Hymns Ancient and Modern,* written in 1860 by William Whiting (1825–78) and beginning: 'Eternal Father, strong to save, / Whose arm hath bound the ocean wave, / Who bidd'st the mighty ocean deep / Its own appointed limits keep / O hear us when we cry to Thee / For those in peril on the sea.'

265:1   *Mary Ann:* Mick Gilligan's bawdy daughter, who in Chapter 1 of Joyce's *Ulysses* (and Chapter 3 of Aiken's *Blue Voyage*) lifts up her petticoats and doesn't give a damn; in *Ultramarine* (64), her paternity is attributed to 'Paddy McGulligan.'

266:1   *Old Blake:* William Blake (1757–1827), poet and engraver, through whom Lowry imbued most of his Swedenborgian ideas; the reference here is to the Song of Experience, 'The Little Vagabond,' which begins: 'Dear mother, dear mother, the Church is cold; / But the Alehouse is healthy, and pleasant, and warm. / Besides, I can tell where I am used well; / Such usage in heaven will never do well.'

267:1   *the Matsue Maru:* one of the steamers belonging to the Mitsui Steamship Company of Japan. The poem itself may be an attempt to compose in syllabic quantities (see **143:T**), though its exact measure is evasive.

268:NOTE   *Undone, it seems are we:* the note is a rather unsettling concoction of Donne's 'Undone,' Shakespeare's 'with old woes new wail' (Sonnet 30), and Shelley's 'drain not to its dregs the urn / Of bitter prophecy' ('Hellas,' ll. 1105–6).

268:1   *The nurse in Medea:* Euripides's *Medea* (431 BC) tells of Medea's passionate reaction when Jason abandons her to marry Glauce, daughter of King Creon of Corinth; she takes her revenge by poisoning Glauce and then killing her own children, knowing that Jason's living grief will be the deeper. Lowry refers to the beginning of the play where the children's nurse is mourning the change in Medea and, fearing the worst, asks their tutor to keep them from their mother's sight.

268:15   *their second war:* that between Finland and the USSR while WWII was yet in progress. The Russians had tried to annex Karelia and get access to the strategic Hankö Peninsula; and the Finns, despite their heroic resistance, were compelled to agree to the first of these demands.

269:T   *A Picture:* the view as seen from Lowry's Dollarton shack, looking out across Burrard Inlet towards the Port Moody refinery on the opposite shore. There is a similar description, with many identical verbal echoes, in the Consul's letter to Yvonne (UV 42–3).

270:T   *T.H.:* Lowry's Cambridge friend, the sociologist Tom Harrisson, the original of the Consul's friend 'Wilson,' who so magnificently disappeared into the jungles of darkest Oceania (*uv* 130). In a 1933 'Letter to Oxford' Harrisson had attacked the bovine mentality of Oxbridge; and Lowry's 'pigs' are a response to the puns on oxen, bulls, and cattle in Harrisson's indictment (although, curiously, the title and the final line appear to have been added later to an already existing poem).

271:1 *a Chinese poem:* though ostensibly the simple description of a moonlit scene (one framed by a window of Lowry's shack), the poem is also a response to a charming little doodle of Lowry's own, the original of which can be found among his working notes for *uv*.

271:8 *Chinese lantern of the sun:* the Chinese ideograph for the sun, 日 , is not unlike a lantern.

271:18 *Evinrude:* a popular make of outboard motor; the original of the figure is probably Jimmy Craige.

271:36 *Gastown:* i.e., Vancouver (see **213:T(var)**); Lowry responding (as so often) to the popular etymology of the name.

272:T *The Plagiarist:* Lowry was constantly haunted by the fear of being exposed as a plagiarist (in 1935, accused by Burton Roscoe, he had been deeply humiliated); and in a later notebook he wrote: 'Frankly, I have no gift for writing. I started by being a plagiarist. Then I became a hard worker, as one might say, a novelist. Now I am a drunkard again. But what I always wanted was to be a poet,' (Day 177). The fear of plagiarism is ostensibly well-founded, but Lowry's compulsion to work with the original phrasing of his sources is part of a literary technique so intricate that plagiarism is not the right word.

273:1 *Plingen plangen:* a nonsense rhyme, uttered mysteriously by the Consul (*uv* 192) as he sets off on his dark journey. In an early draft it is cited as 'klingen klangen,' which implies, remotely, a kind of uproar leading to prison (Ger. *aufgefangen,* 'captured').

273:2 *Swingen swangen:* variants of Ger. *swingen,* 'to do violence to,' 'to compel.'

273:3 *Bootle:* see **101:8**.

273:4 *Nemesis:* to the ancient Greeks, the force of retributive justice.

276:T *Auden:* Wystan Hugh Auden (1907–73), poet of the 1930s, whose absence from England during WWII (Lowry here 'assumes' his guilt) had led to a decline in his reputation and exposed him to public comment (Aiken calls him in a letter 'the renegade poet, W.H. Whoreden').

276:T   *Clare's Snail:* that featured in the poem of John Clare, madman (see **177:6**).

277:T   *Gold:* the definition of 'gold' as 'the most malleable and ductile of all the metals' and the Latin name of the goldeneye (see **277:5**) confirm that the Dictionary in question is *Webster's Second.*

277:5   *goldeneye:* for the description of this duck, see **218:1**; Peterson does not give the name *Glaucionetta clangula,* which is offered in *Webster's,* but he does comment that the bird is known as the 'whistler' from the singing sound made by its wings.

279:T   *Prayer:* another instance of the villanelle (see **138:T**).

280:2   *Beelzebub:* from the Hebrew, meaning 'Lord of the Flies'; in Milton's *Paradise Lost* the demon second only to Satan and, in occult tradition, one of the eight sub-princes of darkness.

280:4   *Pontefract:* sometimes spelled and pronounced 'Pomfret'; a town in the West Riding of Yorkshire, in the castle of which Richard II met his death. Lowry may be using the word in the pseudo-etymological sense of a broken bridge.

281:T   *The Wicket Gate . . . Forty One Doors:* this poem formed part of a Christmas greeting to Conrad Aiken, who called his recently acquired house in West Brewster, Massachusetts, '41 Doors,' as the Lowrys occasionally called theirs 'The Wicket Gate' (in the drafts of *Dark as the Grave,* Sigbjørn gives his address as 'The Wicket Gate, Dark Roslyn, Eridanus, British Columbia').

281:1   *thimbleberries:* the black raspberry *(Rubus occidentalis)* has fruit like small raspberries, but it is disappointing to the taste because it is mostly seeds.

281:1   *frost flowers:* a small herb *(Milla biflora)* with a bulbous root and star-shaped flower, known as 'the floating flower'; but also a phrase commonly used of ice crystals that resemble such a flower.

281:3   *mephitic:* offensive to the sense of smell, poisonous, or noxious, as applied particularly to exhalations from the earth; in Aiken's *Blue Voyage* (103), 'Mephitic vapours escape through cracks in rock.'

281:7   *Orion:* in Greek mythology, the hunter slain by Artemis for making love to Eos and turned into a constellation, one of the brightest in the sky.

282:4   *Herr Ober!:* in a German tavern, a call for the waiter.

284:1   *Roderick Usher:* the central figure of Edgar Allan Poe's story, 'The Fall of the House of Usher' (1839), in which the narrator, a childhood friend, goes to see Usher in his decayed mansion at the edge of a gloomy tarn; after a visit full of Gothic horrors, the narrator rushes from the house; and as he looks back in the moonlight, he sees it split asunder and sink into the tarn. A marginal note in the manuscript mentions celebrating Poe's centenary (i.e., that of his death in 1849); and in the drafts of *Dark as the Grave* Sigbjørn cites the opening couplet of the poem and comments: 'Nay, what was the House of Usher but a hangover . . . No, the House of Usher was the state of his soul in such a hangover, the tarns and the mists were his hideous thoughts, and its fall was his soul's fall.' The poem appears towards the end of

'Through the Panama,' in the context of a raging storm.

284:12–17 *going to vote . . . Baltimore . . . murdered:* alluding to the circumstances of Poe's death, which are as bizarre as those in the poem: in October 1849, on his way to New York, Poe stopped off in Baltimore (where he had been living when he wrote 'The Fall of the House of Usher'). A week after arrival, he was found semi-conscious and delirious outside a polling booth and taken to hospital where he died a few days later of 'congestion of the brain.' It appears that, having broken his temperance pledge, he had fallen into the hands of an electioneering band who had imprisoned him, drugged him, and dragged him to the polls where he was forced to vote; then, having placed the voting ticket in his hand, they left him in the street to die.

285:7 *had ten but buried nine:* a marginal note in the manuscript refers to 'the ten talents of the bible' (see Matthew 25:14–29); and Lowry explains that: 'the idea seems to be to compare the cynical despairing hopeless famous English poets of anthologies – who are in a huge majority – than which only the socially optimistic socialistic ones are worse – to unscrupulous loggers of the slash.'

286:1 *Milton:* John Milton (1608–74), poet and Puritan. His *Il Penseroso* (1631), meaning 'the contemplative man,' describes the rewards of the studious and meditative life; *Paradise Lost* (1667) justified profoundly the ways of God to man; *Lycidas* (1637) mourns the death of Edward King as a premature tragedy; and *Samson Agonistes* (1671) is a poetic drama based on the blindness and death of Samson.

286:9 *Yet Wordsworth said:* see his Sonnet 14 (1802), which begins, 'Milton! thou shouldst be living at this hour,' and states (l. 9), 'Thy soul was like a star, and dwelt apart.'

286:10 *Dryden:* John Dryden (1631–1700), poet and dramatist, who may have changed in his faith but never in his allegiance to Milton, whose influence may be traced in every major work.

286:11 *Blake:* although William Blake claimed that Milton was of the devil's party without knowing it, he also wrote a long Prophetic Book called *Milton* – a complex allegorical work that arises from his own interpretation of *Paradise Lost,* whereby the spirit of Milton enters into the world of Blake in an apocalyptic way.

288:1 *Shakespeare's house:* either the house of his birth, in Henley St., Stratford-on-Avon, acquired by the Shakespeare Birthplace Trust in 1847 and carefully restored; or Anne Hathaway's cottage at Shottery, just outside the town; but not the house in New Place, bought by the Bard in 1597 and destroyed by fire in the eighteenth century.

288:2 *curses on his tomb:* there is an inscription over Shakespeare's tomb, in the parish church at Stratford: 'Good frend for Jesus sake forbeare, / To Digg the Dust encloased heare: / Blese be ye Man yt spares thes Stones / And curst be he yt moves my Bones.'

288:3 *Rip van Winkle:* Washington Irving's tale of the good-natured Dutch-American who lives with his termagant wife in the Catskills; one day while hunting Rip meets a stranger, is invited to a gathering, and drinks some liquor that makes him sleep for twenty years; when he awakes the village is much altered, his wife is dead, and his own house, while still standing, has greatly decayed, with its windows shattered and the roof fallen in. Rip's house, never quite completed and finally in ruin, is also the subject of Melville's prose-poem, 'Rip van Winkle's Lilac.'

288:7   *Stonehenge:* a circle of large stones near Salisbury, built during the Late Neolithic to Early Bronze Age (1800–1400 BC), with stones brought at enormous effort from Pembrokeshire for a purpose of druidic mystery. Most of the megaliths still stand.

289:T   *Ship:* a later manuscript note in Margerie's hand reads: 'Malc doesn't like this & he calls it the S.S. Housman, but I, for some reason, do – No, I like it for the last 2 lines – No, I like it.' The verse form, one now notes, is that of 'A Shropshire Lad.'

290:10   *Jules:* perhaps a sailor on the *Oedipus Tyrranous* in *Ultramarine,* though nothing is said there of his loathing the sea.

290:11   *the metro:* the Paris underground, where the sign cited points to a 'correspondance,' or change of line; here, from the *Porte-Maillot / Château de Vincennes* line (l. 1), in the 'direction' of *Porte de Clignancourt* l. 4; changes at *Nation* and *Etoile*).

290:15   *the wild Southern Cross:* a constellation of four bright stars near Centauris, visible in the Southern Hemisphere. The image of crucifixion at the masthead is recurrent in Lowry's poetry (see Poem 233, but also 24, 99, and 173); it may have been stimulated by an illustration at the beginning of Chapter 8 in Lowry's copy of the 1930 Modern Library edition of *Moby Dick* or, more simply, by the death of Billy Budd (Melville cannot resist the comparison).

291:4   *Sokotra:* Lowry's island of mystery (see **68:22–3**).

291:7   *blue water:* that of the open sea.

291:9   *bilged:* in naval parlance, a vessel broken or stove in at its bilges, i.e., at the turn of the hull near the water line. The term is therefore used of failing a test or being dropped from service.

291:10   *felling:* a word used in conscious awareness of Hopkins's Terrible Sonnet which begins: 'I wake and feel the fell of dark not day.'

293:T   *Song:* echoing the imagery and rhythm of a popular traditional song, 'The Fairest May,' and of countless others like it.

294:NOTE   *De Profundis:* L. 'Out of the depths,' the opening words of Psalm 129 (in the King James Version, 130); but also the title given by Robert Ross to the prose apologia (written 1896–7) based upon Oscar Wilde's experiences in prison after being sentenced to two years' hard labour for homosexual practices. Wilde recounts his efforts (tragically, to be of little avail) to arise out of the depths of his ignominy and suffering; and he follows the passage cited by Lowry with the reflection that behind suffering we always find hidden a soul.

294:8   *Clapham Junction:* a station south of the Thames in the London residential district of Wandsworth; Wilde was in process of being transferred from Wandsworth Prison to Reading Gaol.

295:T   *Pentonville:* Pentonville Prison, where Wilde had been taken before being sent to Wandsworth and to which he was briefly transferred from Reading before his release in May 1897.

296:2   *cabbalistic:* the word 'Cabbala' derives from the Hebrew root

'QBL,' 'to receive,' and refers to the mysteries first taught by God to a select company of angels, then after the Fall communicated to Adam that his posterity might regain their pristine felicity; hence, a complex organized body of mystical Jewish wisdom, based upon the principles that Man is a microcosm of the Universe and God and that by rightly interpreting paradigms and signs he might regain union with God.

296:4   *obscure:* invariably used by Lowry (as by the Consul in uv) in the sense of possessing mysterious intimations of the occult.

297:6(var)   *the bloody little man:* a phrase used by Hugh in uv (329) in protest against intolerance and persecution. It derives from Tom Harrisson's 'Letter from Oxford' (see **270:3**), where it is argued that every great movement begins with one man who was crucified, in body or mind.

298:1   *Success:* specifically, the long-awaited triumph of having *Under the Volcano* accepted for publication and met with acclaim, but followed by a pathological fear arising from that triumph. In more general terms, the creative impasse: in the drafts of *Dark as the Grave*, Sigbjørn reflects that the building of a work of art, long perfect in the mind, becomes a vehicle of destruction in the effort to realize it – to transmute it upon paper.

298:1   *disastar:* a deliberate misspelling, to suggest that the fault lies not within ourselves but in our stars.

298:7   *a treacherous kiss:* such as that given by Judas Iscariot to Christ in the Garden of Gethsemane or by Faust to the phantasm of Helen at a critical moment in *Doctor Faustus.*

301:1   *conspiracy about the great:* perhaps an echo of Stephen Spender's 'I think continually of those who were truly great,' which asserts (as Lowry's poem deliberately does not) the renown of those who fought for life, 'And left the vivid air signed with their honour.'

301:2   *Johnson:* Samuel Johnson (1709–84), the writer and critic who was the dominant literary presence of his age and who emerges most vividly in Boswell's *The Life of Samuel Johnson* (1791), where his brilliant conversation and opinionated eccentricities are given full rein. Lowry refers to Boswell's *Life,* Thursday, 11 November 1793, when, dining at Dr. Webster's, Boswell notes the remark and also Johnson's further comment that this will account for many of the celebrated death-bed sayings that are recorded.

301:6   *unknown wool:* by synecdoche, 'unknown sheep,' who went sans protest to slaughter and are commemorated by plaques to the Unknown Soldier. Compare **195:13**: 'a strong sheep.'

301:15   *to be unremembered:* the ultimate humility; advocated by a Christian saint, but it would be an impertinence to inquire whom.

301:18   *the unimaginable library of the dead:* a phrase also used in the 1940 version of uv, as Hugh recites to Yvonne in Chapter 9 an interminable list of past masters whose works live on and says that it was inspired by something he has been reading in Hermann Broch. He is referring to the final words of Broch's *The Sleepwalkers* (1929), in which he invokes 'the voice that binds all that has been to all that is to come' in the sense of a mystical community of the dead.

302:7   *Poltergeists of the ether:* a phrase used in uv (1 57), where Hugh, listening to the radio, gets only static and interference. *Poltergeists* (from Ger. *poltern,* 'to make a great noise,' and *Geist,* 'spirit') are spirits responsible for inexplicable noises; and the *ether,* in occult thought, is a fifth element that can be 'tuned in' only by those sensitive to it. Lowry's understanding probably derives from A.A. Keyserling's *The Recovery of Truth* (1929), which argues (1 1 1) that man encounters only the occurrences attuned to his particular nature, since his unconscious conjures up the accidents that befall him.

303:2   *the weevil:* the boll-weevil, which causes such anguish to cotton-growers and those (such as Lowry's father) in the fabric trade.

305:1   *Those who die young will look forever young:* perhaps a paraphrase of Laurence Binyon's 'For the Fallen' (ll. 1 4–1 6): 'Age shall not weary them, not the years condemn. / At the going-down of the sun and in the morning / We will remember them.'

305:2   *Chatterton:* the 'marvelous boy' who committed suicide at the age of nineteen (see **52:2**).

305:2   *Brooke:* Rupert Brooke, the 'young Apollo' who died at the Dardanelles (see **35:3**).

305:7   *Doughty:* Charles Montagu Doughty (1 843–1 926), author of the magnificent *Travels in Arabia Deserta* (1 888), noted for its exciting but unusual prose style; a similar eccentricity in verse (notably, the six-volume epic, *The Dawn in Britain*) led to his being neglected and unread.

305:7   *Melville:* the earlier novels *(Typee, Omoo, Redburn,* and *White-jacket)* had won Melville fame, but with the publication of *Moby Dick* in 1 85 1 his popularity began to wane; and the later works (such as the esoteric *Pierre* and the long poem *Clarel)* were almost entirely ignored, so that his last years were spent in complete obscurity, his death passing virtually unnoticed.

306:T   *Though I Have More:* an imitation of John Donne's 'A Hymn to God the Father,' which enters roughly in this form into the Consul's thoughts of the cosmic golf course (uv 207).

306:2   *silver king:* a brand of golf ball popular between the wars.

306:7   *divots:* strokes that remove more turf than ball.

307:1 0   *as firemen to seamen:* in terms of a ship's hierarchy (and notably in Grieg's *The Ship Sails On),* a natural opposition; even though the 1 894 *Seamen's Articles* require (point b) that seamen and firemen shall mutually assist each other in the general duties of the ship.

308:8   *compare juniper with dog violet:* according to Mrs. Traill's *Studies in Plant Life in Canada* (9), *dog violet* is a pretty variety of the branching white wood violet (see **1 57:2–3**), distinguished by a long spur, lilac-tinted petals, striped and veined with dark purple, and with a branching stem; it is contrasted with juniper, the evergreen shrub, the berries of which are used in the distillation of gin.

308:1 2   *the purple hills:* throughout uv the word 'purple' is used (by association with W.H. Hudson's *The Purple Land,* 1 885) with the sense of a paradise soon to be lost.

3 1 0:T   *Villanelle:* see **1 38:T**.

313:2 *haciendas:* in Mexico, large estates or ranches; usually associated by Lowry (though not here) with the exploitation of the peasantry and the cry for land reform.

313:9–10 *the groans of the dying . . . the groans of love:* a sentiment experienced by the Consul in the Farolito (UV 350); in the earlier drafts Lowry had intended to contrast the Consul's dying groans with the ecstasy of Hugh and Yvonne (at that point, his daughter) making love beneath the stars.

314:10 *deodars:* an East Indian species of cedar *(Cedrus deodara),* which gives an excellent timber much prized for its beauty.

314:10 *arbor vitae:* L. 'tree of life'; the 'juniper' here is a West Coast conifer (compare 308:8).

314:16 *Sweet fern:* the *complania asplenifolia,* of the Order *myricacae,* to which (says Mrs. Traill, 113), the name of sweet fern is improperly applied. She adds that the smell is evanescent and soon vanishes; but the comment about the seed making us invisible is otherwise opaque.

314:28 *the corduroy road:* literally, a road formed by laying split logs transversally across swampy land, rounded side up; thus, a corrugated road. Here, the Dollar Road, built in 1918 for the sawmill, and giving the Dollarton community access to Deep Cove and Vancouver.

314:41 *as Wolfe remembered Gray:* as James Wolfe, having read Gray's *Elegy,* took the path of glory that led but to his grave (see 84:11).

315:4 *wyvern:* in heraldry, a chimerical winged dragon with the feet of an eagle and a barbed, serpent-like tail.

316:9 *the Oxford Grouper:* a religious caterpillar (see 224:T).

317:NOTE *A.P. Herbert:* Alan Patrick Herbert (1890–1971). Independent M.P. for Oxford and campaigner for such issues as the reform of the divorce laws (*Holy Deadlock,* 1934) and English spelling (*What a Word,* 1935). His best-known novel was *The Water Gypsies* (1931), and he was a regular contributor to *Punch.* His squib, 'Where is young Lance,' was reprinted in Vancouver's *Daily Province* on 14 December 1939 and is here cited in full because Lowry's poem, which appeared in the *Province* of 29 December 1939, is such a direct response to it:

Where is young Lance . . .

By A.P.H. in Punch

Where is young Lance the Leftist, who shouted 'Arms for Spain!'
Who doubted so the fortitude of Mr. Chamberlain;
And if such arms had been dispatched would soon have spent his
[breath
On hissing that his countrymen were Profiteers in Death.
Where are Iseult and Steve, who, hanging posters from their necks,
Marched fearlessly to Downing Street and cackled 'Save the Czechs!'
Who cursed because he did not save the Abyssinian souls,
But thought it very rash indeed to guarantee the Poles?
Oh, where is Spitfire Florence, who confidently swore
That if we threatened war enough there would not be a war?

Where is young Know-all Nesta, so mystically sure
That everything that Russia did was peacable and pure;
And, while of course our Empire caused her honest blood to boil,
Explained that Righteous Russia would not pinch an inch of soil?
Where too is Percy Pink, who backs a loser every race
But, like the happy tipster, loses neither funds nor face?
And where is Modern Mervyn, who was bubbling fire and sparks
But cannot aid the war because it's not in aid of Marx?
And what of Comrade Chris, who thinks democracy such fun –
Always excepting everything our Parliament has done;
And Ermytrude, who wants free speech and voting everywhere,
Although of course in England an election's never fair?
Where are the youthful genii who knew exactly how
The cosmos should be managed? For their chance is surely now.
Where are the New School Knickers who despise the Old School Ties?
What do they do to show themselves more good and brave and wise?
Their sisters are in hospitals; their brothers won't be long:
But they are still explaining where the government was wrong.
Or in the Billius Weekly very lengthily expound
The reasons why they think their 'ideology' is sound.
While Reginald, who actively can not assist the war,
Proclaims the right to know at once what he is fighting for.
Where Mervyn is, or Barbara, we simply do not know:
But Lance, I hear, is lecturing in Prudence, Ohio.

317.2 *J.B.S. Haldane:* geneticist and biometrician (1892–1964), who opened up new paths of research in the science and philosophy of biology. From 1922 to 1932 he was Reader in Biochemistry at Cambridge, where he announced himself a Marxist and for several years edited *The Daily Worker,* though he was later to be disillusioned by the evolution of Stalin's policy. For a short time Lowry was a member of the 'addled salon' run by his wife, Charlotte, who used him as a model for her protagonist James Dowd in her novel *I Bring Not Peace* (1932).

317:3 *Mann:* Thomas Mann (1875–1955), German novelist whose works, such as *Death in Venice* (1912) and *The Magic Mountain* (1924), are preoccupied with the relation of art to reality and whose opposition to Fascism led to his exile from Germany to the US, where he took out citizenship in 1944.

317:3 *Hemingway:* Ernest Hemingway (1899–1961), writer, bull-fighter, and skiamachist (see 201:6), who served with an ambulance unit in WWI and as a war correspondent in Spain during the Civil War (his novel arising from that experience, *For Whom the Bell Tolls,* was soon to be published).

317:12 *the vaunted Bear:* i.e., Russia. The reasons for APH's being startled are unclear.

317:19 *Molotov:* Vyacheslav Mikhailovich Molotov (1890–1970), the Russian statesman who was the major spokesman for the Soviet Union before WWII and who negotiated the infamous German-Soviet Non-Aggression Pact of August 1939.

317:19 *Hess:* Rudolf Hess (1894–1987), Hitler's deputy and confidant and the man largely responsible for the organization of the Nazi Party before the War; he was yet to make his spectacular flight into Scotland in 1941 or to suffer the long years in Spandau Prison.

317:20 *Goebbels:* Paul Joseph Goebbels (1897–1945), minister of propaganda for Hitler and thus with authority over the press, theatre and film, music and the visual arts. He was later to commit suicide.

317:26 *indoor Marxmanship:* parlour politics (see **147:46**).

317:30 *the celebrated vicar:* in an anonymous ballad of the eighteenth century, a self-serving parson who turns his coat and faith to match that of the monarch of the day, claiming that 'whatsoever king may reign' he will remain Vicar of Bray.

317:31 *and ever the twain shall meet:* echoing Kipling's 'The Ballad of East and West,' which maintains that: 'East is East and West is West, and never the twain shall meet, / Till Earth and Sky stand presently at God's great Judgement Seat.'

318:1 *Nine-light windows:* i.e., lead-light windows, divided into nine smaller panes ('Nine-light' appears to be Lowry's invention). In an early draft of *Dark as the Grave*, Sigbjørn and his wife Primrose are rebuilding their burnt house, and Sigbjørn thinks of the big windows they'd wangled from the machine-shop and how proud Primrose was when, with Sam's help, they had fitted them into their frames: 'Nine-light windows that never saw the sun. Now face the east in a house that's scarce begun. Who once lent grudging day to a machine, what joys and agonies would they be someday light within. Too many days, too much light. Or it was, could be, almost, a poem.'

319:14 *Lycidas:* see **154:6**.

319:18 *the bermudas:* islands in the Western Ocean, off the North American coast; referred to as in Marvell's 'The Bermudas' (1653), where they represent a safe and beneficent landing after a long voyage.

320:4 *young Aeschylus:* the Greek tragedian (525–456 BC), author of *Prometheus Unbound* and the Orestean trilogy. In his time he had served proudly at Salamis and Marathon, but (despite the 'young') Lowry seems to be referring to the apocryphal story of his death, when an eagle flying over dropped a tortoise on his head.

320:8 *crepitation:* a crackling noise; here perhaps used in the medical sense of the sound produced by fractured endings of bones moving against one another. The tone is similar to Richard Wilbur's 'The Death of a Toad,' which, however, Lowry's poem probably antedates.

321:T *A Young Fellow Named Crane:* Hart Crane, author of *The Bridge,* who on 27 April 1932 jumped from the *Orizaba* into the Gulf of Mexico. He jumped not at midnight, but noon; an alcoholic, he had been drinking but was not drunk; and, an admitted homosexual (though travelling with Peggy Cowley), he was not likely to be 'awaiting a Jane.' A sense of having disgraced himself in Havana and on board the ship, as well as a lack of faith in himself and his creative future, seems to have prompted him to jump (see **42:1**).

322:T *The Young Man from Oaxaca:* the limerick is repeated in the manuscript of *Dark as the Grave,* where Lowry notes that Cervantes, the proprietor of a Oaxaca cantina, might be referred to as 'El León' (later to be one of Lowry's pet names for himself).

322:2   *Mintaka:* one of the three stars (the others being Alnilam and Alnitak) that form the belt of Orion.

322:3   *Orion:* the hunter killed by Scorpio; and the brightest constellation in the northern winter sky. The phrase 'Dark Orion' is used in Aiken's *Blue Voyage* (1 32), also in a jest about death.

Appendices

Appendix A

IN 1954 THE Lowrys left Dollarton forever, eventually settling in Ripe, Sussex, via Los Angeles, New York, Italy, and the Atkinson Morley Hospital in London, where Lowry underwent psychiatric treatment. In February of 1956 the Lowrys took possession of 'The White Cottage' in Ripe, and except for Margerie's three-month hospital stay in late 1956 and their June 1957 tour of the Lake District, they lived quietly in Ripe until Lowry's death on 27 June 1957.

The ninety-eight poems in this section date from 1949–57, and all except one, 'Lusty Advice of a Fortune Teller' [354], appear in correspondence and notes left around the Dollarton shack or the White Cottage in Ripe. Although 'Lusty Advice' may have been included in a letter, it now exists on a single sheet of 8½ × 11″ white 'Plantagenet Bond' paper, datable to 1957 from its appearance in Lowry's outgoing correspondence for that year. Three poems (plus one version of another) are included with correspondence on various smaller sizes of unmarked white paper; the contents of the letters indicate they were sent from Ripe to London during the period September–November 1956 when Margerie was hospitalized for exhaustion.[1] The remaining ninety-four poems appear with correspondence and notes on pink, blue, green, yellow, and white sheets of 3¼ × 4¾″ note paper. These papers are also present in the *October Ferry to Gabriola* manuscripts, on which Lowry worked during second Dollarton and Ripe periods (1949–54 and 1956–7). Except for 'From *The Gleanings of a Gadwall*' [344], all of the poems in this section exist in only one holograph version; there are no typescripts. As a result, there are few sigla for these hastily composed notes.

In December 1987, these ninety-four 'multicolour' poems were deposited to the Lowry Collection at UBC by Margerie's sister, Mrs. Priscilla Woolfan, who maintains that all this 'love letter' material dates from England. Although her dating hypothesis is verified by the content of *some* of the love letters and although the unified nature of the love letters argues strongly for a single-period composition, it is irrefutable that at least one-third of this new material belongs to the 1949–54 Dollarton period. Evidence for this dating includes some of the content, most noticeably in the poems 'Welcome Home, Oh Sweetest Harteebeeste' [405] and 'With Sweetest Morning Love to Their Beloved Harteebeeste' [420], and the fact that isolated sheets of the small, variously coloured note papers occasionally appear during the Dollarton period, for example, in the manuscripts for 'Beneath the Malebolge lies Hastings street' [178] and in

Lowry's outgoing correspondence for 1950 (2–14). In addition, two of the small papers – the blue and the yellow – bear the 'Chenaux Bond' watermark and are imprinted 'Made in Canada.' Of course, the Lowrys could have taken a stock of this paper with them to England; in any case the dating for these note papers bears further investigation because content is usually not by itself adequate evidence for dating a poem. To accommodate this dating problem and because of their unified, coherent tone, the poems of this section are categorized by genre rather than by chronological period.

Unlike other Lowry poems, the love poems cannot be regarded as either finished or unfinished since they were, properly speaking, not intended to be published. Nevertheless, they have been included because they reveal the private world and language of the Lowrys, a world populated by articulate animals such as Lowry's persona The Pronghorn, Mr. and Mrs. Duck, the Gadwall, the Loving Larks, the Mink, the Seal, and Margerie's *alter ego*, the Hartebeeste. Despite their sensitive nature, they have been included for several reasons. First, this material extends the range of possible critical analyses into Lowry's English period. Critics will be able to establish links with typically Lowryan imagery, especially the nature imagery that developed during the Dollarton period. In addition, and perhaps more importantly, they will also discover new techniques in Lowry's poetic attempts, most noticeably his increased experimentation with concrete or spatial poetry. Second, because they were composed during the same period, these poems might be of great interest to those critics and scholars working on *October Ferry to Gabriola*. Third, biographical critics require access to this material in order to help piece together the events of the final years of Lowry's life. Finally, these poems evoke a strange atmosphere of contentment and yearning: contentment in Lowry's obvious great love and concern for Margerie, and yearning, expressed through the imagery, for the idyllic life on the beach at Dollarton.

Because the correspondence in which these poems appear almost always lacks specific dates, they are arranged alphabetically, including articles. Except where specific dating does occur or can be determined, the poems are dated 1949–57. Although they could have been composed at any time during this period, because the Lowrys travelled from 1954 to 1956, 1949–54 and 1956–7 are the most likely periods of composition; the tone and content of these poems reflect the fact that, during their composition, Lowry was stationary at 'The Lovecot.' Because the poems themselves often form the content of the entire note, the closing salutations present an editorial problem. In this edition, the salutations are generally omitted unless they form part of the rhyme, syntax, or content of the poem, in which cases they are preserved. As usual, Lowry's tendency towards initial line capitalization in the later versions of his multiple-version poems provides the justification for emending to capitals in this section. Left unemended is the spelling for Margerie's animal persona, 'The Hartebeeste,' which Lowry frequently spells 'Harteebeeste.' It is possible that Lowry has simply misspelled the word, but equally possible is the theory that he changed the spelling to suit the rigours of scansion, emphasis, and tone. Therefore this edition retains his various spellings of the word.

NOTE

1   The three poems are: 'Half of the harm that is done in this world' [346], 'How overjoyed I am to get your letter' [348], 'Though we are all a little disappointed. . . ' [392]; plus one version of 'From *The Gleanings of a Gadwall*' [344].

1949–57   A CONCLUSION – POEM   [323.1]

And though it is possible there are many
        Other fine antlered animals in
    Existence such as the Texas Longhorn
        May I ask you humbly where one is to
5   Be found, oh my most best belovedest
    Harteebeeste, always excepting her, at once
        So musical,
            So amusing,
                With so many accomplishments.

1949–57   [324.1]

            A lapis dawn is gleaming
            Over Port Moody steaming,
            And a silver dawn is crashing
            Where hangs the ghostly washing
5   The morning bird is whistling
            Within the raspberries bristling.

3   324.1: A silver dawn is crashing
6   324.1: Within the sagebrush bristling.

1949–57   A LITTLE DITTY FOR THIS DAY   [325.1]
                TO THE BELOVED HARTEEBEESTE

        Dear golden eyes
        Are bold and wise
        El Leon is unmatcheable
        And the Pronghorn gay is a way away
5   But the Seal, she is uncatcheable
        Her home is strange, on the watery range
        And they say, it is unthatcheable,
        But the Seal, she is uncatcheable.

1949–57   A MYSTERIOUS HINT   [326.1]

The seal and all the fishes green
The panther puss with shining eyen
The little flowers with golden sheen
And he of cats the lordly dean
5   Who lately up a tree was seen
But nonetheless maintains his mien
The loving larks with trills so keen
The pronghorn with his knowing beam
And other beasts upon the green
10   Will call, *if asked,* on Hallowe'en

1949–57   A SIMPLE SEABIRD'S TRIBUTE   [327.1]
                 TO HER HARTEEBEESTE

Cold-cold-are the sabre wings of the Jaeger
Warm-warm-is the little heart of the Jaeger.
Chill-chill-are the long ways of the Jaeger,
As he cleaves the ocean, but when he so cleaves the
5   Ocean, thinking ever of his beloved Harteebeeste:
Warm-warm-are the sabre wings of the Jaeger
And warmest of all,
                Is the little heart,
                        Of the Jaeger.

1949–57   [328.1]

A sweet night
And sleep thin
Because of the cat
Who will sleep fat.
5   And great luck
From Harlequin –
(Mr and Mrs) – Duck –

1949–57   A TRIBUTE TO   [329.1]
              THE RENOWNED HARTEEBEESTE

By rocky shores
We have heard of thy fame
By wintry shores
We have heard thy name
5   So bringing you all
Kinds of love and luck,
We paid you a call –
The Harlequin Duck.

5–6 329.1: So bringing you all kinds
          Of love and luck,

1949–57   AFTERNOON NOCTURNE   [330.1]

          The evening day is churning
          The room, it is a muddle,
          The fire at last is burning
          But the porch is but a puddle
5   The arrowy rain is slanting
          The arrowy wind is blowing
          For chow we cats are panting
          But at least it is not snowing.

4 330.1: But the porch is just a puddle

1949–57   AND WHO IS IT THAT WITH SNOW-FREAKED   [331.1]
          ANTLERS VICARIOUSLY MUSHETH

And who is it that with snow-freaked antlers
          Vicariously musheth through the frozen tundra
Beside his heroic Harteebeeste at the chamois
          Gait of one who ascendeth the sombre Matter
5   Horn? But yours more respectfully, more
Worshipfully, more dutifully, more admiringly
And yet more waggishly than ever,
                    Your,
                The Pronghorn

1949–57   [332.1]

And who is it through the forest after the
New Year tottereth with antlers
Feeling approximately about the weight of the Matterhorn
Through the early afternoon resembling nothing so
5   Much as a leaden dawn
To greet his beloved Harteebeeste in tones amorous and lovelorn
          But yours more beamingly than ever
                Your The Pronghorn.

1949–57   AS FROM ALL THE LITTLE ANIMALS   [333.1]

          The morning fog is bracing
          The morning dog is pacing
          The morning gull is pacing
          The cat is not us gracing
5   The bird doth far away sing

But not the cat is pacing
The day is very silent
The fog makes us an island
Off, say, the coast of Thailand.

1949–57   [334.1][see 375]

As to report,
Within his court
El Leon holds sway
Tail dipped in quink
5   With scholarly paw
And tender roar
Has eschewed all drink
And prepared to think
And lay down the law
10   Re the problem which
Greater lesser and least
Have already been solved
While his great tail revolved
By the Harteebeeste
15   We won't tell him so
But all of us know
Or at least suspect
That he thinks that the Night
Being tender in effect
20   Is something to bite
And for lions a treat.
– So off in our sleigh
Through the wind woods away
With snow white hocks
25   And immaculate brush
And sound of pock-pocks
Away in a rush
Goes the Arctic fox
Bearing words of love
30   From below and above
In her snow-white socks
Whisks the
Arctic Fox.

1949–57   BILLETIN   [335.1]

The morning bird is singing
El Leon he is training
The greenfinch she is winging
Her way neath a moon awaning

5   The morning bird is singing
        And the morning rain is raining.

1949–57   BILLETS DOUX FOR   [336.1]
      THE BELOVED HARTEEBEESTE

       We feel my dear
       The seal was here
       And not on even keel, my dear

1949–57   !BULLETIN!   [337.1]

       El Leon is swimming
       The shearwaters skimming
       The larks are a'larking
       The linnets are sparking
5   The butterfly stampeth
       The Jaeger he campeth
       On the roof the rain dampeth
       The windbell is chiming
       The pronghorn's song rhyming
10   And none of them shrinketh
       For all of them worketh...

1949–57   [338.1]

     But we little animaux have gone
     With our darling Harteebeeste every
     Step of the way and from the bottom
     Of our loyal and tender hearts wish you all
5   The love in the world from
        2 wise (wise because El Leon is
     Slightly, or was, in 'roar,' feeling bad,
     Take no notice of him) little raccoons.

1949–57   COMMUNAL MESSAGE [339.1]

       Dry thy tears
       My pretty dears
       Nor death nor slaughter
       Fear...
5   *The Shearwater*

       But upward move
       And think on love
       With love
          The Dove

 6 339.1: But think upward

1949–57   DUCKTURNE   [340.1]

The evening bird is singing
The evening bell is ringing
The evening rain is soughing
And the evening grebe is coughing.

4   340.1: And the evening duck is coughing.

1949–57   EL LEON SENDS HIS GREETINGS   [341.1]

All night in dreams I wrestled with an Uck
Reflecting upon how much better twas to be a duck
Eftsoons I held his life in pawn
While he had time to reflect upon how much
5   Better it would have been all round
For him had he instead been born

1949–57   FOR OUR SWEETHARTEEBEESTE ON   [342.1]
                 HARTEBEESTE DAY

The morning tea is boiling
The morning boards need oiling
The morning breakfast threatens
To replace its patterns
5   As the Morning Bed rewettens
The morning bacon greasy
Is gulphed by stomachs queasy
And eek a second plateful
For which most are ungrateful
10   As though they found it hateful
Ourselves, we find all splendid
Our troubles all but ended
As on this day auspicious
We banish naggings vicious
15   And o'er our marmite yeasty
SALUTE OUR HARTEEBEESTE.

11   342.1: Myself, I find all splendid

1949–57   FRAGMENTS FROM THE DUCK ANTHOLOGY   [343.1]
            TO GREET OUR BELOVED HARTEEBEESTE
                 IN THE MORNING WATCH

The morning bird is singing
El Leon is in training
The greefinch she is winging
Her little beak outcraning
5   The morning bird is singing

The morning gull complaining
But the morning rain, refraining.

Saint Leon of Ripe
And Prince of Tripe
The Baron of Gripe,
And Lord of Snipe
5   (Lord Protector of Snipe)
Rose up in his drawers with a loud 'Hup Hipe.'
And said 'By God I'm a peculiar type' –
As he lit his breakfast and cooked his pipe
And gave his arse a hell of a wipe –
10   'To be at once Lord Protector of Snipe
And Lord of Snipe
The Baron of Gripe
The Prince of Tripe
And Saint Leon of Ripe!'

344:2: Saint Leon of Ripe,
     The Prince of Tripe
     The Baron of Gripe
     The Lord of Snipe
     (Lord Protector of Snipe)
     And Count of Gripe
     Rose up in his drawers and cried 'Hup Hipe.
     By God, I *am* a peculiar type,'
     (As he lit his breakfast and cooked his pipe
     And gave to his arse a wipe
     The baronial backside a princely swipe
     The saintly seat a hell of a wipe)
     'To be at once the Count of Gripe
     (Lord Protector of Snipe)
     The Lord of Snipe
     The Baron of Gripe
     The Prince of Tripe
     And Saint Leon of Ripe!'

344.3: Saint Leon of Ripe
     The Prince of Tripe
     And Baron of Gripe
     And Protector of Snipe
     And who rose in his drawers with a lound 'Hup, Hipe!'
     And he gave his arse a princely wipe
     As he lit his breakfast and cooked his pipe
     And said 'By god, a peculiar type
     Am I to be Protector of Snipe
     And Baron of Gripe
     And Prince of Tripe.
     And not to mention Saint Leon of Ripe!'
     (So said (so they say) good Saint Leon of Ripe!)

1949–57   GOOD MORNING TO   [345.1]
            OUR SWEETEST HARTEEBEESTE!

> A little note we were going to write you last night
> For the morning to greet you instead we do write
> To greet you with loving words in duck-like song
> Wishing you all luck, et avec les dents
> 5   Especialement, avec les dents!
> With devotion, sweetest concern, nimble and
> Delighted brooding and love from all the little animals.

1949–57   [346.1]

> Half of the harm that is done in this world
> Is due to people who want to feel important.
> They don't mean to do harm – but the harm does not
>   interest them.
> 5   Or they do not see it, or they justify it
> Because they are absorbed in the endless struggle
> To think well of themselves.

1949–57   HAPPIEST OF HARTEBEESTE   [347.1]
        DAYS AND DEVOTED LOVE ETERNE

    DE TOUS LES PETITES ANIMAUX SANS EXCEPTION TO OUR
        SWEETHARTEEBEESTE

> The morning bird is warbling
> The kettle it is dawdling
> The morning rain is dripping
> The sea's bereft of shipping
>
> 5   – Still, all of this is ripping
> The weather shall no 'fash a man
> We're bound away for Rashiman.

1956   [348.1]

> How overjoyed I am to get your letter
> To hear that you are very nearly better
> The days are long and they are getting longer
> But within a song, like you, is getting stronger
> 5   So perhaps the days are short and getting shorter
> Although one must admit they didn't oughta
> But long or short, of him known as THE CARPER
> The claws are sharp, and they are getting *sharper*.

1949–57   [349.1]

> I am speeding through the northern lights
> On my snow-white skis, in my snow-white tights,

With my snow-white sleigh behind so keen
Bearing glasses for foxtails of rosy sheen
And Harteebeeste presents for Hallowe'en.

1949–57   [350.1]

      i am very small
      i write very little
      but you have said
      kind things about me
5   and my friends speak
      with love about you
      no speak English very well
      but the loving larks are
      delivering this special
10   message of love from me
      the dear ducks send love
      too

1949–57   [351.1]

    I bet you don't know who I am
    Though I am your oldest friend –
    The trouble being, have lately been in Siam
    Thither my ways during the late cold weather
5   It having been necessary for me to wend.
    Now my ways in the other sense as concerns
        Letter writing I am just about to mend.
    O bountiful Harteebeeste!
    Please forgive your oldest friend!
10   O beautiful Harteebeeste! Very soon
    I shall come back gracefully, with thee
        In the forest to bend!
    Meantime, all love to those in the lovecot
    To all those who therein livest of a dimension
15   Me high above cot
    Very soon through the forest again of spring
        With love to you will resound my song-horn
    And meantime my belovedest Harteebeeste
        Allow myself to sign myself thine with
20   The very greatest of devotion thy oldest friend
            The Pronghorn

1949–57   JUST A MERRY LITTLE DITTY OF WELCOME   [352.1]
        FOR THE MOST BELOVED HARTEEBEESTE
           ON EASTER SATURDAY

    El Leon's mane is a mythical mane
    And though real, it is unpatcheable,

And the door to these things is a mythic door
And though real, it is unlatcheable,
5   And this note so sweet is a mythic note
Dispatched, and yet undispatcheable;
And the Gadwall's egg is a mythic egg
And though real, is yet unhatcheable;
But the seal is a seal is a seal is a seal
10   And though seal, she is uncatcheable.
For the seal, she is uncatcheable.

1949–57   [353.1]

Just some love and kisses
From a very sleepy seal
One who never misses
The Harteebeeste's appeal
5   However large the fish is
Or tempting, the sea-abysses
He's one who never misses
The Harteebeeste's appeal
With earnest love: The Seal.

1957   LUSTY ADVICE OF A FORTUNE-TELLER   [354.1]

The Titanic called at Cherbourg at dusk.
And so, the morning before the fire
We swept the floors of our funeral pyre
In the house of our hopes that by night was their husk.

5   This miserable thought I excise from my work.
The voyage of triumph has Cherbourg on schedule.
The day before love finds you fate finds it, death
You'll most certainly find in a week.
You're more likely to find in a week.
10   The doomed man for breakfast had brandy and kippers and tea,
Next hour was reprieved, and the month after that, found not
                               [guilty, moreover was free.

The house was rebuilt and it stands again, happy, if lonely.
But loved. So I charge you, sweet reader, to think of this only.

T 354.1: Lusty Advice of a Tea-cup Reader
7 354.1: The day before love finds you fate reads its dead
        The day before love finds you fate reads as dead
8 354.1: You'll more certainly find in a week.

1949–57   LYRICAL MORNING POEM   [355.1]

The morning bird is eating
The snow it is a'melting

And everywhere retreating
That yesterday was pelting
5   The gulls have finished pelting
And have new grey cloaks, with white fronts,
                                    And white belting.

1949–57   [356.1]

May well befall the common weal
May good attend thy every meal
In health increasingly to feel
And on a fairly even keel
May you maintain yourself, The Seal.

1949–57   MORNING ADDRESS OF LOVE TO   [357.1]
              THE BELOVED HARTEEBEESTE

The morning bird is shrilling
The morning sea looks chilling
As a poem by L. Trilling
The morning sky is leaking
5   The seagull babe is skreeking
The fire – well, words are lacking
We ducks we keep on quacking.

1949–57   MORNING SONG FOR THE HARTEEBEESTE   [358.1]

The morning bird is throstling
The morning sea is jostling
The morning oil tanks gleaming
Like organ-pipes, great steel boots abeaming
5   The morning roofs are ateaming
The day is in good fettle
Not so, the morning kettle.

1949–57   MORNING SONG OF EL LEON   [359.1]

The morning finch is chirping
(But El Leon he is burping)
The day it is a question
(But the night was indigestion)
5   The morning sea is oily
And the kettle will not boil – *Hee!*

1949–57   MY BELOVED HARTEEBEESTE   [360.1]

How sweet and dear it was of
You to let me take you, my beloved

Harteebeeste, to the cinematograph.
How sweet and dear you looked
5   With hooves and horns all honed
And eating peanuts and raisins so sweetly
Even if the film was not *quite* as good
As Living with Lions. How sweet to
Eat enchiladas à la Leon with you. We
10   Wish to say that we have falled mane over
Paws in love with you all over again.

1949–57 [361.1]

Never seek to tell thy stove
Love which never told can be
For the metal fiend doth move
Silently, invisibly

5   I told thy stove, I told thy stove
I told her all, all my heart
Trembling, cold, in ghastly fears
Ah, she doth depart.

Soon as she was quite gone out
10   I stood with wordless cry,
Silently, invisibly,
She blew up with a sigh...

5 361.1: I told my stove, I told my stove

1949–57 [362.1]

Oh and
Who is it unforlorn
Beaming, and just round the
corn –
Er, hath slipped this note
For his belovedest Harteebeeste
With love for a sweet sleep till morn –
Ing but your merrily and
devotedly and truly
The Pronghorn

1949–57 [363.1]

Oh love
Oh Shame, we are late
With our message of love,
But the gadwall was buried
5   In a snow slide, we had

To make a feathered chain
To find her, and you know
The rest – she had
Laid, but a double
Yoked egg this
Time –

10

1949–57   [364.1]

Oh Storms
Oh The Seal!
Oh Love!
Oh Boats!
Oh Logs!

1949–57   [365.1]

Oh the Harteebeeste is *dear* to us
Oh the Harteebeeste is *cheer* to us
And ever far more *near* to us
Beloved Harteebeeste!

5   Oh the Harteebeeste is *near* to us,
Oh Harteebeeste, *appear* to us
Though elsewhere this won't be *queer* to us,
At least O Harteebeeste...

O the Harteebeeste is *here* again
10   Nor more our hearts have *fear* again
Nor in yellow leaf fall *sere* again
But like yeast, oh Harteebeeste!
Oh wise beast! O Harteebeeste!

1949–57   [366.1]

Oh welcome Home
To thy cot by the foam
Please excuse this pome
Tis of love increased
A thousandfold for our Harteebeeste

1949–57   [367.1]

Platinum sun rising.
Platinum frost on porch.
Slight grue on water.
Imperceptiblue grue of perhaps
5   Vanishing [?meridian]

Many tired but very loyal little
Animals all waking simultaneously.

Moonsail...

1949–57   [368.1]

Poor Butterfly that stamped,
My boots are all cold and cramped,
And the little flowers whereon I have camped,
Are fast asleep...

5   Poor butterfly that stamped,
How should she stamp again,
In her poor boots so cold and cramped,
In the murk and rain...

The minutes pass into hours
10   And the hours into days –

1949–57   REPORT ON CONDITIONS   [369.1]

The morning day is hazy
Though to rain there is no clue,
(In fact, a glorious view)
So the weather man is crazy.
Or so thinks the little bill blue.

1949–57   REVEILLE   [370.1]

The morning bird is singing –
El Leon feels religious
His mane about him flinging
With gestures strange and hideous
5   (Yet with kindly mien fastidious)
The morning rain is refraining
The moon is slightly waning
And the kettle, hugely trying.

1949–57   [371.1]

Singing.
The morning bird.
(Humphum!)
– sing –
ing
(O, his,)
– Bips –
in the cool dawn
FISH.

1949–57   SPARK POETRY   [372.1]

The morning bird is honing
Some sort of dawn is breaking
El Leon is agroaning
His matted mane is shaking
But still manages to convey you
Love from all the
Little animals to
Their Harteebeeste

1949–57   [373.1]

     still speeding to your heart
     oh beloved harteebeeste great
     love to all at the love cot
     a little dove on the mast has
5   taken this message from me
     while I rested

1949–57   SWEET GOOD NIGHT POEM TO   [374.1]
                 OUR BELOVED HARTEBEESTE
                 FROM ALL THE LITTLE ANIMALS

Noses to grindstone!
Beaks to the Northstar!

Though we may find no Kaiser-i-*Hind* stone
Yet shall we *fare forth far!*

1949–57   [375.1] [see 334]

     The Arctic fox
     With snow white hocks
     And glistening locks
     Despite the rocks
5   And other shocks
     With immaculate brush
     Comes in a rush
     In her gleaming sleigh
     To sing hey hey
10   Upon this day
     And to report
     Within his court
     El Leon holds sway
     Tail dipped in quink
15   And leonine wink
     With scholarly paw
     And tender roar
     Has eschewed all drink

And prepared to think!
20   And lay down the law
Re the problems which
Greater, lesser, and least
Have already been solved
By the Hartebeeste,
25   (While his tail revolved.)
– We won't tell him so
But all of us know
Or at least suspect
That he thinks that the Night
30   Being tender i' effect
Is something to bite,
In short, to eat,
And for lions a treat.
– So off in our sleigh
35   Through the wild woods away
With snow-white hocks
And immaculate brush
And sounds of pock-pocks
Away in a rush
40   Leaving words of love
From below and above
For the Harteebeeste dear
Without any peer.

1949–57   [376.1]

The deal was here
Oh love alas
The floor unswept
The wood uncut
The lamps unfilled
The cat unfed
The fire unlaid
And ourselves half dead

1949–57   THE HARTEBEESTE BOTH GRAVE AND GAY   [377.1]

The Harteebeeste is very good
And oft times wears a merry snood
Such soft times she is very gay
And charms all beasties' troubles away.

5   But when El Leon gives a growl
She then assumes a monkish cowl
With monkish cowl and spookish hood
Though charming still she may not seem good.

But with monkish cowl or merry snood
10   She really is so very good
In mien grave or mien gay
In this resembling God's own Day.

1949–57   [378.1]

The Harteebeeste with flying hoof
Hath kicked El Leon on the hoof
With mien low and mane all shrunk
Beneath the bushes he has slunk.
5   So with purring tactful cat-like voice
Sing to this creature of your choice
And then once more both clip and kiss
And then there will be naught amiss.

1949–57   [379.1]

The morning bird is bathing
The morning sky is grue
The morning gull is scathing
The morning sea is pew
5   But the morning wind mas puro
Blows swift and soft and true
This lovenote from the bureau
Of the little mink to you.

1949–57   [380.1]

The morning bird is singing
The morning cat, unhinging
The morning grebe is fluting
The morning gull, commuting.
5   Five goldeneyes, in motion
Slide sweetly toward the ocean.
Though the evening cat displeases
With an appetite for cheeses
All things they wait to greet thee!
10   With love they wait to meet thee!
Though El Leon he is roaring
And the morning rain, is pouring.

1949–57   [381.1]

The morning bird sits mutely
The weather absolutely –
The day is full of wishes

The sink is full of dishes
5   The morning floor is dusty
The morning throat is rusty
The morning stance is tilty
The conscience slightly guilty
And battered as the oven
10   But the morning heart is loving.

1   381.1: The morning bird sings mutely

1949–57   [382.1]

The morning rain is rained
The morning gull complained
No morning craft are seined
(The morning leg, half pained)
5   The morning moon is waned
The morning coffee drained
Say not O Lord in vained
Insaned, insaned.

1949–57   [383.1]

The morning rain is raining
A morning pain is paining
The morning gull is cruising
While this duck tries to sing
5   Unlike the morning kettle
Which is in chilly fettle
Just like Popocatapetl.

1949–57   [384.1]

The morning rain is raining
The morning leg is paining
The morning grebe is swimming
The morning gull unhymning
5   The morning lion is working
The morning coffee, perking...

1949–57   [385.1]

The morning rain is sleeting
The morning hail is snow
Yet through all this our greeting
– Our sweetest warmest greeting –
5   To the sweet Harteebeeste doth go.

1949–57   [386.1]

– The morning rain is weeping –
The morning brain is blue
The morning dew is keeping
A consistency of glue
5   (While the morning sea is pew)
But despite this dolorous scene
To the lovecot warm and neat
Comes this message wishing greener
Days to the Harteebeeste so sweet.

1949–57   [387.1]

The morning sleet is sleeting
The morning quay is miring
The picture is defeating,
At least, is not inspiring –
5   But through the slush and uckery
With compassed beaks and true
We bear this note of duckery
Of dearest sweetest duckery
To sweetest, dearest you.

1949–57   [388.1]

The morning sneat is snewing
The morning feet are blueing
The morning seat is glueing
But the kettle is not stewing.

1949–57   [389.1]

The morning stove is wheezing
The morning gull is dovey
(This note is for my lovey –)
At least it's not so freezing.

1949–57   [390.1]

The morning tanker gleameth
El Leon he a'schemeth
(Life being as he deemeth
Much stranger than it seemeth)
5   The day, meanwhile, a'beameth
And the kettle, it a'steameth.
But the seal, she is uncatcheable.

1949–57   [391.1]

     Thou was not born for death, immortal Duck
     No hungry generations tread thee down:
     The quack I heard this passing night, with luck
     Was also heard by Emperor and clown:
5   Perhaps the self-same quack that found a path,
     Through the great heart of El Leon, when sick for you
     He roamed with roars about the Cariboo...

1949–57   [392.1]

   – Though we are all a little bit disappointed this year there
                                  [won't be any fireworks
   We know that is but because we are all willy-nilly engaged in
                                  [higherworks
   And though it cannot but be with a little sadness that we shall
                            [not see this year fly off our beloved
                            [Harteebeeste's Roman Candle
   That is no reason why we should to put it succinctly fly off the
                                    [handle
5 For as El Leon sagely observes what this year we shall miss as
                                [to wild celebration
   We shall in all senses make up for by what might be called
                                [mild cerebration
   And though this year shall bring us no splendid burgeoning of
                                [rockets
   To come down to brass tacks all that means is that we shall
                    [burn the midnight oil down to its sockets
   So let us not regard these things, oh sweetest and most beloved
                [Harteebeeste with haggard and sallow e'yne
10 But look upon them as tokens of an even finer and by no means
                        [laggard Hallowe'en
   And all this with oh so much love is as from the hearts of *all*
                      [your faithful little animals torn
   Who join in sending more love than ever in entire concert by
              [their ancient and waggish ambassador your
                                      Affectionate
                                    The Pronghorn

8   burn] burning

1949–57   [393.1]

          Though we are but *sea* birds
          Not much grammar having
          We send unto *thee* words
          Full of sincere loving

1949–57   [394.1]

       3 Happy little ducks
       Swimming in the rain
       Thinking not of bad lucks
       And feeling no pain.

5   O feeling no pain
       Thinking not of bad lucks
       Swimming in the rain
       3 Happy little ducks, ducks, ducks
       3 Happy little ducks!

1949–57   [395.1]

       Two frozen claws
       In two frozen mittens
       Send warmest love
       That was ever written
5   – To our beloved Harteebeeste

1949–57   [396.1]

       Waking wassails of wistful welcome
       Upon this woebegone Wednesday wan!
       We wise waterbirds wish waking well-being
       Wading wearily wobbling waterwards
5   Whether we – oh, the uck with it.

1949–57   WELCOME HOME OH GLADSOME   [397.1]
              SPRINGHORNED BELOVED
            AND FAMED HARTEEBEESTE

    With sweetest protective dotings
        Of affection, and comradely featherly
           Solidarity
        Nearly all the little animals have gone
5   In with you this day to have their plummage shined.

1949–57   [398.1]

   Welcome Home oh Harteebeeste beloved who doth with thy
   Delicate and unparalleled presence all the verdant scene adorn
   And who with it holdeth likewise our hearts in fee
        If not literally in pawn
5 And without whom none of us are worth one might say
       Figuratively speaking even a prawn.

1949–57   [399.1]

        Welcome Home oh Harteebeeste mio
        Welcome home, oh Harteebeeste – klio! –
        So full of love are we
        We await thee by every tree!
5   As thou steppest through the forest so neatly!
        Oh, illiterately, we greet thee!
        But with undying love we meet thee!
        With this expression of our hearts unfeatly!
        But sweetly!

1949–57   WELCOME HOME – OH MOST   [400.1]
                 BELOVED HARTEEBEESTE

        The smooth mink, the swift seal
        Do their bit for the common weal
        The smooth seal, and the swift mink
        Do more for their Harteebeeste, *than you think.*

1949–57   WELCOME HOME OH MOST LOVED   [401.1]
                 AND FAMED HARTEEBEESTE

        – big wood, small wood, little wood, bark;
        big lamp, small lamp, little lamp; hark
        to the sound of the Harteebeeste's distant hooves!
        then who is it that, through the wildwood, moves?

1949–57   WELCOME HOME OH OUR   [402.1]
                 BELOVED HARTEBEESTE

        This illuminated address
        To that noble animal we all love the best
        Wishing her all devotion and luck
        Was designed by Mr and Mrs
5   Affectionately yours   *Harlequin Duck*

1949–57   WELCOME HOME OH OUR   [403.1]
             MOST BELOVED HARTEEBEESTE

        And my socks, they are immatcheable
        And my shoes, they are unpatcheable
        And my house, it is unthatcheable
        And you dear Seal she is
5   uncatcheable...

1949–57   WELCOME HOME OH OUR   [404.1]
                 SWEETEST HARTEEBEESTE BELOVED

                    For though our disapproval
                    Shakes every wing and finlet
                    We plan on no removal
                    From *our* stations on the inlet
5   Chorus: So never mind the weather
                    But hiss in every feather etc

1949–57   WELCOME HOME, OH   [405.1]
                   SWEETEST HARTEEBEESTE

                    from our shoved up bank,
               with our faces to the air,
                    ringing our bells,
                        or hiding snugly in the shack,
5   we greet you with love
               from the bottom of our hearts.

1949–57   WELCOME HOME OH SWEETEST   [406.1]
           HARTEEBEESTE WITH QUADRUPLE DEVOTION
              FROM ALL THE LITTLE ANIMALS

                    Oh we are running!
                    The dear ducks are running!
                    We hear thy hoofs
                    On the grassy-er-poufs
5   And glimpsing from roofs
                    See thy horns so splendid
                    With the foliage blended
                    Oh we are running
                    The dear ducks are running
10   So t'is time we ended.

1949–54   WELCOME HOME OUR OWN   [407.1]

          Welcome Home, Harteebeeste, from far off Vancouver
          We watched o'er thee each moment (tho' not like Edgar Hoover)
          Close beside thee we went when thou wentst to stove,
          Sitting hard by the ram, and oh dear it was raw,
5   And then through the forest we followedst thy spoor
          Little animals 3 – carry one – that makes 4.

1949–57   WELCOME HOME OH HARTEEBEESTE   [408.1]

          Welcome oh Harteebeeste, back from town
          With your twinkling feet and your eyes so brown

With ponderous tomes and Tolstoy grim
And geranium pots and a bottle of gin.

1949–57   WITH A GREAT GOODMORNING KISS   [409.1]
                AND LUCK AND LOVE
              TO OUR BELOVED HARTEESTE
             FROM ALL THE LITTLE ANIMALS

            – and moreover,
                A gorgeous widgeon
                Who got religion!
                He send Hosannas to you!
5   Hot duck!
                He send Hosannas to you!

1949–57   WITH DEAREST LOVE ENFOLDED AND   [410.1]
            ENCLOSED FROM *ALL* THE LITTLE ANIMALS

            And who is it that through the watery woods
            Wanderest unwanly and wonderfully
            With his stiff upper horns wisely clenched
            At the north star, and warbling winsomely
5   Of his belovedest Harteebeest in tones so
            New as to be almost unborn
            But yours more adroitly and faithfully and
            Waggishly than ever – your
                        Affectionate Pronghorn –

1949–57   WITH DEAREST MORNING LOVE AND KISSES   [411.1]

                The morning is maturing
                The frosty sun – t'is a pure ring –
                The poor gulls are a vulturing
                (That is, they are shivering)
5   But at least it is not pouring.
                And El Leon, he is roaring...

1949–57   WITH DEVOTION ENTIRE FROM ALL YOUR   [412.1]
                LITTLE ANIMALS WE THOUGHT FIT
                TO REVIVE THE FOLLOWING DITTY

            Ducks of oak, ducks of distinction
            Ducks of *the* red white and blue
            Ducks who'll never know extinction
            Ducks of get-up-and of go. Ducks of oak etc.
5   Ducks of progress, ducks of daring
            Ducks of labour, ducks of fun
            Ducks of land and of sea-faring

Oh the Ducks of Dollarton – Ducks of oak etc.
Ducks of Leo, Ducks of Taurus
10   Ducks from all the Zodiac
All join now in one loud chorus
In one great triumphal quack. Ducks of oak etc.

4   <u>... Ducks of oak etc.</u>] [missing end punctuation]

1949–57   WITH GREAT LOVE OH BELOVED   [413.1]
HARTEEBEESTE FROM EL LEON

Quarrels make up, quarrels end
But LionCola always is your friend,
Friendships dwindle, friendships wane
But Lionlittle liver pills is always
5   In the morning of excesses
Of the night before, the bane.

1949–57   WITH MIDSUMMER DEVOTION FROM   [414.1]
ALL THE LITTLE ANIMALS TO
THEIR BELOVED HARTEEBEESTE

The engine tells the knell of parting day
El Leon homeward prowls with mane forlorn
But who is it upon the forest way
Dancing this midsummer an even fancier
5   Step as he prances under the moon in honour of
His beloved Harteebeeste but yours
Fayly
The Pronghorn

1949–57   WITH SWEET DEVOTION AND TRUE   [415.1]
FROM ALL THE LITTLE ANIMALS

But who is it who the forest leapeth
Blessings and gratitude upon his Harteebeeste beloved heapeth
To array himself in that which replaceth so
Gaily his accoutrements outworn
5   But yours more devoted than ever
Before and waggishly your
The Pronghorn

1949–57   WITH SWEET SWEET LOVE FROM   [416.1]
ALL YOUR AMUSED LITTLE ANIMALS

But who is it that through the salmonberry wobbleth
That through the huckleberry hacketh and hacketh
That through thimbleberry thrasheth and smacketh

In such a manner that had he been any one else
5 He would have presented a mien as of the ram newly shorn
But yours more craggishly
More staggishly
And more *waggishly* than ever
Your devoted, your dear The Pronghorn

1949–57   WITH SWEETEST LOVE AND WELCOME   [417.1]
               FROM ALL THE LITTLE ANIMALS

The stove it is – well – patcheable
And the dear Gadwall's egg is – well – hatcheable
The door it is – just – latcheable
But the Seal – she is uncatcheable

1949–57   WITH SWEETEST LOVE FROM ALL   [418.1]
          THE LITTLE ANIMALS AS FROM 2 OLD FRIENDS

When the Harteebeeste is on the horse
Then woe to the sluggard on his course –
El Leon pads then to tactful lair,
(The Lion 'tis said has gone to prayer)
5 The defection, though, to say the least,
Is not confined to this noble beast;
Yet with merry cries, and madrigals,
Come flying all the animals –
To do her bidding with dispatch,
10 To paint the door and to shine the latch –
And of all those who with cries, songs, barks
Her call to action gladly harks
None gayer are than the loving Larks.

1949–57   WITH SWEETEST LOVE FROM ALL THE   [419.1]
          LITTLE ANIMALS TO THEIR BELOVED HARTEEBEESTE

With infinite feather-poultices
And hot shearwaterbottles of love
And brooding attention and care
For your poor toothache in the hope
5 That a great magic may be worked by
Morning and *all* your pain may be vanished
With a mutual ducklaration of concerns
Sweet affection from all the little animals

1949–54   WITH SWEETEST MORNING LOVE   [420.1]
          TO THEIR BELOVEDEST HARTEEBEESTE

The morning bird is singing
The morning wind is new

The morning rag is clinging
The morning oil is 'grue'
5   The morning gull bedecked is
In all his breakfast finery
And the morning train unwrecked is
Beneath the oil-refinery.

Appendix B

SONG LYRICS

THE FIFTEEN ITEMS in this appendix span the whole of Lowry's literary career. Music, about which Lowry was genuinely knowledgeable, was an important element in his life, and it contributed significantly to his personal mythology. Accounts of his early life in Bowker, Bradbrook, and Day always include a depiction of Lowry with his battered ukulele or 'taropatch.'

Of the fifteen songs included in this section, six are juvenilia. 'I've Said Good-bye to Shanghai' [427] and 'Three Little Dog-gone Mice' [433] were printed as sheet music by a vanity publisher in London in 1927. The date of 'Ballad' [422] cannot be bibliographically ascertained because no manuscript has surfaced; however, in 1960 Margerie Lowry sang and transcribed the song for Philip Thomas, explaining that Lowry had written it as a joke on his professors while at Cambridge.[1] In 1932 Chatto and Windus published Charlotte Haldane's *I Bring Not Peace*, in which Lowry appears as the drunken, ukulele-playing James Dowd; Haldane dedicated the volume to Lowry as well as crediting him with the authorship of Dowd's three songs.[2] However, one of the Dowd songs, 'And When I Die,' properly titled 'That's What I Mean' [431], is a fragment of a song Lowry contributed to the Cambridge Footlights Dramatic Club's 1932 production of *Laughing at Love*. The production's programme (33–18) credits Lowry as the lyricist for 'Tinker Tailor,' but no such song exists in the British Library's copy of the libretto. The last two songs dating from the apprenticeship period, 'Give Me the Money' [425] and 'Rich Man, Poor Man' [429], appear in Haldane.

The three songs datable from the Dollarton period come from eclectic sources. 'Song for a Marimba' [430] is a typical Dollarton poem in terms of its manuscript development – the holograph and typescript drafts appear on newsprint – but it is included in Lowry's 1952 manuscript of 'Through the Panama' (25–7). 'Happy Birthday' [426] exists only in Lowry's outgoing correspondence and was composed for James Stern's birthday in 1950, while 'Nagging at Myself Something Awful' [428] appears in a 1952 letter to Albert Erskine (2–14, 3–2, respectively). The six remaining songs appear in the 1949–57 'Love Poems.' These six ditties have been separated from the love poems in this edition on the basis of Lowry's conception of them as musical entities; in the accompanying correspondence, Lowry either explicitly refers to them as 'ditties' or 'songs' or surrounds them with drawings of musical notes and symbols, thereby underscoring their musical nature.

The bracketed dates indicate that a published version has been used as copy-text; in these cases the lack of manuscripts renders it impossible to determine the precise dates of composition, which for some songs span almost a decade. Given this wide margin for dating, the songs are arranged alphabetically.

NOTES

1 Philip Thomas, personal interview, 18 September 1987.
2 Charlotte Haldane, *I Bring Not Peace* (London: Chatto and Windus 1932) 69, 262, 263.

1949–57   [421.1]

       Au clair de la lune
       Harteebeeste Mio
       Pretez-moi ta plume
       Klio! Klio! Klio!
5   Though we are but *sea* birds
       Little grammar having
       We inscribe to *thee* words
       Full of sincere loving. . .

[1929–32]   BALLAD   [422.2]

       Twas in the springtime of the year
       On such a May morning
       Me and my wife did make good cheer
       And men love women

5   Aye, Aye, the wind doth blow
       Nor shall I see my love no mo
       On such a May morning

       I sought her in the town and mead
       I sought her in the sky
10   And sorree did my heartee bleed
       Nor would my love come neigh

       Aye, Aye, the wind doth blow
       Nor shall I see my love no mo
       On such a May morning

15   I sought her east
       I sought her west
       I sought in a far countree
       And I prayed Jesus to give me rest
       For sweet charity

20   Aye, Aye, the wind doth blow

Nor shall I see my love no mo
On such a May morning

And with Tennybreath now my head
And I'm a wax and woe
25   And pray that I might be dead
To Jesus Son of God

Aye, Aye, the wind doth blow
Nor shall I see my love no mo
On such a May morning

30   But now I've found my love evis
A child upon her knee
The mother of God my leman is
The blessed virgin she

No more the wind doth blow
35   I'll see my love for ever more
On each a May morning.

[Margerie Lowry's recollection]

  1   422.1, 2: [chorus begins song]
17   422.1, 2: I sought her in the sky
18   422.1, 2: And I prayed Jesus did give me rest
19   422.1, 2: Nor would my love come neigh
34   422.1, 2: Aye Aye no more the wind doth blow
35   422.1, 2: I'll hear my love for ever more
36   422.1, 2: On each May morning

1949–57   DUCK TRAIN – VOCAL ARCTIC FOX-TROT   [423.1]

(LEON AND PRONGHORN)

Duck train!
Duck train!
Quackitty quack
Quackitty quack
5   On a floating piece of slag,
Quackitty quack quacking along!
Singing a song –
(On our way to town
Blow the man down!)
10   Duck train!
Duck train!

[1932]   [424.1]

Give me the money,
Give me the money,
Give me the money and I'll go-oh,

Give me the money,
5   Give me the money,
Give me the money and I'll go.

And when I die it'll be just the same
I'll have to borrow somebody's name,
So give me the money,
10   Give me the money
To buy the undertaker a hoe
To get me the garden, the hearse and the parson,
Give me the money and I'll go.

1949–57   GOOD LUCK   [425.1]

– WITH SWEET DEVOTION FROM ALL THE LITTLE ANIMALS –

Oh Happy Days are here again
In Happy ways we'll cheer again
Our Hearts shall dance to 'rire' again

No valse Triste
5   On Harteebeeste
– Like yeast
Oh Harteebeeste!

1950   [426.1]

Happy birthday to you
Happy birthday to you
Though it's deferred it's
sincere it's
5   A message worth two.

And if it is but our fate
To celebrate it late
Please look forward
– hard to starboard! –
10   To that royal date!

[1927]   I'VE SAID GOODBYE TO SHANGHAI   [427.1]

VOCAL FOX-TROT

Moonlit river way out there in old Shanghai,
Makes me shiver, and I'll tell you why.
Took my girl home ev'ry night just to hand her in,
Till I found that she'd been foolin' with a mandarin.

5   I've said good-bye to Shanghai
P'raps that's why I'm pinin',
Shady trees, buzzin' bees,

Yes I've said so long to ev'rything Chinese,
I left my girl in Shanghai,
10   Said she'd marry me. My!
But as I knew the things she'd do,
It's bye-bye to old Shanghai.

I adored her underneath the Chinese moon,
How I bored her when I settled down to spoon.
15   She would stamp her tiny foot and give me a frown,
Now I realise she never meant to settle down.

I've said good-bye to Shanghai,
P'raps that's why I'm pinin',
Shady trees, buzzin' bees,
20   Yes I've said so long to ev'rything Chinese,
I left my girl in Shanghai,
Said she'd marry me. My!
But as I knew the things she'd do,
It's bye-bye to old Shanghai.

1951   [428.2]

Nagging at myself something awful
Nagging at myself something fearful
All because we ain't used to cheerful news

Nagging at myself blues
5   Those old Judas blues...

Nagging at myself something gruesome
You're nagging too so it's a twosome
And all because we ain't used to good news

Nagging at myself blues
10   Those old Judas blues...

3   428.1: And all because we ain't used to cheerful news
8   428.1, 2: All because we ain't used to good newsome news

[1932]   [429.1]

Rich man, poor man, beggarman, thief,
All agree in this belief:
What makes the world go round is Love.

1940–52   SONG FOR A MARIMBA   [430.6]

Oa-xa-ca! Oa-xa-ca!
Oa-xa-ca! Oa-xa-ca!
It is a name like
A bro-ken

5   A broken heart at night.
       Wooden wooden wooden are those faces at night.
       Wooden wooden wooden are those faces at night.
       Broken hearts are wooden at night.
       Wooden, are wooden, at night.

T   430.1–3: In the Wooden Brothel the Band Plays Out of Tune
6   430.1–3: Wooden wooden wooden are the faces at night

[1932]   THAT'S WHAT I MEAN   [431.1]

       Our destiny takes us, and binds us and breaks us,
       Leaving life confused and hating the sun.
       Our responses are musty, our Shakespeares are dusty,
       The need we brought to seek for beauty has gone.
5   I sit and murmur word for stupid word,
       Hoping I may not be overheard

       For this is the music that's within my soul,
       I know I can't express it as a whole:
       It's just simple music that my soul has seen,
10   That's what I mean.
       I was always dreaming when the day was done,
       My childhood broke through chords of music and of sun,
       Dreaming of the might-have-been and used-to-be;
       That's what I mean.
15   If I could tell, I'd tell you just what then befell:
       But night and day I hide – it's courage and pride.
       Now if you solve this beauty you would see the man
       Behind all that I try to say and never can,
       And share the simple music that my soul has seen:
20   That's what I mean.

1949–57   THE HARTEEBEESTE IS HERE AGAIN   [432.1]

                   (PRONGHORN AND LEON)

       The Harteebeeste is here again
       Oh the Harteeste is here again
       And our hearts they rise, my dear again
       Like the yeast, oh our Hartebeeste!

4   Hartebeeste!] hartebeeste!

[1927]   THREE LITTLE DOG-GONE MICE   [433.1]

       JUST THE LATEST CHARLESTON FOX-TROT EVER

           We gotta story, we gotta story,
           It will int'rest you,

An' there's not faddin' about Aladdin,
Or the woman who lived in a shoe;
5   It's just a fable, a little fable,
We didn't get on the farm,
Old Mother Hubbard's dead in the cupboard,
An' we don't give a darn;

For Three little dog-gone mice,
10   See how the little devils run,
They bought a little motor car,
Wouldn't do its advertised miles per hour,
They turned it into a cocktail bar,
Did the three little dog-gone mice.

15   Now old Marconi, ate macaroni,
And made the wireless set,
Why did he do it, if you only knew it,
To Broadcast this you bet!
What did Asquith, what did Asquith,
20   Say in eighteen eighty three,
Was it politics, or was it folly?
No just wait and see;

Oh! Three little dog-gone mice,
See how the little devils run,
25   Wifey's first night she was wed,
She gave a little scream and quickly said,
Jack dear, help, for we're in bed
With three little dog-gone mice.

We're gonna finish, we're gonna finish
30   Off this little song,
We're awfu' sorry, to tell the story,
Of the three little mice who went wrong;
It's simply tragic, and only magic
Could make them reform,
35   Whate'er the weather they cling together,
And keep their tootsies warm;

Oh! Three little dog-gone mice,
See how the little devils run,
Afraid that we must say goodnight,
40   Some fool will soon put out the light,
We're not possessed with second sight,
Said the three little dog-gone mice.

OPTIONAL TRIPLETS [chorus: lines 3–5 inclusive]

They opened up a sausage store,
Folks rolled in and wanted more,
Into a great big hole in the floor ran the, *etc.*

They tickled the whiskers of a priest,
On the day of a ceremonial feast,
They should apologise at least – should the, *etc.*

They watched the movements of a cow,
When it slipped on an orange peel, dunno how,
They all can do the Black Bottom now, can the, *etc.*

Just one step and then a pounce,
Cat thought 'Gee, I'll catch a mouse,'
So Let's all go to Mary's House, said the, *etc.*

Invited some friends for a drink or two,
They said 'We've got a case of flu,'
'Alright we'll drink it up for you,' said the, *etc.*

They went to the room of a movie star,
Lordie only knows that they went too far,
And made her spill her I-cil-ma did the, *etc.*

1949–57   WITH SWEETEST DEVOTION FROM *ALL*   [434.1]
            THE LITTLE ANIMALS TO THEIR
            MOST BELOVED HARTEEBEESTE

!Hammer and tongs! !The ducks are creating!
!Clamour and songs! ! In short, cerebrating!
        Ah miraculous stuff!
        Oh, supernalest wuff!
5   And t'is never enough...
For we're never so happy as when with brains sappy
Our thoughts they go mounting in measures past counting
From depths of absurdity unknown to birdity
To heights of profundity – marvellous fecundity –
10   Singing !Hammer and Tongs!
            !Clamour and Songs!

1949–57   WITH SWEETEST LOVE AND SUNDAY   [435.1]
            ANTHEMS OR SWEETEST GOODNIGHT
            FROM ALL THE LITTLE ANIMALS

        Wonderful love
        Beautiful love
        Love to the Harteebeeste, – like yeast, –
        Are all our hearts
5   Burgeoning hearts.
        Burgeoning hearts, like yeast,
                    like yeast,
                    like yeast,
        Oh, love to our Harteebeeste!

Appendix C

FRAGMENTS

THE ITEMS IN this section are classified as fragments for various reasons. Many appear as insertions in Lowry's prose manuscripts. For example, the first page of a 1950 newsprint paper draft of 'Present Estate of Pompeii' bears the address 'Ye Pow'rs who make mankind your care' [474]. Fragments, ditties, and casual couplets abound throughout the manuscripts; this section presents a representative selection.[1]

Some of Lowry's poetic fragments are not truly poems, even though the content is couched in the form of verse. His 1944 telegram 'Betty and Gerald Noxon' [446] and the advertisement 'Personal' [455] are good example. Another interesting fragment, – 'My two hands broke in two: and they' [477], appears in Lowry's own copy of John Sommerfield's 1937 novel *Volunteer in Spain,* now owned by Hilda and Philip Thomas of Vancouver. Although the inscription was obviously composed between 1937 and 1957, it is unfortunately impossible to date it more precisely. Of the last three poems in this section, all undated, the original manuscript for 'No prayer for the people' [478] is missing.[2]

Two of the items are classified as fragments because they are 'hearsay' poems, preserved only in contemporary reminiscences. Both of these fragments – 'Hindu Babe' [436] and 'Marching down the road to China' [437] – are songs attributed to Lowry's seagoing and jazz-composing apprenticeship period.[3] Related to the 'hearsay' poems is the dubious poem entitled 'The Voyage of Kevin O'Riordine' [469], inscribed in Lowry's hand on a 1950 letter from Albert Erskine, but by Lowry attributed to 'H.D. Barton,' who may be apocryphal.

Equally dubious because of their marginal poetic value are the items included in some letters, especially to Margerie: the 1939 items 'And Samson said if yo' shave ma hair' [445], 'The asperin tree outside told me to say' [461], 'The only thing that Jack had' [465], 'The Slough of Despond' [467], 'to account for this, but it cannot be' [473], and, from 1956, 'Cold Roast Hamlet Blues, Blubberhouses Blues, Ugley [sic] Blues' [476]. 'Ten fifty eight *may* arrive' [459] is a nonsense poem from a dated 1954 letter to Albert Erskine; the numbers refer to Erskine's error in addressing his last letter to Lowry. In 'The thing to know is how to write a verse' [468], Lowry dispenses some poetic advice to Conrad Aiken, which the older man must surely have appreciated. 'Yvonne stood there silently' [475] appears on the verso of a 1945 draft letter; Lowry may have been revising the corresponding section of *Under the Volcano* at that time.[4]

Almost half of the forty-four items in this section are drafts so rough that they can only be classed as fragments. 'Pacific is a feeble symbol of death' [440] (popularized by Earle Birney as 'Be Patient for the Wolf') probably contains more than one draft, but the chaotic state of the manuscript – extending over five pages of 8 × 10″ 'Pegaso' notebook paper – makes it impossible to reconstruct the final poem as Lowry envisioned it. As a consequence, the entire draft is reproduced. Similarly, 'The wild-duck swam in the gold-fish pond' [470] is clearly a first draft of 'Golden-eye and Goldfish' [218]; because the variants and length differ so radically from the final version, collation serves no purpose, and the draft is printed here as a parallel fragment.

This section is divided into the chronological periods of the main text; the poems included within each period are arranged alphabetically. This section aims merely to collect representative fragments; no emendations have been made nor sigla recorded. Readers particularly interested in the relationship between the fragments and prose should examine Chris Ackerley's preface to the explanatory annotations.

NOTES

1   Ten other fragments in this section come from various prose manuscripts. The poem numbers are: 443, 444, 450, 451, 454, 457, 458, 460, 471, 472.
2   Prof. F. Asals of the University of Toronto kindly shared with me his transcription of the elusive manuscript. His transcription provides the copy text for this edition. 'Poets are Godlike in that they' [479] appears on a paper with an unidentifiable watermark and thus cannot be dated at this time.
3   Bowker, 23 and 33, respectively.
4   Three other fragments in this section appear in correspondence. The poem numbers are: 449, 453, 464.

Apprenticeship

[1927]   [436.1]

Hindu Babe [fart]
I love you [fart]
I love you [fart]

[1927]   [437.1]

Marching down the road to China,
You will hear me singing this song,
Soon we'll be aboard an Ocean Liner sailing for Hong Kong,

And when we've put these Yellow Faces in their proper places,
5   We'll be home once more,
And I'll take my Alice to the Crystal Palace at the end of the
[China War.

Mexico

1938   A CURSE   [438.1]

how shall we apostrophise the vileness of women
who dissemble their idleness though death
is a kinsman and the abortion of
a household god. No pen
5   will ever prick your baseness
to its inner womb and no ten
thousand lines of prose or verse
no stanza, no paragraph, may anatomise
what is evil in its purest form
10 because all your children will be born dead.

1937–8   [439.1]

Elsinore was the battlements of Oaxaca:
Hotel Francia: Oax, mec: the silver miner
typed his mind out in the next estate
dinner was at six and death at eight:
5   Juarez disguised as the statue of liberty
and in the Ochas Farolito night
shook a frosty torch at Monte Alban
For Crane where is your bridge and Tennyson your bar
For [?Arlarcon] a Taxco in Guadalajara
10 for time and Timon meek and was both
for lies a liar and for truth a troth
alas poor Herrick and poor Conrad's youth
And Aase on the roof
Alas poor Yorick not in the first three.

1938   [440.1]

Pacific is a feeble symbol of death:
The final smile of California skies
is a smile pried open of the frightened actress.
Image of her hard faked
5   at the beginning of the inferno, in the middle of our life
of the wood, the image teeters between mother and sea.

though more survive its petulant note . . .

This is a world of worthless mysteries:
fire cannon and blast up who sunk with lead
10 whose tones are overdressed even in death.
Even in dust.

Be patient for the wolf is ever with you
Listen my little one to the sound of your desire

God will come out of such ignorance as this
15   not like a jack-in-the-box but like a tree
turned weeping father in delirium
he will say that such and such will happen.
Be patient because the wolf is patient.
The squeaks and woes of night all have their place.
20   And you'll find your blood warm cave and rest at last
and oil for your dispersed and aching limbs
whose small shadow has stopped here.
Be patient because of the wolf. Be patient
His soft steps are now your own, and you are free, being bereft.
25   He will say that such and such will happen;
the woes of night all have their tragic place
half the face of god seeks its face:
the meadow waits for rainbow to say god:
the shadows wait, for you to say the word:
30   the two pillows, wait for love to save the world:
the charter waits: the ship freezes in the fjord.
The angel waits his heart an aching hand
to win you from the wolf to the evening land
where no one ravens but where things are made:
35   The redbreast waits for redress from the dark
The swallow waits for autumn to say now:
and Echo, for Hero not to reply, no.
Only the bell that follows does not wait
galloping motherfaced across the shadowy fields
40   across the shadowy fields at nightfall
to abrase you to the bone with rough chime:
the bell not to the aged sea
but to the dear kind wolf pay allegiance
Be patient for the wolf is with you.
45   Listen little idiot for the sound of your desire.
Do not be deceived as it is not the sea.
The wolf is madness but the moon is light.
God will come out of such ignorance as this.
not like a jack-in-the-box but like a tree
50   turned weeping father in delirium.
He will say that such and such will happen.
The woes of night all have their tragic place.
and he will find your genius in the dark
and give it back without bondsman.
55   Forget the shrieking of the drunkard's wife,
the contemptuous sea curling its lip all day
strident as factories of shattering glass
Pass by the sleek unvintageable sea
for those who drink her deepest are the drowned.
60   Be patient for much much much is patient.
The meadow waits for rainbow to say god:

the shadows, for you to say the word.
The pillows, think that love will save the world
The moonlit collier reels at a foul anchor.
65 The charter waits: the ship freezes in the fjord.
The angel waits his heart an aching hand
to win you from us to the evening land
where no one ravens but where things are made
but where is no wolf is nor no moon nor thought of blood
70 Be patient child for the wolf is ever with you
Listen my little one to the sound of your desire.
God will come out of such ignorance as this:
not like a jack-in-the-box but like a tree
turned weeping father in delirium.
75 He will say that such and such will happen.
The woes of night all have their tragic place.
and you   half the face of god seeks half its face.
your blood-warm clot of rest at last.
God will find your genius for you in the dark:
80 and give it you back again without a bondsman.
The shadows wait for you to say the word.
Think: you will never have to read another book.
You will have oil for your dispersed, aching limbs
whose small shadow has stopped here . . .
85 Be patient, because of the wolf, be patient;
His soft step is your own now, you are free, being bereft.
The sea is foolish, curling its lip all day.
Listen to my little one, to his soft, cunning, step.
to the aged sea,
90 The foolish sea curling its lip all day.
No attention to the unvintageable sea.
for those who drink it deepest are the drowned.
The contemptuous sea curling its lip all day
noisy as factories of shattering glass.
95 Reel not towards the unvintageable sea
for those who drink it deepest are the drowned.
The redbreast waits too for redress from the dark:
The swallows press for autumn to say now:
And Echo, for hero, to say, no.
100 only the bell that follows does not wait
Galloping across the fields at nightfall
Vast, mother-faced, across the shadowed fields
to abrase yet the bone with soft toll
Try your teeth on iron nipples how you will
105 But your small shadow has stopped here.
Listen to your own strange cunning step.
The shadows jump: they know
you are going with them.
The wolf's step is your own, now being bereft.

110   to forget the shrieking drunkard's wife sea
       the contemptuous sea curling its lip all day.
       strident as factories of shattering glass.
       Pass the rough unvintageable sea.
       For those who drink it deepest are the drowned.

1937–8   [441.1]

       The crane over seas and forests seeks her home
       No bird so wild only has its quiet nest
       When it no more would roam
       The sleepless billows on the ram's breast
5   Break like a bursting heart and die in foam.

Canada

1940–54   [442.1]

       A cap and gown instead of a sweatrag,
       And a chainbreaker singlet and worse food
       Instead of bad. I'll have these buggars blood
       One day, though. Or will I. The soul of a fag
5   Is a bad thing to carry around a University.
       Perhaps I have the soul of a deck boy.
       I have been a cod trimmer though. Shitty
       Is this place and that face is too that passeth. Oy
       It said. Oy. Fake proletariat.
10   And to the id of –
       . . . The coast of Sokotra stormy between spells
       And long and dark the wharves at Singapore.

1940   [443.2]

       A mackerel shouldn't take
       Shouldn't take the water for granted
       Yet if you suggested to him
       It would be better to live in the fresh air
5   To meet in an alien element
       The lone sniper cormorant
       The depth charge pelican
       The harpoon gannet
       And the rapacious seagull
10   To grow fine fluted wings
       That put flying fish to shame
       If someone suggested to him
       That he should have another name
       For a fish that swims and sings
15   For a little fish that swims and sings

To say the least he would gape
In a manner habitually submarine
In a manner habitually submarine!

1942–4   [444.1]

And partly they deserve dishonest death
Who guard our frontiers, and wholly they
Who forge the weapons for a rise in pay
And double, treble, those whose stinking breath
5   Hangs above the world in a fouler wreath
And pass on half thoughts every day
God is there not some way, not some way
To show men what untruth beneath
This heavy sabbath of hypocrisy
10   For any wish will not show them nor will pace
God curse on all the cancerous [?remarks]
Will merely shower ruin down in vain
Upon these loathsome quite determined faces
That gave the world these, its [?doom]

15   Whatever heroes are, I might be bold,
To say they're not, who do what they are told.

1939   [445.1]

And Samson said if yo' shave ma hair
Jus' as clean as ma *hade*
Ma strength-a will become-a like a *natcherl* man
For Gawd's-a g'wine t'move all de troubles away
For Gawd's-a g'wine t'move all de troubles away.

1944   BETTY AND GERALD NOXON   [446.1]

Delighted excited journeying youward
tourist arriving Oakville eight-thirty a.m. Monday
Margie unhurt myself fit
though back fried no
5   stiff upper lips or Nordic
glooms saved Branches Detectives Volcano Purgatorio
Noxon photos also Betty's pictures thousand
pages Paradiso what I lost will reimburse
gently you are saints please
do not dread
                            Malcolm

1940–54   FRAGMENT   [447.1]

The dead tree that, frozen, utters at the top
Meadowsweet to heaven this winter day . . .

1939–40   [448.1]

     Got a date with a bottle of
       gin
     When its over I've
       another date playing alone
5   too –
     For when I'm
       through with
       that bottle of
        gin
10   I haven't got a
       date with
        you –

     But I'd far rather
     sit and just play the
15   blues –
     you may think this
     gloomy but it
     just ain't so

     Got a date with a
       bottle of
20   scotch,
    And then a blind date,
      for two.

1943   [449.1]

    Here [*sic*] him play
    That sinister melody
    That's what the people say
    When they hear those weird chords
5   The mice run out of the worn old boards
    To hear him play
    That sinister melody . . .

1949–52 [1938–9]   [450.1]

   I don't want to criticize war
   to criticize war
   to criticize war
   I don't want to criticize war
5 And I don't say I want to hate you . . .
   Just want to see the sergeant dance
   The sergeant dance
   The sergeant dance
   Just want to see the sergeant do his bloody ballet dance
10 his bloody belly dance

his bloody belly dance
I want to see the sergeant do that bloody ballet dance
Which I read about in Yeats

1949–54   [451.1]

My love now lies upon his rump
And wrestles with a stomach pump
My love he hath a broken spine
And never more will he be mine

1940–54   [452.1]

No wonder it feared peace, the knees of years
knocking together, trembling hands of treaties,
The coronation of the rat, and the hyena,
And the great tossing moosehead of America's idiot son
5   To make the world
bullfrog, croaking of honour,

Bullfrogs croaking in clean pools of honour

For all I care succeed, in your gruesome joke
To give the world one bullfrog and one croak.

1949   [453.1]

No words assess, no pencil knows
No picture is, no music gives
A meaning, inkling, parallel,
To that which drew this soul from hell
5   And made it thus transcend its laws.

1949–54   [454.1]

Oh the Pyrrus boys are we
Oh the Oedipus boys are we
We'll diddle your sister
And diddle your mother
5   For sixpence half pennee . . .
But the Pyrrhus boys are we –

1940–54   PERSONAL   [455.2]

Bill, Kath and family gone.
Am very sick, all alone.
Please come and see me.
– Skinny.

1939–40   [456.1]

        Playing alone

        Drunk and bored –
        Sometimes a chord

        Touches your heart

5   – piercingly –

1949–54   [457.1]

Rocksie Ann was a Roxy and she live on Histon, Eng.
And she didn't give a goddam for the says of Dean Inge
To stick her finger up her arse it was her daily wont
And every year at Christmas she gave her friends her cwont

1949–52   [458.1]

    Sadness is so much a part of me
    May not.... encumbered ... dare hope
    That I am ... may ...
    My grief is like a battered old cookstove

1954   [459.1]

      Ten fifty eight *may* arrive
        on the date
      But fifteen o' eight will
        always be late
5   Land on *no*body's plate
      Save its senders who wait
      – Oh indirectorate
      With a hand on't like fate!
      – Or some Bartleby fate
10   For po' fifteen o' eight!

1946   [460.1]

    That she could cook
    He had no doubt
    Until she creamed
    His bristle sprout
5   with Burma Shave

1939   [461.1]

   – the asperin tree outside told me to say
   her leaves were trembling for your good beauty

but the pingpong bird and the scissors man were in the vicinity
as they have trembled since it wore the cross
5   you didn't know Christ was crucified on an asperin tree but so
[he was

she since has trembled both in gale and calm
for me I am unable to reply
too boiling with malaria am I
besides which I am too goddamned hungry
10   for you and far too parenthetical too –
we are simple lovers who love the rain
but a poem no I did not mean it
for christ and all deciduous things we love the sun –
and as for you you love what is sane in man
15   and I I too what is sane in woman.
– perhaps perhaps perhaps we love the sea?
that rose you wore in the sargasso sea?
well damn it that was another thing again
which brings us to the ubiquitous insane
20   that nauseous trap where love and hate are two
or are they one? and yeah, what about Thomas Chatterton?
and who made grey days grey and St. Louis blue? –
but all I wished to say was I love you
not only at sunset: and this is no sonnet.

1952   THE BIRD IN THE TREE   [462.1]

Meantime a bird in a tree
Sings something unlike a song as could be
Or something that is very unlike a song to me.

1940–54   THE COMMUNIST   [463.1]

You may praise this bloody awful world
Or divide it into
To me the whole thing stinks:

1947   [464.1]

– the margeries and the malcolms did
so bugger the squawks from the fools who chid –
Who all seem singularly full of shid
and we liked the Kid, we loved the Kid

1939   [465.1]

The only thing that Jack had
lacked

in life
— besides an understanding wife —
5   was tact.

1939–40; 1945–6   [466.1]

The port has a sweeter name than Saigon
And Cathays flags do command it wholly
Whitman loved it well but so did Shelley
Keats and the sardonic Chatterton
5   The soul of Adonis dwelt in that town

1939   THE SLOUGH OF DESPOND: [467.1]
                  OR THE HOUSE OF HOPE

I hate the dogs, the cats, the road, the weather, the shadows,
                              [everything that seems
to be conspiring to keep me from you.
I know what you must be feeling, my precious, but since
                              [love is the only thing that
can mount in this cockeyed world, we will win out and we
                              [will be together soon,
5   I know, somehow.
I am still waiting for further news from England.
The only thing that keeps me alive are your letters.
Oh my dearest sweet tender darling, I know this waiting is
                              [hell for you.
But with a fair wind, you won't have to wait much longer: I will
10   find a way, in any event, and take any risk.
For the present still try and be patient. Do things you've put
                              [off doing,
and all that sort of bunkum.
Please be true and to the thought of me. It is still the
                              [reasonable thing to
do to wait; I shall be bound to hear before the week is out,
                              [and if
15   there is an unfavourable reply, I'm just going to figure
                              [out the means of
getting to you anyhow, as I said. I am deliberately curbing
                              [myself in our
future interest from rash, independent, action, so far.
I'm trying to work desperately at stories so that I can make
                              [enough to
be with you independent of this bloody control: the war has
                              [knocked
20   most everything else on the head in the Labor Depart. The
                              [trouble is, I'm

so anxious to be with you, our personal problems keep
[intruding, my
work won't sit down and be objective.

1939   [468.2]

The thing to know is how to write a verse
Whether or not you like it, whether or not
The goddamn thing will put you on the spot
And Petrarch will not save you from the curse.
5   You may be circumambient or terse

, for better or worse
A thousand lines without a single blot.
Christ the great psalmist cannot save us here
He lisped in Numbers but no numbers came

10   Eliot and Pound were prosing all the time
And Whitman (Walt), alas, did much the same.

[1950]   THE VOYAGE OF KEVIN O'RIORDINE   [469.1]

H.D. BARTON

The chronometer fell in the bilge and was useless
We ran out of water and broke out in boils
O'Riordine cursed himself, being abuseless
We lashed ourselves forward and lashed ourself aft
5   And the last of the seven gales stove in the craft.
The ranges shrivelled, and the eggs they were loud
Wars splintered the top of the cabin
In a thirty foot sloop, single-masted and [?primed]
They sailed out of Falmouth and docked in New York

[perhaps apocryphal]

1952–4   [470.2][218]

The wild-duck swam in the gold-fish pond.
The gold-fishes' owner came waving his hat,
of those gold fish both being equally fond
Though in different ways. 'Might taste good at that
5   Though they're gold sort of things,' the duck seemed to say
While the man cried 'Shoo, you duck. Beat it. Scat.'
And much more beside   again in vain inveigh.
While the gold-fish swam and the wild duck sat
Sage eyed serene in the midday sun.

10   Now that goldfish pond was artificial
But that old goldfish instinct, was initial.

1949–52   [471.1]

       The years standing round in a ring.
       Then all at once they make a gibbering.
       Not till this year have I observed a spring
       And yet this stone must sing –
5   To which Sigbjorn had added, enigmatically, why?

1942–4   [472.1]

           There was an old Consul called Firmin
           Who alas was infested with vermin
           But for this man obscene
           Was prepared a ravine
5   To spend all the rest of his term in.

1939   [473.1]

      to account for this, but it cannot be
      lipstick, unless it is teleportedly yours:
      perhaps you were putting on a face, as
      I wrote. Please wait for me so that
5   you will be all mine. I haven't
      thought of anybody else since leaving
      you. The sheer pain of wanting you, of
      desire for your loveliness, for the smoothness of
      your body and your breasts, is unbearable:
10   if you must suffer, please suffer with this
      pain as I do, which we can soon
      assuage. Oh god, my darling, want me
      as I want you, want me to take you.

1950   [474.1]

           Ye Pow'rs who make mankind your care
           And dish them out their bill o' fare
           Auld Scotland wants no skinking ware
           That jaups in luggies
5   But, if ye wish her gratefu' prayer
           Gie her a haggis!
               Still ere

[1945]   [475.1]

     Yvonne stood there silently,
     the roar of the plane still in her ears,
     the buffeting of wind and rain in her face as they left the
                        [sea behind:

in her mind's eye the roads before were still climbing and
[dropping,
5 the little towns shakily passed with their humped churches,
the cloudless sky glowed toward the east and there was the
[sudden
onslaught of sunlight
while the earth turned, yet in shadow,
then mountains filed on mountain,
10 a river flashed and was gone,
a gorge wound darkly beneath,
the volcanoes wheeled into view from nowhere
And Quahuanhuac with all its cobalt swimming pools
rose stupidly to melt them, Quahuanhuac, her town of
cold mountain water swiftly running.

England

1956   [476.1]

Cold Roast Hamlet Blues, Blubberhouses Blues, Ugley Blues,
Hard to come by Blues, Make-em Rich Blues,
Tadley God Help Us Blues, Little in sight blues,
Wide-Open Blues, King Edward Horsenail Blues,
5 Shippobottom Blues, Wig-wig Blues. Leaping Wild
Blues. [?Penny]-come-quick Blues.

Undated

[477.1]

– My two hands broke in two: and they
broke me!
Our hands were broken anyway, but
the thumbs
5 Said this: at least we are here with
our two
Cool moons, unclench those tyrant fathers
as you will
... We waited long for you to do something good
10 But though we had no songs we still are spokesmen
And what we wish to speak neither is little nor rough
Perhaps it is in southeastern port,
Davenport, Samarkand
– and, if you are lost, well, Billy-be-damned,
15 You are at a loss anyway, – with wine? –
but yet thumbs were once
fingers...
– and we were the great

[478.1]

No prayer for the people,
And no curses either;
The soaring steeple
should be a shaft rather.

5   It's damp in the well:
and its bold on the steeple
and its cold on the wire
where the bullets must ripple.

Cramped in heaven or hell
10   it is wiser to tipple
Much wiser to tipple than topple, sir, better,
to tipple than topple.

[479.1]

Poets are Godlike in that they
May write their agonies away

But most are mute; and in their hearts
Expression moves by fits and starts.

5   Or not at all: yet greater these,
And greater still their agonies,

Who no assuagement have, nor light
Save that which moves our Lord himself to write.

Appendix D

THIS PAPER CHART is intended as an aid in dating Lowry's poetic manuscripts and typescripts. Restricted to papers preserved in UBC's collection of Lowry's outgoing correspondence, it cannot be regarded as complete. However, because such a high proportion of Lowry's outgoing correspondence is undated, paper evidence often provides the only clue for accurately placing the manuscripts in a chronological sequence. The chart is included as a convenience to Lowry scholars working on his manuscripts who do not have ready access to the UBC collection and who, for purposes of dating, may wish to compare their manuscript papers with those in the outgoing letters.

The chart is organized by year. If no paper colour is listed, the paper is white. Type is black unless otherwise stated.

PAPER	INSCRIPTION
1937	
unmarked 8½ × 11″	pica type
blue-lined, pink-margined (on one side) 8½ × 11″	pencil
[?Xochimilco] Bond 8½ × 11″	black ink
Mercantile Bond 8½ 11″ (Hotel Francia, Oaxaca letterhead)	black ink
blue-lined notebook paper 5½ × 7″	purple pencil
1938	
blue-lined notebook paper 8 × 10″	pencil
blue-lined notebook paper 5½ × 7″	purple pencil
1939	
unmarked thin 8½ × 11″	green ink; elite type
blue letter paper 8 × 10″	black ink; pencil

PAPER	INSCRIPTION
unmarked thick 8½ × 11″	black ink; pencil
newsprint blue-lined notebook paper 7 × 9¼″	black ink; pencil

1940

NOTE: 8½ × 11″ unmarked newsprint bearing various types of inscription regularly appears in Lowry's outgoing correspondence and manuscripts for the 1940–54 Dollarton period. Because of its frequent appearance, this paper has not been included in the chart.

PAPER	INSCRIPTION
Colonial Bond 8½ × 11″	pencil; pica type
Wilson Stationery 8½ × 11″	blue pica type
blue-lined pink-margined notebook paper 7 × 9¼″	pencil
unmarked thick 8½ × 11″	pica type

1942

Great West Bond 8½ × 11″	pica type

1944

Cheneaux Bond 8½ × 11″	purple pencil

1945

blue-lined pink-margined notebook paper 7 × 9¼″	pencil
blank newsprint notebook paper 7 × 9¼″	pica type

1946

blue-line pink-margined notebook paper 7 × 9¼″	black ink; pencil
illegible watermark in flowing script extremely thin 8½ × 11″	pencil
unmarked 8½ × 11″ two ring	black ink; pica type
unmarked 8½ × 11″	black ink; pica type
blank blue notebook paper 3⅛ × 4¾″	pencil
blank notebook paper 3 × 5″	pencil

1947

blue-lined notebook paper 3¼ × 5½″	pencil
illegible watermark 8½ × 11″	pica type

PAPER	INSCRIPTION
Victory Bond (large watermark) 8½ × 11″	pencil; pica type
Great West Bond 8½ × 14″	pencil
unmarked 8½ × 11″	pica type

1948
blue-lined notebook paper 3¼ × 5½″	pencil

1949
Cheneaux Bond 8½ × 11″	blue ink; pica type
unmarked thick 8½ × 11″	pencil

1950
Rockland Bond 8½ × 11″	pica type
blank blue notebook paper 3¼ × 4¾″	pencil
unmarked thick 8½ × 11″	pencil
unmarked 8 × 10″ torn from pad	pencil

1951
unmarked thick 8½ × 11″	pencil
Rockland Bond 8½ × 11″	pica type
Genoa Bond 8½ × 11″	pica type
unmarked 8½ × 11″	pica type
unmarked thick 8 × 10″ torn from pad	blue ink
Victory Bond (large watermark) 8½ × 11″	pica type
thin 5¾ × 8½″ torn from pad	blue ink

1952
Victory Bond (small watermark) 8½ × 11″	pica type
Cheneaux Bond 8½ × 11″	pica type
thick 8 × 10″ torn from pad	pica type
unmarked 8½ × 11″	pica type
thick 8 × 10 torn from pad	blue ink

1953
unmarked 8½ × 11″	elite type
blank yellow notebook paper 3⅛ × 4¾″	pencil
thick 8 × 10″ torn from pad	pencil; blue ink

PAPER	INSCRIPTION
5½ × 7¼″ torn from pad	blue ink
Bell-Fast Bond 8½ × 11″	pica type
unmarked 8 × 10″	pencil

1954

unmarked 8 × 10″ torn from pad	pencil; blue pen; elite type
thick 8 × 10″ torn from pad	pica type
Extra Strong Bond 8¾ × 11¼″	blue pen

1955

Extra Strong Bond 8¾ × 11¼″	blue pen; pink pen
blue-lined notebook paper 3¼ × 5¾″	blue pen
unmarked thick 6 × 8¼″	pencil
illegible watermark 9¼ × 11½″	pen

1956

blank notebook 3¾ × 5″	pencil
blank notebook 5¼ × 7″	pencil
Waterton Bond 8 × 10″	pencil

1957

Plantagenet Bond 8½ × 11″	black ink; elite type
unmarked 8½ × 11″	pencil
unmarked 8 × 10″	pica type

Appendix E

MARGINALIA

LOWRY'S POETIC MANUSCRIPTS, particularly the holographs, are laden with marginalia, some of which are vital to a full comprehension of the poetry or Lowry's compositional method, and some of which are interesting for biographical or other reasons. A transcription of all the marginalia is impossible for the purposes of this text; it would easily double the length of the edition. Chris Ackerley's explanatory annotation necessarily refers to some of it, but scholars interested in close analysis of its relationship with the poetry are encouraged to visit the manuscript collections, especially those at UBC.

This Appendix comprises reproductions of five manuscript sheets chosen to exemplify the major categories of marginalia in Lowry's poetic manuscripts. The first, one page from the lengthy fragment 'Pacific is a feeble symbol of death' [440], demonstrates the possible extent of marginalia for one page. Of course, not every holograph draft is so heavily inscribed, but a great many are, particularly those found on the torn-apart notebook sheets. The marginal comment on the penultimate version of 'The Canadian Turned Back at the Border' [167], the second reproduction, is interesting because it is characteristic of the 1947 selection, which Lowry annotated with pencilled comments before he sent it to Albert Erskine on 7 November 1947; some of the sheets bear Erskine's pencilled reply. The marginalia on these 1947 sheets provide fascinating insights into Lowry's critical and compositional method, in this case, with special reference to the poem's literary influences and the purpose of its complicated sestina form. The third example, 'And partly they deserve dishonest death' [444] comes from a medial version of *Under the Volcano;* this reproduction provides a typical example of Lowry's habit of composing fragments of poems on the edges of prose manuscripts. The manuscripts for *Dark as the Grave* and 'Through the Panama' are also rich in this category of marginalia. Many of the poetic manuscripts contain marginalia interesting for biographical reasons. For example, the fourth reproduction is the verso of the El Petate restaurant menu discussed in *Dark as the Grave* (84–5), on which two drafts of the poem 'Some years ago he started to escape' [108] appear. The manuscript also contains, in the top left corner, Lowry's bar bill reckoning. The fifth reproduction, an early draft of 'I sing the joy of poverty' [223] provides one of Lowry's marginal drawings; such sketches appear throughout the manuscripts.

Reproductions of manuscript sheets on the next five pages are courtesy Special Collections, UBC Library.

Manuscript page from 'Pacific is a feeble symbol of death' [440]

The Border

I

A singing smell of tar, of the highway,

Fills the grey Vancouver Bus Terminal,

Crowned by dreaming names, Portland, New Orleans,

Spokane, Chicago, and Los Angeles!

City of the angels and my luck,

Where artists labor to insult mankind

With genius coeval to the age,

And city of my love, come next Sunday.

Out of a flag-hung shop a sleeked puppet

Hands me a ticket and my destiny.

II

The blue exhaust speeds parting's litany.

Then, with pneumatic bounds we herd the street.

The lights, symbolic, nictitate in day.

Cautious, but with mechanic persiflage,

- Rolando's horn could no more strangely wind -

Past Chinatown and names like Kwong Lee Duck,

Our bus treads asphalt with the noise of bees,

By taverns mumbling of skidroad scenes,

Then double-declutched my heart through neutral

And sang it into high for U.S.A.

Manuscript page from 'The Canadian Turned Back at the Border' [167]

Manuscript page from Under the Volcano, *containing 'And partly they deserve dishonest death'* [444]

Restaurant menu on which two drafts of the poem 'Some years ago he started to escape' [108] appear

Blessed are the poor in spirit.

But none will heed my song nor have [they] ears.

I sing the joy of poverty, not such
as war insults with ruins of...
evil. But...
Before the spirit, bare still ....   rich

The walls are bare of learning, and the trees
of leaves: both stand, beautiful:

innocent of ships.
NN with a twist, but with a poet

who lived before the God's were born
where were the images there, I long to teach
NN all their hypocrisy destroyed ...

There is a nakedness here
The soul scuttled to the

Ships are there

touch smell, out of the pages of a book
whose... the sense

Here on the ruined wharf I feel
such thoughts... live
... that they will die to young;

*Manuscript page from an early draft of 'I sing the joy of poverty' [223],
which includes one of Lowry's sketches*

Appendix F

THIS SET OF twenty-four poems, most of which are from *The Lighthouse Invites the Storm*, forms the final chapter of Lowry's typescript draft of *Dark as the Grave* (UBC 9–23), on which he worked during the late 1940s and early 1950s. It does not appear in the published version of the novel, and I have reproduced it particularly for Lowryans interested in the relationship between his prose and poetry. Because the *Dark as the Grave* selection is part of a discrete text, it plays no bibliographical role in the full poetic volume, nor does the full *Lighthouse* command textual authority here.

There are no substantive editorial emendations; silent changes in accidentals are limited to spelling and punctuation corrections and respacing to clarify divisions within the text. Pencilled editorial marks in the manuscript appear to be Birney's and thus have no textual authority.

Chapter XV: The Poems

THE LIGHTHOUSE INVITES THE STORM.

APRIL 1937 IN THE OAXACA TRAIN.

When maguey gives way to pine
What ae've seen from the train is kinder
'This is England,' or, of the Rhine,
'That' is a reminder.

Then when it is dark, from the train
Nor forest nor field may we see
So within from the dark flies the pain
Of the maguey, the strength of the fir tree.

But when pine gives way to cactus
What we see, someone says, is brutal
To smashed maguey's patterns react us
From wooled thought of Bonn or of Bootle.

To settle in toiler's faces
In the faces of those who recline
In the faces of those who have laboured
In maguey, or up in the pine.

Yet what hope in this plunging compartment!
As they sleep, it is set like a sign
Of hope that still flickers in England
But vanished along the Rhine.

NOVEMBER, 1937

And did this all begin, and why am I here
At this arc of bar with its cracked brown paint?
Papegaii, mescal, Hennessey, cerveza,
Two slimed spittoons, but no company but fear
Fear of light, of the spring, of the complaint
Of birds, and buses flying to far places.

And the students going to the races,
Of girls skipping with the wind in their faces
But no company, no company but fear,
Fear of the blowing fountain, and all flowers
That know the sun are my enemies
These dead hours.

BEGUN IN CUAUTLA, JULY, 1937, FINISHED IN THE FAROLITA JAN. 1938

This ticking is most terrible of all
You hear the sound I mean on ships and trains
You hear it everywhere, for it is doom;
The tick of real death not the tick of time
The death watch beetle at the rotten timber of the world
And it is death to you though well you know
The heart's silent tick failing against the clock,
Its beat ubiquitous and still more slow
But still not the tick, the tick of real death
Only the tick of time – still, only the heart's chime
When body's alarm wakes whirring to terror
– In the cantina throbs the refrigerator
While against the street the gaunt station house
What can you say fairly of a broad lieutenant
With bloody hand behind him a cigarro in it,
But that he blocks a square of broken sunlight
Where scraps of freedom stream against the gale
And lightning scraps blue shovels against coal?
The thunder batters the Gothic mountains;
But why must you hear, hear and not know this storm
Seeing it only under the door
Visible in synecdoches of wheels,
And khaki water sousing down the gutter?
In ripples, like claws tearing the water back?
The wheels smash a wake under the jalousie
The lieutenant moves, but the door swings too . . .

— What of all this life outside, unseen by you
Passed by, escaped from, or excluded
By a posture in a desolate bar?
No need to speak, conserve a last mistake;
Perhaps real death's inside, don't let it loose.
The lieutenant carried it into the back room?
The upturned spitoons (may) mean it, so may the glass?
The girl refills it, pours a glass of (real) death,
And if there's death in here there is in me.
On the pictured calendar, set to the future,
The two reindeer battle to death, while man
The tick of real death, not the tick of time
Hearing, thrusts his canoe into the moon
Risen to bring us madness none too soon.

OF THE FRANCIA.

Where has tenderness gone, he asked the mirror
Of the Biltmore Hotel, Cuarto 216, Alas,
Can its reflection lean against the glass
Too, wondering where I have gone, into what horror?
Is that it staring at me now with terror
Behind your frail tilted barrier? Tenderness
Was here, in this very bedroom, in this
Place, its form seen, cries heard, by you. What error
Is here? Am I that rashed image
Is this the ghost of love you reflected?
Now with a background of tequila, stubs, dirty collars
Sodium perborate, and a scrawled page
To the dead, telephone off the hook? In rage
He smashed all the glass in the room. (Bill $50)

Shakespeare should have come to Acapulco
Here he would have found a timeless hell
He who leaves all, Dean Donne said, doth as well —
(There is no rhyme for foul Acapulco
Nor reason, expletive save — Acapulco!)
— As he who eats, devours. He scarcely would have left all
Fruits here in this 'seascape in a bottle'
— (Or escape into a million) — quotes: Wells Fargo
Paraiso de la Caleta, seduce him to your bed!
Suppose it, he would have held no horses,
Written no plays. What creditor wants verses?
Globe? No Globe here, not a scenical sound
All that could be said is what Marston said
Rich happiness that such a son is drowned.

But never fall from fealty to light
You said, Melville? Now by God sir, why not?

The fall is comfortable enough, as soon rot
There as another place; once being well met
The beauty of the Turk is there's no sight
Of that light you speak of: what lamps are lit

Save no falling from fealty to it
When once accepted wholly by the night
It is a treachery to suggest, a treason
Against the inferno whose judgement will
Fit the crime; whose mercy is tempered
With fire – light enough for those unhampered
By day. And true to unreason.

     I have known a city of dreadful night
Dreadfuller far than Kipling knew, or Thomson
This is the night where hope's last seed is flown
From the evanescent mind of winter's grandson

The policeman's shadow swings against the wall
The lantern's shadow is darkness against the wall
And on the cathedral's coast slowly sways the cross
(Which are) wires and the tall pole moving in the wind.

     In the dungeon shivers the alcoholic child
Comforted by the murderer, since compassion is here too
The noises of the night are cries for help
From the town and from the garden which evicts those
                    [who destroy!

     And I crucified between two continents

But no message whines through for me here, oh multitudinous
To me here (where they cure syphilis with Sloan's liniment
And clap, with another dose.)

THOUGHTS WHILE DROWNING (ACAPULCO)

Let others quarrel alone about my grief
Raven like wolves over a cache of meat
Long self-starved it is on relief;
Many of these with surfeit of happiness need it.
The evening darkens with a sense of guilt
Like a thunderstorm blackening the promontory
Smearing the remembered headland of a life
With a child's scrawl of chaos against the night
The tourists wait with fatuous smiles of triumph
With bereaved arms upon the gossiping shore
Having known the corpse they are for a moment great.
(Hart Crane again – this should come after 'In home his Morro
Castle poem...)

PERHAPS FOR ERIDANUS

Like a rotten old ladder
Cast adrift from a dismantled sawmill
To float, shoulders awash, the rest
Waterlogged, eaten by teredos,
Barnacle-encrusted, shellfish
Clinging in blue bravelottes
Stinking, heavy with weeds and the strange life
Of death and low tide, vermiculated, helminthiatic,
Seems my conscience
– gregarine –
hauled out to dry in the sun
leaning against nothing
leading nowhere –
but to be put to use perhaps
salvageable – to be graved –
up and down which
each night my
mind meaninglessly
climbs.

Born ailing on a hemisphere apart
But tremulous, to acquire a heart
This soul still has its awkward music
And will not be stayed by contempt:
No legend roots in my obscurity
Tradition rests not on it: nor do words
Like flame ripple in its wake
Spawn of the doomed freighter and the ruined street
Spewed from the maw of the Great Hypocrite
Accidentally conjured out of defeat
Into a spate of nameless trees and birds
Not till this year have I observed a spring
And yet this stone must sing. . .

Give way, you fiends, and give that man some happiness
Who knelt in Wesleyan prayer to beget a fiend
Builder of a gabled house with daffodils
Flattened by the webbed foot of false April
Father of four steel gaunt sons minus one
Who, hearing the great guns faltered not at all.
In church his rock, in home his Morro Castle
In golf his chess in poetry capital
(And in the gulf his youngest abortive beauty)
For him and for the woman of his choice
Replace the love which those most displaced me
And from the wild choir over the freezing estuary

Bear him one humble phrase of love at last
Some childhood supplication never to be lost
As I am lost whose lips had formed its shape.

ON READING REDBURN.

Children brave by day have strange fears at night
But when they wake in the morning light
Their fears dissolve in sun between warm sheets:
Or, freezing in winter, become icy thoughts, –
The compulsory game in frost, – the impossible boast
The geometry lesson, the primer stolen or lost...
– How often, Redburn, lovers wake in nightmare
Bedded with what seems hatred and despair
Only to turn to ecstasy like de Maupassant
To find yet one more morning is triumphant!
– There is no constant here, such is our condition
In dark to know conquest too, in light no hope.
At dawn the girl, at midnight the horned owl.
– But what of the waking of the brave race of Man
After the unvintageable terrors of its sleep
To find the mildew still upon its soul?

PIJIJIAPAN

Time entered the stuffed court, slowly swearing
– I have, he added, dripped my soft snow
Too long for those who find our life past bearing
Treading down in the year's drifts their black woe;
And long enough have turned the day to dollar
For soldier spendthrift rogue and battered scholar
Been spelled, by the echoing bell, in the ship's pitch
Tolled agony to far schoolmates in green velvet
For all that I am a faked healer of cracked hearts
Vampired and counterwhored by a false name
Most merdurinous; and so the fates
Contrived, for a poor dream, a famous crime
Though love's wrenched houghs my cataplasms have known
Now that I love, my lord, I must be slain.

Informal ('dancing on the zebra floor')
Seemed first – it was an electric sign – 'Infernal'
Then, the next street to the bar, came Vigil
Which was really Virgil by Vermont
St. Vitus of the City of the Angels!
Wurlitzer turned 'Howitzer', from it hung
Blasted a boisterous bomb at the bar.
At the blue clock, with vermillion pendule (pendulum)
Hung (hangs) man's public inquiry of the hour.

The goose blue cloak swings high against the door...
On that travel agent's window, indistinct: 'Quest for beauty?'
And one thinks how two sable steeds were lost
Through gaps in hearts unvoyaged through by Dante
But delirium's on the march, we are wrong
Nevertheless those three dark words proved right.

Love which comes too late is like that black storm
That breaks out of its season, when you stand
Huddled with upturned tentative hand
To the strange rain. Yet sadly no sane calm
Succeeds it as when all the surprised form
Of nature is restored to a surprised land
Or the poor flowers thirst again and the sand
Sifts drily once more; and the abnormal norm
Of a parched world wholly returns. But say
It is like anything else; for let this love strike
You blind, dumb, mad, dead, your untimely fate
Will not be altered by your simile.
It slakes no thirst to say what love is like
Which comes too late, my God, alas, too late...

You were in hell fire? had been all your life?
And thought that nothing had been forged there?
I see a weapon mounded from that fire
Stronger than any sword: that deadlier knife
Of keen wisdom which flayed your soul strife
With flame in the pit could not wholly tire
Take that soul and strip it down to the core
With new steel as others who burnt before
For their knowledge or ours, or gain or loss...
There is a fellowship some pilgrims think
Between all in disastrous fight, yet few
Know their truest guardians in darkness.
Get out to your tavern, drink your nauseous drink
And read these lines, then pray to those like you.

A dried up river is like the soul
Of a poet who can't write, yet perceives
With imperfect clarity his theme, and grieves
To parched death over the drought. Set his goal
Once a wholesome sea of clearest crystal
Recedes, grows grey in heartseye, like old love leaves
Leaves the mind altogether. He conceives
Nothing to replace it: only at the pole
Of memory flickers some senseless compass
So the river, by her grey pitying trees
Is an agony of stones, horrors which sank

But are now declaused, bleached. For it is these
These stones and nothingnesses that possess
When the river is a road and mind a blank.

Resurgent sorrow is a sea in the cave
Of the mind – just as in the poem
It gluts it – though no nymphs will quire a hymn
Abandon it! Take a trip to the upper shore. Lave
Yourself in sand: gather poppies, brave
The fringe of things, denying that inner chasm.
Why the hush of the seas in the seashell, in the limb
Of the smashed ship its tempest, and your grave
The sand itself if you'd have it so. Yet glare
Through a sky of love all day still must you receive
In the cave the special anguish of your life
With the skull of the seagull and the wreck you may fare
Well enough, but will not escape the other surf
Remorse, your host who haunts that whirlpool where
The past's not washed up dead and black and dry
But whirls in its gulf forever, to no relief.

The ship is turning homeward now at last.
The bosun tries to read but dreams of home.
The old lamptrimmer sleeps, the engine thrums
Home. Lamps are set to light as from the past
To a near future unmysterious as this mast
Whose bulk we recognize and finite aim
Patient iron! But beyond the mainstruck, dumb
Blankness, or the twitch of reeling stars cast
Adrift in a white ocean of doubt.
Perhaps this tramp rolls towards a futurity
That broods on ocean less than on the gall
In seaman's minds. Is that star wormwood out
Among love's stars? This freighter eternity?
Where are we going? Life save us all.

(From this, on the whole, moving melange of Louise Bogan, (un-
mysterious) Joseph Conrad, Beddoes, Dostoevsky, Nordahl Grieg, and
Herman Melville (Poor Jimmy Rose, God save us all) – Sigbjørn,
wondering at these singular moments of purity induced by mescal, turned
to be one that seemed sadder and more personal, and once more in his
queer versification, the distinguishing feature of which seemed to be a
series of attempts to write a sonnet, and when in doubt for a rhyme, any-
thing will do)

He prayed to his ghost for a vision of the sea...
Which would harbour it strictly in the mind
For all time, that he might be resigned

To it, and not haunted eternally;
The ghost nodded his head, and said gravely:
Forget, thus you would lose your only grief and find
You had composed your tears, landlocked your heart;
You would pray for the roar of the sea wind
And darkness then, call us wrong or right,
You must always claim its unrest and its monotony,
Its mist on your breast. – – His ship in harbour
Loaded sweet timber from the high-piled wharf
He looked at her long, and then with a laugh
Climbed on board and was seen no more.

He was, however, seen some more: for on the next page under the heading, In the Farolito, 4 A.M. was written these words:

– the out-of-the tavern of the dark ejected sun
who darkness drank all night
while I have just begun...

I tried to think of something good
That I had thought or done or said
But in my life seemed only food
For such thoughts as awake the dead
To send them howling down a gulf
Of their own selfishness and dread
Each hunted soul its Beowulf
For the grave is but a drumming bed
Of nightmares I had understood
From spirits who had been misled
In life by self, for such as they
Who threw in life their death away.

– But at this point I heard a voice
Which said, 'My boy – you have a choice
Tomorrow there is left and right
Tomorrow there is day and night.
Tomorrow there is right and wrong
and death-filled silence, life-filled song.
So get down on your drunken knees
And thank God for the choice of these
And after that, get up, I think
Your father needs another drink.'

So delighted by this gruesome drollery was Sigbjørn, that without reflecting that he had done, for him, anything remarkable, he had produced a pencil and in a few minutes added these lines by way of conclusion:

– Miraculous such nights as those
Should be survived, how, no one knows
Far less, how one reached finer air
That never breathed on such despair.

Appendix G

THE SMALL LOWRY listing at Harvard's Houghton Library contains a manuscript entitled 'Eridanus.' While examining the manuscript for her edition of Lowry's letters, Sherrill Grace of the University of British Columbia came across two poetic fragments, which she has generously passed on to me for inclusion in this edition. I received them while the book was in production, and so must attach them here as an appendix. Both items were composed in 1945 and are reproduced without any editorial emendations. I would like to thank Sherrill Grace and the Houghton Library for their permission to reprint this material. The first item is a draft of 'The Wounded Bat' [320].

A NOTE

Bat: On a summer's afternoon, hot,
and in the dusty path, a bat
With injured membranes & little hands,
a *contact* that would have knocked young Aeschylus flat
5   She looked at the twig;
Its red mouth, helpless, like a mouse
A buzzing, like a buzzer, electric.
Pathetic crepitation in the path
It hooked to the twig, I laid it in the shade
10   With compassion, yet with blind terror
            praying that not too soon
Death might care to do for me as much.

'Portly & middleaged' can never
Refer to us, although we are both
Portly & middleaged. Nothing loth
to be old though; have we ever
5   Been anything else indeed? Clever
poets! Disgusted with our sloth
at twenty-one,
Were we not one year older than Chatterton
And still was no work done
10   at 27 beating Keats by two
And still there was far too much work to do.
Then at some remembered second-hand remorse
To drink again the sorrow of being young.

Bibliography

THIS BIBLIOGRAPHY INCLUDES only English language material. Check the standard Lowry bibliographies by New and Woolmer, and the annual bibliography in *The Malcolm Lowry Review*, for foreign language material.

Primary Sources

SIGNIFICANT MANUSCRIPT COLLECTIONS – POETRY

Malcolm Lowry Papers. University of British Columbia, Vancouver
Malcolm Lowry Papers. McFarlin Library, University of Tulsa, Tulsa
Malcolm Lowry Papers. Harry Ransom Humanities Research Center, University of Texas at Austin
Conrad Aiken Papers. Henry E. Huntington Library, San Marino
Lord Chamberlain's File. British Library, London
Earle Birney Papers. Fisher Library, University of Toronto, Toronto

PRINTED WORKS

BOOKS (FIRST EDITIONS ONLY)

Ultramarine. London: Jonathan Cape 1933
Under the Volcano. New York: Reynal and Hitchcock 1947
Hear Us O Lord from Heaven Thy Dwelling Place. Philadelphia: Lippincott 1961
Selected Poems of Malcolm Lowry. Edited by Earle Birney with the assistance of Margerie Lowry. San Francisco: City Lights Books 1962
Selected Letters of Malcolm Lowry. Edited by Harvey Breit and Margerie Bonner Lowry. Philadelphia: Lippincott 1965
Lunar Caustic. Edited by Earle Birney and Margerie Lowry. London: Jonathan Cape 1968
Dark as the Grave Wherein My Friend Is Laid. Edited by Douglas Day and Margerie Lowry. New York: New American Library 1968
October Ferry to Gabriola. Edited by Margerie Lowry. New York: World Publishing 1970
Malcolm Lowry: Psalms and Songs. Edited by Margerie Lowry. New York: New American Library 1975
Notes on a Screenplay for F. Scott Fitzgerald's 'Tender Is the Night' (with Margerie Bonner Lowry). Bloomfield Hill, MI: Bruccoli Clark 1976

The Letters of Malcolm Lowry and Gerald Noxon. Edited by Paul Tiessen. Vancouver: UBC Press 1988

The Cinema of Malcolm Lowry: A Scholarly Edition of Lowry's 'Tender Is the Night' Edited by Miguel Mota and Paul Tiessen. Vancouver: UBC Press 1990

POETIC CONTRIBUTIONS TO ANTHOLOGIES

Davenport, John, et al., eds. *Cambridge Poetry 1930.* London: Hogarth Press 1930. One poem

Smith, A.J.M., ed. *A Book of Canadian Poetry.* 2nd rev. ed. (rpt. 1957). Toronto: Gage 1948. Seven poems (rpt. four poems)

Gustafson, Ralph, ed. *The Penguin Book of Canadian Verse.* Harmondsworth: Penguin 1958. Two poems

Smith, A.J.M., ed. *The Oxford Book of Canadian Verse in English and French.* Toronto: Oxford University Press 1960. Four poems

Williams, Hugo, ed. *London Magazine Poems 1961–66.* London: n.p. 1966. Three poems

Larkin, Philip, ed. *The Oxford Book of Twentieth Century English Verse.* Oxford: Clarendon Press, 1973. Two poems

Colombo, J.R., ed. *The Poets of Canada.* Edmonton: Hurtig 1978. One poem

Atwood, Margaret, ed. *The New Oxford Book of Canadian Verse in English.* Toronto: Oxford University Press 1982. Four poems

Safarik, Allan, ed. *Vancouver Poetry.* Winlaw: Polestar Press 1986. Three poems

Geddes, Gary, ed. *Vancouver, Soul of a City.* Vancouver: Douglas and McIntyre 1986. One poem

POETIC CONTRIBUTIONS TO PERIODICALS

PUBLISHED DURING LOWRY'S LIFE

'Der Tag.' *Leys Fortnightly* 49 (1925):186

'Homoeopathic Blues in J.' *Leys Fortnightly* 50 (1926):150

'The Old Woman Who Buried Cats.' *Leys Fortnightly* 51 (1926):26–7

'The Rain Fell Heavily.' *Leys Fortnightly* 51 (1926):78–9

'The Glory of the Sea.' *Leys Fortnightly* 52 (1927):94–5

'The Cook in the Galley.' *Leys Fortnightly* 52 (1928):230

'Number 8 Fireman.' *Leys Fortnightly* 52 (1928):256–7

'In Cape Cod with Conrad Aitken [sic].' *Festival Theatre Programme, Cambridge* 7, 16 (1930):10

'Those Coke to Newcastle Blues' (with Conrad Aiken). *Festival Theatre Review, Cambridge* 4, 68 (1931):8–9

'Where did that one go to, 'Erbert?' *The Vancouver Daily Province,* 29 December 1939: 4

'In Memoriam: Ingvald Bjørndal.' *Atlantic Monthly* 168, 4 (1941):501

'Sestina in a Cantina.' *Canadian Poetry Magazine* 11, 1 (1947):24–7

'Salmon Drowns Eagle.' *Contemporary Verse* 21 (1947):3

'The Glaucous Winged Gull.' *Contemporary Verse* 21 (1947):4
'Stoker Tom's Ukulele.' *Contemporary Verse* 21 (1947):4
'The poignance of a quarrel in the post.' *Contemporary Verse* 21 (1947):5
'This evening Venus sings alone.' *Contemporary Verse* 21 (1947):5
'Old Freighter in an Old Port.' *Canadian Poetry Magazine* 11, 2 (1947):24
'Port Moody.' *Canadian Poetry Magazine* 11, 2 (1947):25
'Indian Arm.' *Canadian Poetry Magazine* 11, 2 (1947):25
'These animals that follow us in dream.' *Contemporary Verse* 24 (1948):6
'Sunrise.' *Outposts* 10 (1948):7
'Sestina in a Cantina.' *Arena* 1 (1949):79–80
'Nocturne.' *Arena* 1 (1949):81
'Glaucous Winged Gull.' *Arena* 1 (1949):81
'Port Moody.' *Arena* 1 (1949):81
'Turned Back at the Border.' *Arena* 2 (1949):58–60

POSTHUMOUS

'The Flowering Past.' *New York Times* 109, 37, 150 (11 October 1959):section 4, 10E
'No Still Path.' *New York Times* 109, 37, 201 (1 December 1959):38
'To Three in London.' *Moment* 1 (1960):9
'Sestina in a Cantina.' *Moment* 2 (1960):7
'Imprisoned in a Liverpool of Self.' *Contact* 7 (1961):83
'The Glaucous-Winged Gull.' *Contact* 7 (1961):84
'Mr. Lowry's Derivative Good Friday under a Real Cactus.' *Contact* 7 (1961):85
'Don't, Have One for the Road.' *Contact* 7 (1961):85
'Eye-opener.' *Contact* 7 (1961):85
'The Flowering Past.' *Contact* 7 (1961):86
'Old Freighter in an Old Port.' *Contact* 7 (1961):86
'The Pilgrim.' *Contact* 7 (1961):87
'Heat Wave.' *Hip Pocket Poems* 4 (1961):unpaginated
'Harpies.' *Hip Pocket Poems* 4 (1961):unpaginated
'What Sigbjørn Said.' *Hip Pocket Poems* 4 (1961):unpaginated
'A Lament – June 1944.' *Canadian Literature* 8 (1961):20
'In Tempest's Tavern.' *Canadian Literature* 8 (1961):20
'After Publication of *Under the Volcano*.' *Canadian Literature* 8 (1961):21
'Hypocrisy.' *Canadian Literature* 8 (1961):21
'Lupus in Fabula.' *Canadian Literature* 8 (1961):22
'The Dodder.' *Canadian Literature* 8 (1961):22
'Autopsy.' *Canadian Literature* 8 (1961):23
'Strange Type.' *Canadian Literature* 8 (1961):23
'Joseph Conrad.' *Canadian Literature* 8 (1961):24
'The Devil's Kitchen.' *Massachusetts Review* 2, 3 (1961):412

'The Exile.' *Massachusetts Review* 2, 3 (1961):412–13
'Bosun's Song.' *Massachusetts Review* 2, 3 (1961):413
'Because of No Moment.' *Tamarack Review* 19 (1961):42
'The Volcano Is Dark.' *Tamarack Review* 19 (1961):43
'The Paths of Wolves.' *Tamarack Review* 19 (1961):43
'Vigil Forget.' *Tamarack Review* 19 (1961):44
'Christ Walks in This Infernal District Too.' *Tamarack Review* 19 (1961):44
'Alternative.' *Tamarack Review* 19 (1961):45
'Draft Board.' *Tamarack Review* 19 (1961):45
'The Dollarton Bus Stop.' *Tamarack Review* 19 (1961):45
'There Is a Tide in the Affairs of Men.' *Tamarack Review* 19 (1961):46
'Blepharipappus Glandulosus or White Tidy-tips.' *Tamarack Review* 19 (1961):46
'A Wounded Voice over the Telephone.' *Tamarack Review* 19 (1961):47
'Jokes in the Galley.' *Tamarack Review* 19 (1961):48
'Lines on the Poet Being Informed that His Epic about the Philistines Needed Cutting.' *Tamarack Review* 19 (1961):48
'Note for a Poem.' *Tamarack Review* 19 (1961):48
'The dead man sat in the sun.' *Tamarack Review* 19 (1961):49
'No Time to Stop and Think.' *Tamarack Review* 19 (1961):49
'Semicolon Technique.' *Tamarack Review* 19 (1961):49
'The Magic World.' *Canadian Forum* 41, 487 (1961):112
'Tashtego Believed Red.' *Canadian Forum* 41, 487 (1961):112
'Song.' *Canadian Forum* 41, 487 (1961):112
'Nocturne in Burrard Inlet.' *Canadian Forum* 41, 487 (1961):112
'Doggerel.' *Canadian Forum* 41, 487 (1961):113
'Those Were the Days.' *Canadian Forum* 41, 487 (1961):113
'Be Patient for the Wolf.' *X: A Quarterly Review* 2, 2 (1961):85–6
'Hebephrene's Steep.' *X: A Quarterly Review* 2, 2 (1961):86–7
'Delirium in Vera Cruz.' *X: A Quarterly Review* 2, 2 (1961):87
'Reading Don Quixote.' *X: A Quarterly Review* 2, 2 (1961):87
'Queer Poem.' *New York Times* 110, 37, 827 (17 September 1961):section 4, 10E
'The Unborn.' *Virginia Quarterly Review* 37, 3 (1961):396
'There Is a Metallurgy.' *Virginia Quarterly Review* 37, 3 (1961):397
'Poets Are Godlike.' *Virginia Quarterly Review* 37, 3 (1961):397
'Comfort.' *Paris Review* 26 (1961):28
'Mercy of Fire.' *Paris Review* 26 (1961):28
'Death of an Oaxaquenian.' *Paris Review* 26 (1961):29
'From Helskinki to Liverpool with Lumber.' *Review of English Literature* 2, 4 (1961):37
'A Marathon of Gulls.' *Harper's Bazaar* 3000 (1961):181
'It was not so.' *Harper's Bazaar* 3000 (1961):181
'No Kraken Shall Be Found till Sought by Name.' *American Scholar* 30, 4 (1961):530
'Foul Acapulco.' *Carleton Miscellany* 2, 4 (1961):34
'You Think You Are a Man.' *Carleton Miscellany* 2, 4 (1961):34–5

'Hypocrite! Oxford Grouper! Yahoo!' *Carleton Miscellany* 2, 4 (1961):35

'Quartermaster at the Wheel.' *Dalhousie Review* 41, 3 (1961):383

'This Bitterest Coast.' *Dalhousie Review* 41, 3 (1961):384

'This Dead Letter.' *Dalhousie Review* 41, 3 (1961):384–5

'Whirlpool.' *Dalhousie Review* 41, 3 (1961):385

'Some Sword for Me.' *Epoch* 11, 3 (1961):157

'One Flying Line.' *Epoch* 11, 3 (1961):157–8

'Correcting Manuscript.' *Epoch* 11, 3 (1961):158

'On Reading Melville's Redburn.' *Epoch* 11, 3 (1961):158

'Injured Choriant or Paeonic.' *Epoch* 11, 3 (1961):159

'Thirty-five Mescals in Cuautla.' *Minnesota Review* 2, 1 (1961):24–5

'Walk in Canada.' *Queen's Quarterly* 68,3 (1961):418–19

'The Western Ocean.' *Queen's Quarterly* 68, 3 (1961):420

'The Wild Cherry.' *Queen's Quarterly* 68, 3 (1961):420

'Venus.' *Western Humanities Review* 15, 4 (1961):332

'Life in Death.' *Western Humanities Review* 15, 4 (1961):333

'Look Out! The Bloody Bosun!' *London Magazine* 1, 9 (1961):27

'Byzantium.' *London Magazine* 1, 9 (1961):27

'Visiting the Wreck: An Able Seaman Explains.' *London Magazine* 1, 9 (1961):28

'No Company but Fear.' *Arizona Quarterly* 17, 4 (1961):360

'The Ex-poet.' *Saturday Review,* 6 January 1962:21

'Thoughts While Drowning.' *Audience* 8, 3 (1962):42

'The Lighthouse Invites the Storm.' *Audience* 8, 3 (1962):43

'In the Shed.' *Delta* 17 (1962):9

'Loathing.' *Delta* 17 (1962):9

'On Reading Edmund Wilson's Remarks about Rimbaud.' *Delta* 17 (1962):10

'Quatrains.' *Delta* 17 (1962):11

'Men with Coats Thrashing.' *Exchange* 2, 3 (1962):10

'Foul or Twenty-Five!' *Raven* 10 (1962):5

'The Sun Was Almost Shining.' *Raven* 10 (1962):6

'For *Under the Volcano.' Evidence* 4 (1962):81–2

'Self-Pity.' *Evidence* 4 (1962):82

'Prayer (for his father).' *Evidence* 4 (1962):83

'Rilke and Yeats.' *Evidence* 4 (1962):83

'Doctor Usquebaugh.' *Evidence* 4 (1962):84

'Hunger.' *Northwest Review* 5, 1 (1962):60

'Iron Cities.' *Northwest Review* 5, 1 (1962):61

'The Doomed in Their Sinking.' *Northwest Review* 5, 1 (1962):62

'The Ship Is Turning Homeward.' *Northwest Review* 5, 1 (1962):63

'S.S. Housman.' *Northwest Review* 5, 1 (1962):64

'At the Bar.' *Northwest Review* 5, 1 (1962):64

'Sunrise.' *Northwest Review* 5, 1 (1962):65

'Wind Blowing through the Shack.' *Northwest Review* 5, 1 (1962):66

'The Wounded Bat.' *Northwest Review* 5, 1 (1962):66

'Eels.' *Northwest Review* 5, 1 (1962):67

'Fragment II.' *Northwest Review* 5, 1 (1962):68
'Hangover – Reading Rilke, Schnitzler or Someone.' *Northwest Review* 5, 1 (1962):69
'The Drunkards.' *New Yorker* 38, 11 (5 May 1967):46
'Kingfishers in British Columbia.' *Atlantic Monthly* 209, 6 (1962):55
'Happiness.' *Ladies Home Journal* 79, 6 (1962):88
'Poem.' *Fiddlehead* 52 (1962):8
'The Coiled Heart.' *Fiddlehead* 52 (1962):8
'The Ship of War.' *Fiddlehead* 52 (1962):9
'Love Which Comes Too Late.' *Perspective* 12, 4 (1962):172
'Injured Stones.' *Perspective* 12, 4 (1962):172
'Saint Malcolm among the Birds.' *Tamarack Review* 23 (1962):39
'He Liked the Dead.' *Tamarack Review* 23 (1962):40
'Epitaph.' *Tamarack Review* 23 (1962):40
'For the Love of Dying.' *Harper's Magazine* 225, 1348 (1962):38
'Thunder beyond Popocatepetl.' *Southwest Review* 47, 3 (1962):230
'Prayer from the Wicket Gate for Forty One Doors for Forty Two.' *Prairie Schooner* 37, 4 (1963):333–4
'On Board the Matsue Maru.' *Prairie Schooner* 37, 4 (1963):334
'The Sun Shines.' *Prairie Schooner* 34, 4 (1963):334
'Wrecker of Gardens.' *Prairie Schooner* 34, 4 (1963):335
'Number of Fireman.' *Études Anglaises* 18, 4 (1965):394
'Conversations with Goethe.' *A Malcolm Lowry Catalogue,* Focus Series 2 (1968):12
'Reflection to Windward.' *A Malcolm Lowry Catalogue,* Focus Series 2 (1968):13
'Midnight denies poursuivant of the dawn.' *Canadian Literature* 121 (1989):56
'I met a man who had got drunk with Christ.' *Canadian Literature* 121 (1989):57
'Sun, Aeroplane, Lovers.' *Canadian Literature* 121 (1989):58

Secondary Sources

BIBLIOGRAPHY

New, William H. *Malcolm Lowry: A Reference Guide.* Boston: G.K. Hall 1978
Woolmer, J. Howard. *Malcolm Lowry: A Bibliography.* Revere, PA: Woolmer/Brotherson 1983

BIOGRAPHY

Day, Douglas. *Malcolm Lowry: A Biography.* New York: Oxford University Press 1973
Bowker, Gordon, ed. *Malcolm Lowry Remembered.* London: Ariel Books (British Broadcasting Corporation) 1985
Salloum, Sheryl. *Malcolm Lowry: Vancouver Days.* Madeira Park, BC: Harbour Publishing 1987

CRITICISM

Ackerley, Chris, and Lawrence J. Clipper. *A Companion to Under the Volcano.* Vancouver: UBC Press 1984

⁻. 'Slips that Pass in the Type... ' *Malcolm Lowry Review* 26 (1990):5–6

Birney, Earle. 'The Unknown Poetry of Malcolm Lowry.' *British Columbia Library Quarterly* 24, 4 (1961):33–40

⁻. 'Malcolm Lowry's Poetry.' *Contact* 7, 2 (1961):81–2

⁻. 'Five Signallings in Darkness.' *Evidence* 4 (Winter 1962):76–8

⁻. 'Foreword' to 'Twelve Poems by Malcolm Lowry.' *Northwest Review* 5, 1 (1962):57–9

⁻. 'Against the Spell of Death.' *Prairie Schooner* 37, 4 (1964):328–33

⁻. 'Malcolm Lowry's Poetry.' Conference of Canadian Studies, University of Texas at Austin, March 1974

⁻. 'Malcolm Lowry's Search for the Perfect Poem.' *Poetry Canada Review* 7, 1 (1985):3–4, 20–1

Bradbrook, Muriel. *Malcolm Lowry: His Art and Early Life.* Cambridge: Cambridge University Press 1974

Bromige, David. 'Reviews.' *Northwest Review* 6, 1 (1963):113–15

Bubbers, Lissa Paul. 'The Poetry of Malcolm Lowry in Relation to the Fiction.' MA thesis, York University, 1976

Cogswell, Fred. 'Lord Jim as Byron.' *The Canadian Forum* 42 (1963): 230

Colombo, J.R. 'Poetry and Legend.' *Canadian Literature* 16 (1963): 61–3

Costa, Richard Hauer. *Malcolm Lowry.* New York: Twayne 1972

Easton, T.R. 'The Collected Poetry of Malcolm Lowry.' Graduating essay, University of British Columbia, 1968

Edelstein, J.M. 'The Voyage That Never Ends.' *New Republic* 147 (1962):22–3

Grace, Sherrill E. *The Voyage That Never Ends.* Vancouver: UBC Press 1982

⁻, ed. *Swinging the Maelstrom: New Perspectives on Malcolm Lowry.* Forthcoming.

Kim, Suzanne. 'Les Oeuvres de jeunesse de Malcolm Lowry.' *Études Anglaises* 18 (1965):283–94

⁻. 'Genetic Criticism: The Figures in Lowry's Poetic MSS.' International Lowry Symposium, University of British Columbia, 14 May 1987. Revised version to appear in *Swinging the Maelstrom,* ed. Sherrill E. Grace

Leavis, F.R. 'Cambridge Poetry.' *Cambridge Review,* 16 May 1930:414–15

Lopos, George J. 'Selected Poems of Malcolm Lowry.' *Poet and Critic* 5 (1968):41–2

Lowry, Malcolm. 'A Letter.' *Wake* 11 (1952):80–90

Mathews, Robin. 'Canadian Poetry and Fiction.' *Queen's Quarterly* 70 (1963):282–3

Matthew, Michael. Review of Stories and Poems. *British Columbia Library Quarterly* 26, 4 (1963):31–3

Peter, John. 'Selected Poems of Malcolm Lowry.' Canadian Broadcasting Corporation, 11 September 1962

Purdy, A.W. 'Dormez-vous? A Memoir of Malcolm Lowry.' *Canada Month* 2, 9 (1962):24–6

Scherf, Kathleen. 'Problems in Editing the Collected Poetry of Malcolm Lowry.' International Lowry Symposium, University of British Columbia, 14 May 1987. Revised version published as 'Issues in Editing Malcolm Lowry's Poems,' *The Malcolm Lowry Review* 23/24 (1988/9):32–9

–. 'Three New Poems by Malcolm Lowry, with a Textual Introduction.' *Canadian Literature* 121 (1989):55–8

–. 'The Collected Poetry of Malcolm Lowry: A Critical Edition with a Commentary.' PH.D. dissertation, University of British Columbia, 1988

–. 'Unearthing Malcolm Lowry's Two Unknown Volumes of Poetry.' *Paper of the Bibliographical Society of Canada* 29, 1 (1991):7–22

Skelton, Robin. 'Let's Ban the Myth of the Poet Drowning in Alcohol and Guilt.' *The Vancouver Sun,* 10 October 1962:5

Sugars, Cynthia. 'The Letters of Conrad Aiken and Malcolm Lowry.' MA thesis, University of British Columbia, 1988

Thomas, Mark. 'Weaving Fearful Vision: Malcolm Lowry's Poetry.' MA thesis. College of William and Mary, 1984

–. 'Strange Type: The Shoddy Commentary on Malcolm Lowry's Poetry.' *American Notes and Queries* 23, 5–6 (1985):84–5

–. 'Lowry's "In Tempest's Tavern."' *Explicator* 47 (1988):36–7

–. 'Under the Shadow of the *Volcano:* Malcolm Lowry's Poetry.' International Lowry Symposium, University of British Columbia, 14 May 1987. Revised version to appear in *Swinging the Maelstrom: New Pespectives on Malcolm Lowry,* ed. Sherrill E. Grace

Wilbur, Robert Hunter. 'Conrad Aiken: An Interview.' *Paris Review* 42 (1968):97–124

Indices

THERE ARE THREE alphabetical indices: for poems identified by first line, for poems identified by title, and for poems retitled by Birney. In the first two indices, Birney's titles appear in square brackets. The entries are keyed by poem number.

Index of First Lines

Index of Titled Poems

Index of Birney's Titles

Copy-Text Location File

THE LOCATION FOR each copy-text appears below; the list is keyed to poem numbers in this edition. Unless otherwise stated, box and file numbers refer to the Malcolm Lowry Papers at the University of British Columbia. If there is no file number, the text is listed in the indicated library's regular index system. Abbreviations are listed in the Preliminaries; book titles in the bibliography.

1	British Library (BL)	25	6–7	55	6–51
		26	4–14	56	6–51
2	BL	27	6–55	57	6–51
3	33–19	28	6–55	58	6–46
4	33–10	29	5–10	59	6–9
5	BL	30	6–51	60	6–51
6	BL	31	6–51	61	5–98
7	BL	32	6–51	62	6–51
8	H Aik 2489	33	6–51	63	6–51
9	H Aik 2489	34	6–51	64	5–81
10	H Aik 2489	35	6–51	65	6–51
11	H Aik 2489	36	6–51	66	4–81
12	33–15	37	6–51	67	6–51
13	Queens College, Rosenthal Library, Flushing, NY (QC)	38	6–51	68	5–55
		39	4–97	69	6–51
		40	6–55	70	6–51
		41	6–51	71	5–5
		42	6–51	72	6–51
		43	6–14	73	6–51
14	QC	44	6–51	74	6–51
15	5–63	45	4–11	75	6–26
16	5–12	46	4–56	76	4–120
17	4–103	47	6–51	77	4–87
18	4–3	48	6–51	78	6–19
19	5–28	49	6–51	79	6–55
20	6–34	50	6–51	80	6–55
21	5–101	51	6–51	81	4–37
22	4–29	52	6–51	82	4–21
23	5–33	53	6–51	83	5–40
24	4–107	54	6–4	84	6–51

85	628	133	UTML	181	4–26
86	6–51	134	UTML	182	4–27
87	5–13	135	UTML	183	H Aik 2521
88	5–105	136	UTML	184	4–32
89	6–1	137	UTML	185	6–56
90	5–23; 4–45	138	7–2	186	4–35
91	5–111	139	7–2	187	4–36
92	5–104	140	7–2	188	4–40
93	UTML	141	UTML	189	4–41
94	4–45	142	UTML	190	4–42
95	6–55	143	UTML	191	4–43
96	6–41	144	UTML	192	4–45
97	6–51	145	UTML	193	4–46
98	4–9	146	UTML	194	4–47
99	4–23	147	UTML	195	4–48
100	9–21	148	3–13	196	4–52
101	6–55	149	UTML	197	4–54
102	4–17	150	UTML	198	4–60
103	5–34	151	UTML	199	UTML
104	5–41	152	UTML	200	4–65
105	9–21	153	UTML	201	Tiessen 57, 58
106	1–75	154	7–2	202	4–67
107	1–75	155	UTML	203	UTML
108	WTP 1–24	156	6–31	204	4–69
109	1–75	157	7–2	205	4–71
110	6–13	158	UTML	206	4–72
111	12–14	159	7–2	207	3–7
112	6–32	160	UTML	208	4–74
113	6–36	161	UTML	209	4–76
114	UTML	162	UTML	210	4–77
115	UTML	163	UTML	211	UTML
116	UTML	164	UTML	212	4–79
117	UTML	165	UTML	213	4–80
118	UTML	166	UTML	214	5–45
119	UTML	167	7–2	215	4–86
120	UTML	168	UTML	216	4–88
121	UTML	169	4–4	217	5–91
122	UTML	170	4–5	218	4–93
123	UTML	171	4–6	219	4–94
124	UTML	172	4–7	220	4–99
125	7–2	173	22–23	221	4–101
126	7–2	174	6–33	222	4–102
127	DM 1–9	175	4–10	223	6–56
128	UTML	176	4–12	224	4–106
129	UTML	177	4–15	225	5–109
130	UTML	178	4–38	226	4–20
131	UTML	179	4–19	227	4–20
132	UTML	180	4–24	228	4–108

229	6–21	277	5–75		354, are as yet	
230	4–109	278	5–79		unprocessed	
231	4–110	279	5–80		at UBC	
232	UTML	280	UTML	354	5–22	
233	4–5	281	5–83	421	unprocessed	
234	UTML	282	5–114	422	McConnell	
235	UTML	283	5–87		Papers, UBC	
236	4–119	284	UTML		1–10	
237	4–121	285	5–95	423	unprocessed	
238	4–122	286	5–96	424	Haldane, *I*	
239	5–8	287	UTML		*Bring Not*	
240	UTML	288	5–102		*Peace,* 262	
241	20–23	289	UTML	425	unprocessed	
242	5–14	290	4–45	426	2–14	
243	UTML	291	5–106	427	photocopied	
244	5–17	292	5–107		from Sherrill	
245	5–18	293	5–112		Grace, private	
246	5–19	294	5–113		collection	
247	DM 1–9	295	5–114	428	3–2	
248	5–26	296	UTML	429	Haldane, 263	
249	UTML	297	4–44	430	4–116	
250	5–30	298	5–118	431	Haldane, 69	
251	5–32	299	5–50	432	unprocessed	
252	4–54	300	5–120	433	Grace, private	
253	5–36	301	6–3		collection	
254	5–37	302	5–85	434	unprocessed	
255	H Aik 2517	303	6–8	435	unprocessed	
256	5–38	304	4–16	436	Bowker, 23	
257	5–39	305	6–10	437	Bowker, 33	
258	5–43	306	6–11	438	WTP 1–24	
259	5–46	307	6–12	439	4–98	
260	5–47	308	6–16	440	4–17	
261	5–48	309	4–95; 6–18	441	1–76	
262	UTML	310	6–21	442	5–8	
263	5–50	311	6–22	443	26–2; 30–13	
264	4–105	312	6–23	444	26–19	
265	20–23	313	6–24	445	1–78	
266	5–52	314	UTML	446	2–1	
267	5–54	315	6–29	447	6–56	
268	5–61	316	6–33	448	6–56	
269	5–64	317	33–24	449	Tiessen, 57	
270	5–66	318	6–38	450	9–21	
271	22–23	319	6–40	451	22–19	
272	5–68	320	6–42	452	6–56	
273	UTML	321	6–49	453	22–20	
274	5–70	322	6–50	454	22–19	
275	4–110	323–420	inclusive,	455	5–62; 4–95	
276	5–73		except for	456	6–56	

457 22–19
458 9–22
459 3–7
460 7–7
461 private
     collection
462 5–82
463 6–56
464 H Aik 2489
465 1–78
466 6–56

467 1–78
468 1–77
469 1–21
470 22–26
471 9–21
472 T, VI, 54,
     verso
473 1–78
474 22–25
475 2–2
476 3–11

477 Hilda and
     Philip
     Thomas,
     private
     collection
478 Frederick
     Asal's
     transcription;
     ms missing
479 5–77